D062607

Also by Taras Grescoe

Sacré Blues

The End of Elsewhere

The Devil's Picnic

Bottomfeeder

STRAPHANGER

STRAPHANGER

Saving Our Cities and Ourselves from the Automobile

TARAS GRESCOE

HARPERCOLLINS PUBLISHERS LTD

Published by HarperCollins Publishers Ltd

First Canadian edition

The author gratefully acknowledges the support of the Canada Council during the writing of this book.

Map credits: © 2011 Metropolitan Transit Authority. Used with permission (page 19); courtesy and copyright of the Los Angeles County Metropolitan Transit Authority (page 50); courtesy and copyright of Valley Metro (page 79); courtesy and copyright of the RATP (page 105); courtesy and copyright of Metroselskabet (page 132); courtesy and copyright of Artemy Lebedev, Egor Zhgun, Ludvig Bystronovskiy (page 158); courtesy and copyright of Hisagi (page 178); courtesy and copyright of Nueva era (page 208); courtesy and copyright of TriMet, Portland, Oregon (page 231); courtesy and copyright of Southeastern Pennsylvania Transportation Authority (page 259); courtesy and copyright of STM (page 288).

HarperCollins books may be purchased for educational, business, or sales promotional use through our Special Markets Department.

HarperCollins Publishers Ltd
2 Bloor Street East, 20th Floor
Toronto, Ontario, Canada
M4W 1A8

www.harpercollins.ca

Library and Archives Canada Cataloguing in Publication

Grescoe, Taras
Straphanger : saving our cities and ourselves from the automobile / Taras Grescoe.

ISBN 978-1-55468-624-7

1. Commuting—Environmental aspects. 2. Local transit—Environmental aspects. 3. Urban transportation—Environmental aspects. 4. Environmental protection—Citizen participation. I. Title.

TD195.T7G74 2012   363.73'1   C2011-905706-9

Designed by Meryl Sussman Levavi

Printed and bound in the United States
RRD 9 8 7 6 5 4 3 2 1

To Desmond,
who arrived, unexpectedly, after
his parents rode the 80 bus to the
hospital for a routine ultrasound.

Contents

Shanghai, China

For first-time car buyers on the floor of the Shanghai Auto Show, the future looks bright, if not downright dazzling. Throughout the cavernous showrooms, lithe motor-showgirls in shimmering nylon evening gowns and leatherette miniskirts drape themselves over aerodynamic fenders, like molten watches drizzled over branches in a Dalí landscape. On rotating platforms, surrealistic concept cars languidly pirouette: the Geely McCar, a tiny hybrid with an outsized hatchback that pops up to release a three-wheeled electric motorcycle, and the chrome-grilled Engrand GE, which features a V-8 engine, rear seat massagers, and a built-in refrigerator that, according to the brochure, "gives access to mobile joy."

Caught in the crush, a visitor is torn between amusement and awe; it's hard not to chuckle at cars with names like the Great Wall Wingle Pick Up, the Jiangling Landwind, or the Book of Songs. At the same time, the audacity of China's carmakers is impressive: the Noble is a near replica of Daimler's Smart, the Lifan 320 appears to be a clone of a Mini Cooper, and the Dongfeng Crazy Soldier looks like the love child of a Humvee and a Tonka truck. Every few minutes, cameras flash and applause ripples through the showrooms as another "delivery ceremony" is completed: a proud owner is presented with flowers, a framed photo, and a bag of gifts as he is handed the keys to his brand-new Lavida, Cowin, or Beauty Leopard.

The lust to buy is almost palpable. Fourteen million cars were sold in China last year, which means the country has overtaken the United States as the world's largest automobile market. Over eight days, three-quarters of a million people will pass through the seventeen hangar-like halls of the Shanghai Auto Show—which has now surpassed New York's to become the world's largest—lining up for their chance to caress vinyl, shift gears, and slam doors, publicly dreaming of owning modernity's ultimate consumer item: the private automobile.

The big news at this year's auto show is that subcompacts are no longer at center stage, and major manufacturers have relegated hybrids and electrics to the sidelines as they promote old-fashioned gasoline-powered sedans. For years, the Chery QQ, a fuel-efficient, jellybean-shaped bumper car that retailed for less than $5,000, was the nation's most popular automobile. Lately, though, the aspiring middle class has set its sights higher. China's best-selling car is now the BYD F3, a four-door sedan that bears more than a passing resemblance to a Toyota Corolla, with a sticker price of $9,300. The popularity of the F3, which sold over a quarter of a million units in 2010, is a sign that Chinese consumers have made the Great Leap Forward from economy to midsize.

On the showroom floor, a silver F3, complete with power sunroof and dash-mounted perfume dispenser, has attracted the attention of Chen Shuli, a young mother from Shanghai's Jing'an district, who has come to the show with her husband.

"We have a small child, and we've heard that the F3 is very safe and sensible," says Chen. "We're just looking, and we're not really sure we can afford it. At the moment, we don't have a car. I don't work, but my husband has a job with an engineering company and gets there by metro, which takes about forty-five minutes. I'm not sure his commute would be any quicker by car." The husband in question has wandered off to investigate the BYD S6, an SUV that retails for twice the price of the F3. "Mainly, though," Chen continues, "we'd use a car to see my parents, who live in a small town in Zhejiang Province that we have to take two buses and a taxi to get to. Not many of my friends have cars yet; they get around on buses and the metro."

For Chen Shuli and her husband, the cars on display promise a future of status, freedom, and convenience. Those who came to the auto show by car, however, drove through a present already markedly diminished by the automobile. On the city's double-decked Inner Ring Road, a scrim of smog obscures even the taillights of the cars ahead, and the congestion has turned the Yangpu Bridge to Pudong, one of the world's longest bridges, into a six-lane parking lot. China's air pollution, exacerbated by coal-fired plants, is already the worst in the world: 656,000 citizens die prematurely of smog-induced lung and heart disease every year. In a grim coincidence, *Shanghai Daily* reports that the week of the auto show has brought the city's "worst air quality to date." In this car-choked metropolis of 23 million, the air people breathe has officially become a health hazard.

Only twenty-five years ago, automobile traffic in Shanghai was limited to chauffeur-driven Hongqi limousines for Communist Party officials. Such was China's isolation that, during the Cultural Revolution, the Red Guards floated a proposal to make red stoplights signify "Go." Today, there are two million cars on the streets of Shanghai. To ease congestion, a high price has been set on car registration, and bicycles have been banned from main streets. Backups in China can make even Los Angeles traffic look positively bucolic: in 2010, drivers northwest of Beijing were stuck for ten days in a jam that stretched 60 miles across two provinces. To increase mobility, China has built a 33,000-mile system of expressways in the last twenty years. Already larger than the network that connects the European Union, it will be more extensive than the United States' freeway system by 2035. By then, carbon dioxide emissions from China's transport sector will easily be the highest in the world.

China is compressing a century of Western automotive history into a few years, but it is not alone. In India, automaker Ratan Tata has launched the Nano, a 5-foot-wide micro-car with a top speed of 60 miles per hour, whose $2,500 sticker price puts it within reach of India's burgeoning middle class, currently 300 million strong. Tata says he believes every Indian should own his own car, but in such cities as Bangalore and Hyderabad, the addition of hundreds of thousands of low-cost cars has already created a state of near permanent gridlock. At this rate, the global automobile fleet is expected to increase from its present high of 600 million to almost three billion by midcentury. Many, if not most, of these new cars are going to be Chinese- or Indian-made. China's Geely recently bought Volvo; Tata purchased Jaguar and Land Rover; and the maker of the F3, Shenzhen-based BYD—one of whose main shareholders is the legendary investor Warren Buffett—has set the goal of becoming the world's largest car manufacturer by the middle of the next decade.

When it comes to escaping the throngs at the auto show, a visitor has a choice: hail a taxi and brave Shanghai's murderous traffic, or ride the metro. For even as China embarks on history's most ambitious bout of highway building, it is also making a huge investment in urban mass transit and intercity rail. In Chongqinq, Hangzhou, and Chengdu—the names are little known in the West, but each is a metropolis more populous than Chicago—brand-new subways with thousands of miles of tracks are nearing completion. China's major cities are already connected by 5,000 miles of tracks for high-speed trains—among them "The Harmony," which *averages* 220 miles per hour between Guangzhou and Wuhan—a network the government plans to triple by 2015. Only fifteen years after opening its first station, Shanghai's metro already counts eleven lines and 261 miles of track, making it the largest subway system in the world.

The BYD F3 or the metro: when it comes to building its future, China is planning for both the private automobile and public transport. Yet the fate of the planet may depend on which option future leaders in the developing world embrace. If they draw their inspiration from Western cities built around cars, freeways, and sprawl, the prognosis is not good. If they look to places that bet on public transport, trains, and walkable neighborhoods, there may still be hope.

For today, at least, Chen Shuli and her husband have made the practical choice. After their afternoon at the auto show, they walk the few hundred yards to the metro station, pass through the turnstiles, and wait on the platform, watching ads for maternity wear and iced coffee on overhead screens as the seconds count down to the next train. A single ride costs the equivalent of 45 cents, and trains come every minute and a half. The train is crowded, it's true, and there is the usual scrum of elbows and knees as people jockey for a seat, but the Bombardier-made trains are clean, well-lit, and air-conditioned. The couple find some floor space in the middle of the car, grab the straps hanging from an overhead railing, and in less than half an hour, they're back in their apartment in Jing'an.

Cars may be good for daydreams, but they may not be the best way to get around the rapidly growing cities of the future. In twenty-first-century Shanghai, the metro is definitely the fastest way to get home.

Any man of forty who still rides the métro is a loser.

—Salvador Dalí

A man who, beyond the age of twenty-six, finds himself on a bus can count himself as a failure.

—Margaret Thatcher

Confessions of a Straphanger

I admit it: I ride the bus.

What's more, I frequently find myself on subways, streetcars, light rail, metros, and high-speed trains. Though I have a driver's license, I've never owned an automobile, and apart from the occasional car rental, I've reached my mid-forties by relying on bicycles, my feet, and public transportation for my day-to-day travel. If you credit the U.K.'s late prime minister Thatcher, that makes me a failure of almost two decades' standing. Dalí, who depended for locomotion on a fleet of chauffeur-driven Cadillacs, is kinder: according to him, I've only been a loser for a couple of years. Far from being ashamed of my fare card, I consider it a badge of honor: I'm a straphanger, and I intend to remain one as long as my legs will carry me to the corner bus stop.

I'm not alone. Though there are 600 million cars on the planet, and counting, there are also seven billion people, which means that for the vast majority of us getting around involves taking buses, ferryboats, commuter trains, streetcars, and subways. In other words, traveling to work, school, or the market means being a straphanger: somebody who, by choice or necessity, relies on public transport, rather than a privately owned automobile.

Half the population of New York, Toronto, and London do not own cars. Public transport is how most of the people of Asia and Africa, the world's most populous continents, travel. Every day, subway systems carry 155 million passengers, thirty-four times the number carried by all the world's airplanes, and the global public transport market is now valued at $428 billion annually. A century and a half after the invention of the internal combustion engine, private car ownership is still an anomaly.

And yet public transportation, in many minds, is the opposite of glamour—a squalid last resort for those with one too many impaired driving charges, too poor to afford insurance, or too decrepit to get behind the wheel of a car. In much of North America, they are right: taking transit is a depressing experience. Anybody who has waited far too long on a street corner for the privilege of boarding a lurching, overcrowded bus, or wrestled luggage onto subways and shuttles to get to a big city airport, knows that transit on this continent tends to be underfunded, ill-maintained, and ill-planned. Given the opportunity, who wouldn't drive? Hopping in a car almost always gets you to your destination more quickly.

It doesn't have to be like this. Done right, public transport can be faster, more comfortable, and cheaper than the private automobile. In Shanghai, German-made magnetic levitation trains skim over elevated tracks at 266 miles an hour, whisking people to the airport at a third of the speed of sound. In provincial French towns, electric-powered streetcars run silently on rubber tires, sliding through narrow streets along a single guide rail set into cobblestones. From Spain to Sweden, Wi-Fi–equipped high-speed trains seamlessly connect with highly ramified metro networks, allowing commuters to work on laptops as they prepare for same-day meetings in once distant capital cities. In Latin America, China, and India, working people board fast-loading buses that move like subway trains along dedicated busways, leaving the sedans and SUVs of the rich mired in dawn-to-dusk traffic jams. And some cities have transformed their streets into cycle-path freeways, making giant strides in public health and safety and the sheer livability of their neighborhoods—in the process turning the workaday bicycle into a viable form of mass transit.

If you credit the demographers, this transit trend has legs. The "Millennials," who reached adulthood around the turn of the century and now outnumber baby boomers, tend to favor cities over suburbs, and are far more willing than their parents to ride buses and subways. Part of the reason is their ease with iPads, MP3 players, Kindles, and smartphones: you can get some serious texting done when you're not driving, and earbuds offer effective insulation from all but the most extreme commuting annoyances. Even though there are more teenagers in the United States than ever, only ten million have a driver's license (versus twelve million a generation ago). Baby boomers may have been raised in *Leave It to Beaver* suburbs, but as they retire, a significant contingent is favoring older cities and compact towns where they have the option of walking and riding bikes. Seniors, too, are more likely to use transit, and by 2025, there will be 64 million Americans over the age of sixty-five. Already, dwellings in older neighborhoods in Washington, D.C., Atlanta, and Denver, especially those near light-rail or subway stations, are commanding enormous price premiums over suburban homes. The experience of European and Asian cities shows that if you make buses, subways, and trains convenient, comfortable, fast, and safe, a surprisingly large percentage of citizens will opt to ride rather than drive.

For those who prefer their lives bubble-wrapped in gated communities, sports utility vehicles, and security-patrolled malls, public transport will probably always seem seedy, dangerous, and inconvenient. But around the world, there is a revolution going on in the way people travel. It is rewriting the DNA of formerly car-centered cities, making the streets better places to be, and restoring something cities sorely need: real public space.

The Great Oil Shock

The United States is the most extravagantly motorized nation in the history of the world.* At the end of the first decade of the twenty-first century, the

---

* Transportation scholars use the term "motorization" to describe a nation's level of vehicle ownership. Mass motorization is said to occur when there are 400 vehicles per 1,000 population. The United States achieved mass motorization in 1958, and Canada would follow in 1972; China, which currently has 123 vehicles per thousand, will achieve it in 2050.

country was home to 255 million registered vehicles, but only 196 million licensed drivers; in other words, cars and trucks now outnumber drivers by a factor of 5 to 4. The average American household owns 1.9 cars, and spends $16,700 a year keeping them running—not counting parking and tickets—more than it spends on food and health care combined.

In the summer of 2008, the price of a barrel of crude oil spiked to $147, a historic high. Since then, a gallon of gas, which could be had for under a dollar for most of the 1990s, has routinely retailed for $4.50 at some pumps. The shock waves produced by this price hike have been as dramatic as any initiated by the energy crises of 1973 and 1979. Two of the world's largest automakers went into bankruptcy; General Motors, once the world's largest corporation, is, after receiving $50 billion in taxpayers' money, now part owned by the U.S. Treasury. While the causes of the late-2000s financial crisis were complex, and included financial deregulation and subprime mortgage lending, many economists believe skyrocketing gas prices provided the critical body blow to consumer confidence that deepened the crisis into a worldwide recession.

Demotorization, which for twenty years has been a fact of life in Japan, may now have come to the United States. In 2009, Americans bought ten million cars, but scrapped fourteen million; this net loss of four million vehicles was the first time the total automobile fleet has shrunk since the Second World War. (In Canada, sales of cars and trucks plateaued in 2002 at 1.73 million units and fell to 1.46 million units in 2009. At the beginning of 2012, new vehicle sales remained well below their pre-recession levels.) Per capita vehicle miles traveled, the most reliable indicator of automobile dependence available, began to decline in mid-decade, and are now at their lowest levels since 2000. On the manufacturing side, the cradle-to-grave security of the auto sector is a thing of the past: with unemployment in Detroit near 20 percent and thousands of homes being bulldozed, parts of the onetime Motor City are returning to wilderness as beavers build dams in abandoned subdivisions minutes from downtown.

Putting money on the recovery of the automobile sector would be a sound bet were it not for the grim prospects ahead for energy production, especially when it comes to fossil fuels. Long the domain of conspiracy theorists, "peak oil"—the notion that the world is on the verge of using up half its reserves—has lately been accepted as an imminent reality by mainstream geologists, financiers, and oilmen. In 2010, the highly conservative International Energy Agency announced that output of conventional oil would peak within ten years if demand continued to grow on a business-as-usual basis.

"Even if oil demand were to remain flat," Fatih Birol, the agency's chief economist, conceded in 2011, "the world would need to find more than forty million barrels per day of gross new capacity—equal to four new Saudi Arabias—just to offset this decline."

As old fields are sucked dry, oil from such unconventional sources as Alberta's tar sands is coming on line; the extraction process, which requires enormous amounts of water and natural gas, is energy-intensive and punishing to the environment. Hydraulic fracturing, used to extract natural gas from shale deposits, is already a suspected cause of widespread contamination of groundwater across North America. The Deepwater Horizon spill, which blackened the Gulf of Mexico with 200 million gallons of oil over three months in 2010, highlighted the desperate measures already being taken to track down the planet's last remaining reserves of oil. The simple fact is, we have already burned too many fossil fuels for the good of the planet, too quickly. Using what is left in the ground would release three trillion tons of carbon dioxide, enough to bring on the most nightmarish scenarios of global warming: the melting of ice caps and glaciers, the acidification of oceans, and the inundation of coastal cities. "Business-as-usual," in other words, is a recipe for global disaster.

Too much of the oil now being used—the oil that may soon be gone—goes to keeping cars and trucks on the roads. Ninety percent of every barrel of oil in the world is used for transportation fuel, and American cars and trucks alone use nine million barrels of oil a day, one-tenth of the world's daily production.* While the global car industry tries to rebrand itself with plug-ins and hybrids, the widespread use of electricity as an alternative fuel is problematic in its own right: half of the electricity in the United States comes from burning carbon dioxide–emitting coal, a proportion that rises yearly.

Peak oil was not responsible for the summer of 2008 price spike—the rise in demand from China, India, and other developing nations was the more immediate cause—but the high prices were an augury of things to come. Unrest in the Arab world has led to intense volatility in gas prices,

---

* Though airplanes are significant guzzlers of oil, there are far fewer vehicles in the sky than on the ground. It is estimated that aviation accounts for 3 percent of greenhouse gas emissions. Automobiles alone—not including trucks or motorcycles—are responsible for 10 percent; after electricity generation, cars are the single leading manmade cause of global warming.

and some economists predict a barrel of crude could cost $200 by mid-decade, meaning $10 a gallon gas at the pumps. Any way you look at it, the prognosis for cheap energy is not good. Sooner rather than later, three-car garages in far-flung suburbs are going to become unimaginable luxuries, and car culture will undergo a radical transformation.

Even now, some modern-day Edison could be putting the final touches on a low-cost, portable cold-fusion reactor in a workshop in Kansas. But even if a zero-emission miracle sedan, running on tap water and yielding only lavender-scented exhaust, appeared in dealerships tomorrow, it would not solve the fundamental problem with cars.

The automobile was never an appropriate technology for the cities of America. As a form of mass transportation for the world, it is a disaster.

The End of Bliss

On September 13, 1899, a real estate dealer named Henry Bliss was alighting from a streetcar at West 74th Street and Central Park West, a block from his home, when a taxicab, swerving to avoid a truck in the right lane, ran him down, crushing his head and chest. He died of his injuries the next day. In North America, the first victim of the automobile was Bliss.

You would be hard-pressed to track down the name of the latest victim: in the last minute alone, two humans somewhere on the planet have had their lives cut short by cars. Year in, year out, automobiles kill 1.2 million people around the world, and injure twenty million.* It is a hecatomb equivalent to a dozen fully-loaded jumbo jets crashing every day, with no survivors, yet one so routine the majority of fatalities go unreported—as though being crushed by glass and metal had become just another of death's "natural causes." War, in comparison, is an inefficient scourge of the human race: among people aged ten to twenty-four, the automobile long ago beat out armed conflict as the leading cause of death.

A case against the automobile can be built purely on the grounds of public health. In spite of improvements in emission standards, pollution from automobiles still kills 30,000 Americans a year. Car ownership has been proven to make you fat and lazy: a survey of drivers in Atlanta found that each additional hour spent in a car per day was associated with a 6

---

* In spite of airbags and seatbelts, automobile accidents still claim over 40,000 lives a year in the United States, and cost the economy $433 *billion* annually.

percent increase in obesity. (In 1969, when half of American children got to school by foot or by bicycle, childhood obesity rates sat at 14 percent. Today, when 84 percent of children are driven to school, 45 percent of American kids are considered overweight or obese.) Time spent in a car is also correlated with social isolation: every ten minutes spent in daily commuting cuts involvement in community affairs by 10 percent. North Americans now spend so much time in cars that oncologists say drivers have significantly higher rates of skin cancer on the left side of their bodies.

But the automobile's most insidious impact is on the built environment. Between cul-de-sacs and hundred-acre Wal-Mart parking lots, metropolitan areas now eat up mind-boggling amounts of land. The cities of Dallas and Fort Worth, for example, have merged into a single conurbation the size of the nation of Israel. A large percentage of Americans now live in what is considered sprawl—tracts of low-density, single-family homes scattered over the urban fringes with little planning oversight. The result is utter car dependency. Between shuttling kids to school, visiting the mall, and driving to work, the average household generates eleven separate car trips a day. And asphalt really is as bad a land-gobbler as it seems: if all the pavement in America were merged, it would create a parking lot the size of Georgia.

Even in recessionary times, the propaganda for car culture is all-pervasive. Car ownership, consumers are constantly told, brings freedom: the freedom for restless rebels to flee stifling Main Street for cross-country road trips on Highway 66; the spontaneity for the city-weary to seek weekend respite in national parks; the autonomy to go south, literally, when things go south, figuratively. From the mattress-laden jalopy in Steinbeck's *Grapes of Wrath* to the Dean-driven '49 Hudson in Kerouac's *On the Road*, from the Great Red Shark in Hunter S. Thompson's *Fear and Loathing in Las Vegas* to the pimped-out Hondas of the latest from the *Fast and Furious* franchise, the iconic car of pop culture is a ticket to adventure. (One ad shows a young man setting his alarm for four in the morning so he can take his new Volkswagen out for a cruise. That's about right. In most metropolitan areas, the wee hours are the only time left when roads are actually uncongested enough to enjoy.) The personal automobile has, dramatically and enduringly, broadened our horizons. In the process, however, it has completely paved them over.

How did things get this bad? In North America, decades of government policy have made the private automobile the de facto mode of public transportation. Nine out of ten American commuters get to work by car, and more than three-quarters of these car commuters drive to work alone. Thanks to congestion, the average commute in the United States is now 51 minutes a day, and 3.5 million Americans qualify as extreme commuters, spending three hours or more getting to and from work. Economists have actually managed to quantify the absurdity of this situation. According to the Texas Transportation Institute, congestion costs the American economy $115 billion every year in wasted time and fuel—or $808 per person, a figure that, in spite of recession, has increased by 50 percent in the last decade. And time spent commuting turns out to be a powerful predictor of unhappiness. A study of German drivers who commute for two hours or more has shown they would have to make 40 percent more income to be as satisfied with their lives as a non-commuter is, and couples in which one partner commutes for longer than 45 minutes are 40 percent more likely to divorce.

The automobile is not going to disappear any time soon. At once cocoon and workhorse, it ingeniously reconciles two contradictory human impulses: the desire for home and security and the longing to roam and experience the world. Crucial for its load-carrying capacity in remote and rural areas, irreplaceable for many of its functions in cities, it is too useful an invention to ever completely vanish. Indeed, thanks to generations of car-centered development, living a car-free life—particularly for those raising young children—can seem like an impossible dream. Given the way most metropolitan areas are currently configured, calling for a ban on cars may seem tantamount to urging people to trade their refrigerators for iceboxes, or swap their vacuum cleaners for brooms. But car culture has hit a wall—and that may be a good thing. It is time to reconsider the dream of free-flowing freeways for all, spacious suburban living for the masses, and an SUV in every garage.

Another long-term trend is working against the automobile. Thanks largely to the ongoing industrialization of agriculture, for the first time in human history more people live in urban areas than in rural ones. Over the next thirty years, the population of the world's cities is expected to grow by three billion. The future is urban, which could well be a boon for the planet: dense city living not only spares countryside and wilderness undue human impact, but it is also more energy efficient than dispersed suburban settlement. But if urbanization means longer traffic jams, never-ending metropolitan sprawl, higher carbon emissions, and global grid-lock, we are going to have to face a simple reality.

If we don't start imagining a future with fewer cars, there might not be much of a future left to imagine.

Tracks and Taillights

My animus against automobiles runs deep, but I come by it honestly. When I was a boy, my parents moved to the West Coast, and something about the way cars bombed up our street, wrecking games of street hockey and kick-the-can, must have awakened in me an embryonic ambition toward city planning. After pacing out our block I built a kraft-paper model, with Monopoly hotels standing in for the houses, that showed how our street could be closed to automobiles and the back lanes used for deliveries and local traffic. I brought the model to a local television station, where I earnestly made the case for turning streets into parks—an eight-year-old urbanist with a white turtleneck, a Prince Valiant haircut, and some strong opinions about traffic calming.

Later, downwardly mobile in my early twenties, I got a job working as a delivery driver for a dental lab. The work was hardly glamorous: I punched in, spent my days circling for parking and riding elevators in office blocks with dripping bags of false teeth, and punched out. Forty hours a week, I watched the world from behind glass, getting angry at shiftless pedestrians and unpredictable cyclists, a Travis Bickle in the making. At the end of the workday, I would unlock my bicycle and become a quick-flip hypocrite, cursing cars and their exhaust all the way home. In six months of driving I was rear-ended twice; my shoulders ached, my belly spread, and the unspent adrenaline from day-to-day near misses turned my blood prematurely bilious.

Heading back to the lab near the end of one shift, I glanced in my rear-view mirror and saw the compact car behind me come to a complete stop, the victim of a blow-out or a stall. We were on a long, visibility-reducing curve on a stretch of downtown expressway, and I instantly knew the driver was in trouble. I briefly caught a flash of panicked face, and then saw his body go flying through the window as he was rear-ended by the 18-wheeler behind him. I never saw the aftermath—everybody knows you don't stop on a shoulderless freeway—but I will never forget the look of utter shock on his face in what were surely the last seconds of his life. After punching out that day, I put in my notice.

Cars, I decided then, would not be a major part of my life. It was not just the drudgery of driving for a living. It just felt wrong, as though every hour I spent cocooned in plastic, fiberglass, and metal was an hour I had failed to spend living. My subsequent career as a traveling writer has only confirmed my intuition: planes, sure, as a means to an end; trains and boats, always; but cars—only as a last resort, when there really is no other choice. The places that meant the most to me were almost always the ones I got to on foot.

Don't get me wrong—my experience as a delivery driver was no formative trauma; it did not scar me deeply enough to make me a rabid autophobe. I live in the real world, which means I dutifully renew my license, and rent cars when I need to. As a teenager, I fetishized Detroit's coolest rides, and a well-preserved Citroën DS can still stop me in my tracks. But for me, the seductive ease of mobility without effort, available at zero dollars down and $299 a month, is the beginning of a spiral through selfishness, road rage, and anomie, one whose ultimate goal is the mall and the gated community. If you really want to be free in this world, I have come to believe, then whatever you do, don't buy a car.

In the last few years, a tectonic shift has been occurring in the North American landscape. In Florida, Nevada, Arizona, and California, the fallout from the subprime mortgage fiasco has left boomburgs, "drive-till-you-qualify" subdivisions, and edge cities, most built on the assumption that fossil fuels would always be cheap, in a state of crisis. As newspapers filled with stories of ranch-style homes being turned into meth labs and scavengers stripping abandoned "starter castles" of pipes and copper wire, demographers announced, in a turnaround that would have been unthinkable a generation ago, that the suburban poor now outnumber the urban poor. Lately, the reviled "inner" city is starting to look like a good place to live. Factories and their pollution have fled old urban centers for the interstates, and though traffic still plagues city streets, urban smog has diminished over the last two decades thanks to ever more stringent automobile emission standards. The average life expectancy in New York City is now actually one and a half years longer than in the nation as a whole.

"For too long, federal policy has actually encouraged sprawl and congestion and pollution, rather than quality public transportation and smart, sustainable development," President Barack Obama announced at an urban affairs summit in 2009. Under his administration, policy began to shift some public resources to cities, with a strong emphasis on improving transit. From Los Angeles to New York, miles of new subway tracks are being laid, and rail transit is again becoming symbolic of progress and municipal achievement. Streetcars, long vanished from the American streetscape, are cropping up in such unlikely places as Houston, Denver, and Salt Lake City. After a long hiatus, miles of new subway and light rail tracks are finally being added to Canada's largest cities.

In many ways, we are entering a golden age of urban transit: sophisticated software and GPS allow for better dispatching of buses and trains, higher ridership is funding service improvements, rechargeable fare cards allow effortless transfers, and smartphones empower commuters with up-to-the-minute scheduling information. And as people drive less, demand is growing: in 2010, transit ridership in the U.S. hit a fifty-four-year high of 10.2 billion annual rides. For people like me who believe we need alternatives to a life centered on the private automobile, all this is excellent news.

This book is, in part, the story of a bad idea: the notion that our metropolises should be shaped by the needs of cars, rather than people. A slow-motion exodus from cities began when old, coherent neighborhoods were divided and degraded by on-ramps and overpasses, and highways were cut into the living tissue of the metropolis. By diminishing public space, the automobile has made once great cities terrible places to live.

This book also tells the story of some very good ideas. Around the world, energetic and idealistic people are working hard to reclaim neighborhoods once left for dead. The movement goes under a variety of names: transit-oriented development, smart growth, new urbanism. In the wrong mouths, these are just buzzwords; in the wrong hands, they can serve as the justification for boondoggles as bad as any hastily thrown-up boomburg. But the advocates of livable cities and walkable small towns may be on to something—by investing in development that includes well-conceived transit, we can create more sustainable and, crucially, more *civil* communities.

A caveat for readers: I am not a rail fan, a juicehead, or an aficionado of doodlebugs. (Rail fans are also known as "foamers" because they tend to foam at the mouth when talk turns to bogeys and pantographs; they may or may not be "juiceheads," whose knowledge of vintage electric streetcars and even "doodlebugs," the streetcar's gas-powered equivalent, tends to be encyclopedic.) While I love the gritty allure of a great metropolitan subway, and consider a rail trip one of life's great pleasures, my interest in transportation technology runs a distant second to my love of cities. Simply put, I like subways, buses, and trains because I believe they make better places than cars and freeways.

There's something else, too. Over the last twenty years, I've gotten to know a lot of cities. I spent the early '90s in Paris and, in my travels, many months living in the great metropolises of Europe, Asia, and the Americas. While I've watched friends and family opt for the suburbs or the country, I've never lost faith in the old city centers. Even though I've seen how rents could be high, pollution bad, break-ins frequent, and traffic horrific, the rewards of urban living have always seemed worth the aggravations. And things are clearly getting better. In only a few years, I've seen how intelligent urbanism, transportation policy, and changing demographics could transform cities whose quality of life had been merely tolerable into genuinely great places to live.

When I discovered Montreal, which seemed to have much of what I was looking for in a city, and met Erin, a woman who made me want to stay put, my perspective really started to change. Recently, Erin and I got married and bought a home together. Even more recently, Erin told me she was pregnant. When I began mapping out this journey, parenthood was just an idea. Now that I'm going to become a father, the questions I've been asking myself about the future of cities seem a lot less abstract. I find myself wanting to know whether Erin and I have made the right choice; whether my parents' generation was right to give up on the increasingly traffic-clogged, smog-choked, and often crime-ridden cities of the twentieth century; or whether, with a little imagination and will, we can remake them into places where people will want to live, thrive, and raise families in the twenty-first.

To answer the question, I know, I'm going to have to see what people around the world are doing to make their cities better places to live. It's only a hunch, but I figure I'll find the kinds of places I'm looking for by following tracks and sidewalks, rather than taillights and freeways.

Any time we don't have crowding during rush hour, there'll be a receiver sitting in the mayor's chair and New York will be a ghost town. Why, they talk about the rush hour and the crash and noise. Why, listen, don't you see that's the proof of our life and vitality? Why, why, that is New York City!

—Mayor Fiorello LaGuardia, 1943

1. The Subway that Time Forgot

New York, New York

Something impossibly big and powerful was moving beneath the city.

In a portable office at a construction site in Chelsea, I could already sense its presence as a low rumbling rising through the soles of my rubber boots. As I rode a steel cage fifteen stories down a circular abyss, the physical shudder became an all-encompassing roar. The elevator touched down on the floor of a high-ceilinged chamber blasted out of gray rock, where a makeshift factory was abuzz with activity. Beside me, an arc welder's torch cracked and sizzled; a crane hoisting stacks of precast concrete overhead emitted piercing beeps; a construction train juddered to a halt and shook a couple of dozen tons of broken rock onto a conveyor belt. Underneath it all, the earth-rattling roar never abated. At the chamber's north end, where the ceiling lowered into parallel tubes as smooth and round as twin shotgun barrels, the tunnel on the right thrummed like Hades' didgeridoo. It was hard to shake the feeling that a living thing had been unleashed, and was gnawing its way through the bedrock of Manhattan.

"It's up ahead, about a thousand feet!" my guide yelled into my ear. Rich Redmond, a consulting engineer for New York's Metropolitan Transportation Authority (MTA), and the man responsible for day-to-day operations on this site, walked ahead of me into the tunnel. I squinted into the distance, but the tube darkened and narrowed at the limits of my vision. As my mind conjured visions of sandworms and minotaurs, I followed Redmond into the gloom.

We splashed through murky water that purled around the ties of a single railway track, a rivulet constantly fed by groundwater seeping through the concrete walls. Ahead of us, the end of the tunnel was plugged by a vibrating disc fitted with red and green lights. Just as moving forward was becoming physically painful—it sounded like the world's biggest wood chipper was grinding its way through a petrified forest—the roar stopped. Redmond paused and shouted back: "They must be done with the shove. If you want to see it, now would be a good time!" Quickening our pace, we came to the end of the line: a floor-to-ceiling framework of horizontal walkways and vertical ladders, draped with a cat's cradle of coiled wires and dangling tubes.

The monster at the end of the tube was a Herrenknect Double Shield tunnel-boring machine—a TBM for short. "This is the trailing gear," explained Redmond, as we clambered aboard the back end of the machine. "It's about three hundred and fifty feet long; it houses the ventilation, the pumps, the electrical systems." Custom-made for the job at a workshop in Germany, the thousand-ton TBM was so massive that it arrived in New York in three separate transatlantic shipments; reassembling it, once it had been lowered down the excavation shaft, took two and a half months. The machine's immediate goal was the cavern of a new station at Thirty-fourth Street. From there, it would veer from Eleventh Avenue, boring under Penn Station's Amtrak tunnels, before connecting to the 7-line platform at Times Square. The 7-line extension, as the project was known, would ultimately allow New Yorkers to commute to jobs at the Javits Center and elsewhere on the far West Side.

Weaving through pipes and beams, we came to the TBM's nerve center, a small booth where an operator in green coveralls sat in front of computer screens monitoring the monster's progress. "The screens show the thrust, applied pressure on the rock, and the torque of the machine," said Redmond. Guided by GPS, lasers, and radar, the operator was responsible for adjusting hydraulic levers to keep the machine's cutting-head on course.

Though it is made of metal and powered by electric motors running on 13,000 volts, the tunnel-boring machine moves like a living organism. Its rotating cutting-head resembles the circular maw of a lamprey eel, with forty-four spinning discs of alloy in the place of pointed teeth. Bracing itself against the tunnel walls with two convex grippers, the machine uses pistons to force the cutting-head forward; the crushed rocks fall into chutes behind the discs and are ferried away by a central conveyor belt. When the TBM has completed a five-foot "shove" into solid rock, the grippers are released, and, like a colossal caterpillar, the machine shifts its entire thousand-ton bulk forward by lifting and dropping its multiple feet.

Climbing a ladder, Redmond and I ducked beneath the ceiling of the tunnel, and scuttled toward the business end of the TBM. Three workers in hardhats and overalls were on their sides, grunting and cursing as they tightened the bolts on a curved, five-foot-wide segment of precast concrete; a half-dozen such segments made one complete circle of tunnel wall. On a good day, said Redmond, the machine could complete a shove in half an hour, lengthening the tunnel by 60 feet over three eight-hour shifts. On a bad day, when unexpected conditions were encountered, everything ground to a halt. As we backtracked through the trailing gear, Redmond reached into an open rail car and passed me an arrowhead-shaped piece of broken rock, flecked with glints of mica. "This is the muck train," he yelled. "Muck is vernacular for mined rock. You're holding a piece of pure Manhattan schist in your hands." The TBM makes short work of the large-grained whitish-gray rock, as it does granite, which accounts for much of the bedrock undergirding the skyscrapers of New York. In less predictable ground, however, other techniques are necessary.

"We ran into water-bearing glacial material at the very start of tunneling," said Redmond. "We had to drill holes and run tubes from the surface, fill them with liquid brine, and use a freezer plant to bring them down to thirty below zero. They basically turned the soil into a giant block of ice—which made it solid enough to mine." Once the freezer was turned off, grout was injected between the concrete walls and the rock, sealing the tunnel against seeping groundwater.

All around us were sandhogs, New York's legendary urban miners, broad-shouldered, stocky men in jeans and safety vests thoroughly begrimed with gray slurry. The sandhogs refer to the tunnel-boring machine as "the mole"—a nickname that is not entirely affectionate. For generations, the power behind the cutting-head was almost entirely human. Since laying the foundations of the Brooklyn Bridge in 1872, the sandhogs have dug every important sewer, water, and train tunnel in the city. These storied laborers, many of them Irish, African American, and Italian, dug the Lincoln and Holland tunnels, shored up the collapsing Trinity Church, and excavated the city's subway lines, blasting with dynamite, tightening bolts with 75-pound wrenches, often clearing away muck with their bare hands. Working in pressurized tunnels when they dug beneath New York's riverbeds, they died by the dozens in cave-ins and catastrophic blowouts.

The sandhogs are still a force to be reckoned with beneath the streets of New York. An Irish flag hangs at the entrance to the excavation shaft, and before digging on the 7-line extension could begin, the city's new Roman Catholic archbishop paid a visit, tracing the sign of the cross over bowed hardhats. Automation, which began when New York's first TBM was lowered into the shaft of the Third Water Tunnel in 1970, has been both a blessing and a curse. With the coming of the "mole," the most dangerous part of the sandhogs' jobs, digging into potentially unstable ground with picks, shovels, and percussion drills, was eliminated—but so were a good number of jobs. At the turn of the last century, it took almost 8,000 men, working for two dollars a day, to excavate New York's first subway lines. Today's sandhogs are paid far more—over $100,000 a year, with benefits—but only a few dozen are needed on each eight-hour shift. The mole, the steam-powered hammer to the underground miners' John Henry, has turned out to be the biggest, toughest sandhog of them all.

Around the world, hundreds of such machines are now at work, chewing through geology in an unprecedented push to increase human mobility. In Beijing, Madrid, Delhi, and Los Angeles, TBMs are drilling beneath the feet of urbanites, in one of the most astonishing bursts of transit infrastructure building in decades. As the planet enters a new phase of urbanization, cities are looking to advanced transit systems as the way out of congestion, pollution, and economic stagnation. The mole may have taken the danger, and thus the glamour, out of tunnel digging, but it is allowing cities to build new lines on time and on budget, with no loss of human life. The fact that New York—which for decades stood alone among great cities in that its total track mileage was actually decreasing—is finally digging a new tunnel, is a sign of the times. After half a century of freeway building, the subway is back.

If all goes well, Redmond explained to me as we rode back to the surface, the work would be completed some time late in 2013. According to its critics, the 7-line extension, which will add exactly one stop to the existing network, is a "subway to nowhere"—a waste of precious resources in recessionary times. It was intended to serve a stadium for the 2012 Summer Olympics, but when New York lost the bid to London, plans for a second stop for Hell's Kitchen—a neighborhood sorely in need of another stop— were dropped. The line will terminate at the largest undeveloped patch of real estate in Manhattan: the Hudson Yards, twenty-six acres of switches and marshaling tracks the MTA sold to Related Companies and Goldman Sachs in 2009 for a cool billion dollars. The developers plan to turn it into a $15 billion enclave of office towers, apartment buildings, a hotel, parks, and retail businesses. According to Mayor Michael Bloomberg, it is such long-term investments in infrastructure that will transform areas full of promise into "neighborhoods full of residents, park-goers, office workers and shoppers." Critics call it a boondoggle—one that will mostly profit the mayor's developer friends. The price tag for extending New York's subway network by just one mile in the early years of the twenty-first century? Just over two billion dollars.

The project, by any calculus, is ridiculously expensive. Thanks to the tunnel-boring machine, the actual excavation work is not a big provider of employment for the city. But laying new subway track—even a controversial project like the 7-line extension—may be the smartest investment New York has made in its own future in decades.

Take the "T" Train

Were it not for the subway, New York as it is today would not exist. At a crucial time in the city's history, the engineers of this ingenious subterranean railroad cleared the streets of impossible congestion and decanted the population of the teeming, insalubrious tenements of the Lower East

Side to the farthest corners of the boroughs. Because it was able to move so many people so quickly, the subway became the ultimate urban density amplifier, allowing the apartment buildings and office towers of Manhattan to be built side-by-side, and turning a 26-square-mile island of gneiss, marble, and schist into one of the world's greatest metropolises, where millions could live and trade services, goods, and ideas swiftly and efficiently.

Given how badly it was neglected in the twentieth century, it's a miracle that New York's subway survived into the twenty-first at all. In the mid-1950s, when the underfunded system's rolling stock was already forty years old, the city adopted an official policy of deferred maintenance, kicking off a long decline that tracked the city's sagging fortunes. The nadir came in the early '80s, as motors fell from brackets and trains burst into flames with depressing regularity. In one of the worst accidents, an antique signal failed, causing a Manhattan-bound local to slam into the back of a train waiting in a Brooklyn tunnel, killing the motorman and injuring 135 riders. When author Paul Theroux spent a week riding the rails in 1981, he discovered a Dickensian underworld of loopers (car-hopping purse-snatchers), skells (vagrants), shooflies (undercover transit cops), and lushworkers (drunk-rolling pickpockets), where transit workers were burned alive in token booths for kicks.

"What is amazing," Theroux concluded, "is that back in 1904 a group of businessmen solved New York's transport problems for centuries to come. What an engineering marvel they eventually created in this underground railway! And how amazed they would be to see what it has become, how foul-seeming to the public mind." It was as though Theroux had stumbled upon a rusty *musée mécanique* in the jungle, kept running, barely, by the local tribespeople.

Something had to change, and it did. Shortly after Theroux's visit, the Transit Authority declared war on graffiti, hauling in cars nightly and scrubbing them clean of the day's accumulated Wildstyle tags. (Spray paint is now a thing of the past: the modern vandal has resorted to etching the windows with acid.) Antique and defective trains were replaced by Canadian-made cars that now average 690,000 miles between breakdowns—one hundred times the '80s norm. In the last thirty years, $75 billion has been poured into the system.

Not that grit has entirely disappeared. Among the subways of the world, New York's is a utilitarian system. With a few exceptions, the stations are shallow: on the avenues, trains can be heard clattering through the sidewalk grates, raging uptown and down only a few yards beneath the feet of pedestrians. "There's the smelly essence of New York down there," intoned Manhattan's pop-poet laureate Lou Reed in the days of subway vigilante Bernhard Goetz, and the underground has retained its velvety stench of soot and sweat, mixed with the roasted nut odor of dust from overheated brake shoes settling on the puddles of rainwater between the tracks. On the concourses, freckled black with the chewing gum of the ages, pillars cut off sightlines, the ceilings seem to be only inches overhead, and the dry heat and jaundiced light enfold you, forcing you into a new, almost theatrical relationship with the city.

For anybody who grew up with stories of a system going to hell beneath a crumbling metropolis, it is remarkable just how well the New York subway works. Most trains are air-conditioned, and on the Grand Central platforms, giant overhead air-cooling units create an oasis that, on hot days, actually tempts you to linger underground. (I've spent a couple of Julys in New York. That people here rode the subways for most of the twentieth century without air-conditioning is a testament to their fortitude. That Parisians and Londoners are still asked to do without it should be considered cruel and unusual punishment.) These days, almost everybody takes the train; depending on the traffic, it can be faster than hailing a cab. Even billionaire mayor Michael Bloomberg sometimes rides the express to City Hall on the Lexington Avenue line—perhaps as often as twice a week.* Subway ridership, which bottomed out in 1977 at a billion rides a year, is once again approaching the record highs of the post-war years, when two billion trips were taken on the elevateds and subways.

Most important, New York is finally building more transit infrastructure. In addition to the 7-line extension, the East Side Access tunnels, which are being drilled beneath the Waldorf-Astoria Hotel and the Seagram Building at a cost of $7.2 billion, will allow Long Island Rail Road commuters to arrive at Grand Central Terminal, saving a half hour of backtracking to East Side offices from the usual terminus at Penn Station. And the warren of corridors and stairs at Fulton Street in Lower Manhattan, which local transit campaigners have wryly dubbed a "funhouse that's

* *New York Times* reporters who spied on Bloomberg for six weeks in 2007 discovered that the "straphanger mayor" was actually met outside his Upper East Side town house by a pair of Chevrolet Suburbans and driven 22 blocks to the stop outside Bloomingdale's, so that at least a quarter of his commute was by chauffeured SUV.

no fun," is finally being rationalized into an easy-to-use east-to-west concourse. (The Access to the Region's Core Project, whose three tunnels between New Jersey and midtown Manhattan would have doubled the number of rush-hour commuter trains serving Penn Station, was canceled by New Jersey's governor in 2010. Since then, the Bloomberg administration has reportedly been at work on implementing a further extension of the number 7 line across the Hudson River to New Jersey, a plan that would make the line significantly more cost effective.)

But the most eagerly awaited project of them all—one in the offing since the fare was a nickel and the Brooklyn "Trolley" Dodgers were hitting homers at Ebbets Field—has got to be the Second Avenue subway. When the widely hated elevated tracks on Second Avenue were torn down for scrap iron during the Second World War, and the Third Avenue El was demolished fifteen years later, it was with the understanding that a subway would soon replace them. Despite a number of promising starts, the Second Avenue subway never got built. The Lexington Avenue line, meanwhile, has had to do all the heavy lifting on the east side: its number 4, 5, and 6 trains carry 1.7 million people a day—equal to the ridership of Boston's "T," Chicago's "L," and Washington's Metro combined—making it the busiest transit line on the continent. Estimated price tag for the Second Avenue Subway, when it is completed, maybe, in 2016: seventeen billion dollars.

Does Manhattan really need this much subway? Definitely. In a week riding the Lexington Avenue line during the rush hour, I never got a seat. In fact, there wasn't a morning I rode when the trains weren't at crush load, which means 160 people were crammed into cars built for 110. Even with a train arriving every two minutes, commuters stand five deep on the main platforms. The infrastructure, meanwhile, is showing its age. At Union Square, the curved tracks make arriving trains squeal (at 98.6 decibels, the *New York Post* discovered, enough to cause hearing damage) and result in an 18-inch gap between train and platform at many doors. To solve the problem, early Industrial Age technology was mobilized: moving metal flanges snap into place from the edge of the platform when the train arrives. There is no way to decrease the headway—the amount of time—between trains; thanks to analog relays and signals that date from the 1930s—and look, as one subway commentator told me, "like the switchboard at the Grand Hotel"—trains are already running as close together as is safely possible. New York's subway may be running better than it has been in decades, but compared to many European and Asian systems, it is still in shockingly bad shape.

The rationale for the Second Avenue subway has always been a simple one: scooping up commuters on the far East Side will significantly reduce the atrocious crowding on the overtaxed Lexington. So far, however, work has been delayed by, successively, the Depression, the Second World War, the Korean War, and the fiscal meltdown of the '70s. This time around, work has actually begun beneath the streets of the Upper East Side, and the sand-hogs have lowered a tunnel-boring machine into the launch box at 96th Street. Riding the "T," as the new line will be called, will likely be a disori-enting experience for veteran straphangers: the bright, well-lit stations will have column-free mezzanines and dizzyingly high ceilings—more like Washington's Metro than the claustrophobic stations New Yorkers are used to.

That is, if this apparently cursed subway ever sees the light of day. Given the state of civic finances, its future is by no means guaranteed. With the real estate taxes that are the source of much of the MTA's fund-ing in serious decline, the authority announced in 2010 it was facing a $900 million budget shortfall, and would have to cut basic service on three subway lines. Which raises the question: If the MTA can't even keep existing lines running, how can it afford to build a new one?

In a city this compact, populous, and wealthy, sustained investment in transit should be a no-brainer. Only 5 percent of daily commuters to Manhattan's central business district arrive by car; the rest get to work by foot, bicycle, or on some form of transit. The subway is the *sine qua non* of Manhattan; it keeps the economy of the city, the state, and the entire Northeast thrumming. Shut it down, even for a day, and New York City turns into Podunk.

When it comes to transit, though, some people just can't seem to do the math. *It never pays its own way*, goes the refrain; or *The crooks that run the system are making money hand over fist*; or the classic *We should take all that money and use it to build more roads*. It is the kind of reasoning that has turned the Second Avenue subway, a simple replacement project that should have been completed half a century ago, into the line that time forgot.

As a brief look at the history of public transport in New York shows, it has ever been thus.

"To Harlem in Fifteen Minutes!"

Every city has its phantom tollbooths, spots on the map where the space-time continuum does not seem to apply. In New York, there is a certain subway train that, after the last passenger has gotten off, makes a brief stop at a ghost station: a spectacular, century-old chapel of rapid transit that has been sealed like King Tut's tomb since the end of the Second World War.

This is the old City Hall station, a legend among transit historians. In order to visit it, I had to promise a spokesman for New York City Transit that I would not reveal the number—or letter—of the train that stops there. James Anyansi met me at the end of a damp subway platform in Lower Manhattan, and after showing his ID to the operator of a train emptied of its passengers, took me on a short, wheel-shrieking ride around a sharp bend in the track. The doors opened, and we emerged into a time capsule: a station of the Interborough Rapid Transit Company (the IRT), looking much as it did when it first opened to the public on October 27, 1904.

It took a few seconds for my eyes to adjust to the diffuse light cast by the frosted globes of multi-armed chandeliers. We were standing on a sweep of platform curved like a sultan's scimitar. Unlike the simple, post-and-lintel construction of most subway stations, there is not a straight line to be seen in the old City Hall station: a succession of arches curved out of sight, as in the crypt of a Romanesque church. Between the semicircular ribs, a her-ringbone pattern of glossy cream and emerald tiles bordered skylights of leaded glass; incandescent bulbs illuminated the station's gloomier cor-ners. As the train pulled away, leaving us alone in the station, an elaborate bronze plaque on the other side of the tracks was revealed. Between seated damsels bearing the dates 1900 and 1904, it paid homage to "This first municipal rapid transit railroad. . . . Authorized by the state / Constructed by the city," and bore the names of Cornelius Vanderbilt and August Bel-mont. We walked up a broad staircase to a domed mezzanine crowned by a glass oculus, once the spot where "ticket choppers" collected fares from commuters. Anyansi directed his flashlight beam up a staircase sealed by heavy metal doors. Had we been able to open them, we would have emerged next to the statue of Nathan Hale outside City Hall.

When the City Hall station opened, a *New York World* reporter called it "a cool little vaulted city of cream and blue earthenware like a German beer stein," which just about gets it right. In all New York, there is only one other place remotely like it: the time-warp temple of hygienic tile that is the Grand Central Oyster Bar. Both were designed by a Spanish architect known for bringing the technique of tiled vaulted ceilings common in Catalonia to America. During the Second World War, the station's magnificent leaded glass ceiling was blacked out in anticipation of air raids; it closed permanently in 1945, because its platform was too sharply curved to handle longer trains.

Waving his flashlight at waist height, Anyansi signaled the driver of the next train to pick us up. We rounded another curve, and, in a Viewmaster's click, were back from the rabbit hole to the workaday, no-nonsense domain of the MTA.

New York's early subway boasted other touches of elegance, most of them effaced during the twentieth century. Oak ticket booths, with elaborate bronze fittings, were supplanted by cages of Plexiglas and steel. Glass-bricked sidewalks that allowed light to pour in from street level were gradually paved over. More than one hundred arched iron and glass kiosks, modeled on Turkish summer houses, were removed when motorists complained they blocked their view of traffic. (The kiosk that shields commuters from rain and wind at Astor Place is a faithful contemporary re-creation.) In total, August Belmont Jr., the financier behind the IRT, allowed half a million dollars for ornamentation of the entire system, a paltry sum even then—he spent more operating his private subway car, the *Mineola*, which featured mahogany from the Philippines, sliding leatherette curtains, over-stuffed couches, and its own motorman.

The Sunday after its grand opening, one million New Yorkers lined up to ride the IRT, which bored north from City Hall along Broadway all the way to 145th Street in Harlem; queues at some stations stretched for two blocks. Its express trains reached speeds of 40 miles an hour, making it the fastest mass transit railroad in the world—it is still one of the world's only subways with dedicated express tracks. Public enthusiasm for the new system was genuine. In a chronically congested commercial center, freedom of movement had been a long time coming.

Gridlock is a function of New York's geography and history. It is, after all, an urban archipelago whose islands are divided by tidal estuaries and rivers; the charming muddle of narrow, frequently off-bias streets in Lower Manhattan is a legacy of colonial and even Dutch pre-industrial settlement. In 1811, state commissioners laid out a street plan that became the template for all future growth: 155 streets that spanned the island from river to river, crosshatched by eleven 100-foot-wide avenues, creating a gridiron that extended from Greenwich Village to Harlem, with little provision for green space. Broad north-south avenues were fretted with narrow, closely spaced streets, their width best suited for buildings of one to four stories. Broadway, which followed an old Native American footpath, threw a diagonal across the grid, introducing confusion at key intersections.

At a time when Central Park was still swampy bog and Harlem a distant village surrounded by the estates of wealthy farmers, the commissioners' plan must have looked like a fond dream. But, as the port boomed, so did New York's population, doubling from 1820 to 1840, and again from 1840 to 1860—and yet again by 1890. With 3.4 million inhabitants, New York at the turn of the century was the second-largest city in the world, and by far the densest. With almost 5,000 people crammed into an average city block, the Lower East Side, staging ground for America's immigrants, was the most crowded patch of real estate on the planet.

In the first decades of the nineteenth century, New York had been a walking city, crossable on foot in less than half an hour. As the city stretched north of 14th Street, and travel times increased, the city's first transit entrepreneurs competed for passengers' nickels. Swiping an idea from the French, a stable owner in the 1820s introduced horse-drawn omnibuses running on fixed routes and schedules. The New York and Harlem Railroad, the world's first horse railroad, upped the ante by sinking iron rails into the Bowery: the tracks reduced friction, allowing more passengers to be pulled faster, and with fewer horses, than the poky omnibuses.

By 1860, when fourteen horse-railway companies were carrying 38 million passengers a year, conditions on the streets of Manhattan had become unbearable. As there were no separated lanes, traffic moved any which way, and progress was glacial. Such was the confusion of drays, butcher carts, and grocers' wagons that it was said crossing Broadway at Fulton Street could take twenty minutes. Mark Twain, writing for a California newspaper in 1867, captured the sheer folly of the situation:

> You cannot ride unless you are willing to go in a packed omnibus that labors, and plunges, and struggles along at the rate of three miles in four hours and a half, always getting left behind by fast walkers, and always apparently hopelessly tangled up with vehicles that are trying to get to some place or other and can't. Or, if you can stomach it, you can ride in a horse-car and stand up for

three-quarters of an hour, in the midst of a file of men that extends
from front to rear (seats all crammed, of course)—or you can take
one of the platforms, if you please, but they are so crowded you
will have to hang on by your eye-lashes and your toe-nails.

Getting any business done in New York, Twain concluded, involved
devoting an entire day to fighting traffic.

In a city at a virtual standstill, schemes for improved transit prolifer-
ated like patent medicines, filling the pages of scientific journals and illustrated weeklies. Some of the follies actually got built. The West Side and
Yonkers Patent Railway, a scheme straight out of Dr. Seuss, consisted of a
single track suspended thirty feet above Greenwich Street (in what would
later be known as the Meatpacking District) by slender wrought-iron stan-
chions. Steam engines hidden beneath the sidewalk powered loops of continuously whirring wire rope threaded through giant pulleys; passengers
filed into a car, a gripman pulled a lever, and padded claws grasped the
cable, jerking the car into motion along half a mile of track. The "rattletrap
line," as the dailies dubbed it, was constantly breaking down, leading to
comical scenes in which commuters stranded three stories above street
level had to be rescued by ladder. After only two years of unreliable service,
the entire apparatus was sold for $960 at sheriff's auction.

As long as William "Boss" Tweed ran Tammany Hall, efficient rapid
transit didn't stand a chance. The impossibly corrupt commissioner of
public works had a vested interest in keeping transit on street level: a
major investor in omnibuses, Tweed made a fortune dispensing 999-year
franchises to the owners of the horsecar lines. Despairing of political
approval for a subway, and inspired by the success of London's underground, inventor Alfred Beach decided to build a subterranean railway in
secret. A team of workmen, digging at night and carting away dirt in wagons from the basement of a clothing store at Warren Street and Broadway,
managed to excavate a 300-foot-long tunnel without being detected. In 1870
Beach triumphantly unveiled his Pneumatic Railway. The curious waited in
an underground parlor furnished with settees, chandeliers, and a grand
piano, and then filed into a horseshoe-shaped car that fit snuggly into an
8-foot-diameter tube. A giant fan, used for ventilating mines, blew the car
and its passengers down the tracks at six miles an hour; almost half a million people would eventually pay 25 cents a head to ride the Pneumatic.
Tweed tried to bring suit against Beach, but shortly after the opening, Tweed

was imprisoned for life on corruption charges. Unfortunately, the Panic of 1873, in which railroads across the continent failed, killed off investment in new schemes, and the Pneumatic was sealed up and forgotten. When sandhogs digging a subway line to Brooklyn forty years later broke into the subterranean parlor, where the piano still sat, they might as well have been Morlocks stumbling on a Victorian time machine.

The Pneumatic turned out to be an idea before its time: it would take a generation of in-fighting before construction of another underground railway began. In the meantime, New York had to make do with its balky surface transportation. Cable cars ran up many avenues, but they were notoriously dangerous. Electric trolleys, which began replacing horsecars in the 1880s, were soon ubiquitous, but their progress on Manhattan's crowded streets was always painfully slow. The stopgap solution for rapid transit was the elevated railroad, and soon the "Els" ran up four major avenues. They seemed like a natural solution in the laissez-faire nineteenth century: private enterprise could throw them up quickly and cheaply, without government help. By 1890, New York's trolleys and Els were carrying a billion passengers a year, more than all the other railroads in the Americas combined.

Widely used, Els were also widely hated. What's wrong with an El? Nothing—unless it happens to run through your neighborhood. Brooklyn retains many stretches of elevated tracks, and to get an idea of what an intrusion they can be, I rode the Q train to Coney Island one afternoon. Four El tracks run right down the middle of Brighton Beach Avenue. At the best of times, strolling past the Russian delis and nail salons is an intense experience: the tracks overhead cast the street into perpetual gloom and amplify the honking and revving of cars and trucks at least twofold. I watched as a Manhattan-bound train arrived, its contrapuntal clacking mounting to a teeth-gnashing crescendo as the wheels screamed on the curve over Coney Island Avenue. When two trains went by at once, it was like being in a basement suite beneath Valhalla's bowling alley.

Living on Second Avenue in Manhattan in the 1890s must have been even more trying. The trains passing overhead weren't powered by electricity, but by coal. Pedestrians were splattered with axle grease, or blinded by iron filings from brake shoes, and chunks of burning coal routinely fell to the pavement. A visiting Australian travel writer complained it was like having an "ever-active volcano" overhead, and posed "a severe trial to the average nervous system." Though they reduced property values in their immediate vicinity, the Els succeeded, as the streetcars had before them, in reducing the extreme density of Lower Manhattan. Gradually, tenements spread northward past Central Park, as people moved to less crowded neighborhoods and rode to work downtown.

Building an underground railway was another matter, and opposition to Manhattan's subway came from all quarters. Property owners on Broadway feared foundations would be undermined and entire department stores swallowed up, and papers published scare stories about women suffocating in the pestilential atmosphere of the new London Underground. And citizens were afraid—quite rightly, after decades of Tammany corruption—that municipal involvement would mean sweetheart deals and kickbacks for developers and pols. Then, early one March, as the debate raged, a vicious nor'easter blew in from New Jersey, piling snow to the second floor of brownstones. Ferries stopped running, steam engines were extinguished, and piles of snow blocked the tracks of every horsecar and elevated line in the city. The commercial capital of the Western Hemisphere had been paralyzed after only two days of inclement weather. "New York," the *Times* marveled, "was as completely isolated from the rest of the world as if Manhattan Island was in the middle of the South Sea."

The Great Blizzard of '88 clinched the deal: New York would have its subway. The mayor came up with a formula by which private enterprise would build and operate the trains, with nominal ownership in the hands of the city. Though this put transit in control of the business elite and beyond effective democratic control, voters approved the formula in a referendum by a factor of 3 to 1. On February 21, 1900, August Belmont Jr. signed Contract No. 1, to build and operate the IRT—at a guaranteed nickel fare—for the next fifty years. One month later, an honor guard fired a 21-gun salute in City Hall Park. Between each volley, Joseph Pulitzer's paper reported, "the *World*'s watchword, 'To Harlem in Fifteen Minutes,' ran from lip to lip and swelled into a splendid chorus."

It had been a long time coming, but New York's first subway was finally getting built.

The Second Avenue Saga

One hundred and ten years after the groundbreaking, the subway is still under construction. Joe Pecora wouldn't mind so much, but the work is being done right outside the front door of his restaurant.

The lunch rush was over at Delizia 92, a neon-fronted Italian restaurant at the corner of Ninety-second Street and Second Avenue that's been serving Upper East Siders calzones and cannolis since 1978. Pecora cast a baleful eye over the espresso on the table in front of him toward the sandhogs sipping filter coffee next to a rectangular scar in the pavement. Delizia 92, you see, has the misfortune to be located next to the launch box, where a tunnel-boring machine had just been lowered to start digging the first phase of the Second Avenue subway.

"They notified us by mail first," Pecora told me, "but we didn't really believe it was going to happen, because they'd started building the Second Avenue subway twice before and never finished it. Then the fences started going up." The construction, he said, was causing no end of grief. His electricity had been cut without warning, destroying valuable equipment. Vibrations turned hairline cracks in the floor into alarming gaps. Pipes in his basement burst. His clients couldn't find parking. "And it's going to be like this for the next *seven years*."

This stretch of Second Avenue once ran through Germantown, a multiethnic enclave of Germans, Hungarians, Russians, and Irish; the Marx Brothers grew up around the corner, in one of the tenements built after the El opened the neighborhood for development. When the El was torn down in 1942, Second Avenue began to get denser, as new high-rises were built in anticipation of the long-promised subway. This is not the Upper East Side of robber baron mansions and Madison Avenue boutiques; it remains home to such working-class institutions as the Heidelberg Restaurant and the half-century old Dorrian's Red Hand bar.

As head of the Second Avenue Business Association, Pecora gets to hear all the grievances. Several businesses have already shut down, and a hundred-year-old residential building had to be evacuated when it began to tilt dangerously. "The MTA is giving the store owners peanuts," complained Pecora. At least fifty-two tenants had already been relocated to make room for subway entrances.

It sounded like a classic case of big government ramming a mega-project down the throats of reluctant locals. But this time nobody involved—not even the organizer of the resistance—appears to be against the subway project itself. "Definitely, I think there's a need for it," said Pecora, "but they should compensate the businesses much better." And he just wished the station wasn't being built in his front yard. "The ideal place for the launch box would have been at Ninety-sixth Street." In other words, four blocks north—right where Harlem begins.

The MTA, for its part, feels it's being more than fair. It has set aside $10 million to compensate those who want to move; if a tenant chooses a more expensive apartment, the MTA will pay the difference in rent for the next three and a half years. "The interesting thing," Michael Horodniceanu, the president of the authority's capital construction company, told me, "is that we're bringing three hundred workers to that area on a daily basis. And a lot of them end up stopping in for a slice of pizza at Delizia." There are only a few stretches along Second Avenue, it turns out, where the tunneling will affect life on the surface—and Delizia 92 happens to be on one of them. According to Peter Cafiero, the MTA's director of rail service design, "Any point we're coming up to the street, where the station areas are, we've got a highly concentrated visibility. But once we're drilling through rock with the tunnel-boring machine, most people won't even know we're there."

Compared to the initial round of transit construction in 1900, the work now being done on Second Avenue is positively painless. Half of the original IRT was the product of "cut and cover," a technique pioneered in building the subways of Budapest and Boston. Sandhogs literally ripped the tops off major thoroughfares, exposing and rerouting sewers and gas mains as they dug rectangular trenches down Broadway, Forty-second Street, and Fourth Avenue. Adjoining buildings had to be shored up, and wooden bridges built to support the weight of streetcars, which continued to roll over the heads of men laboring below. Accidents were frequent. A dropped candle ignited a quarter-ton of dynamite in Midtown; the resulting blast defaced Grand Central Terminal, and caused building facades to collapse into the crater, laying bare the bathtubs and boudoirs of dignified brownstones. Between explosions and tunnel collapses, forty-four men died building the first subway.

Were the long-term results worth the short-term pain? There is no question that the new system met an urgent need. In its first month, the IRT was handling 425,000 people a day, and newspapers were already bemoaning the birth of the "subway crush." Within four years of its opening, cars were packed 30 percent over capacity.

The subway had an even bigger impact on the shape of New York than elevateds and electric trolleys. The old walking city soon tripled in area. Realtors bought up farmland in northern Manhattan and the Bronx, building "new law" tenements—more spacious and better ventilated than Lower East Side walk-ups, with airshafts and courtyards—for working-class families. The "chariot of the poor" encouraged the creation of decent, walkable neighborhoods—places like Jackson Heights in far-flung Queens, conceived as a prototypical garden suburb (and later the lumpen Shangri-la of television, inhabited by the likes of Frank and Estelle Costanza). In the outer boroughs, virtually all new construction clustered within a quarter-mile of the tracks. By following the taproots of mass transit, the working poor were able to escape industrial squalor for greener pastures. Before the subway, over half of all New Yorkers lived in Manhattan; forty years later, only a quarter lived there, and Brooklyn had become the city's most populous borough.

While the subway reduced population density in Manhattan, it also intensified downtown commercial development. "The most spectacular consequence of the subway," observed William Parsons, its chief engineer, "has been the skyscraper." Without it, neither the Chrysler Building nor Rockefeller Center would exist: the horizontal technology of rapid transit, combined with a nineteenth-century breakthrough in vertical transportation—the safety elevator, first installed in a five-story building on Broadway in 1857—made closely spaced skyscrapers truly practical. The underground railway enabled the astonishingly rapid shift of Manhattan's commercial center of gravity from Wall Street to Midtown, as Times Square and Grand Central were stitched together by the Forty-second Street Shuttle. Along with the federally funded irrigation system that built Los Angeles, the New York subway is considered the single greatest improvement to urban real estate ever undertaken.

And yet, from day one, many New Yorkers took the subway for granted. "While the crowds were still enthralled by the strangeness of it all," a *New York Times* reporter wrote not long after opening day in 1904, "the men on the trains were quietly getting out at their regular stations and going home, having finished what will be to them the daily routine for the rest of their lives. It is hard to surprise New York permanently." Familiarity with the trains quickly turned to resentment, producing one of Gotham's most durable tropes: that fat cats were making a fortune packing commuters into rattling sweatboxes.

There was truth to the complaint, at least in the early days. In 1913, the city signed "dual contracts" with the IRT and Brooklyn Rapid Transit, extending subway lines across the East and Harlem rivers and doubling track mileage. In the pages of his *New York Evening Journal* William Randolph Hearst fulminated against the deal made with the "Traction Trust," arguing for municipal control of the entire system. The real-life Citizen Kane was right about the dual contracts: they were a bad deal for the city, allowing the subway kings to rake in the nickels while leaving the city responsible for all the debt. But Hearst was mistaken about the profits— quite quickly, the subway turned into a money loser. By the 1920s, the "Traction Trust" was struggling to make interest payments on its capital debt and was forced to lay off thousands of guards and "ticket choppers."

Civic traditions of kvetching aside, the subway was a sweet deal for New Yorkers. For fifty years, anybody with five cents in his pocket could ride the train to Coney Island, Yankee Stadium, or Times Square. At that fare, commuting six days a week, the head of a working-class household had to devote only 1 percent of his gross annual income to transportation.* Yet it was this nickel fare that doomed the subway as a moneymaking venture: inflation in the '20s led to a massive city transit deficit, and when ridership briefly declined during the Depression, the IRT went bankrupt. The cost of a ride only increased to a dime in 1948, long after it had risen in every other city in America.

For years, populist politicians had been proposing municipal ownership of the subway. Fiorello LaGuardia, first elected in 1933, oversaw the completion of the Independent Subway System (the IND), the last significant addition to the subway network in the twentieth century. Conceived as a municipally run alternative to the private lines, the "People's Subway" was great for Manhattan, but, outside of Queens, failed to foster much expansion into the outer boroughs. The IND's routes, starting with the Eighth Avenue subway, often paralleled and directly competed with existing private lines; at best they filled in gaps in the system. What's more, it was a financial disaster: for every nickel ride taken, the city lost nine cents. The IND's existence as an independent entity was short-lived. LaGuardia spearheaded the unification of the IND with the bankrupt private companies into a single system. (On today's subway, you know you're on the old IND if you're riding a train lettered from A to G. Numbered trains follow old IRT routes; generally speaking, trains lettered J to S follow the former Brooklyn-Manhattan Transit routes.) In 1940, LaGuardia donned a cap and as Motorman No. 1 took a ceremonial ride on the new, city-owned

* Today, car-dependent American households spend 25 percent of their income on transportation.

New York Transit System. For the past seventy years, the subway has belonged to the people of New York.

The idea that New York's subway was born out of private entrepreneurial genius is hyperbole; it was in fact the product of what would now be called a public-private partnership. The system could never have been built without municipal financing or New York's bond-raising capacity; the city gave August Belmont Jr. $35 million to lay the tracks and dig the tunnels, and another $1.5 million to buy the land for stations. And private companies ran the system for as long as it was profitable—less than two decades. Yet even after private ownership ended, the ideology of business management prevailed. In the 1950s, Paul Windels, a Republican lawyer, helped create a highly bureaucratic agency, the New York City Transit Authority, that removed the subway from direct democratic control. The Metropolitan Transportation Authority, a state-level super-agency, took over operation of the NYCTA and the region's commuter railways in 1968. The hoary civic cliché that somebody was making money hand over fist from the straphangers' misery became even more entrenched when the policy of deferred maintenance sent the system into decline, and New Yorkers grew increasingly alienated from their own subway.

The real estate industry has long resisted the notion that property taxes should subsidize transit. This is the height of ingratitude, considering that the subway increased the values of apartment buildings, bringing fortunes to developers. "The subway represented an indirect municipal subsidy to the private construction industry," Clifton Hood cogently argues in *722 Miles*, his history of the building of New York's subway. "Without violating the laissez-faire taboo against direct intervention in the private sector, city government helped provide decent accommodations for working-class families. The subway's enduring legacy was that the lives of New York's poorer citizens became fuller and more productive."

Back on Second Avenue, the long-delayed subway is still causing Joe Pecora no end of grief: the chain-link along the sidewalk, the vibrations, the heavy equipment being lowered into the launch box—the disruption to neighborhood life is likely to continue until late in this decade. (In the meantime, you could do worse than dropping by Delizia 92 and placing an order. Pecora makes a mean spinach calzone.) But when the Second Avenue subway opens, it will handle a half-million passengers a day, providing long-needed relief to a system that has been overcrowded since the day it opened. For a city as compact as New York, digging a subway is essential surgery, worth the expense and short-term pain. The wounds are soon sutured, and when they heal, they leave the city stronger, more efficient, more bound together than before.

Highways are a completely different story. They are open wounds that never heal—and they tear cities apart.

The Meat-Ax and the Metropolis

A century ago, New York City was on its way to becoming a remarkably good place to live. Gracious apartment living, first pioneered in such Gilded Age upper-income buildings as the Stuyvesant Apartments (1869) on Eighteenth Street and the Dakota (1884) on Seventy-second, encouraged a dense, class-mixed urban environment, where working families lived within walking distance of their employers. The addition of Frederick Law Olmsted's Central Park—based on the "People's Garden" in Liverpool, the first public urban park—provided a welcome respite from the gridiron, and more block-sized parks were being created all the time. The wealthy Progressives of the City Beautiful movement successfully lobbied for civic art and enduring public monuments inspired by Classical architecture (and against ads in the subway—a battle they lost). Indoor plumbing, electric lights, and improvements in public health made the city a cleaner, more pleasant place to live. The trend was global: along with the Eixample of Barcelona, the Champs-Elysées in Paris, the Gold Coast in Chicago, the Recoleta in Buenos Aires, and the Bund in Shanghai, Fifth Avenue became a proving ground for the latest manifestations of elegant urbanism. New York's working class, meanwhile, was enthusiastic about the nascent "wonder city" of skyscrapers of Midtown, which seemed to embody the loftiest civic aspirations while maximizing efficient land use. The subway tied the metropolis together, and the visionary urbanists of the Regional Plan Association, founded in 1922 to rationalize the growing city, drafted ambitious plans to expand the subway (including a line along Second Avenue) and create a rail system that would allow people to travel throughout the region quickly, cheaply, and pleasantly. The future seemed very bright indeed.

Then something happened that would reshape the city like a slow-motion tsunami. It started slowly, with the appearance of a few curious, sputtering, backfiring flivvers, the playthings of wealthy dilettantes. By 1932, however, there were 790,000 motor vehicles in the city, and New York was again choking on its traffic. This time it was not butcher's carts and horsecars clogging the streets, but Fords, Chryslers, and Chevrolets. The greatest enabler of the automobile invasion would be Robert Moses—the man who made the modern metropolis safe for the car.

It's possible to put a positive spin on the career of Moses, and recently, in a radical reassessment of his legacy, historians, curators, and journalists have been doing just that. Here is the authorized, sugar-coated biography of the man. Born to wealth in 1888, the recipient of a blue-chip education at Yale, Oxford, and Columbia, Moses campaigned against patronage in city government and pioneered the parkways to Long Island—often by expropriating land from the wealthy—which allowed the working class to escape the sweltering city for Jones Beach and other coastal playgrounds of his making. He used New Deal funds to finance the awesome Triborough Bridge, and brilliantly employed the legal concept of the authority to guarantee an independent revenue stream from highway tolls, allowing him to fund further public works—among them the Verrazano-Narrows Bridge, the world's longest suspension bridge when it was completed. As his influence grew, Moses brought the city the United Nations, two World's Fairs, and Lincoln Center, which jump-started the revival of the Upper West Side. His magnificent swimming pools conferred grandeur on poor neighborhoods, his parks and playgrounds helped the city breathe, and his one thousand mostly low-income apartment houses helped solve the housing problem for all New Yorkers. In his forty-four-year career, which spanned the administrations of five mayors and six governors, he built 15 expressways, 16 parkways, the West Side Highway, the Harlem River Drive, and Shea Stadium. He thought big, and got big things done: without his expressways, New York would be gridlocked into economic irrelevance. Robert Moses, from this perspective, was indeed the master builder of twentieth-century New York, a man who, in the words of one revisionist, "made Baron Haussmann look like a subcontractor."

Here's an alternative to the hagiography, gleaned from the pages of Robert A. Caro's masterful, and massive, biography *The Power Broker*. Raised in privilege, Robert Moses was always cushioned from real life; from the age of nine, he slept in a custom-made bed and was served dinner prepared by the family's cook on fine china. As Parks Commissioner, he swindled Long Island farmers and homeowners out of their land to build his parkways—essentially cattle chutes that skirted the properties of the rich, allowing those well-off enough to own a car to get to beaches disfigured by vast parking lots. He cut the city off from its waterfront with expressways built to the river's edge, and the parks he built were covered with concrete rather than grass, leaving the city grayer, not greener, than it had been before. The ambient racism of the time hardly excuses his shocking contempt for minorities: of the 255 new playgrounds he built in the 1930s, only one was in Harlem. (Physically separated from the city by one of his highways, the playground featured trellises decorated with wrought-iron monkeys.) In the decade after the Second World War, he caused 320,000 people to be evicted from their homes; his cheap, sterile projects became vertical ghettoes that fomented civic decay for decades. If some of his more insane schemes had been realized—a highway through the sixth floor of the Empire State Building, the Lower Manhattan Expressway through today's SoHo, the Battery Bridge whose approaches would have eliminated Castle Clinton and Battery Park—New York as we know it would be nearly uninhabitable. There is a name for what Robert Moses was engaged in: class warfare, waged not with armored vehicles and napalm, but with bulldozers and concrete.

Whichever version you accept—Moses the master builder or Moses the master villain—one thing is clear: the man had no time for public transport, or the people who used it. He tore up the city's trolley tracks to improve traffic flow, and made the overpasses on his parkways a foot too low for buses to use, so only car owners could reach Jones Beach (Moses himself lived on Long Island). Ignoring the Regional Plan Association's recommendations, he refused to make room for transit tracks on bridges or in the center malls of highways, making it impractical to reach Idlewild Airport (later JFK International) and many other locations by train.

"By building his highways," Caro wrote in *The Power Broker*, "Moses flooded the city with cars. By systematically starving the subways and the suburban commuter railroads, he swelled that flood to city-destroying dimensions. By making sure that the vast suburbs, still rural when he came to power, were filled on a sprawling, low-density development pattern relying primarily on roads instead of mass transportation, he insured that that flood would continue for generations if not centuries, that the New York metropolitan area would be—perhaps forever—an area in which transportation—getting from one place to another—would be an irritating, life-consuming concern." If the Second Avenue subway is only now getting built in the twenty-first century, it is because public funds were monopolized by Moses to build bridges and highways, rather than transit, during the twentieth.

Most critically, Moses, who never learned to drive and was chauffeured in an air-conditioned Packard limousine, ignored the emerging problem of gridlock. By making it easier for people to drive and to live in suburbs that could be reached by cars, he foredoomed the city to paralysis. He enabled the suburbanization of Long Island, where mass-produced, car-based suburbs like Levittown, built just off his Wantagh State Parkway, ate up villages and farmland. The Triborough Bridge was meant to solve New York's traffic problems; instead, congestion on all the city's other bridges actually *increased* in the months after it was built. Moses's bridges and city-spanning highways provided the first demonstration of the theory of induced traffic: build more highways, and they will fill up, almost instantly.

Perhaps Moses should be judged not for what he built, but for what he destroyed. The saddest story was East Tremont, in the heart of the Bronx. This working-class neighborhood of Jews, Italians, and Irish who had escaped the congested Lower East Side included a thriving strip of butcher shops, bakeries, delis, and movie palaces. The district's apartments were famously roomy and affordable; beautiful Art Deco buildings with streamlined facades lined the Grand Concourse, and were a short walk from the lake, tennis courts, and baseball diamonds of Crotona Park. Few families owned cars; an IRT line ran right to Manhattan's garment district, where most people worked. Then Moses drew a line on a map and declared East Tremont to be in the way of his seven-mile-long Cross-Bronx Expressway. In spite of protests, he refused to move the highway by even one block, boasting, "When you operate in an overbuilt metropolis, you have to hack your way with a meat-ax." In theory, families had 90 days to leave their buildings; in practice, as soon as the top floor of apartments was vacated, his work crews would begin tearing off the roof. When the expressway was completed, East Tremont was riven by an uncrossable, 225-foot-wide swath of concrete. All told, 1,530 families were evicted, and a once vibrant neighborhood had to stand by as its heart was torn out.

Moses's blind spot was community, the little people who never showed up on his models and plans. Appropriately, it was those little people who eventually ruined him. In 1956, his plan to build a parking lot on Central Park's beloved Tavern-on-the-Green was foiled when a bulldozer driver refused to cross a line of well-dressed women with baby carriages, a scene reported by every major media outlet in the city. When he tried to have part of Greenwich Village declared a blighted slum, protests by residents reinforced his new image as a destroyer of communities. "There is nobody against this," he was heard to splutter when his plan to ram a four-lane roadway through Washington Square Park was foiled. "Nobody, nobody, nobody but a bunch of, a bunch of mothers."

One of those mothers, of course, was the great urban theorist Jane Jacobs. From her home on Hudson Street, the author and activist orchestrated theatrical opposition to Moses's projects, burning cars in effigy in Washington Square, and tossing the stenographer's paper around the stage of a public hearing to protest the building of the Lower Manhattan Expressway. In *The Death and Life of Great American Cities*, she pinpointed the appeal of such neighborhoods as Boston's North End and her own Greenwich Village, arguing that it was the disorderly vestiges of nineteenth-century street life—shops and residences cheek by jowl, with the bartender sweeping his sidewalk keeping an eye on the neighbors' kids playing hopscotch—that made them safe and viable urban spaces. Small blocks, buildings of six stories and less, a mixture of commerce and residences, and lots of foot traffic, were not symptoms of blight, but vitality. In the car-loving, city-fleeing culture of the 1960s, Jacobs's prescriptions were heresy: she actually believed New York should make it *harder* for people to drive, on the grounds that dense neighborhoods function better when people rely on bikes, transit, and their feet.

In the long run, it is Jacobs's worldview that appears to be triumphing. After 1968, no new highway would be built in Manhattan, and a wave of grassroots protests killed highways in Baltimore, Milwaukee, New Orleans, and Philadelphia. Moses, meanwhile, lived to witness his Triborough Bridge Authority become a mere unit of the MTA, New York's bankruptcy, and his reputation destroyed by Robert Caro's biography. His grandson, the one person Moses really seemed to dote on, died on a highway when his car smashed into a culvert as he drove back to Long Island from Stanford University.

While Jacobs defended successful old neighborhoods, she never believed they should remain inviolate. Quite the contrary: she fought for the hundreds of subsidized apartments in the West Village Houses and, after she'd moved to Canada, dense mixed-income housing in Toronto's St. Lawrence neighborhood. Yet her writing has too often provided ammunition not only for the NIMBY (not-in-my-backyard) movement but also for BANANAs (build-absolutely-nothing-anywhere-near-anything). Jacobs wasn't particularly interested in "heritage" buildings or specific architectural details. She fought for social complexity over the steamroller of modernist sterility, and for the *people* who make up a neighborhood—the more diverse the better. Though her name has been invoked in fights against subway lines, she was a walker and a defender of transit.

If the century-old promise of North American cities as good places to live is finally being revived, it is exactly because mothers like Jacobs had the courage to oppose what people like Robert Moses spent their careers trying to impose: cities built for cars, rather than people.

Amsterdam-on-the-Hudson

On a Monday afternoon early in summer, I stood in the middle of Broadway, enjoying what felt like a lovely pedestrian city. The last time I'd been to Times Square, the sheer volume of people on the sidewalk regularly forced me to step off the pavement into oncoming traffic. This time around, seven blocks of Broadway were closed to traffic, and I spent a leisurely half hour picking my way among lawn chairs scattered through a vast pedestrian plaza, filled with New Yorkers from nearby offices eating lunch and tourists snapping pictures of the parading neon. Two days before, I'd walked up the middle of Madison Avenue, eating a fajita bought from a taquería stand located in a parking lane devoid of parked cars, a portion of seven miles of Manhattan streets closed to automobiles as part of the Summer Streets program.

Not everybody was happy about the lane closures. At Thirty-seventh Street, I overheard the driver of a Ford pickup complain to a cop, "The thing is, they're taking up two lanes of traffic!" He waved vaguely at the green bike lane and the benches at a pop-up café where a family was sipping iced drinks in the curb lane. "Don't get me wrong, it's nice and all, but one day an out-of-control truck is going to plow into those benches, and that'll be the end of that." He didn't look entirely displeased by the prospect.

If Manhattan's streets are more walkable than they have been in a century, it is largely thanks to Janette Sadik-Khan, the fast-talking commissioner of New York City's Department of Transportation, and the woman responsible for the city's 6,000 miles of roadways since 2007.

"New Yorkers are very passionate about their streets," Sadik-Khan told me, at a conference room on the ninth floor of 55 Water Street. A youthful-looking woman with gaminesque bangs, she is known for her rapid-fire delivery and command of figures. "At any given time, it feels like I'm dealing with over eight million traffic engineers, because everybody's got an idea of how the streets should be used. In the next twenty years, the city's going to grow by a million people. We're not going to be double-decking our road system. The only way we're going to be able to deal with the demand is by building more efficient mobility into our network. That means buses. That means bike lanes. And that means better walking environments. They really all go together."

Sadik-Khan gave me a quick rundown of the statistics: 95 percent of commuters get to Manhattan's central business district by transit, bicycle, or on foot. Fifty-four percent of New Yorkers don't even own a car. To cope with this reality, the DOT has created 200 miles of bike lanes in the last three years. In the Bronx, they have already introduced the Select Bus Service, an express route where prepaid fares speed up bus loading, and are consulting with underserved communities to introduce at least eight other rapid-transit bus corridors. New legislation will force the owners of commercial buildings with freight elevators to provide indoor bicycle parking.

And yet, I pointed out, apart from such highly visible sites as Times Square, private automobiles seem to have the run of New York, a city where curbside parking is still largely unmetered. Sadik-Khan countered she had done her best to limit traffic. As a policymaker under David Dinkins, she saw her project for tolls on East River bridges mothballed. Under Bloomberg, she worked hard to introduce a charge for cars entering Manhattan. By charging a new bridge toll, New York would have followed England's example, where an £8 charge for every vehicle entering central London has decreased congestion by almost a third (the charge is used to fund public transport). The New York City Council passed the legislation, but it was defeated by the state legislature in Albany.

Which raises the question: If only 5 percent of commuters get to work by car, who are all these drivers clogging the streets of Manhattan—the ones who presumably oppose congestion pricing—and where do they come from? About 750,000 motor vehicles enter the central business district every day. Thanks to Moses, who made sure that almost every major highway in the region led to Manhattan, one-fifth are just passing through; a solid majority come from areas in Queens, Brooklyn, and Long Island that are poorly served by transit.

Once you eliminate delivery vans, trucks, "black cars" (limousines and car service vehicles), and taxis, though, most of the drivers on the road are employed at some level of government. A startling 35 percent of New York's government workers drive to work: free parking has long been considered one of the perks of public service. Agents almost never ticket cars with parking placards, which in theory are for city and state workers on official business. In 2010, *The New Yorker* outed a justice and former senate majority leader who used placards to park beside a fire hydrant and avoid feeding a meter outside Barneys. The practice creates a strong conflict of interest among the lawmakers in Albany: Why vote to limit automobile access to Manhattan—or, for that matter, to approve funding for a new subway line—when a placard gives you a golden key to the city?

When I asked Sadik-Khan about the issue, she flashed a slightly frayed smile. "Under Mayor Bloomberg's watch, we've cut across the board thirty percent of the placards for city workers. And the Department of Transportation is moving forward with a pilot car-sharing program. If it works out, it could have huge applications citywide."

Sadik-Khan is facing an uphill battle. While the Department of City Planning has rezoned 20 percent of New York under Bloomberg, most of it to higher densities and within a half-mile walk of transit stations, nothing has been done to limit car use. Moses-era regulations requiring new construction to include off-street parking spaces still prevail—and the more parking there is, the more people tend to drive. Over Sadik-Khan's shoulder I could see the rusting piers of the Brooklyn waterfront and the multiple lanes of traffic on the Bronx-Queens Expressway, a Moses project that kick-started the decline of the Red Hook neighborhood.

"We've stopped looking at the streets as these utilitarian, 1950s-style corridors for moving cars as fast as possible. We really look at them as valuable public spaces. In many ways, the Department of Transportation is the largest real estate developer in New York City." To her credit, Sadik-Khan is capable of enacting change on the streets as rapidly as she talks. "In certain areas, we can transform pavement to plazas in a matter of days. I think New Yorkers are really tired of waiting ten or fifteen years to see any kind of change. Whenever we create a public space, it's amazing: people just materialize out of thin air in minutes."

After talking to Sadik-Khan, I strolled over to the Meatpacking District, and climbed several flights of stairs to the High Line, a disused New York Central rail line that has been turned into a gorgeous elevated promenade. Among rail spurs that curved into bricked-up warehouses, sumac, smokebush, and other native plants emerged from the joints between pre-cast concrete planks; office workers with loosened ties and unbuttoned blouses lolled on benches, catching some sun. The absence of traffic brought to mind sociologist Paul Goodman's plan to ban private cars from Man-hattan, leaving avenues open for electric buses and taxis. "It can easily be a place as leisurely as Venice," he wrote in a 1961 manifesto, "a lovely pedes-trian city." And it was hard not to read the High Line as a pointed com-mentary on car culture: after piercing the modernist slab of the Standard Hotel, it detours into tiers of benches facing a glass wall that seems to be suspended over Tenth Avenue. The glass makes the roadway a piece of framed kinetic art, contrasting the very human scene of mothers with strollers with the vista of taillights of taxis and trucks rushing uptown.

About halfway along the High Line's three-mile course, I came across one of those automated parking garages where cars are stacked in an open steel framework five high, like so many battery hens in wire-mesh cages. With their wheels suspended in the air, the immobile Lexuses and Mer-cedes looked faintly ridiculous—like relics of primitive urbanity, on dis-play in some future museum of otiose technology.

Tepper Is a Straphanger

As I rode the number 1 train downtown to the West Village one afternoon, sharing a bench with some excited Spanish tourists laden with Blooming-dale's bags and a street performer dressed as Spiderman, I remembered how, when I was a teenager, I thought New York's subway was the scariest place on earth. I'd seen its graffiti-covered, crime-ridden trains in count-less movies on late-night television. If you were to credit *The Warriors*, deserted Union Square station was roamed by gangs of roller-skating punks; *The Taking of Pelham One Two Three* showed commuters on the Lexington Avenue line being terrorized by gun-toting robbers wearing fake mustaches; and, according to *The Incident*, if you rode from Brooklyn to Times Square you were bound to be traumatized by ducktailed, switchblade-carrying psychopaths.

Hollywood scriptwriters (many of them escapees from New York) really knew how to play on America's fear of the city. In reality, the heavily patrolled subway was always safer than the streets above. Even when violent crime peaked in 1981, there were only 17 murders in the subway, versus 1,832 on the streets; more people died that year from vehicular homicides—being run over by cars—than underground.

The subway has changed, but so has New York. The new Greenwich Villages are a train ride from Manhattan, in Astoria, Corona, Boerum Hill, Sunset Park, Carroll Gardens, and Ridgewood, walkable old neighborhoods, now being colonized by families, that Jane Jacobs would have appreciated. Tens of thousands of condos built at the height of the real estate boom are being turned into affordable rental housing. These days, New York resembles nothing so much as New York of the late '40s, when municipal population and vitality were at their peak. With a twist: 40 percent of the population is now foreign-born, and the pace of immigration is eclipsing the Ellis Island days. The fact that all classes, races, and ages are once again mingling on the subway bodes well for the future.

Calvin Trillin, who has been living in the West Village since 1961, could probably be numbered among the first wave of urban pioneers—or gentrifiers, depending on how you look at things. The longtime *New Yorker* writer's Federal-style townhouse, on a dog-legged street west of Seventh Avenue, was built in the 1830s. Trillin used to rent; now he owns. (I didn't dare ask how much his place was worth, but a couple of blocks away, Jane Jacobs's modest Hudson Street home, declared "blight" by Moses and company fifty years ago, recently sold for $3 million.) Pulling down a folding staircase from the ceiling, Trillin invited me to climb to his roof, where we sat beneath a sycamore tree. You might assume the author of *Tepper Isn't Going Out*, a novel about a New Yorker who becomes a kind of grumpy guru of Gotham for camping out in his Chevrolet, would be a die-hard driver. (He does own a Volkswagen Passat, which he uses to get to a summer home in Nova Scotia.) But Trillin has a secret: he mostly gets around by bicycle and subway.

"I almost never take a cab anymore," said Trillin. "It's almost always the subway. There are maybe a few people I know who don't take the subway because they consider it 'mass' transit. They're essentially snobs." The number 1 line, Trillin told me, was his warhorse; there was a station two blocks from his front door. "Last night I had to emcee a benefit across the street from Grand Central, and it's an enormous pain to get there any other way than the subway." He rode the train in a tuxedo. "People just assume I'm a waiter. My late wife didn't like to take the subway at night when she was all dressed up in high heels and fancy clothes. She didn't mind that people took me for a waiter; she just didn't want to be somebody *with* a waiter." In almost five decades of riding the trains, he said, he had not witnessed a single serious crime, nor even been stuck in a tunnel.

"Sure, there were times I thought the subway was unpleasant, especially the graffiti. And it was only fairly recently that they put maps outside the cars. You used to have to get into the train to find one, and then you needed a degree from the Royal Institute of Cartography to read it. By then, you realized you were going in the wrong direction. The next stop was Queens Plaza. For some reason, it was *always* Queens Plaza." All in all, though, the service was better than he could remember it ever being. "Really, in New York, it's just dumb not to take the subway."

If I lived in New York, I'd be a full-time straphanger, too. When I was in my thirties, I toyed with the idea of relocating, and Erin and I still talk about spending a year or two in Manhattan—an idea that gets more appealing as more streets get pedestrianized, the network of bike paths grows, and parks like the High Line open. The reality is we'd probably end up in more affordable Brooklyn, where some of our friends now live. In the meantime, we get to visit, and our first order of business almost always involves ducking into a subway station, to charge up our MetroCards.

After all these visits, the subway is still revealing its secrets to me. This time around, I took an almost bucolic excursion to Far Rockaway, riding along the causeway past wood-framed boathouses, where wading herons speared frogs on rocky beaches. At the 34th Street–Herald Square station, I came across a virtual xylophone that lit up when I waved my palm in front of photo-sensors, splashing the station with the electronic tones of marimba, flute, and birdsong. Riding the D train from Brooklyn, I looked up to see the illuminated image of a cartoon rocket taking off in the tunnel: it was the Masstransiscope, a 300-foot-long strip of hand-painted panels installed on an unused subway platform by artist Bill Brand, the images animated, zoetrope-like, by the motion of the train.

And though the disturbances remain—the hard-luck litanies of panhandlers, the hard sells from roving battery and chocolate bar salesmen— they are outweighed by the little pleasures. My favorite is the dreamy feeling I get gazing out the window of an uptown local, hypnotized as the ridged roof of the swaying express on a parallel track lowers itself into the hidden depths of New York City.

> I used to like this town. . . . Hollywood was a bunch of frame houses on the inter-urban line. Los Angeles was just a big, dry sunny place with ugly homes and no style, but good-hearted and peaceful. It had the climate they just yap about now. People used to sleep out on porches. Little groups who thought they were intellectual used to call it the Athens of America. It wasn't that, but it wasn't a neon-lighted slum, either.
>
> —Raymond Chandler, *The Little Sister*, 1949

2. Only Connect

Los Angeles, California

If you know just one thing about Los Angeles, it's probably this: in the City of Angels, a person just can't get by without a car.

Here's how the story, as it is usually understood, goes: by accepting a devil's bargain that exchanged public transport for an urban freeway network, Angelenos enjoyed the gift of unlimited mobility—all points accessible to anybody who could afford the wheels. For a few blessed decades, it seemed to work, and the winter-weary came from across the country to dump their dreams, and their life's savings, into ranch-style homes within easy striking distance of surfing beaches and snowtopped mountains. But gridlock's technological fix, the urban highway, all too quickly succumbed to paralysis. The well-engineered freeways that have made Los Angeles the cradle of smog alerts and "slurbs," road rage and drive-by shootings, and the most polluted city in the United States, are now the nation's most congested.

But what very few people know is that the western metropolis that, according to the old East Coast put-down, has never amounted to anything more than "seventeen suburbs in search of city," is belatedly coming around to the gospel of old-fashioned urbanism. Multifamily apartment buildings are being built within walking distance of light-rail lines, and an incipient subway system is set to double its track mileage in the next decade. Against a background of looming statewide bankruptcy, a popular mayor has won local and federal funding for the most ambitious transit plan in the United States, one intended to achieve a goal long thought beyond human reach: getting Angelenos out of their cars, and on to buses and trains.

Though reclaiming Greater Los Angeles from the empire of the automobile is a fine and ambitious idea, it may be the product of delusional thinking. Anybody who has seen Southern California from the air knows that a sea of pavement, interrupted only by a few inconvenient patches of subdivision-repelling mountains, stretches from Santa Barbara to the Mexican border.

This is one city that even the most visionary planners and politicians might not be able to redeem.

The Billion-Dollar Taco

On a sunny winter morning, a Metro Gold Line train pulled into the platform outside Union Station, bells clanging and headlights flashing, as if it were hauling a presidential Pullman on a whistle-stop tour. It was a sleek Italian number, carefully styled for maximum retro appeal: with its elegantly chamfered cab, stainless-steel doors, and speed lines painted on the front like Cubist cat's whiskers, it recalled the aerodynamic styling of some silver-sided Jazz Age turboprop. I found a seat in the lead car of two—not difficult, as apart from a woman and her infant daughter, I was the only other passenger—and the train left the station with a piping *phew-phew!*—a perfect electronic reproduction of an old-fashioned steam whistle. Instead of the usual recorded English and Spanish announcements warning riders to keep their feet off the seats, the driver provided his own chipper commentary.

"A very good morning to you!" he said, in great-to-be-alive tones that seemed to channel all the Southern California sunshine through the train's loudspeakers. "This Atlantic-bound train will be making all station stops. Just a little safety announcement: never, never, *never* run across the tracks—you never know when a train might be coming the other way. Our next stop will be Little Tokyo–Arts District!"

And so began a window-seat flipbook of the cultural juxtapositions of East Los Angeles. After following a sinuous viaduct over the thin trickle of the concrete-bound Los Angeles River, we passed, in rapid succession, the tiered pagoda of the Hompa Hongwanji Buddhist Temple, the primary-colored murals of the Boyle Heights Christian Center, the sun-baked pan-tiles of the city's oldest tortilla factory, and the ranks of club-tipped crosses in the Serbian Cemetery. After the tracks dipped beneath the Santa Ana Freeway, the light rail became a subway, flashing through a mile and a half of tunnel, before bursting back into the sun-drenched landscape of drive-through pharmacies and cell-phone towers disguised as palm trees.

For a buck and a quarter a ride, the Gold Line delivers Cadillac service at Kia prices. A textbook example of well-executed light rail—"light" refer-ring not to the size of the vehicles, which can be as long as subway cars, but to the fact that they carry relatively light loads at high speeds—it makes even the newest city bus feel like the lurching, cramped, traffic-snagged, second-class ride that it is. The train accelerated with smooth electric vigor, and red lights turned green at our approach. The Gold Line is cheap, com-fortable, and because cross traffic is held back to let it pass, very fast. It is hard to imagine why anybody who had the choice would prefer to drive.

At Atlantic Square in Monterey Park, I got off with the train's only remaining passengers, two teenage Latino hipsters, who had wheeled their immaculate fixed-gear bikes onto the train at Mariachi Plaza. The end of the line was a no-man's-land, its highlights a McDonald's drive-thru and a Pep Boys auto parts store—a landscape for drivers, not walkers. Fortu-nately, I was in East L.A., where great Mexican food is never far. Spying a taco stand in a strip mall, I scampered across two lanes of traffic toward Manny's El Loco Restaurant.

"I'm here to pick up nine chicken tacos!" the guy in front of me at the counter boomed. I recognized the cheerful voice from the train's intercom: it was the driver. When I introduced myself, Running Hawk, of the Apache Nation, gave me a gladiator-style forearm handshake, and said: "Man, you came to the right place! Manny's is the best. I always call in my lunch order from my cell phone when I'm coming this way." He asked me what I thought of the Gold Line. I told him it was a great ride; too bad nobody seemed to be using it.

"It's true!" he said, with a laugh. "It makes my job a bit easier. But you've got to keep in mind, the line's only been open for a few months. People haven't caught on yet." When his order arrived, he spontaneously offered me a foil-wrapped taco from his horde.

Maybe Running Hawk was right, and ridership would increase over time. But the Gold Line to East L.A. seems to suffer from the fatal flaw that afflicts transit lines in many Sun Belt cities: too often, they run along under-used corridors, chosen by officials because there will be little local opposition, rather than because they serve areas that are actually dense enough to support transit. The Gold Line wends its way through neighborhoods of single-family homes on small lots, the commerce-free no-man's-lands around freeways, strips of auto-body shops, and thousands of acres of parking lots. For now, the closest it gets to the heart of downtown is Union Station, the gorgeous Mission Revival terminal that also serves as a hub for commuter and Amtrak trains, a mile from the skyscrapers of Bunker Hill.

Don't get me wrong: I'm happy to be given any opportunity to visit East L.A., and this part of town deserves the best transit it can get. The catfish in my soft flour taco was beautifully grilled, and I exchanged a grin with a mustachioed dad at the table next to me when his preschool-age son gripped a plastic seat and executed a perfect hip-swiveling salsa to the rhythm of the Champs' "Tequila." But building the Eastside Extension's nine stations and seven miles of track took five years and cost $900 million, and it has yet to come anywhere near its projected ridership of 13,000 people a day. (To put this in perspective, New York's Lexington Avenue line handles as many riders every fifteen *minutes*.) That's a lot of money to spend on a line whose primary benefit, so far, seems to accrue to downtown condo owners in search of the perfect fish taco.

For transit in Los Angeles to work, the city will have to change in several crucial ways. The first is already happening: the system of existing subways, light rail, and rapid buses is being expanded and interconnected. The second will depend on Southern California's economic future, which is by no means assured: a significant amount of new, and dense, construction will have to happen near transit lines for truly walkable neighborhoods to be carved out of the sprawl. Unfortunately, a third key change, significantly reducing free parking in new development, isn't even being considered.

In other words, Los Angeles will have to become something many Angelenos never wanted it to be: a city, rather than an unplanned convention of suburbs.

The *Roger Rabbit* Theory

Once upon a time, according to a persistent urban legend, Los Angeles was a tranquil constellation of residential villages on the Pacific shore, unafflicted by freeways, congestion, or smog. In the 1988 feature *Who Framed Roger Rabbit?* an urchin asks gumshoe Eddie Valiant, played by Bob Hoskins, why he isn't driving a car.

"Who needs a car in L.A.?" replies Valiant, as he insouciantly hops on the rear bumper of a passing streetcar. "We've got the best public transportation system in the world!"

The plot hinges on the dastardly plans of Judge Doom, who wants to pave over Toon Town (which bears a marked resemblance to Watts) so he can build an empire of tire salons, fast-food restaurants, and billboards along a new kind of high-speed roadway: "Eight lanes of shimmering cement— they're calling it a freeway!" Valiant reacts with disbelief. "Nobody's going to drive this lousy freeway when they can take the Red Car for a nickel!"

This much is true: the Red Cars really existed, they really went everywhere, and the fare really was five cents. If you credit the Judge Doom version of history, a cabal of automobile interests tore up tracks in Los Angeles and across the country, and replaced efficient electric streetcars with polluting diesel buses in an effort to make the internal combustion engine the king of the road. This conspiracy theory, though it makes for compelling pop history, is at least a couple of notches too simplistic. The real story behind what happened to the Red Cars, and why Los Angeles has become a byword for sprawl and congestion, is a little more complex and a lot more interesting.

Contrary to popular belief, Los Angeles owes its sprawled, horizontal form to railways, rather than freeways. Founded in 1781 as a New Spanish ranch town by mestizo and mulatto settlers, the city remained an obscure dot on the map until railroads brought a tidal wave of settlement from the Midwest; by the mid-1880s, fare wars between the Southern Pacific and

Santa Fe brought down the cost of a one-way ticket from Kansas City to a single silver dollar. A railroad right-of-way to San Pedro, which became the city's deep-water port in the 1890s, extended the city limits 20 miles southwest from downtown. The building of the Owens Valley aqueduct—a story of civic corruption loosely told in Roman Polanski's *Chinatown*—permitted the annexation of the San Fernando Valley, and the discovery of oil dispersed centers of industry, and population, throughout the region. By 1930, Los Angeles was the fifth-largest city by population in the United States—and the largest in area in the entire world.

The budding metropolis really began to grow thanks to the adoption of a marvel of nineteenth-century technology, the electric streetcar. In 1887, inventor Frank Sprague outfitted Richmond, Virginia, with a system of forty sparking trolleys that drew power from a cat's cradle of overhead wires. Streetcars quickly became the dominant mode of urban transportation in North America, carrying eleven billion passengers a year by the end of the First World War. The wires extended deep into forest and farmland, making the electric railroads de facto intercity highways; after nightfall in the countryside, farmers would signal drivers to stop by burning a rag next to the track. The network of interurbans, as the big intercity cars were known, was eventually so dense that a determined commuter could theoretically hop interlinked streetcars from Waterville, Maine, to Sheboygan, Wisconsin—a journey of a thousand miles—exclusively by electric trolley.

In Los Angeles, Southern Pacific heir Henry Huntington bought up dozens of shoestring streetcar companies to create the Pacific Electric empire. The Red Cars, as the big interurban trolleys were known, could be seen swaying through orange groves between Santa Monica and Arrowhead Hot Springs, and clattering over the sandy margins of Newport Beach all the way up to the tavern at snowtopped Mount Lowe; on a straightaway, they could hit 60 miles an hour. At their peak in 1926, they laced together four counties and fifty communities, mostly along private rights-of-way; together with the Yellow Cars—Huntington's network of smaller streetcars, which ensured local service in central Los Angeles—they constituted the most highly ramified public transport system in the world, with over 1,500 miles of track.

The Red Car system wasn't the product of high-minded philanthropy—the tracks had a suspicious tendency to go straight to land owned by Huntington and his cronies—but it did produce an appealing urban landscape with pockets of factories, bungalows, Safeway supermarkets, and Owl drugstores within walking distance of the streetcar lines. "The efficiency and convenience of the Big Red Car interurban system," wrote rail historian Spencer Crump, "whisking people to the contrasts of the orange groves, seashore, mountains, villages and cities, and showing them the opportunities, encouraged people to vacation permanently in Southern California. . . . Of the thirteen cities incorporated in Los Angeles County during the decade which ended in 1919, all but one was located on a Pacific Electric line." The city's horizontal spread, which was also encouraged by the dispersed location of oil fields and refineries, and a preference for detached houses brought by migrants with roots in small towns and family farms, resulted in a new kind of city, where walkable residential centers were physically distant from downtown, but still within easy commuting distance of department stores and office buildings. As long as the Red and Yellow Cars were running smoothly, Los Angeles delivered its residents both spacious living and a modicum of urbanity.

The golden age of urban rapid transit ended with the coming of the motor age. The car's arrival in cities across America was hotly contested, and with good reason: it turned public streets into killing fields. In one year alone, 1925, seven thousand children were killed by cars and trucks. Reckless motorists were attacked by mobs in Philadelphia and "death drivers" were denounced in major city newspapers. In a Milwaukee parade, a streetcar pulled a flatbed trailer displaying a wrecked car driven by a likeness of Satan; in St. Louis, flowers were scattered from an airship over a monument that bore the names of thirty-two child victims of automobiles.

In a sustained and concerted effort, thoroughly documented in Peter Norton's excellent study *Fighting Traffic*, car manufacturers, auto clubs, and traffic engineers banded together to usurp citizens' ancient supremacy of the street, successfully confining pedestrians, now recast as "jaywalkers," to corner crosswalks and turning roadways once shared by stickball players, bicycle riders, and street vendors into motor thoroughfares and parking lots for private vehicles. Motordom's greatest triumph, as Norton shows, was a slow war of attrition that all but banished the cheap, nonpolluting streetcar from the American streetscape.

Jazz Age Los Angeles was a key battlefront in the contest. Automobiles were not a hard sell for Southern Californians, many of whom had made the long trek across the desert from the rural Midwest in farm trucks and jalopies. By the mid-1920s, Los Angeles counted one driver for every three people—essentially a car in every garage, making it by far the most motorized city in the world. As dispersed as the city's industrial and residential areas were, its downtown was one of the most substantial in the nation, concentrating banks, offices, and retail into 300 square blocks of Beaux Arts skyscrapers and palatial department stores. As car commuters and shoppers joined the half-million workers who converged on the downtown every day, traffic ground to a halt, and Huntington's Red and Yellow Cars routinely ran sixty minutes late during rush hour. To unclog the streets, the newly formed City Planning Commission took a radical step: on a hazy spring day in 1920, they decided to ban on-street parking during business hours.

The plan worked—at least at first. For the first time in years, the street-cars ran on schedule, and workers got to their offices on time. But the following day, tens of thousands of enraged motorists descended on the downtown, led by silent movie star Clara Kimball Young, and parked their cars in protest. The doe-eyed actress told newspaper reporters that brutish bureaucrats were restricting the freedom of middle-class women to shop and attend downtown matinees. (It was no coincidence that Young's latest picture had its debut at the Rialto that very weekend, and the parking ban threatened to play hell with the box office.) After the protesters had exhausted the police department's supply of tickets, the pro-automobile *Los Angeles Times* ran an article declaring the planners' parking ban a fiasco, with the headline: "No-Parking Law Proves Motor Cars Absolutely Essential." (Which was nonsense: eight years later, Chicago would success-fully implement a daytime ban on curb parking in the Loop.) A publicity-seeking actress had won the day, the ban was lifted, and streetcars were once again stuck in a morass of barely moving traffic.

The question still remains: Did streetcars die a natural death? The *Roger Rabbit* theory, it turns out, has a surprising amount of truth in it. After a sales slump hit the auto industry in 1924, motordom explicitly iden-tified the lack of "floor space" in crowded downtowns as its chief impedi-ment to expansion, and targeted streetcars as the vehicles standing in the way. In the '30s, General Motors, Firestone Tires, Standard Oil, and Mack Truck really did buy up an obscure midwestern intercity bus company to form National City Lines. This front company, which eventually scrapped streetcar systems in forty-five cities, secretly and illegally agreed to buy an equal number of buses from GM and Mack Truck. In 1944, a subsidiary of City Lines bought up Huntington's Yellow Cars and replaced them with "motor coaches" running on Standard Oil diesel and Firestone rubber tires. ("From our standpoint," a Standard Oil executive would later testify, "it was going to create a market for our product—gasoline, lubricating oils, and greases.") Two years later, a federal grand jury found the corporations that owned City Lines guilty of antitrust violations and fined their directors one dollar each. The conviction, it is important to note, was not for conspiring to rid America of streetcars but for colluding to agree to buy only GM and Mack buses. After the war, GM and the other conspirators sold their stock in City Lines and got out of the transit business altogether.

Some transportation scholars argue that streetcars would not have survived on their own, pointing out that ridership was in decline by the '30s, and that after years of neglect, the rolling stock of many private companies was in terrible shape.* The streetcar, from this perspective, was so much roadkill, a victim of the irresistible American love affair with the automobile. Trolleys, it was true, were having trouble operating as automobiles brought them to a near standstill in downtowns across the United States. Pacific Electric, forced to keep its fares at a nickel and maintain service on low-demand lines, saw its business stolen on profitable routes by unregulated "jitneys" and bus companies; the company's efficiency was further reduced by accidents as reckless drivers crisscrossed the tracks. General Motors and its co-conspirators were not solely responsible for the death of the trolley—but they did manage to deliver the decisive coup de grâce.

Streetcars, in other words, didn't simply fall off the cliff. Like the bison of the great plains, they were stampeded, recklessly and prematurely, to near extinction. The fact that extensive systems continue to run in Toronto, Melbourne, and dozens of European cities shows street railways can function effectively in modern urban settings. Public ownership and expansion of the Pacific Electric system—of the kind that guaranteed the future of the subway in Fiorello LaGuardia's New York—could well have saved the Red and Yellow Cars. But Huntington and other real estate barons were complicit in their demise. As historian Peter Hall summed it up in *Cities of Tomorrow*, "Los Angeles allowed its light rail systems to be built by buccaneer capitalists chiefly interested not in supplying transportation but in massive land speculation; then, it abandoned the system to its fate." In 1925, transportation experts proposed a plan to separate trains

---

* These are half truths—at best. The Depression did send transit ridership into freefall, but the Second World War made many systems profitable again, including Pacific Electric, which also earned significant revenues from transporting freight in the Greater Los Angeles area.

from traffic on elevated lines emanating from downtown, but planners, politicians, and the public imagination were already fixated on a surefire cure-all for the city's congestion problems: a kind of express highway completely separated from slow-moving surface streets—a freeway!

The last interurban made its final run to Long Beach in 1961. The Red Cars of the world's greatest streetcar system would end up in a scrapyard at the end of the Long Beach freeway, stacked like cordwood.

One afternoon, strolling downtown near Pershing Square, I caught a flash of yellow out of the corner of my eye, and left the sidewalk to investigate. Against all odds, one of Huntington's vintage trolleys has survived into the twenty-first century; it languishes on blocks beneath a tarp, evidently being restored by a local historical society. All riveted steel, canary yellow below, key-lime-pie green on top, it beckoned me to enter with two italicized words painted beneath its single headlight: "*Enter Front.*"

I was tempted to clamber aboard, but the solitary Yellow Car was in the middle of a parking lot—boxed in by automobiles—and an attendant was already closing in on the trespasser on his territory. I made my escape, jaywalking across Olive Street. The sight of the streetcar must have put me in some kind of Toon Town reverie, because, as I crossed the lanes of traffic, I narrowly missed being run over by a late-model SUV.

I'd forgotten. In real-life Los Angeles, it was Judge Doom and his freeway, not Roger Rabbit and the Red Cars, that ultimately triumphed.

Torture-of-the-Freeway

By the 1960s, Los Angeles had become the most up-to-date metropolis in the world, thanks to the omnipresence of limited-access expressways within the city itself. Freeways in older cities function mainly as conduits to suburbs and other communities. L.A.'s thousand miles of urban freeways are more like arteries, the equivalent of other cities' main streets and boulevards. Within a block of where half a million cars converge every day at the intersection of the San Diego Freeway and Route 101, the busiest interchange in the world, you'll find children playing on residential sidestreets.

According to persistent Southern Californian lore, there was a golden age, right before everybody *else* arrived, when the freeways were empty and the driving was good. You sense the power of the myth when Randy Newman comes on the car radio, rhyming off the freeways in "I Love L.A." as he cruises Santa Monica Boulevard with a nasty redhead in an open-top Buick. Or when you pass the space-age sign of an In-N-Out Burger and dig the Googie architecture on Sunset that looks so good at 40 miles an hour (and like so much cheap plaster when you get up close). Or when you come across Joan Didion rhapsodizing in *The White Album*: "The freeway experience is the only secular communion Los Angeles has. . . . Actual participants think only about where they are. Actual participation requires a total surrender, a concentration so intense as to seem a kind of narcosis, a rapture-of-the-freeway."

Driving Los Angeles's roads can still be a rapturous experience—provided you do it at three in the morning. Any other time, you are guaranteed to get stuck in the worst gridlock in North America. One Saturday morning I decided to take what Angelenos call the "surface roads," rather than the freeways, from downtown to Venice Beach. On Venice Boulevard, the congestion was so bad I was repeatedly passed by the same posse of retirement-aged cyclists at major intersections. Every street within a mile of the coast was locked in rigor mortis, a multilane perdition of screaming children and steaming parents. On Pacific Avenue, shirtless dudes held aloft cardboard signs hawking off-street parking in vacant lots and front yards for twenty-five bucks. It took me half the morning to make the trip, and most of the lunch hour to find a parking space. The ultimate goal of all this motorized suffering, amazingly enough, was a casual stroll with other human beings along a car-free boardwalk.

As I became intimately acquainted with the bumper of the Mazda ahead of me on the I-10 all the way back to my hotel, I heard the traffic woman on the AM station wonder aloud: "Where are those hovercars they promised us?"

Don't hold your breath. A driver in Los Angeles spends an average of 72 hours delayed in traffic annually, the equivalent of almost two full weeks of work. (That's not total travel time—that's just the time spent stuck in traffic. Calculating an average of 18.5 hours a week, an American will spend nine years of his life in a car.) And congestion really is getting worse: since 1982, when there were 44 hours of delays, Los Angeles has consistently ranked first as the most congested city in North America. The Hollywood Freeway is officially the worst automobile commute in America, with average speeds a mere 14 miles per hour in bottlenecks.

Come to think of it—do hold your breath. Thanks to its freeways, Los Angeles is also the filthiest city in America. Angelenos have been living with car-caused air pollution since at least Black Sunday, the day late in the summer of 1943 when pea-soup smog reduced visibility to three blocks throughout the region, causing crops to wither and provoking rumors of a Japanese chemical attack. Stricter emissions standards have cleared the air slightly since then, but a cloud of toxic diesel exhaust still emanates from the trucks that rumble north from Long Beach, and research has revealed a new threat: ambient particulate matter. The tiny particles from tire rubber, brake metal, and exhaust pipes can penetrate air-conditioning filters and double windows, and cause hardening of the arteries, premature births, and lifelong lung damage in children. The effects are especially severe for those who live within a block of major roads, but "cancer corridors" can extend a mile on either side of freeways—and not many neighborhoods in Los Angeles are less than a mile from a freeway. All told, particulate matter is estimated to kill 24,000 Californians a year prematurely, about six times the number who die in car accidents.

In the next thirty years, the five counties in the metropolitan area are expected to grow by 6.3 million residents. Los Angeles is clearly going to have to adapt or face paralysis and suffocation. Short of triple-decking the freeways and installing giant fans along the ridgeline of the San Bernardinos to blow all the smog to China, its best hope lies in transit.

After a few days stuck in this torture-of-the-freeway, I decided to rely exclusively on Metro's buses and trains. It wasn't rapture, and parking my rental car meant there was a lot of the city I wasn't seeing. But what I did see, I saw better; and, at the end of the day, I was a hell of a lot more relaxed.

The Bus Riders vs. the Subway Mayor

"We think that mass transit is a human right," said Sunyoung Yang, of Los Angeles's Bus Riders' Union (BRU). "It is a social service that needs to be provided, and it should be publicly funded. And the number one way to increase ridership and encourage more people to use transit is by lowering fares—not by digging expensive subway tunnels and building more light rail."

I was a bit confused. Or maybe I just wasn't used to the polarized rhetoric of class conflict on the West Coast. Yang, an emphatic young woman in charge of the BRU's Clean Air campaign, was sitting in a corner office on the twelfth floor of the Pellissier Building, which offered a panoramic view of a half-dozen or so Metro Rapid Buses frozen in traffic up and down Wilshire Boulevard. I'd arrived by subway from Pershing Square, a trip that cost me a buck and a quarter and took exactly ten minutes. The day before, I'd ridden a Japanese-made light-rail train through the security-barred bungalows of Compton and Watts on the Blue Line, a comfortable and, unlike the Gold Line, heavily used light-rail service that makes the 22-mile run from Downtown to Long Beach through some of the city's poorest neighborhoods. And I'd just read that, against heroic odds, the mayor had obtained funding to build a subway line deep into the Westside that promised to ease congestion for the entire city. It seemed to me that what this desperately congested city needed was as much transit as it could get, and as soon as it could get it.

So run that by me again, I implored Yang. What exactly does the Bus Riders' Union have against building more rail transit?

"You have to understand," she replied, "we took on the whole transit issue in the early nineties, not because we wanted better transit—well, of course we want better transit—but because it was a clear civil rights and environmental justice issue for many of the community members that we organize. Over eighty percent of bus riders are black, Latino, and Asian people who make less than twelve thousand dollars in average annual household income. The buses are basically the feet of the poorest of the working people in Los Angeles. We sued Metro to make sure they used the cleanest fuel available, and we won.

"Now Metro wants to build more light rail and a new subway line, but they have a history of not securing enough operating funds, and they end up cannibalizing current bus operations to run them." The result, said Yang, is that the middle class gets expensive but underused rail lines, while the poor have to rely on an inferior bus system that faces constant service cuts. "It's boondoggle capital expansion," she told me. "And you shouldn't buy a new house if your current house is falling apart."

Yang was making a valid point. Los Angeles's interurban Red Cars and local Yellow streetcars worked well when the city was young, but the twenty-first-century metropolis is an altogether different kind of city. Los Angeles, as urbanist William Fulton has written, was settled "as a kind of national suburb for old-line Protestants wanting nothing to do with the immigrant politics of big urban cities elsewhere in the country." By 1930, 94 percent of all dwellings in the city were suburban-style single-family houses, largely inhabited by the "middle-aged middle class from the Midwest"—who were also the world's earliest and most enthusiastic adopters of the private automobile. As of the 2010 census, however, L.A. is a majority Latino city, and a further 20 percent of the population is African and Asian American. The city's enormous population of working poor, many of whom live in car-dependent subdivisions built for past generations of migrants, is disproportionately dependent on transit. The money the city is about to spend on a new subway line, this argument goes, could buy working-class Angelenos a whole lot of buses. Ironically, it is a line of reasoning that puts the far-left Bus Riders' Union in the same camp as libertarians who oppose "big-government"-built rail transit, and favor privately owned buses as the market-driven, and fittingly second-class, solution for those who can't afford cars.

Yet Metro, the county's public transport agency, seems to be working pretty hard to build a network that serves all Angelenos. Against heavy opposition from homeowners associations, they built a two-line subway that runs heavy-duty, standard gauge trains through cavernous downtown stations. The "Metro Liner" buses of the Orange Line, which look like high-tech centipedes dreamed up by the set designer of *Robocop*, are fast and frequent, shooting deep into the heart of the San Fernando Valley along a dedicated busway. Downtown, the subway and light-rail systems are stitched together by the peppy, half-sized DASH buses, which cost a mere twenty-five cents to ride. With its half-billion boardings a year, Los Angeles ranks second in the country in sheer numbers of transit trips, but there is clearly room for improvement, especially when it comes to attracting commuters: only 1 in 16 Angelenos currently get to work by bus or train.

The main problem is that, for the time being, there are too many gaps in the network for it to function effectively. The misnamed Rapid Buses, which always seem to be snarled in traffic, are bright-orange billboards for transit inefficiency. The rail network currently goes nowhere near rich Westside neighborhoods, so a domestic worker from East L.A. who cleans house in Beverly Hills faces a two-hour ride to work by bus, light rail, subway, and then bus again. When using public transport means doubling your travel time and suffering through interminable transfers, only the desperate will ride it.

Transportation, as author Alex Marshall noted in *How Cities Work*, is a system: "You can't have a little bit of transportation. One cannot have a half-mile of a bus route, and then a half-mile of rail, and then a half-mile of Interstate." New York's subway and Paris's métro are true systems: by offering coverage of virtually an entire urban area—and linking to national passenger rail stations and airports—they come close to mimicking the anywhere-to-anywhere efficiency of the private automobile.

Metro is trying to create such a network. They are building a Regional Connector, a short subway that will allow Gold Line riders from East L.A. and Pasadena to get to the heart of Downtown. The 15-mile Expo Line through Culver City is already under construction; when it is completed, it will be the first Los Angeles rail line that ends within walking distance of a public beach. Metro is gambling that building a network that connects Hollywood Boulevard, UCLA, the airport, Santa Monica Pier, and eventually high-speed trains that make the trip to San Francisco in less than three hours will make it possible for a significant number of Angelenos to get by, if not altogether without cars, at least with fewer per household.

Which is why the Bus Riders' Union's position on rail transit is so short-sighted. For the first time since the 1920s, the political will exists to bring the citizens of Los Angeles a modern, highly integrated transit system. Amazingly, the Bus Riders' Union refused to support Measure R, a half-cent sales tax intended to guarantee a $22 billion revenue stream for public transportation over the next thirty years. Since they also campaign for lower fares, I pointed out to Yang, their stance would guarantee bankruptcy for transit in Los Angeles for decades to come.

"Our position," she objected, "was that if they were willing to create a first-class, extremely well operated, viable, and equitable bus-centered system, we'd support them. *Then* they could invest whatever billions they had left over to build this lofty thirteen-mile subway project."

I didn't see anything especially "lofty" about the planned extension of the Purple Line. Buses, it's true, can be excellent forms of transit, especially when they run along dedicated rights-of-way, as they do on the Orange Line. (And as I would discover later in my travels, citywide rapid transit bus networks are providing superior service in developing-world metropolises.) But subways are permanent infrastructure that benefit the working poor and middle class alike—and unlike bus lines, which can be cut overnight when civic budgets get tight, rail transit *lasts*. No subway system in the world has ever permanently stopped running.

Most Angelenos support the subway. In 2010, they ignored the Bus Riders' Union position on Measure R, and voted 68 percent in favor of the transit-supporting sales tax. The man behind the push for better transit was Antonio Villaraigosa, Los Angeles's mayor since 2005, who is gambling that the "Subway to the Sea," and eleven other transit projects, will become the initiatives that will define his mayoralty. The idea is to extend the stublike Purple Line west along Wilshire Boulevard, with stops at Rodeo Drive, Century City, UCLA, Westwood, and eventually even to the waterfront at Santa Monica—potentially over a dozen miles of new track, at an estimated cost of $9 billion.

I met Mayor Villaraigosa in the high-ceilinged mayoral suite on the third floor of City Hall. Villaraigosa is a compact man who carries little extra weight on his trim frame; if it weren't for the lines deeply furrowed into his forehead, he would look younger than his 58 years. He is passionate about public transport, an issue he has been thinking about since his first political appointment to the Los Angeles's Transportation Board twenty years ago, and has developed a declamatory style that leaves little room for interruption. When Villaraigosa seemed a little shaky on the math of it all, he turned to deputy mayor Jaime de la Vega, who was seated on the edge of a sofa alongside the mayor's armchair, a sheath of papers in his hands.

"Let me go over a couple of things first," began Villaraigosa. "I said Los Angeles was going to be the safest big city in America. Homicides are now down to 1952 levels—I'm sorry," he said, glancing sideways for corroboration from De la Vega, "*violent crime* is down to 1952 levels. Two, I said we would make L.A. the greenest big city in America, and we have now reached and surpassed the Kyoto standards for carbon emissions. Three, I said we would make gridlock and public transit a priority, and we broke ground on the Expo Line and inaugurated the Orange Line, which is probably the most successful busway in the United States."

Interjected De la Vega, "It's really the *only* busway in the country. It gets about twenty-six thousand riders a day."

"And we projected only about seven thousand," continued Villaraigosa. "Now, in the middle of a recession, with opposition from every part of this county, we got a bill through the legislature that would allow a half-penny sales tax that would provide twenty-two billion dollars for public transportation. That's *our* money, *local* money. No other city in the country is spending that kind of money.

"The most significant project of the dozen we're working on is the Subway to the Sea. We're going to build it along Wilshire Boulevard. Wilshire connects the two biggest job centers in California, downtown Los Angeles and Santa Monica—with Century City and Beverly Hills in between. The I-10 freeway that links them is one of the most congested in the county. The Subway to the Sea, without question, is going to be the system's heavy hauler. Up to one hundred and fifteen thousand passengers a day are going to ride it, and it will remove tens of thousands of cars from the Wilshire corridor."

If Villaraigosa succeeds, getting the Purple Line extension built will be an historic achievement. Opposition to the route has long come from the rich Westside districts strung out along Wilshire Boulevard. After the 1992 riots that followed the police beating of Rodney King, "neighborhood preservation" became paramount and Hancock Park, Fairfax, and Beverly Hills opposed any form of transport that threatened to bring the teeming masses into their enclaves. Exaggerated fears over underground methane pockets were exploited by local politicians to stall federal funding for new subway construction. But lately, the zeitgeist has changed. When fetching a quart of milk means suffering through half an hour of bumper-to-bumper traffic, even the most blinkered citizens are seeing transit's potential to reduce congestion. Villaraigosa seems to sense the popular support for his plans, and he's in no mood to compromise.

When I brought up the Bus Riders' Union, Villaraigosa became vitriolic. "If they had their way, we wouldn't build any light-rail lines! Look, I recognize the magnet that low fares are to get more people into the system, and I recognize the fact that we have a large transit-dependent population. But they get upset when we close down a bus line when there are only fifteen people riding it. I mean, come on!" Villaraigosa rejected the idea that rail was somehow middle class: "When you look at the economic demographics of rail and bus in this city, they're not much different. And two-thirds of the people that are going to use the subway will be coming from East L.A., South Los Angeles, Koreatown—not the Westside."

Now that Villaraigosa has a guaranteed stream of local money from the sales tax, he wants to complete the subway in ten years, rather than thirty—a program he calls his "30/10" plan. For that, he'll need more money. There is no looking for funding to the state government. California, once proverbial for creditworthiness, is facing one of the nation's worst budget crises, and the state can barely afford to maintain basic infrastructure. Villaraigosa has made several trips to Washington to secure loans, pitching the benefits of "30/10," which he believes will create

166,000 well-paying construction jobs. President Obama welcomed the plan, calling it "a template for the nation."*

For a city known around the world as a car-addicted basket case, I pointed out, this is striking progress.

"Look, man," said Villaraigosa, "we've got to join the rest of the world. And we're doing it. In the quintessential city of sprawl, we're seeing transit-oriented development. We're moving vertical now. Not anywhere like New York or Chicago—but it's only been a few years. The reason Los Angeles became the epicenter of the single-passenger automobile is that until now we've listened to every naysayer who said 'no' to new transit. And we're now focused on 'yes.' *Yes* to a subway to the sea. *Yes* to a public transportation system that begins to move us away from being the car capital of America."

I agree with Villaraigosa: It's time the Bus Riders' Union ended its knee-jerk opposition to rail transit. Their campaigns brought real improvements in the early '90s, when the city's decrepit buses were nearing the end of their fifteen-year life spans, and they remain a useful watchdog when service is cut. But their rhetoric is tired. The largest city in a state with a nation-sized economy deserves something better than traffic paralysis. What it really needs is a combination of comfortable, frequently scheduled feeder buses, preferably operating in reserved lanes, which would allow riders to transfer seamlessly to the biggest subway network the city can afford.

After my interview with Villaraigosa, I rode the elevator to the open-air observation deck atop City Hall. For almost four decades after it was completed in 1928, this blinding white, pyramidal-roofed tower was the city's tallest building. A little chunk of Metropolis on the West Coast, it doubled as the *Daily Planet* skyscraper in *The Adventures of Superman*. Seen from the twenty-seventh floor, the challenges facing Los Angeles are obvious.

Outside the thicket of downtown skyscrapers, what you see is the horizon-to-horizon smear of a horizontal city, an endless vista of single-family houses veined through with strip malls, two-story dingbats, and taxpayer blocks, all blanketed in a patina of russet-colored smog. Between

---

* In the months after I talked to Villaraigosa, the Subway to the Sea was scaled back to become the Westside Subway Extension, whose more modest route would end in Westwood, several miles shy of the Pacific. Construction of another project, the 16-mile Exposition Line, however, was well under way, and its completion will eventually allow people to ride light-rail cars from the University of Southern California to within a few blocks of the Santa Monica Pier.

the San Gabriel Mountains and the Pacific, it is quintessentially dense sprawl. Not the luxuriantly land-hogging subdivisions of an Atlanta or a Houston, but hundreds of thousands of houses shoehorned onto surprisingly small lots, except where the canyons, golf courses, and hilltops supervene.* In spite of the density, there is also a vast amount of concrete-covered land dedicated to parking and driving, bleak acres of paved dead space that make the pedestrian experience tedious, and even dangerous. Projecting from downtown in every direction are freeways whose names evoke freedom and open roads—the Santa Ana, the Golden State, the Harbor—yet even at three in the afternoon, they are jammed.

As it stands now, Los Angeles's transit network is painfully deficient. Yet if even a fraction of the money allocated to maintain the freeway system every year went to transit, Los Angeles could build itself the best public transport network on the continent.

Some Angelenos see their mayor as an ambitious politician cannily using Democratic Party connections in Washington to build a rail empire, one bound to make him popular with a heavily unionized, and highly unemployed, electorate. But I think Villaraigosa is on the right track—though it's going to take a lot more than a few miles of new subway track to solve this city's problems.

The Los Angeles region's best hope for the future is planning for more, rather than less, density: more like Downtown, and less like Orange County. To get there, the city will have to abandon the suburban ethos on which it was predicated—changing, some say, the very DNA of Los Angeles.

And that's not going to happen without a fight.

The Trouble with Downtown

In spite of heroic efforts at revival, downtown Los Angeles can be a pretty forlorn place, filled as it is with polo-shirted security guards on Smith & Wesson mountain bikes fruitlessly trying to herd panhandlers back to the "Nickel," the city's skid row. If you know where to look, though, you can catch glimpses of the future Los Angeles once imagined for itself, of

---

* A little-known fact, and one completely counterintuitive for most easterners, is that Los Angeles is the nation's most densely populated urbanized area. New York's five boroughs are of course far more intensely settled, but the *average* density of the tri-state metropolitan region is actually 25 percent lower than the density of Greater Los Angeles—a landscape whose every nook and canyon is packed with houses, mostly on small lots, giving it densities high enough for rapid transit.

enduring architecture and walkable public places, stitched together by rail rather than roads. My favorite piece of Southern California retro-tech is Angel's Flight, a funicular railway whose two slant-floored cars still haul passengers 300 or so feet up to Bunker Hill, the skyscraper, museum, and concert hall–topped incline that is traditionally considered the heart of Downtown. On Broadway, a plaque in the sumptuously restored Bradbury Building, whose skylit interior is all lacquered filigree and exposed cog-works, informs visitors that its architecture was inspired by the 1888 novel *Looking Backward*, whose author imagined a future in which densely set-tled American cities would be full of colossal public buildings. One block away, on Hill Street, the words *Subway Terminal Building* are engraved in the pavement outside an old commercial building that has been con-verted into upscale condos and lofts. This was where the now-condemned Hollywood subway used to emerge from underground, a mile of tunnel completed in the 1920s in an attempt to solve the congestion problem once and for all by channeling streetcars beneath the pavement and out of the way of cars.

It is a reminder that Los Angeles was supposed to turn out a lot differ-ently. Even as engineers were planning the freeway system that would blow the metropolis apart, ambitious rail schemes were being devised to reassert the hegemony of downtown. After the war, hundreds of business owners campaigned under the slogan "Rail Rapid Transit—Now!" to have mass transit rights-of-way built alongside freeways. In 1963, the Alweg Monorail company of Germany even offered to build Los Angeles a 43-mile monorail operation, for free. "Between 1948 and 1980," writes trans-portation historian Martin Wachs, "at least six different plans that included some form of rail transit were placed before the citizens, and all failed to be enacted."

Given the competition between streetcars and automobiles downtown, something new had to emerge. It took the form of the Miracle Mile, a rhi-zome of commerce projecting from Downtown, and the first significant mutation of urban structure directly attributable to the automobile. Realiz-ing that affluent motorists from Westwood and Beverly Hills no longer wanted to brave downtown traffic, department store owners built branches in the bean fields along Wilshire Boulevard. The first, Bullock's-Wilshire (1929), a block-sized, terra-cotta sheathed behemoth two and a half miles west of Bunker Hill, still stands, and its innovation is obvious: by building porte cocheres that provide access to huge parking lots in the rear, the department store's owners made it as easy for clients to get to their store by car as by streetcar. The result was America's first linear downtown, a boulevard of two-story "taxpayer blocks"—the ancestors of modern strip malls—punctuated by fifteen-story buildings stretching from Fairfax to La Brea.

To many, it was an abomination. Unlike downtown, whose gridwork encouraged strolling, the Miracle Mile was not built to serve pedestrians. To his horror, science-fiction writer and lifelong non-driver Ray Bradbury was stopped by a police car on Wilshire Boulevard because he was on foot, an incident he turned into the 1951 short story "The Pedestrian." (Though the cop involved didn't write a ticket, he advised Bradbury not to walk anymore.) The Miracle Mile successfully competed with Downtown and Hollywood, until, in its turn, it was made uncompetitive by the definitive Motor Age retail innovation: the freeway-supported shopping mall.

The Greater Los Angeles that has emerged is what urbanists call a "polynucleated" metropolis, with at least eight distinct centers of employment and commerce. Periodic attempts have been made to connect the scattered nodes. In *Magnetic Los Angeles*, historian Greg Hise details the postwar efforts to create a string of small industrial suburbs—places like Torrance and Whittier—each with its own adjoining bedroom community, and within a two-mile walking distance of a commercial core. In the 1980s, visionary city planning director Calvin Hamilton came up with the "centers strategy," which would have concentrated high-density commercial and apartment development in thirty-five nodes in the city, to be linked by mass transit. But the region has resisted rationalization. The economy of Orange County, for example, has for most of its history been a slow-motion Ponzi scheme based on the conversion of vast tracts of former ranch lands into a centerless edge city of endless suburbia, with minimal provision for culture or public space. While a city like New York or Chicago can bank on commuters riding trains to a central business district to sustain public transport, Los Angeles's freeway system has dispersed employment centers to office parks alongside interchanges.

In spite of the geographic realities of modern Los Angeles, faith in downtown never died. The potential for a livable downtown was always there: compared to eastern cities, Los Angeles developed late, and its central business district was never home to noisy, polluting factories. At least 200,000 people work downtown every weekday, and 40,000 now live there, a number that has doubled in a decade. (Nonetheless, its population is still smaller than the tiny slice of Manhattan that is the East Village). Many historic buildings, converted into swank condos during the boom years, are now filled with half-vacant rental properties. Though a supermarket opened in 2007, there are still no public schools, making it a hard sell for parents. Spring Street has a decent stretch of hip bars, but few lights seem to be on in residential buildings in the evening, and it is difficult to find a café open on a Saturday. For now, the gridwork of downtown L.A. mostly seems to serve as a stunt double for eastern cities in Hollywood action films.

Many believe the real trouble with Downtown, and all of Southern California, is the glut of parking. According to law, new development in downtown Los Angeles has to be built with a minimum amount of off-street parking spaces. Frank Gehry's soaring, silver-skinned Disney Hall is considered a world-class contribution to the urbanity of Los Angeles, but a concertgoer can drop her car off at one of the six levels of parking, ride interlinked escalators to the show, and leave without ever setting foot on a sidewalk. Downtown Los Angeles requires, at minimum, fifty times more parking than downtown San Francisco allows at *maximum*. Which means that while most San Franciscans ride transit to get to work, in Los Angeles land is gobbled up for the needs of the car, creating pedestrian-repelling dead zones.

"What sets downtown L.A. apart from other cities is not its sprawl," writes UCLA urban planning professor Donald Shoup, "or its human density, but its high human density combined with its high parking density." The math is simple: an office worker requires, on average, 250 square feet of space, whereas his car requires 400 square feet. A downtown where most people commute by automobile needs to set aside one and a half times as much land for cars as for people. If all the parking spaces in downtown Los Angeles were spread out in a single surface lot, they would cover 81 percent of the central business district's land area (versus 31 percent in San Francisco)—the highest parking coverage ratio on earth. Free parking, as Shoup puts it, "is a fertility drug for cars." He and his followers, the self-styled "Shoupistas," believe that many urban congestion problems stem from civically mandated parking minimums. An enterprising mayor who wanted to permanently revolutionize the city's form, and force a huge spike in transit ridership, would have to enact one simple policy change: limiting, or eliminating, off-street parking requirements in new developments.

It would also be a good way to get tossed out of office. A fundamental—and self-fulfilling—belief among developers is that the average American will not walk more than 600 feet to get to a parked car.

No Vacancy

There is something fatally dingy about the catchphrase "transit-oriented development" (TOD). For too many people, the whole notion of living in close proximity to transit carries the stink of cabbage-scented tenements in the overcrowded slums of some nineteenth-century industrial city.

The term, popularized by architect and urban planner Peter Calthorpe, describes relatively high-density neighborhoods with a mix of residences and businesses, often with an emphasis on multistory and multifamily dwellings. In theory, a transit-oriented dwelling is located within half a mile of a light-rail platform, a subway station, or a high-frequency bus line. It should also be close enough to shopping and schools so that residents can reduce their driving, or even get by without a car altogether. In practice, following TOD principles has led to both *Blade Runner*–style cityscapes of high-rise condos towering over subway stations, and *Our Town*–like neighborhoods of closely spaced bungalows.

Los Angeles, it turns out, has both kinds of TOD. Boarding a northbound Gold Line train at Union Station—this time riding away from East L.A.—I took a fifteen-minute ride and stepped off the platform into what looked like small-town America. South Pasadena is only seven miles from Bunker Hill, but it feels half a continent and a whole century away. On a street of Arts and Crafts–style houses (one of which did duty as the house where Jamie Lee Curtis was pursued by Michael Myers in the first *Halloween*), a pair of boys dropped their bikes next to a lamppost and ran into a candy store that sold saltwater taffy and gumdrops. Next to the level crossing, people lined up at the counter of Buster's, "The Coffee Stop By the Tracks," according to a mural on a brick wall depicting a steaming cup of Joe cradled in a lace-collared hand. As crossing gates fell, the sound of clanging bells made it feel like a crossroads in a sleepy midwestern town—one with palm trees and parrots rather than oaks and squirrels.

"This is like the best of Americana," said developer Michael Dieden, who had agreed to show me around Mission Meridian, a transit-oriented complex of sixty-seven condominiums. "There's a beautiful public library within a five-minute walk of here, and last night there was a farmer's market. They show movies outdoors next to the station in the summer."

Built on an acre and a half rectangular lot, Mission Meridian begins, closest to the Gold Line tracks, with a two-story commercial block, faced with bricks of subtly varied hues. The upper floor has artists' lofts with high ceilings, the ground floor features a restaurant, lawyers' offices, and a gym, and an old-fashioned neon sign points the way to the parking lot in the basement (including 143 spaces, subsidized by Metro, for commuters on the Gold Line). Next to the commercial building is a city block of duplexes with gable dormer windows that advance like row houses along Meridian Avenue. The density nearest the station averages forty units to the acre; by the end of the block, where the condos become full-sized houses, it has declined to a dozen units to the acre. The complex shades from urban to near suburban densities, blending with the century-old bungalows that stand eight dwellings to the acre on adjoining streets.

Many locals, Dieden told me, did not like the idea of multifamily, mixed-use residences being built in the midst of single-family houses. South Pasadena is wealthy and conservative; this was Richard Nixon's home base, and the national headquarters of the John Birch Society can still be found down the road.

"I got a call from one woman who was all exercised about how this was going to attract all kinds of minorities. She gave the example of Koreans not speaking English, and affecting test scores in local schools. When I told her units were going to start at about three hundred thousand, she paused and said, 'Well, I can't afford that. I guess I don't have any problem with your project at all.' I never heard from her again."

Given the genteel finished product, it is hard to imagine anyone making a real stink about Mission Meridian. The courtyards are sheltered from the street and shaded by maple trees, so traffic noises disappear and the splashing of fountains and birdsong predominate. That, and the sound of a guitar: a teenage girl was seated on a stoop outside one condo, teaching herself the chords for "House of the Rising Sun." We watched as a trio of high school–age boys on their way to the station sat down with her for a couple of minutes.

The entire complex sold out during construction, the larger units going for $850,000. "The interesting thing is that in spite of the recession they've held their value. And we've actually started to outperform the single-family homes across the street; one unit is on the market for almost a million dollars."

The key question, of course, is whether the residents of Mission Meridian have actually cut down on their driving. A reporter from the *L.A. Times* counted the cars coming out of the complex's parking lot and concluded that many residents continued to drive to work rather than use the Gold Line. A survey of residents, however, found that 55 percent bought the condos precisely because they were next to the Gold Line, and even if they didn't use light rail to commute, they leaned on it pretty heavily for other trips.

As we walked back to the station, Dieden said, "You know, this is the kind of community Sarah Palin should really represent." It wasn't something I expected to hear from a man who had organized liberal icon Tom Hayden's state assembly campaign in the '80s. "No, I really mean it. The conservative movement is all about building community, and the way I see it, trains do a much better job of holding neighborhoods together than the automobile, which disperse and individualize people."

Many Angelenos oppose TOD because they believe that, because it boosts neighborhood densities, it just makes traffic worse. But the evidence shows that walkable, transit-served neighborhoods significantly reduce total vehicle miles traveled, the crucial factor in a city's overall congestion.

"Most congestion doesn't come from density," Roger Moliere, the head of Metro's property development section, told me at the agency's headquarters in an office tower next to Union Station. "It comes from *sprawl*. In a dense city like New York or Chicago, people walk downstairs and hop on a subway or bus. Here, people live in Rancho Cucamonga or wherever, and all those cars accumulate until a freeway like the I-10 is clogged up all the way to Downtown." Metro's strategy for change is incremental, and is not only limited to building new transit, but also the places where people are going to live. "Congestion is actually our friend. People are starting to figure out that if you live near a subway or other transportation lines, you can avoid the enormous waste of time of driving." Metro, which was created through the merger of several agencies that held large parcels of city land in the form of rights-of-way, owns a lot of incredibly valuable acreage. Much of Metro's TOD is what is called "infill"—it involves filling in the blank spaces on the city map, many of them sprawling surface parking lots. "Our object," says Moliere, "is to create spaces that will make it more convenient and attractive for people to get out of their cars and take public transport."

All told, Metro has used public-private partnerships to build twelve major transit-oriented developments in Los Angeles, and two dozen more are in negotiation or under consideration.

Not all of them have the small-town feel of Mission Meridian. Later that day, I emerged from a Red Line subway station into a far more urban setting. I was at Hollywood and Vine, right in the middle of the Walk of Fame; beneath my feet was the star of Ozzie and Harriet, television's quintessential suburbanites; across the street was the electric-deco marquee of the Pantages Theatre. I crossed the red-carpeted lobby of the W Hotel to the courtyard, across which a power cable snaked to a Tesla Roadster convertible.

A salesman named Nelson, nattily dressed in a charcoal suit and golden tie, gave me the tour of 1600 Vine, Metro's latest-born transit-oriented project. We visited a one-bedroom condo overlooking the hotel's courtyard. Compared to Mission Meridian, it was sleek and urban, with exposed concrete walls, high ceilings, and an open loft-style layout.

Down the hall was a lounge whose leopard-skin upholstered furniture made it look like James Brown's rec room, and on the tiered roof, which promises to be a bit of a party scene, Nelson showed me a swimming pool and a huge barbecue pit, as well as two helipads. Scattered through the market-rate apartments, Nelson said, were 78 units for low-income families, which rent for between $600 and $900 a month.

"Our mayor loves to brag about things like this. What he's saying to the working people of this city is, 'You can live here too. You're a resident.' Just the same as the guy who's eating the five-course meal." The city gives developers a density bonus, allowing them to build more units on a lot if 15 percent of the development is set aside for low-income renters.

So far the presence of affordable housing hasn't put off other renters. Of the three hundred market-rate units, sixty-two had been leased in the first two months. "At this rate, they'll all be leased in nine months," said Nelson. "And that's pretty good in this market."

"I tell people," he continued, "come up to Hollywood and Vine, because we have a Trader Joe's in the building for your groceries. You walk two blocks—walking, I'm saying—and you've got the Arc Light Theater, a reserved-seating high-end movie theater. And when you want to go to work downtown on Monday, you take the Red Line to work." It was a pretty good pitch. I could see that it might be fun to have a pad in the heart of glamorous Hollywood. Only a couple of years ago, 1600 Vine was just a surface park-and-ride lot; now it is a bustling urban community, one that is bringing riders to transit rather than more drivers to the road.

As Metro's Roger Moliere sees it, "There's a catalytic effect with transit-oriented development. The people who own the Pantages Theatre across the street from Hollywood and Vine are now going to develop the whole block. There's an old office building next door, and a private developer did an adaptive reuse and made it into high-end condos."

But Metro is getting one crucial aspect of the equation wrong: they are building too much free parking into their transit-oriented development. Every apartment at 1600 Vine includes one off-street parking space *per bedroom*. (Even the project's salesman told me, "This is Los Angeles, man. You *gotta* have a car.") If even the municipal transit agency's buildings are oversupplied with parking, changing the city's DNA is going to be a long haul. Study after study has shown that when parking is free, people are less likely to use transit, even when they've got a high-frequency subway line in their basement.

Metro's TOD isn't going to be for everybody. Some Angelenos will recoil from the idea of raising young children in an apartment building—though New York City is full of people who thrive in them, and there is an elementary and middle school within walking distance of Hollywood and Vine. Nor is all TOD as high quality as Mission Meridian and 1600 Vine; too little is being built in the lower-income areas that really need it, like South L.A., and as the *LA Weekly* has reported, the few that are being built in such districts tend to be unhealthily close to freeways. On the other hand, not every family wants, or can afford, a single-family house with a yard—and Los Angeles is seriously oversupplied with those. The only land left to build new cul-de-sacs is 80 miles east of Downtown, on the far side of the San Gabriel Mountains. Since Los Angeles can't keep growing out, it's time it started to grow up.

There are worse things in life, after all, than sharing walls, and sidewalks, with other human beings.

The L.A. Brand

The debate over transit and freeways is just the latest iteration of a very old struggle, one that has pitted rail-hopping Okies against orchard-owning citizens, Venice Beach surf bums against Slow-Growth homesteaders, and the shotgun apartments of South Central against every gated Rolling Hills or Malibu Beach Colony worthy of its restrictive covenants. It's a struggle over the identity of the North American city and whether that city is going to be a coherent entity with the capacity to generate prosperity and community, or a patchwork of enclaves of self-segregated home owners.

"Los Angeles, it should be understood, is not a mere city," historian Morrow Mayo wrote back in the 1930s. "On the contrary, it is, and has been since 1888, a *commodity*; something to be advertised and sold to the people of the United States like automobiles, cigarettes, and mouth wash." Not only the United States—thanks to Hollywood, the Los Angeles lifestyle has become a global brand. From the days that Buster Keaton cavorted around freshly laid-out subdivisions in a jalopy to the latest episode of *Entourage*, images of this house-and-driveway–dominated cityscape have been broadcast around the world as the prototype of up-to-date urbanism. The city's leading developers have physically exported the brand, turning much of Arizona and Nevada into Los Angeleses (or more accurately, Orange Counties) in the desert. And when ranch-style homes pop up on the outskirts of Dubai, Beijing, and St. Petersburg, it is largely thanks to the propaganda for the good life relentlessly transmitted via screen and satellite.

One thing is certain: it is time Los Angeles altered its self-image. It is more urban than it thinks. Sixty percent of the city's residents are now renters rather than owners. Twenty-five percent of Angelenos don't even own cars. And the city's future is going to be even more Hispanic and Asian American—both groups with fewer hang-ups about transit, and more prone to settle near rail stations, than white Angelenos. At the same time, the districts undergoing the most rapid gentrification, like Koreatown, Westlake, and Echo Park, are both multiethnic and transit proximate.

The best way forward might involve looking backward, and from this perspective transit-oriented development is a return to the kind of place Los Angeles originally hoped to become. The city still retains traces of this ideal. For example, there is Abbot Kinney's turn-of-the-century "Venice of America," where sidewalks and arching footbridges bind together serried homes that back onto canals filled with ducks and rowboats. The postwar Baldwin Hills Village, where traffic is confined to the periphery and 600 row houses and apartments are dotted through a serene wooded superblock, is still a vibrant, and ungated, urban neighborhood. Hidden among the metropolis's overpasses are walkable town centers that could once again be reinvigorated by a revived rail network.

"The freeways," as the boosterish architecture critic Reyner Banham observed forty years ago, "seem to have fixed Los Angeles in canonical and monumental form, much as the great streets of Sixtus V fixed Baroque Rome, or the *Grands Travaux* of Baron Haussmann fixed the Paris of *la belle époque.*" It's the freeways, too, that make Los Angeles a place my wife and I can't imagine living. Friends of ours moved to L.A. recently, and when we visit we always have a good time. There are jewels scattered everywhere—this time, I got out to the Museum of Jurassic Technology, ate Welsh rarebit at Musso and Frank's on Hollywood Boulevard, and drank soju at a bar in Koreatown where nobody spoke English and every-body smoked—but the ratio between experience and pavement is all wrong. Whenever Erin and I get back home, we say, "That was great—but it feels like we spent the whole time in the car."

And I'm not convinced that transit's newfound support among middle-class Angelenos is as forward-thinking as it seems. The enthusiasm for the subway, especially in the rich Westside, may just reflect a desire to get the working poor off the roads and restore the city to the days when the free-ways were empty and the driving was good. In the sprawled American West, public transportation is the ideal solution—as long as the other guy is using it.

And that's too bad, because Angelenos could use all the extra connec-tion they can get. Nelson, the real estate agent at 1600 Vine and a lifelong Angeleno, surprised me by waxing philosophical on the subject. We were standing on the roof of the complex, looking toward the smog-blurred Hollywood sign.

"I've got a friend who's a film director from England," he told me. "He said to me once, 'The one thing I noticed when I got to L.A., is that you guys are completely cordoned off from each other. In Chicago, New York, even San Francisco, people are undoing their ties together at 5:15, riding the same trains. But here, you're in your cars. You've got your BlackBerry grafted to your ear. You've got these things going with your little iPods.' And he goes, 'You guys are like *so* not connecting.'"

My thoughts exactly. But I wish Los Angeles well, I really do. When it comes to transit, it's got the density, it's got the legacy of urban rail, and, crucially, it's got the *need*. If Angelenos build even a tenth of what they've already dreamed for themselves, one day they'll wake up to find they've got a real city between all those freeways.

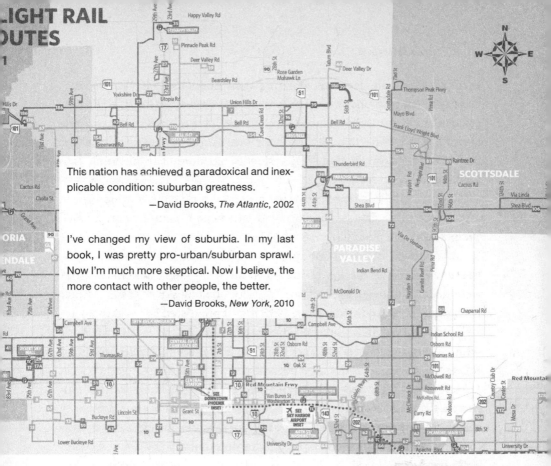

This nation has achieved a paradoxical and inexplicable condition: suburban greatness.

—David Brooks, *The Atlantic*, 2002

I've changed my view of suburbia. In my last book, I was pretty pro-urban/suburban sprawl. Now I'm much more skeptical. Now I believe, the more contact with other people, the better.

--David Brooks, *New York*, 2010

3. The Highway to Hell

Phoenix, Arizona

The future, as envisioned by America's greatest architect, was supposed to look so much better than this.

By this point in the twenty-first century, we were meant to be living in flat-roofed houses distributed over the countryside, each with its own carport and acre of cultivated land. On Sunday mornings we would fly to farmers' markets to sell our surplus pumpkins and pears in family helicopters, called aerotors. For day-to-day travel, there would be fish-shaped three-wheeled road machines, whizzing along multitiered landscaped highways at 150 miles an hour to reach garden schools, factory units, and drive-in churches. Gone would be the dirty, crowded downtowns of the past: the city of the future was to be at once everywhere and nowhere, with even the biggest centers of ten thousand residents harmoniously blending into verdant fields and forests.

There is a hillside in Arizona that gives you both a panoramic view of modern-day Phoenix, and an idea of exactly what became of Frank Lloyd Wright's city of the future. Amid the washes and whipsnakes of the Sonoran Desert stand the buildings of a utopian community meant to be the nucleus of a revolution in the way Americans—or Usonians, as they were to be known—lived. Taliesin West, founded by Wright as his winter home and school in the desert in 1937, is still populated by an aging coterie of true believers, who defend the master's rubblestone walls, plywood wing chairs, and loopier schemes from the depredations of the desert and posterity. It was here, during afternoon naps on the patio of the Great House, that Wright dreamed up Broadacre City, his remedy for the malaise of the citified citizen made "sidewalk-happy" by too much big-city centralization. The key to the success of the new, deconcentrated city was to be the universal adoption of the private automobile.

"The new standard of space in Broadacre City," wrote Wright in *The Disappearing City*, "refers to the motor car and not to walking, nor to riding a horse." The Usonian of the future would drive to automobile inns, filling stations-cum-supermarkets, and banks with drive-up teller windows. On the economy and administration of Broadacre, Wright remained vague. But the wooden model constructed by Wright's acolytes makes it clear that a compound much like Taliesin West was to occupy the highest ground, offering a lordly overview of the workers' districts. Not surprisingly, this would be the headquarters of the county architect, the man who, wielding a T-square and mechanical pencil, would have the ultimate say over the shape and appearance of his fellow Usonians' homes. In 1943, Wright sent a petition urging the Roosevelt administration to adopt the principles of Broadacre; among its sixty-four signers were Albert Einstein, Nelson Rockefeller, and New York's master builder, Robert Moses.

Before Wright could build his city, however, the old city caught up to him. Just beyond the crooked-armed saguaros, which stand like dejected sentinels whose "Who goes there?" has never been heeded, Scottsdale sprawls for forty miles to the north and south, its subdivisions bleeding seamlessly into the suburbs of metropolitan Phoenix. On either side of six-lane Shea Boulevard, the brownish-red roofs of endless Vales and Ranches and Stables cover the reddish-brown terrain, a palate varied only by baby-blue swimming pools and the unnaturally green links of perpetually sprinklered golf courses. When enormous power pylons were erected along the southern border of Taliesin West, an enraged Wright threatened to tear the whole place down.

On the day I visited, Connie, a transplanted New Yorker who daily ushers visitors through Taliesin West's drafting studio and Usonian house, apologized if she seemed a little frazzled: her commute through rush-hour traffic from her home in Maricopa was 92 miles one-way, and it was exhausting her. On my way to Taliesin West that morning, I had bought a breakfast burrito at a filling station, withdrawn money from a drive-up ATM, and picked up a macchiato at the window of a drive-thru Starbucks. There were no aerotors in the desert sky—just the contrails of F-16s over Luke Air Force Base—but the horizontally dispersed Phoenix area was shot through with high-speed highways: with no downtown to speak of, this car-based city of the twenty-first century was simultaneously everywhere around us, and nowhere to be seen. Though it was far from how Wright had imagined it, a kind of Broadacre City had come to pass, and it looked a lot like the sprawl that now surrounded Taliesin West.

Phoenix is my nightmare, the antithesis of any city I could imagine living in. I spent my early teenage years in Calgary, a similarly suburbanized city on the Canadian prairies, and I have driven enough on the outskirts of big American cities to know how sprawl, with its endlessly reiterated clusters of Wal-Marts, Shell stations, and Home Depots can make you feel like you've gotten stuck in a freeway designed by M.C. Escher, sadistically engineered with neither on-ramps nor exits. But even in such paragons of sprawl as Atlanta, Houston, and Miami, the suburbs eventually end, and you reach an historic downtown. I had come to Phoenix because it is a special case, a centerless city built almost entirely after the coming of the automobile. Besides, before I went in search of what people were doing *right* in cities, I figured I needed to see where everything had gone wrong.

In terms of sheer square mileage, low-density, automobile-dependent suburbia has become the dominant built environment on this continent. Yet it turns out that almost everything people think they know about the suburbs is wrong. They did not burble up as a pure product of developers responding to consumer demand, nor were they the result of millions of working- and middle-class families spontaneously choosing to flee the city en masse. They are no longer even the preferred choice of the majority of Americans, but thanks to prodigious overbuilding, Broadacre City, or its modern equivalent, the county-straddling metro area, has become the only affordable option for far too many people. And that is unfortunate, because not only are car-dependent suburbs demonstrably unsustainable, they are also going down—fast.

The Sprawlagists

There is a vocal group of commentators who believe that sprawl is a natural pattern of human settlement, and that the future of the three-car, single-family home is bright.

I decided to talk to Joel Kotkin, probably America's best-known apologist for sprawl. The prolific author, whose editorials appear in the *Wall Street Journal* and the *Washington Post*, believes America's growth will continue to occur in suburbs, and sees such car-based cities as Phoenix as models for the future.

Kotkin is an opponent of federal funding for rail transit, because it offers "precious little that will benefit suburbanites." He believes sprawl is an example of the free market at work: "Suburbs," he has written, "have expanded because people like them." For Kotkin, gated communities, far from being a threat to the public realm, merely "reflect a desire for community that feels secure and that has some controls on interaction." He mocks the British, whose dwellings he says average 850 square feet, for living in "Hobbit houses." While acknowledging that the bulk of demographic growth in America will come from burgeoning Hispanic and immigrant populations, he points to such small cities as Boise, Idaho; Sioux Falls, South Dakota; and Fargo, North Dakota, as prototypes for the growth of the "Heartland" (failing to mention these places are over 90 percent white). In his latest book, *The Next Hundred Million*, Kotkin predicts: "Most of the urban growth will take place not on the older model of New York or Chicago, but along the lines of Los Angeles, Houston, or Phoenix."

Before leaving for Phoenix, I visited Kotkin at his home in Valley Village, a neighborhood of single-family houses in the south of Los Angeles's San Fernando Valley. Kotkin, who is in his mid-fifties, is a short-necked fireplug of a man, with square shoulders and a pugnacious manner. When I met him he was wearing shorts, a faded sweatshirt, and a wary half smile. As we sat beneath a sycamore tree in his backyard, which was full of plastic toys belonging to his two elementary school–age daughters, he laid out the case for the suburbs.

"The aspiration to live in a single-family home is pretty universal," Kotkin began. "We are going to have a hundred million more people in the United States in the next forty years, and immigrants overwhelmingly want to live in suburbs, if you give them half a chance. High density is predominantly attractive to the very wealthy, to the young, and to people without kids. I mean, the chattering class is dominated by people who fantasize about living in the inner city. But you are hard-pressed, outside of the extremely wealthy and the sophistos, to find people who want to live in dense places with kids."

In *The Next Hundred Million*, Kotkin, an energy optimist, predicts that an as yet uninvented technology will avert the "long-prophesied energy catastrophe" of peak oil. When I asked him about the effect rising energy prices could have on sprawl, he smirked. "See, I'm a little older than you; I've already seen this movie before. People have been saying these things for thirty-five years. It's just like the whole climate change thing. Ten years ago, who would've expected we'd find all this natural gas? We have massive amounts of energy, and there's massive improvements you can do in energy efficiency." However, when I pointed out that running cars on biofuels and fossil fuels from shale fields would almost certainly lead to catastrophic increases in carbon emissions, he threatened to end the interview. "Look, if you already have your thesis, then you shouldn't talk to me. Don't waste my time."

Opting for de-escalation, I asked for his take on the future of suburbs, and he warmed to the topic. Kotkin believes that the best hope lies in greening suburbia, creating what he calls "smart sprawl," with village-like centers carved out of existing subdivisions. There would be no need to invest in better transit, because future cars will be more fuel efficient, and telecommuting will become more popular. Kotkin is against government intervention; he believes families need to convince developers to build a coherent community life into their subdivisions, by insisting on parks, bike paths, and sidewalks. "I think telecommuting and the reconstruction of suburbs into more self-sufficient villages is the way to go."

In other words, everybody should live pretty much the way Joel Kotkin lives now. Since he works from a home office, he is freed from a daily commute. Yet in *The Next Hundred Million*, he writes that the only way for the

United States to remain competitive and diminish its enormous industrial deficit will be to revive its manufacturing sector. Now, unless this new workforce is assembling widgets in their garages, people are going to have to get to work somehow—and my guess is that will continue to involve a physical commute, either by automobile or transit. Telecommuting may work for "sophistos," but it can't get workers to the factory or office park on time. And so far, there are no signs that jobs have followed workers to their suburban homes: though figures from the 2010 Census aren't yet available, by 2000 the average round-trip commute to work had increased to 32 miles and took 51 minutes—eight minutes more than in 1980.

Kotkin never tires of pointing out that a slight majority of Americans now live in suburbs. However, according to a 2009 Pew Research Center survey, only a quarter of Americans say suburbs are their ideal community type. A clear majority say they'd prefer to live in a small town or a rural area; the rest say they'd most like to live in a city. In other words, while suburbia is where most people have ended up, it's not necessarily where they want to be. Unfortunately, small towns are no longer where the jobs are; places with populations under 50,000 have been consistently losing residents for decades. That leaves cities as an increasingly popular, and realistic, choice. According to the *Wall Street Journal*, an amazing 88 percent of the Millennial generation, who now outnumber the baby boomers, say they would most like to live in a city.

The launch of Kotkin's book coincided with headlines about a new phenomenon: the suburbanization of poverty. Since the recession began, migration to the Sun Belt has stalled, whereas New York, New Jersey, and Massachusetts are now holding on to residents. There are now twice as many unemployed in suburbs as in cities, and a Natural Resources Defense Council study of 40,000 mortgages in Chicago, Jacksonville, and San Francisco found that the chance of foreclosure was highest in the neighborhoods that were most dependent on automobiles.

Ten years ago, Kotkin was a defender of urbanism: in his book *The New Geography*, he documented an urban revival, comparing revitalized American cities to Renaissance Venice and seventeenth-century Amsterdam. What's changed? One change is that Kotkin, originally from New York, now lives in a neighborhood of single-family homes on the West Coast, the kind of place where house numbers are neatly stenciled onto the curb. Yet Valley Village is not your typical American suburb.

"I guess I live in a single-family house in an urban area," Kotkin acknowledged, as he showed me to the front door, "I can walk to bus rapid transit, which is two blocks away. I'm five minutes from the subway. I ride my bicycle all over, even downtown. We can walk to restaurants." People who live in the sprawled subdivisions Kotkin writes about so glowingly can't do any of these things. Kotkin's house, a rambling ranch-style bungalow that dates from 1937, sits on a corner lot. When it was built Yellow Cars still rumbled down nearby Chandler Boulevard, and developers were still making a nod to community life by building in features like parks and sidewalks. In fact, Valley Village started out as a classic streetcar suburb, the transit-oriented development of its day. As I left, I started walking down the sidewalk at the edge of Kotkin's lot, but the pavement ended in the high hedges marking his property line.

The rest of the houses on his block, more typical of ticky-tacky postwar construction, had no sidewalks at all. Kotkin's house was perfectly placed between a bygone vision of neighborly, sidewalk-and-porch urbanism and the cold-shouldered, driveway-and-garage subdivisions that followed. From his front door, I realized, a person could still maintain the illusion that the American suburb had remained the best of all possible worlds.

Not with a Bang

Driving east along Interstate 10, you hear Phoenix long before you see it, as a kind of nonstop, dyspeptic plaint frothing over the AM dial. Between tirades about Obamacare, Glenn Beck encourages listeners to purchase bullion as a hedge against the impending collapse of the "paper-money economy." A longtime listener, first-time caller on the *Barry "Barely Famous" Young Show* opines that the United States should quit all the talk and just turn Iran into an ashtray, already. Riled up about a mosque, Rush Limbaugh builds up a mouthful of foam and begins to lisp and splutter like Sylvester the Cat.

You see Phoenix soon enough, though. The first signs show up after Quartzsite and Cactus City, ads painted on semi-trailers parked on the far side of the barbed wire, promising sweet deals on 1,200-acre parcels of the Arizona badlands. Just when you are wondering who would be fool enough to buy this far out, the first ghost subdivision appears, a gridwork of curbless streets inscribed on a dry riverbed, sparsely peppered with beige bungalows sitting on one-acre lots. Greater Phoenix starts at the corner of North 311th Avenue and West McKinley Street, and doesn't really stop until it hits the evocatively named mountain range 75 miles to the east, where sprawl finally runs up against the peaks of Superstition.

On the eve of the Second World War, Phoenix, population 65,000, was little more than a rail-stop tank town on the line to California, its tiny downtown a trade and government service center for surrounding farm communities, with fewer residents than even proverbially podunk Peoria, Illinois. Easterners with pulmonary problems came to "The Valley of the Sun," as Jazz Age boosters dubbed it, to overwinter at resorts and dude ranches, but with summer temperatures routinely reaching 120 degrees, even Frank Lloyd Wright and his entourage had sense enough to leave come May.

It took extravagant inputs of electricity and oil for Phoenix to grow. The Hoover Dam started to supply hydro power to the Southwest in 1935, just as primitive air conditioners, called "swamp coolers," appeared on windowsills. Sprawl's big bang came in the late '50s, when construction of Phoenix's first federally funded freeway began, and the IRS allowed home-owners to include central air-conditioning in their home mortgages. (These days, summertime cooling bills for a three-bedroom house can easily top $500 a month.) In a single year, 1959, more houses were built than in the three decades before the end of the Second World War. As late as 1940, Phoenix was a walkable city covering a mere 17 square miles; it even had a small, but popular, streetcar network. After half a century of freeway building and rampant growth, Phoenix is the sixth-most-populous city in the United States. Its metropolitan area, which includes Scottsdale, Tempe, and Mesa, has a population of 4.3 million and covers 17,000 square miles—making it larger than the entire nation of Switzerland.

Phoenix is a new kind of metropolis. New York was structured by its elevateds and subways, Los Angeles by its streetcars and interurbans, but Phoenix was built entirely by freeways and automobiles. If a healthy city grows like an avocado, nurtured by a solid pit of commerce and culture, Phoenix is an onion; remove the successive layers of subdivisions, and there is nothing—apart from an overpriced stadium, some car dealer-ships, and a few half-vacant office buildings—at its core. Phoenix is all "sub": there is no *urbs* to speak of.

"Classical sprawl is when you have a central business district that everybody drives to," Jay Butler, the director of real estate studies at Ari-zona State University, explained to me. "Downtown Phoenix is central, but it has never really been where everything was happening. Motorola set up in the East Valley in the fifties. Intel, one of the largest employers, is in Chandler. Another big employment center is around the Scottsdale Airpark. The regional malls are spread out, as are government offices." A journey-to-work could originate at any one of the region's 1.9 million homes, and finish in any one of thousands of office parks or shopping centers. Not that there are many jobs to drive to: most employment in Phoenix, which lacks a robust indigenous economy, is low-paying assembly-plant and call-center work. "Basically, Phoenix is a production town," said Butler. "Companies have operations here, but no head offices."

As in many Sun Belt cities, Phoenix's economy thrived as long as the subdivisions kept going up. Developers, mostly from Southern California, built such enormous master-planned developments as McCormick Ranch, Sun City, and The Lakes. As long as new arrivals continued to drop nest eggs accumulated in colder climes in the desert soil, the economy looked good. Across the United States, 20 percent of private industry growth between 2002 and 2006 was tied to real estate and construction. In the same period in Phoenix—the height of the city's "hypermarket"—*36 percent* of all growth came from real estate and construction. Since the 2008 recession, employment in construction has fallen by half, and a quarter of Phoenix's commercial real estate now sits empty. The Valley of the Sun is so overbuilt that the current supply of single-family houses will not meet projected population growth until the middle of the century.

That is presuming, of course, the population continues to grow. "Foreclosures are running about four or five thousand a month," Butler told me. "In the hardest-hit areas, like Maryville and El Mirage, about ten percent of homes are foreclosed." Butler estimated that, during my visit in the spring of 2010, at least 50,000 homes were sitting vacant in the Phoenix area. (A year later, that figure had doubled.) "The first wave of foreclosures was the amateur investor who paid too much and couldn't rent out his property. The second was those who got involved in predatory, subprime-type financing. Now you're getting the classic foreclosures: you lose your job, or you don't get those billable hours, so you can no longer afford the payments on your high-end home. The latest buzzword is 'strategic default.' Even people who can afford to make monthly payments are looking at what's happening to the values of the homes around them, they're seeing all the vacancies, and they're walking out on their mortgage." Phoenix was the first major city to see home values fall by more than half from their peak during the hypermarket. In far-flung suburbs like Buckeye, Butler told me, you could pick up a newly built, 1,700-square-foot home for under $40,000.

What happens to a car-based metropolis where two-thirds of mortgages are underwater? Things get weird, fast. As I cruised Phoenix's freeways, the radio dial was full of items about what was happening at the ends of off-ramps and driveways. Police arrested a homeowner in Chandler for cutting a hole in the ceiling of his foreclosed property to remove air conditioners, granite tabletops, and light fixtures before the bank took possession. A Phoenix man, after botching a suicide attempt, continued to live for four days in his foreclosed home with the body of his dead wife on the kitchen floor. On AM-550, a company called Turf-Painter Enterprises—"Lawns to Dye For!"—offered to protect foreclosed properties against break-ins by spray-painting parched lawns green. The city of Gilbert, starved of property tax revenues, announced it was laying off sixty-seven police officers, even as empty ranch-style houses were being converted into methamphetamine labs. In Maricopa, yet another bank had been knocked over; Phoenix, long known as America's kidnapping capital, was fast becoming the hot spot for such serial bank robbers as the "Raggedy Ann Robber" and the "Bad Hair Bandit."

As I drove through yet another zombie subdivision of deserted McMansions, where the only other vehicle on the road was a sheriff's van full of convicts in black-and-white-stripe uniforms, a grim-sounding announcer implored listeners to stay out of abandoned houses, and to report any suspicious activity to the local sheriff.

To me, it was the sound of the suburban dream turning into a nightmare.

From Garden City to Slumburb

Where did all this car-dependent, transit-resistant suburbia come from? Bear with me while I run through a condensed history of sprawl.

The debate over the geographical form the good life should take in the New World has been going on since at least the days of America's founding fathers. For Thomas Jefferson, great cities were "pestilential to the morals, the health and the liberties of man"; an agrarian romantic, he favored a rural republic of citizen-farmers, even as he modeled his Monticello on a *hôtel particulier* in the very heart of Paris. The more hardheaded

Alexander Hamilton, the first secretary of the treasury, imagined "flourishing and increasing towns" of industrious merchants and artisans. Cities, as engines of commerce, the arts, and civilization, clearly had history on their side. But why huddle in coastal towns, slavishly mimicking European urbanism, when there were half a billion acres of arable land between the Rio Grande and the northern border, enough for every citizen to fence off a good-sized plot—and build a miniature castle on top of it?

From the start, the American suburb was an attempt to build the best of both worlds. In Europe, the upper classes had long profited from the excitement of the city in luxurious town houses, and the tranquility of the country in their villas, dachas, and summer estates. The suburbs of pre-industrial cities, often located outside stone walls, tended to be zones for slaughterhouses, tanneries, brick kilns, brothels, and other establishments not wanted in the city. "Even the word *suburb*," writes Kenneth Jackson in *Crabgrass Frontier*, the definitive account of American suburbanization, "suggested inferior manners, narrowness of view, and physical squalor." The destigmatization of the suburbs began when new transportation technology allowed people to live beyond the limits of old walking cities and commute to central-city workplaces. The origin of the Anglo-American suburb has been traced to Clapham, five miles south of London, where, in the 1790s, Evangelical Christians eager to remove their families from the evils of the city began living in what had formerly been their weekend villas, and commuting to the City by private carriage. In the United States, Jackson dates the beginning of the process to 1815, when regular steam ferry service to Manhattan made Brooklyn Heights the nation's first true commuter suburb.

The American suburb, version 1.0, was the brainchild of the elite—progressives, reformers, and other idealists who dreamed of a better future for their fellow citizens. New Jersey's bosky, sinuous-laned Llewellyn Park (1853), generally considered to be the first picturesque suburb, was founded by a member of the Perfectionists, a cult that promoted sin-free living as a way of bringing about the Christian millennial kingdom on earth. West of Chicago's Loop, Riverside (1875), which was similarly built on a curvilinear street plan, was one of sixteen suburbs laid out by Frederick Law Olmsted and Calvert Vaux, the designers of New York's Central Park. These first-wave suburbs, short rides from central cities by commuter train, were built by and for the rich: before the First World War, mortgages were virtually unknown, meaning that only well-to-do families could afford to buy. Llewellyn Park, which housed Thomas Edison's laboratories, was the prototypical gated community: its mansions stood on three-acre lots, and the train station was a two-mile carriage ride away. To this day, access from the surrounding cul-de-sacs of West Orange is limited by security guards manning a stone gatehouse.

Globally, the single most influential figure in the development of prewar suburbs was an Esperanto-speaking reformer named Ebenezer Howard. The son of a London shop owner, Howard first came to the United States at the age of twenty-one to try his hand at farming. While working as a court reporter in pulsating, post–Civil War Chicago—known as the "Garden City" in the days before skyscrapers—he came up with a scheme whereby "town and country [would] be married, and out of this joyous union will spring a new hope, a new life, a new civilization." Published as *Garden Cities of To-morrow* in 1902, Howard's utopian plan centered on removing working-class families from industrial centers by building self-sufficient cities of 32,000 people, surrounded by community-owned greenbelts, and linked to sister cities by rapid rail. A year later, Letchworth Garden City, outside London, was born, to be followed in quick succession by Welwyn and Hampstead Garden Suburb. In the United States, Forest Hills in Queens, Woodbourne in Boston, Chatham Village in Pittsburgh, and neighborhoods in dozens of other cities were inspired by Howard's principles.

Though Argentinian, Australian, German, and Japanese versions of the Garden City were also built, their developers almost always missed the point. Howard was a democratic socialist who wanted to transplant the masses from crowded tenements to greener, but still relatively dense, cities where workers could live within walking distance of factories and workshops. What got built instead were Garden *Suburbs*—residential areas with whimsically arranged streets converging in diagonals on circular parks, but without any nearby source of employment. The Town of Mount-Royal, not far from my home in Montreal, is typical: fenced off from the lower-income neighborhood that adjoins it by hedges and wire-mesh fences, its streets lead to an underutilized commuter train station linked to the office buildings of downtown, where the jobs are. Like most versions of the Garden City, Mount-Royal is a low-density, upper-middle-class suburban enclave where almost everybody gets to work by car. And like all Garden Suburbs I have seen, from England to Japan, it is profoundly soporific, lacking the rudiments of a bustling street life.

Such master-planned communities were the exception. Suburbs that predate freeways most often consist of small houses built on a grid, close to city centers; lately, they have become highly sought-after urban neighborhoods. Cleveland's Shaker Heights, Berkeley's Ashby Station, Boston's Roxbury, and the Globe in Ottawa are all classic streetcar suburbs, with lively mixes of row houses, closely spaced bungalows with front porches, and small shops, located within walking distance of the main arteries where electric trolleys used to run.

The American suburb, version 2.0, was another matter entirely. In the immediate aftermath of the Second World War, when housing shortages meant that six million American families were forced to share living quarters, all pretense of elevating the masses vanished. America needed new homes, fast. The emphasis was on using assembly-line techniques to build vast tracts of cheap housing at the fringes of cities, as quickly as possible. In Levittown on Long Island, former Navy Seabees used their wartime expertise to mass produce four-room Cape Cod cottages with rock-board walls, asphalt floors, and plywood lap, at the rate of one every fifteen minutes. (At an average 750 square feet, they were even smaller than the dwellings Joel Kotkin dismisses as "Hobbit houses.") In Lakewood, south of Los Angeles, similar methods allowed developers to erect fifty preassembled, balloon-frame houses a day. Half as dense as the old streetcar suburbs, the new car-based subdivisions ran roughshod over indigenous architectural styles, as Modified Colonials appeared on the outskirts of Edmonton and split-level ranches dotted the fringes of Charleston. The scale of the exodus to the new subdivisions was astonishing. By 1954, nine million people in the United States had moved to the urban fringes, and the suburban growth rate was ten times that of central cities.

In the popular consciousness, an entire generation of war-weary Americans spontaneously fled tired old Gothams for a lifestyle of lawn mowing, barbecuing, and martini drinking in the shiny Pleasantvilles at the end of newly paved freeways. "The prevailing myth," writes Kenneth Jackson, "is that the postwar suburbs blossomed because of the preference of consumers who made free choices in an open environment. Actually... most postwar families were not free to choose among several residential alternatives. Because of public policies favoring the suburbs, only one possibility was economically feasible."

To ensure the success of suburbia, the federal government dangled carrots and brandished sticks. The carrots, in the form of subsidies for homeownership to families, proved irresistible. By allowing mortgage interest to be deducted from income taxes, the government provided a powerful incentive for buying. During the war, Americans had saved at a rate three times higher than in the decades before or since: these nest eggs, combined with a pent-up demand for housing, led to an unprecedented increase in homeownership. In 1949, a two-bedroom Cape Cod–style house in Levittown, complete with fireplace and washing machine, cost only $7,990. Thanks to the GI Bill of Rights, no down payment was required for ex-servicemen. "Quite simply," points out Jackson, "it became cheaper to buy than to rent."

Washington reserved its sticks for the city. The rise of suburbia coincides with the redlining of low-income inner-city neighborhoods. Researchers have found that maps drawn up by the Federal Housing Administration (created in 1934) surrounded African American, Asian, and Jewish neighborhoods in red ink, indicating the urban areas where mortgages would not be insured. Just as millions of rural blacks were arriving in Detroit, Chicago, Los Angeles, and other big cities, they were cut off from homeownership by the simplest of expedients: banks refused to give them loans. Without money to improve properties in redlined districts, city dwellers found their once stable neighborhoods succumbing to "blight"—further encouraging the flight to such all-white subdivisions as Levittown.

The abandonment of the cities was by no means inevitable. In Europe, governments responded to a postwar housing shortage by building public housing, most of it within an easy transit ride of city centers. Thirty years after the war, public housing accounted for over a third of France's housing market and almost half of England's. In the United States, the comparable figure was 1 percent, and the projects that did get built were often so disagreeable—among them St. Louis's crime-ridden Pruitt-Igoe and Chicago's notorious Cabrini-Green—that they were dynamited after only a few decades of existence.

Zoning, the other great tool in undermining traditional urbanism, guaranteed that people would have to drive long distances between residential and commercial areas. In 1926, the Supreme Court upheld the constitutionality of zoning regulations developed by the village of Euclid, Ohio, to prevent industry from nearby Cleveland impinging on its traditional neighborhoods. "Euclidean" zoning, as it came to be known, separates residential, commercial, and industrial uses. "Zoning," according to Jackson, "was a device to keep poor people and obnoxious industries out of affluent neighborhoods. And in time, it also became a cudgel used by suburban areas to whack the central city." Such ordinances ensured the new suburbs would be free of multifamily apartments and small shops; in the South, they were used to enforce racial segregation. By guaranteeing that exclusively zoned residential areas would be distant from workplaces and shopping centers, Euclidean zoning also made car ownership a prerequisite of suburban life.

By the 1990s, it was clear that a new phenomenon, the American suburb version 3.0, was emerging. "We have moved our means of creating wealth," wrote Joel Garreau in 1991, "the essence of our urbanism—our jobs—out to where most of us have lived and shopped for two generations. That has led to the rise of Edge City." In his book of the same name, Garreau identified two hundred edge cities in the United States, among them Virginia's Tyson's Corner, California's Silicon Valley, New Jersey's Metropark, and Orange County, the prototypical centerless city. The only sure way to identify these paragons of sprawl, he found, was to locate regions with five million or more square feet of leasable office space. (They were often named after stretches of freeway or nearby shopping malls, like Houston's Galleria.) Many could be found in the new exurbs, semi-rural areas where taxes tended to be low. By the mid-'80s, twice as many people worked in manufacturing in the suburbs as in central cities. Thanks to the edge city, the typical commute was no longer from a suburb to a central city skyscraper, but to an office park at the intersection of two freeways, in what, until recently, had been a farmer's field. The most important factor in predicting an office park's location, Garreau found, was usually the location of its CEO's country club.

Written in the techno-booster prose of the '90s, *Edge City* makes for comical reading today. "There is no petrochemical analyst around who thinks there is any supply-and-demand reason—other than war—that the price of oil should go higher than $30 a barrel in this generation," Garreau claims at one point. He devotes a lot of time to scouring Atlanta's office parks and Houston's malls for a decent bagel, cappuccino, or indeed any sign of soul or culture, at one point confessing, "No matter how hard I tried to be fair, more than once, traveling around the country, I found myself in deep despair that the Edge Cities I was looking at would ever amount to anything physically uplifting or beautiful." Then he tells himself to take a deep breath: edge cities are brand-new—culture will follow; even Venice took five hundred years to develop.

In much less than a generation, of course, the price of a barrel of oil quadrupled, and edge cities, far from showing signs of developing lasting culture, have gone into decline as central cities experience a significant revival. At the same time, by portraying edge cities as pure products of boot-strapping entrepreneurs working in a free market, and failing to acknowledge that many of the major employers he chronicled were in defense-related industries, Garreau glossed over the elaborate federal support that props them up.

By profiling affluent African American families on the outskirts of Atlanta, Garreau made a spirited case for late-model edge cities having overcome their racist origins. He missed the point that these suburban enclaves continued to self-segregate by class. Historians have traced the current crisis in states' budgets to California's Proposition 13 (1978), which gained its strongest early support in the suburbs of the San Fernando Valley. This "citizen initiative" slashed property taxes by two-thirds and sparked a nationwide tax revolt that paved the way for Reaganomics and the Tea Party. A generation of well-to-do suburbanites turned their backs on the cities, declaring, in essence, that they had no responsibility for the well-being of their fellow citizens. The ultimate consequence of this self-segregation is that 54 million Americans live in common interest developments, where "government" is by private association. Residents are required to pay fees for private roads, sewers, and garbage collection, which makes them reluctant to support taxation for services that would benefit surrounding communities. In Arizona, where the rich can claim exemptions for country club memberships and private schools, lack of tax revenue has forced the state to furlough 15,000 employees. It is not surprising, as urbanist William Fulton has observed, that "people living inside these suburban cocoons become cocoon citizens, defining the common good as that which benefits only those inside their particular cocoon."

Why did the federal government support suburbanization, to the detriment of central cities? The initial rationale was military. In 1948, the *Bulletin of the Atomic Scientists* published "Dispersal of Cities as a Defense Measure" which posited nuclear war damage as a reason to decentralize the population. (Frank Lloyd Wright frequently argued that his Broadacre City would allow the country to survive enemy attack.) In signing the Federal Highways Act, President Eisenhower noted that a network of high-speed freeways would permit rapid evacuation in the event of nuclear war. It was only when a deadly cloud of fallout blanketed Pacific islands after the Bikini Atoll blast of 1954 that it became clear that no community, no matter how remote, would be safe from a wind-driven pall of radioactive ash.

By then, however, suburbanization had its own momentum. Though Lyndon B. Johnson's Great Society boosted spending in an attempt to fight urban poverty, the riots of the late '60s hastened the flight to the suburbs. With support for conservatives increasingly coming from such suburbanized, low-tax states as Florida, Texas, Arizona, and Nevada, Republicans understood it was in their interest to enact policies favorable to the suburbs. Ronald Reagan became the first suburban president, cutting funding to cities and mass transit, and explicitly favoring investment in highways and sprawled Sun Belt metropolises. During his first term, George W. Bush announced, "We want everybody in America to own their own home," and under his administration Fannie Mae and Freddie Mac radically lowered mortgage purchase standards. Thanks to easy credit, the homeownership rate rose to a historic high, reaching 69 percent of all households by 2004. (By 2012, it is expected to drop to 62 percent, the lowest level since 1960.)

The American suburb, version 4.0, promises to be the least glamorous version of all. In once well-to-do subdivisions, the elderly, immigrants, and minorities are becoming the leading demographics. Nevada and Florida, two of the most highly suburbanized states, now have the country's highest rates of violent crime, and Arizona has the highest rate of property crime. It took a while, but the inner city—or at least the clichéd image of it—has moved out to the suburbs. This signals the end of the baby boomers' dreams of ever-appreciating homes, of always being able to trade up to more square footage in a better subdivision. As shopping centers fill with pawn shops and tattoo parlors, Wal-Mart becomes the world's biggest owner of vacant buildings, and gangs turn empty houses in deserted cul-de-sacs into party pads, the "slumburb" is becoming a common feature of America's residential landscape.

"I think suburbia is becoming a loser's choice," Kenneth Jackson told me. Before coming to Phoenix, I'd met the distinguished historian of the American suburb in a coffee shop in midtown Manhattan. On the future of suburbs, the tweed-jacketed Jackson, whose gravelly voice retains the cadences of his upbringing in Tennessee, was both straight-talking and urbane.

"If you're ambitious, and you're tolerant, and you're vital, and you want to run with the big dogs, the city offers a lot more opportunity in a whole variety of ways. What we're seeing now is that a lot of people who have the option to move to the suburbs are choosing the city. The goal used to be to get out of the Bronx, or Chicago, and move to the suburbs. Now you leave the city because you can't afford it."

Jackson, though a prominent critic of suburbanization, acknowledges that the desire for a freestanding home of one's own has strong cultural roots. But it is not quite as universal as people believe, and he doesn't buy the idea that suburbs are the best environment for raising children. "Look," he said, "humans are social animals. I think the biggest fake ever perpetrated is that children like, and need, big yards. What children like are other children. If they can have space, well, that's fine. But most of all, they want to be around other kids. I think we move children to the suburbs to control the children, not to respond to something the children want. In the city, kids might see somebody urinating in public, but they're much more at risk in the suburbs, where they tend to die in cars."

Jackson insisted on the importance of zoning as a fomenter of sprawl. "Early on, we decided that our schools ought to be here, our shopping centers here, our office parks here, and our houses over here, which guaranteed that if you wanted to get anywhere, you had to rely on the internal combustion engine. But there's a growing perception that a dense environment is more sustainable than a low-density environment. When I was growing up, Los Angeles seemed to be the city of the future. I would say now that you can't be a world city without good public transportation. Probably underground. And even a city like Los Angeles is realizing that."

Jackson's research revealed how suburbanization's heroic creation myth—that it was merely the free market responding to millions of pioneers fleeing the city for greener pastures—was always a self-serving fiction. He put it most succinctly in *Crabgrass Frontier*: "There were two necessary conditions for American residential deconcentration—the suburban ideal and population growth—and two fundamental causes—racial prejudice and cheap housing." The suburban home only remained an affordable option with elaborate support from big government. From the start, the enrichment of the suburbs was contingent on the deliberate impoverishment of cities.

Of course, the biggest boondoggle of all is the one suburbanites most take for granted, and without which suburbia would wither and die: the federally funded freeway system, which, even as it beggared railroads and public transport, came to represent the greatest public subsidy to private real estate in the history of the world.

That is a story, however, that will have to wait for another chapter.

So Wright, so Wrong

As an architect, Frank Lloyd Wright was a giant. As a human being, he was a pygmy. Narcissistic and arrogant, notorious for stiffing his employees, his lack of compassion for his fellow citizens often bordered on sociopathy. I wasn't surprised to learn that the planner of Broadacre City also had a thing for fast cars.

In 1908 he bought a four-cylinder Stoddard Dayton that could do 60 miles per hour. His neighbors called it the "Yellow Devil," and Wright was famous for driving through the quiet streets of Oak Park at twice the legal speed limit. He later acquired a Cord L-29 Phaeton, then the fastest car on the road. While families went hungry in the depths of the Depression, the long-haired architect cut an extravagant figure driving around rural Wisconsin in the exorbitantly priced sedan.

One night in 1933, speeding to a lecture outside of Madison, the architect sideswiped a florist's truck, causing it to flip four times. Wright and his wife were unharmed, but the truck's driver had to be rushed to the hospital to be treated for cuts and back injuries. Wright, who had no insurance, later refused to pay the man's medical expenses. Eight years later, after surviving a head-on collision with a truck, Wright grumbled to a friend, "Highways are now commercialized to such an extent that they are no place for a gentleman with a fine car."

Like many of his generation, Wright was seduced by the glamour of the automobile, a technology that distinguished and shielded him from the hoi polloi. Had it been built, Broadacre City would have made the automobile—not to mention the personal helicopter—the basis of a new civilization. Though Wright's influence on urban form was nowhere near as great as that of Robert Moses, his prestige offered crucial support to proponents of auto-based cities.

Wright scholars tend to treat Broadacre City as an embarrassment, or downplay it as a mere hobby. But from what I could tell, Wright took it pretty seriously. I visited the architecture department of Arizona State University, where a full-scale reproduction of the model hangs on a wall above students laboring over monitors: it is a substantial piece of work, 12 feet square, glazed in glossy earth tones. In the archives of Taliesin West, I spent a morning going through files stuffed with Wright's plans for everything from subterranean highway interchanges to the exact shape of streetlamps. The architect worked on perfecting the scheme for over two decades, and it gets at something deep not only in his character but also in the long love affair that American planners and politicians have had with the decentralized city. Wright, who styled himself a Jeffersonian democrat, shared with the third president a naive faith in the spatial fix, the idea that redistributing the population in bucolic surroundings could resolve all social problems—as if the most intractable challenges of race and class could be remedied by the virtues of fresh country air and rural self-sufficiency.

The defenders of decentralization succumb to the fallacy that one's preferred living arrangement—whether it is a Los Angeles subdivision or a Usonian house on an acre of land—is the only reasonable template for the good life. It's an understandable mistake, one I'm probably a little guilty of myself. People have a vested interest in their housing choices. Buying a home, after all, is a leap of faith, an investment not only in real estate, but in community. The more I talked to people, the more I realized how the places they chose to live could predict their attitudes toward the pros and cons of cities, towns, and suburbs. (The attitudes of Kenneth Jackson, who divides his time between an apartment in Manhattan and a home in commuter-train–served Westchester, seem to me particularly complex. *Crabgrass Frontier* is dedicated to his sixteen-year-old son, who was killed in a car crash when Jackson was close to finishing the book.) Small town, farm, suburb, city: the kinds of places people want to live can change at different times in their lives—when they are hunting for a significant other, raising a family, approaching old age. Having lived in cities for all my adult life, through bad times and good, I have faith in the future of urban living, though I know it's not for everyone.

The trouble is that on this continent government policy has led to the overbuilding of one kind of housing, the subdivision of single-family homes, at the expense of all other possible environments. Yet only a certain percentage of the population wants to live in a suburban house. The baby boom generation is past its child-bearing years, and the proportion of the population in their thirties, the cohort traditionally most likely to buy a house, is at an historic low.

There is a corollary to suburban living: utter car dependency. Although the suburbs we've built for ourselves depend on cars to function, there is another, more subtle symbiosis at work between urban sprawl and the automobile. My time on the road in Los Angeles and Phoenix was probably the longest uninterrupted stretch I've spent in a car in the last decade, and it made me grateful I don't own one. By pitting you against everybody else on the road, driving turns travel itself into competition. After two weeks, I was looking for any excuse to ditch my ride, go for a walk in a park, eavesdrop on a conversation, or just feel the sidewalk under my feet.

Every time you choose to drive you are, in a tiny way, opting out of, and thus diminishing, the public realm. And that, finally, is the problem with suburbs and freeways. In order to gain a spurious freedom, which is in fact just increased mobility, millions of people turn their backs on civility—not just politeness, but also the process of civilization building, in which cities play such a crucial role. Sprawl may end in cul-de-sacs and foreclosures, but it begins every time you slam a car door on the world.

That's why Frank Lloyd Wright was the last person Americans should have looked to for a vision of the future city. With his addiction to fancy cars and his patrician contempt for the masses, Wright excluded neighborliness and interdependence from his vision of the good life. The tragedy is that Broadacre City, or something very much like it, got built anyway.

Is Density Destiny?

Where does all this leave Phoenix?

In a last ditch bid for urbanity, the city recently bought itself $1.4 billion of state-of-the-art public transportation. Since 2008, Metro Rail has been running brand-new Japanese-made light-rail trains on twenty miles of track, from Mesa to Camelback Road. I spent a day riding the smooth-running, air-conditioned, immaculately clean but conspicuously under-utilized trains. The trains were built for 170 riders, but except for a gaggle of undergrads who boarded at Arizona State University, I was one of at most a dozen people on almost all the trips I took. How could it be otherwise? Routed through endless stretches of low-rise strip construction along Washington Avenue, past the high vacancy condos of downtown, and alongside the miles of parking lots on North Central Avenue, Phoenix's light rail doesn't really go anywhere. After two years of operation, daily ridership has barely topped 40,000, an infinitesimal fraction of all journeys made in the area. The fact that Phoenix has kept this system in a recession is amazing, and suggests how hungry people here are for ways out of sprawl. But in an outsized edge city, where offices and factories are as decentralized as residential neighborhoods, it looked to me as if a single light-rail line was bound to be an expensive failure.

Yet some transportation theorists are more optimistic. In *Transport for Suburbia*, Paul Mees, a transport planner in Melbourne, Australia, argues that well-conceived transit can match the anywhere-to-anywhere flexibility of cars and freeways, even in areas dominated by sprawl. "Density," he writes, "is not the main barrier to providing public transport that offers a real alternative to the car; rather, it is a rationalization for inaction." Mees believes that if we wait until our cities densify, we will be waiting a long time. Phoenix is clearly never going to be as dense as Paris, but Mees thinks that state-of-the-art planning can make transit work even in edge cities and exurbs. "Fixing public transport is not simple," he acknowledges, "but it is a much easier task than rebuilding entire cities at many times their current densities."

Mees uses several cities, none of them in the United States, as case studies. Toronto, he believes, has the best suburban transit in North America: the reach of its rudimentary subway system is extended into suburbs—whose sprawl rivals any on the continent—by the intelligent scheduling of extremely frequent feeder buses. But Mees's exemplar of transit excellence is Zurich, a model whose applicability to North America at first seems limited. As Mees points out, however, outside of the central city, the rural canton's density is lower than most American suburbs. Yet every settlement with three hundred or more residents is guaranteed basic transit service, and Zurich's buses even stop in national parks—which, as Mees says, have a population density of zero. Service is frequent, coverage complete, and sophisticated timetabling ensures that buses, trams, and trains mesh like clockwork, making transfers painless. The result is that Zurich area buses and trams carry an incredible half-billion passengers a year, more than all the transit in Boston, whose metro area is ten times as populous.

For Mees, frequency and reliability of service are more important than glamorous transport technology. Zurich, he points out, was able to build impressive ridership on trams dating from the '50s. "The challenge of getting people out of their cars," he told me, "involves providing them with a comprehensive package of alternatives and not getting too excited about which one of them they use."

The key lies in boosting what Mees calls the network effect. Transit agencies need to knit different routes into a single, multimodal network, one where transfers between lines are effortless. Since trip origins and destinations have become increasingly dispersed, transit has to provide links between suburbs, not just between suburbs and downtown. For the network effect to come into its own, and for transit to truly imitate the flexibility of the car, service must be frequent, even if that means vehicles sometimes run empty.

Mees also debunks one of the shibboleths of transportation planning: that transit is only justified when certain minimum residential densities are met. In the 1950s, influential studies set the threshold for economical transit at 25,000 people per square mile, or about forty an acre. Mees argues this number has been repeated mindlessly ever since, often as justification for killing less frequented transit lines; setting the bar this high also ignores the chief benefit of the network effect: busy trunk lines can cross-subsidize sparsely used bus routes through even the lowest-density suburbia.

I'm not as optimistic as Mees about transit's potential for replacing cars in places like Phoenix. The issue for me is not density, but the physical realities of edge cities and sprawled metropolises. Most suburbs repel transit: it is difficult for buses to operate efficiently in the curvaceous streets of the typical postwar American subdivision, and almost impossible in gated communities.

And for now, there's no sign that buses and light rail are making inroads into American subdivisions. In Phoenix, only a tiny minority of residences are within walking distance of light-rail stations, and the city doesn't have the kind of extensive feeder bus system that would expand the streetcars' reach. Even the most comfortable and modern transit may not be enough to save a city built entirely around the needs of the automobile. But one can always hope, and I like Mees's optimism and can-do attitude.

"There's a very unhelpful pseudo-debate going on in America right now," he told me, "between people that reckon their group is the salt of the earth, and that the other group is snobbish and elitist. No matter how much you may dislike suburbs, you can't just wish eighty percent of metropolitan areas away. I leave to others the job of trying to reform human character. I'd be prepared to settle for enabling people to use their cars less, not because it's somehow morally superior, but because we have genuinely made it more convenient to drive less."

I'd phoned Mees at his home in Australia, where the big news lately has been the massive revivals of central Sydney and Melbourne, whose downtown residential populations have doubled in less than a decade. Mees lives in Fitzroy, an old streetcar neighborhood in Melbourne still served by trams.

"Like most middle-class Melbournians who grew up in the suburbs," he acknowledged with a chuckle, "I escaped and now live in an expensive part of the inner city where I can walk everywhere."

Valley Fever

In Phoenix, I quickly gave up on riding transit. To really understand the city, you have to drive. The city's freeway system is impressively overbuilt, with high retaining walls playfully decorated with bas-relief geckos, road-runners, and coyotes. (An allusion, I figured, to all the roadkill you see flattened on Arizona's highways.) It's only when you get off the freeways that you see how the subprime crisis stormed through this city like a tor-nado in a trailer park. "Three Months Free Rent," read the signs on count-less low-rise apartment buildings. Metrocenter, once Arizona's biggest mall and now a crime-ridden shell of vacant big-box stores, is known as the place where rapper DMX was arrested; lately, locals have dubbed it "Ghettocen-ter." But it is in the outer subdivisions, what real estate experts call the "ring of death," that things really get grim. Entire subdivisions in Buckeye, Tolle-son, and Surprise seem to have no residents. The annotations on the for-rent and for-sale signs speak volumes: "Bank-Owned Home"; "Short Sale"; "Price Reduced—Foreclosure."

Queen Creek, located thirty miles southeast of downtown, is typical. This is no Broadacre of spacious lots: these are working-class suburbs, where the houses are packed eight to an acre. Though there are no gate-houses manned by security guards, the subdivisions here have borrowed one aspect of the upscale gated community: they turn their backs on the rest of the city. Each is contained by a seven-foot-high perimeter wall, and often there is only one road in and one road out. Leaving the main boule-vard, you enter a dizzying labyrinth of lanes and drives named after peaks and buttes and creeks; it is like being in a hilltop town in medieval Spain, whose residents have huddled together against Moorish invaders. Desert washes and scrubland just three years ago, Queen Creek is now tan-roofed bungalows presenting blank-faced garages, rather than porches, to the street. There are no trees, just shrubs and cacti, and no lawns, only rectangles of broken brown rocks. Apart from the occasional security detail patrolling the streets, I encountered no traffic, and though it was garbage collection day, only a few houses had beige plastic bins rolled out to the curb. In one empty playground, vultures perched on a swing set. After a while, I started to imagine there were zombies lurking behind the creosote bushes.

After half an hour of cruising, I spied a human figure. Pam Balderas, dressed in a black tracksuit and running shoes, was leaning against the hood of a beat-up Ford subcompact, thumbing a text message into her phone. Her car was parked outside a house with a "Bank-Owned Home" for-sale sign out front, and I asked if she knew what it was selling for.

"It used to be about one hundred and sixty thousand, I think," she said, "but nobody's buying here these days. Everybody's renting. I live with my son, and he pays seven hundred a month." She pointed across the street, where a shirtless man in his late twenties was loading a sofa into a U-Haul truck parked in a driveway across the street.

"I'm here helping him move. We've been evicted," she explained. "The owner only gave us two days' notice. But there are so many places empty, it's not hard to find a new place. We had our choice of five other houses. We're just moving a couple of streets over."

Balderas explained she had come to Phoenix from Chicago fifteen years ago. When the recession hit, she and her husband tried their luck in Texas, where she got work in a coffee shop. But they recently separated, and she'd come back to Phoenix to help her unemployed son with his three kids. She got full-time work at the Fry's Grocery down the road, and chipped in some of her paycheck to help with the rent. She said that it took a lot of her pay just to keep filling up her tank: Queen Creek is an hour's drive from the center of Phoenix.

"I love the climate here," she said. "I hated the winters in Illinois. But it's hard to make a living out here. And being in Queen Creek can get kind of lonely. Everything's so spread out."

Balderas's was typical of the stories I heard in Phoenix. Thanks to the recession, people were moving in with their relatives, walking away from mortgages, and renting when they used to own. Yet this is the city that Joel Kotkin argues will, thanks to its "low-density lifestyle, brilliant sunshine, its lack of social constraints," become the archetype for a new kind of American city. Personally, I wouldn't bet a plug nickel on Phoenix's future. With a hundred thousand houses and a quarter of all commercial real estate sitting empty, it could well be the West's next ghost town. I'm no futurist, but I'd be willing to wager that in the years to come, people will look at aerial photos of Phoenix and other capitals of sprawl and see all the parking lots, strip malls, and overpasses as the manifestation of a pathological addiction to cheap fossil fuels, and wonder how so many people could have been so shortsighted for so long.

Kenneth Jackson realized this over thirty years ago. "The United States is not only the world's first suburban nation, but it will also be its last," he wrote in *Crabgrass Frontier*. "By 2025 the energy-inefficient and automobile-dependent suburban system of the American republic must give way to patterns of human activity and living structures that are energy efficient. The extensive deconcentration of the American people was the result of a set of circumstances that will not be duplicated elsewhere."

In 2008, a delegation from China, on a study tour of American subdivisions, visited the Del Webb development in the Phoenix suburb of Buckeye. Nobody in the local media recorded the officials' impressions, but I hope they weren't too positive. For if even a tiny fraction of the populations of the developing megacities of Asia, Africa, and Latin America pursue the suburban dream of a detached home for every family and a car in every garage, we're in trouble. There just isn't enough planet for any more Phoenixes.

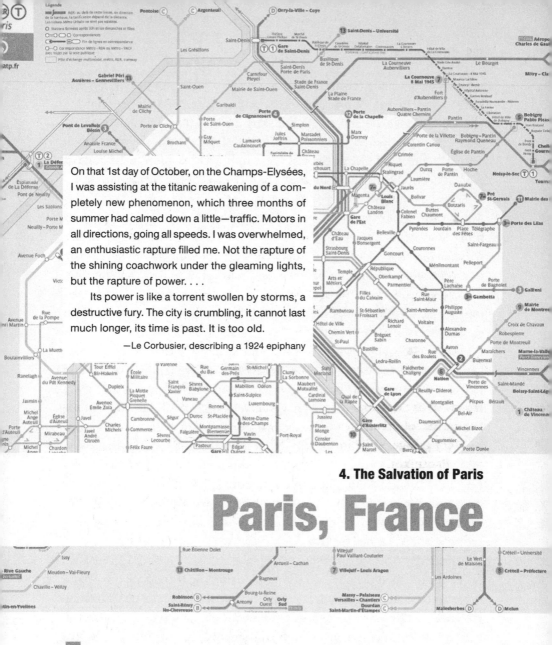

On that 1st day of October, on the Champs-Elysées, I was assisting at the titanic reawakening of a completely new phenomenon, which three months of summer had calmed down a little—traffic. Motors in all directions, going all speeds. I was overwhelmed, an enthusiastic rapture filled me. Not the rapture of the shining coachwork under the gleaming lights, but the rapture of power. . . .

Its power is like a torrent swollen by storms, a destructive fury. The city is crumbling, it cannot last much longer, its time is past. It is too old.

—Le Corbusier, describing a 1924 epiphany

4. The Salvation of Paris

Paris, France

It was a Friday night, late in spring, and it looked like the banks of the Canal Saint-Martin had been taken over by an impromptu country fair. At regular intervals, helium balloons were tied to benches—not to signal some quartier-wide *fête*, but to guide the delivery boys from a nearby Cambodian restaurant to hungry revelers who had placed orders for *bob-uns* and imperial rolls. The more organized had spread blankets over the paving stones, and were picnicking on baguettes, sausages, and Bonne

Maman cookies. On the arching footbridge before the Grange-aux-Belles locks, a tourist couple paused to kiss, and outside the Hôtel du Nord, a woman in high heels and a tight red skirt insouciantly lit a Gauloise after docking a borrowed bicycle at a silver stand. It was as close to a civic idyll as you could get, a mix of classes, ages, and races, gathered with guitars, good food, and cheap wine to share the warm air of the Parisian night.

There has always been a certain magic to the dog-legged Canal Saint-Martin, an urban waterway that injects the odor of salt air and seaweed into the streets of the Right Bank north of the Seine River. During the day, old men in white undershirts sit in lawn chairs, angling for bream, catfish, and eels, while low-riding barges laden with gravel and sand stammer their way through a series of locks and floodgates—a means of transporting freight that is as picturesque as it is low-tech, low-cost, and low in carbon emissions.

Had the technocrats of the twentieth century had their way, the market stalls, café terraces, and waterfront parks where families picnic and old men pitch *pétanque* balls would have been permanently erased from the Parisian streetscape. The plan, hatched by municipal councilors in the late 1960s, was to pave over the canal and cover it with an eight-lane, double-decked highway. Building its on-ramps and overpasses would have meant the demolition of 10,000 dwellings, including most of the dignified nineteenth-century apartment buildings whose balconies overlook the canal. The Axe Nord-Sud, as it was to be known, was to become part of a network of *autoroutes* girding the capital, as ambitious as anything Robert Moses had planned for New York City.

That Paris exists at all is something of a miracle. Notoriously, its Nazi occupiers planned the city's destruction during the Second World War. A lesser-known Armageddon was envisioned by the architect Le Corbusier. He selected the Marais, the area to the west of the Canal Saint-Martin, Paris's historic Jewish quartier, to be the site of an early prototype for his "Radiant City." His Plan Voisin, sponsored by a French car builder, was unveiled in 1925. It called for twenty carefully spaced skyscrapers, each eighty stories tall, on a gridwork of perfectly rectilinear streets. The key to the new city would be universal ownership of the private automobile; the solution to Paris's nascent traffic problems, Le Corbusier believed, lay in elevated high-speed roads running through a partially leveled city. He would spare the Louvre and the Place des Vosges, along with "certain historical monuments, arcades, doorways." But hundreds of acres between the Seine and Montmartre would have to be sacrificed to the bulldozer. "Surgery must be applied to the city's center," declared Le Corbu. "We must use the knife." (Frank Lloyd Wright's scheme for the dispersed Broadacre City, though conceived as a direct riposte to Le Corbusier's high-density vision for his Radiant City, was also predicated on universal automobile ownership.)

Between Nazi explosives and plans for elevated expressways, the streets of Paris barely made it out of the twentieth century without being torn apart in the name of ideology and progress. What held them together, and allowed the city to keep functioning through the decades of depression, occupation, and suburbanization, was what was *under* those streets: the Métropolitain—the métro for short—which, aided by the Réseau Express Régional, the RER, is the most ingenious and efficient urban transit network ever built.

The fact that the system has lately become strained to the breaking point is only a testament to its usefulness. Fortunately, the French are about to make a massive investment in the next generation of public transport, more ambitious than any currently being planned in the Western Hemisphere.

While Paris's system remains publicly operated—for the time being— what is not so well known is that, from Mumbai to New Orleans, French companies are now selling their transit expertise abroad and aggressively expanding into foreign markets. In the not very distant future, many of us could be riding on French streetcars, trains, and buses. And though this may be an improvement over Le Corbusier's corrosive brand of urbanism, anybody who cares about the future of cities should be very concerned about this latest, and most unexpected, French export: the privatization of public transport.

Confessions of a *Fraudeur*

Paris is the city that made me fall in love with cities.

I was twenty-three, bumming around Europe on a post-university walkabout; Paris was the place where my money ran out. The streets of Paris were a revelation: unlike the slapdash North American cities I had grown up in, the entire metropolis seemed to have been designed by some immortal aesthete, following a vast, generation-spanning master plan. The rows of statues in the Tuileries gardens lined up with the chestnut trees of the Champs-Elysées, which in turn aligned perfectly with the Arc de Triomphe, and three miles distant, the ultra-modern arch at La Défense. Every couple of blocks, a quartet of cast-iron caryatids atop a domed *fontaine* Wallace guarded an eternally running thread of potable water; even the newspaper kiosks on the boulevards resembled baroque beach cabanas. I fell in love with a French woman, found work as an English teacher, and ended up living in Paris for four years.

I spent a lot of time walking the streets, but my real key to the city was the métro. At first, it was intimidating, a murky labyrinth full of cutting glances, curt "*pardons*," and sophisticated, corrupt odors (a mixture, it turns out, of cleaning fluid, brake dust, and stagnant water, overlaid by the occasional whiff of Chanel and stale tobacco). But the métro quickly seduced me. The beauty of such a system, as Franz Kafka observed, is that you don't have to speak when you pay or board, making it ideal for new-comers whose language skills are still shaky.

"Because it is so easy to understand," he noted in his travel journals in 1911, "the Métro is a frail and hopeful stranger's best chance to think that he has quickly and correctly at the first attempt, penetrated the essence of Paris."

My job teaching English to doctors, accountants, and high school stu-dents meant that I had to ride the trains every day, to inner-city apartments and suburban villas, and I soon became an expert on the minutiae of the subterranean empire. At the République station, intimidating gypsy camps of *clochards*—panhandlers—clotted the platforms with their impedimenta of mongrels and plastic bags, performing unscripted drunken operettas for passersby. At Saint-Augustin, I would strain to hear the stridulations of the crickets that lived under the tracks, kept alive through the winter by the heat generated by passing trains. When I was too broke to afford a ticket, I would vault the turnstiles—joining the ranks of *fraudeurs*, or fare-skippers—and spend my trip nervously watching for uniformed *contrôleurs*. As an impoverished tutor, I spent hundreds of hours staring out the win-dows of métro trains, catching occasional glimpses of blind tunnels and apparently abandoned platforms, wondering about the mysteries on the other side of the glass.

That is why, two decades after I'd first learned to use the métro, I was so happy to meet Mark Ovenden and Julian Pepinster, two men in their late thirties who have turned their boyhood love of trains into careers. English-born transit chronicler Ovenden is the author of *Paris Under-*

ground, a beautifully illustrated volume on the history and design of the métro. Pepinster, a Parisian born-and-bred, is working on his own book on métro history, but he is also an engineer in the security department of the RATP—the Régie autonome de transports parisiens, the operator of most transit in the Paris area—which means he possesses the keys to unlock some of the metro's most obscure doorways.

Ovenden suggested we meet outside the Châtelet métro stop, at one of the dragonfly-winged *édicules*, or métro entrances, on the cobblestoned square Sainte-Opportune. "This is line one of the métro," noted Ovenden, "which was opened in the nineteen-hundreds with *édicules* built by the architect Hector Guimard. He used this wonderfully laced wrought iron. It looks like the metal has grown from the ground in the way that trees or plants grow. It's very organic-looking; quite advanced for its time, really."

At the Strasbourg-Saint-Denis station, we were joined by Pepinster, a slender, intense man who speaks precise, British-accented English. We walked a few hundred yards to a nondescript stairwell set into the pavement next to the Porte St. Martin, one of the triumphal arches that used to mark the eighteenth-century city limits. Flourishing a set of keys, Pepinster opened the heavy metal doors.

"We're at the entrance of a disused métro station," announced Pepinster, pausing dramatically on the threshold. "It has been closed to service since before the Second World War." Ovenden and I followed him into a well-lit tunnel. "Technicians still come here to do maintenance on the tunnel infrastructure—that's why the lights are on." Pepinster paused in front of a section of wall lined with strikingly colorful ads. Unlike the paper posters for movies and department stores in contemporary stations, these were made of enameled tiles, and were meant to last for years. One, for Javel bleach, showed a silhouette of a slender North African woman hanging a white sheet from a clothesline; black fingers were visible above the sheet, but her body was lighter, as if the bleach had whitened her skin.

"That ad would be quite politically incorrect these days," observed Pepinster.

The Saint-Martin station, as it is known, was taken out of service in 1939 when the opening of stations on nearby lines made it obsolete. As we entered a gloomier section, it became clear that other people had found their way into the forbidden underground before us. The tunnels were covered with spray paint from floor to ceiling, a desecration that made the two métro historians livid. "Each graffiti guy is trying to show that he can piss farther than the other guy," muttered Pepinster. More tiled ads, these for fur coats and defunct brands of disinfectants, were defaced by graffiti of no merit. The tags continued onto the curving walls of what had once been the platform, which had been partitioned off to serve as a homeless shelter in the '80s. An abandoned wheelchair sat in one of the cubicles.

"What's really weird," observed Ovenden, "when you look around you, you realize that you're on a normal Paris métro station platform. Just the other side of this wall, which has been built since this station was closed, there are trains running. And if you look out the window when you're on a train from République to Strasbourg-Saint-Denis, you can see you're going through an old station."

Pepinster led us to the bottom of another staircase. The corridor here was cut in half by a high railing, intended to divide the crowds coming to and from the trains. Pepinster explained that *poinçonneurs*, or ticket-punchers, would have been posted at the entrance to the platform. Leaning around the corner, we found ourselves on a darkened section of platform, just as a métro train clattered past. I caught a glimpse of a young man seated next to a window whose eyes widened as he took in the ghost station. It could have been me twenty years ago, an underpaid tutor daydreaming about the underground's hidden treasures.

Later, over a bottle of wine in Pepinster's apartment in Saint-Germain-des-Prés, Ovenden told me that good transit was one of the reasons he'd moved to Paris. "It's amazing what they're doing with public transport here. Everything's integrated. You can use your métro pass to rent a bicycle and ride it to a station, which is right next to a bus stop; everything links to intercity trains. They'll be spending tens of billions of euros on a brand new métro, and adding eight new tram lines. It's just fantastic."

I'd had the same revelation as a young man in Paris. In a city well served by transit, car ownership becomes optional. What makes Paris unique among world cities is how tightly knit its network is. London's and New York's systems may be more extensive, but Paris has more miles of métro track in its city center, which means you are never more than 500 yards from a station. Tickets are cheap, trains run with headways of only a few minutes, and it is a rare door-to-door journey that takes more than half an hour.

The metro's sinuous Art Nouveau stations are so seamlessly woven into the fabric of Paris that it can sometimes seem as if the system evolved simultaneously with the metropolis. But transit was retrofitted into this historic city with infinite care and trouble, and it was only through constant maintenance and investment that it has continued to function and evolve.

If Paris remains the world's most visited city, and its squares, canals, and arcades are used and loved by its inhabitants, it is because this city, beautiful to begin with, never allowed its history to be paved over. Good transit allowed the city to keep functioning, and prevented its streets from being overrun by automobiles.

Paris, simply put, was saved by its métro.

A Parisian Pilgrimage

If you want to understand why Paris looks like it does today, you'll need to take a little stroll.

A good place to start is the circular metal plaque that marks Kilometer Zero—the point from which all road distances in France are measured—in front of Notre Dame cathedral, on the Île de la Cité, Paris's historic center. (The western part of the island is in the 1st *arrondissement*, one of the twenty boroughs that spiral clockwise outward from the center.) Where tourists gather today, a tribe of Gauls called the Parisii built their dwellings around an *oppidum*, or fortress, before they were subdued by Julius Caesar's legions. Naming the new outpost Lutetia, the order-loving Romans imposed a gridiron street plan, and established the *cardo maximus*, the north-south thoroughfare typical of all Roman settlement, along an old Gaulish road.

Paris's historic *cardo*—the word is Latin for "hinge"—still exists. It is Rue Saint-Jacques, which begins on the south side of the bridge known as the Petit-Pont, not far from where bibliophiles browse through boxes of books outside Shakespeare and Company. For a thousand years, Catholics have walked south along this street, taking their first steps on the grueling pilgrimage road to Santiago de Compostella in western Spain. In its first few blocks, where bagel shops and hole-in-the-wall *crêperies* compete for the custom of tourists, Rue Saint-Jacques skirts the Sorbonne and the Montagne Sainte-Geneviève, once the home of the old Roman forum, and now the site of the hilltop Pantheon.

Strolling on this part of Rue Saint-Jacques 350 years ago, you might have encountered an unusual sight: a horse-drawn carriage, driven by a coachman in the official red and blue livery of the City of Paris, bearing paying customers to a stop in front of the Luxembourg Gardens. At regular intervals, well-dressed gentlemen would have handed the driver a fare of five *sous* as they climbed aboard. The "*carosse à cinq sols*," as it was known, represented the birth of public transport in modern cities. The scheme was dreamed up by the philosopher Blaise Pascal who, using his connections at court, got royal approval to run carriages along five fixed routes. The carriages, he promised, would "be infinitely convenient, leaving at regular hours, even when empty." Launched in 1662 (the year Pascal died), the *carosses* were popular from the start, but turned out to be an experiment before their time. The service, which was limited to the gentry, was suspended after fifteen years.

Early in the nineteenth century, Rue Saint-Jacques was witness to another French first in transportation: the horse-drawn omnibus, the ancestor of the modern city bus. Unlike Pascal's *carosses*, the omnibus could be used by the general public. In 1823, a retired army officer named Stanislaus Baudry opened a steam bath on the outskirts of Nantes; to attract clientele, he ran coaches to his baths along regular routes. Baudry's baths went bust, but the people of Nantes continued to use his oversized carriages. (They owed their name to a nearby hat store named Omnes, whose slogan happened to be *Omnes Omnibus*, Latin for "Omnes for all.") Five years later, Baudry brought his service to Paris, setting up a network of capacious, regularly scheduled public carriages drawn by two or three horses. The unlucky entrepreneur failed—his drivers' pilfering of fares pushed him to bankruptcy, and Baudry drowned himself in the Canal Saint-Martin—but his idea proved a durable one. A year after they had appeared in Paris, 20-seat omnibuses were offering service from Paddington to the Bank of England in London. Three years later, they could be seen running up Broadway in Manhattan. After a period of savage competition for riders, dozens of Parisian omnibus companies were merged in 1855 into the Compagnie Générale des Omnibus, then said to be the largest private cavalry in the world. But the double-decker omnibus, essentially an urban stagecoach that averaged five miles an hour, was soon replaced by a smoother, faster ride.

The tramway, as streetcars are known in Europe, would revolutionize the shape of cities. For the first couple of millennia of urban history the size of cities had been limited by the distance a person could conveniently cover on foot or horseback; even Rome, whose population reached a million by the end of the Republic, was little more than three miles across. Putting horse-drawn omnibuses on iron rails reduced friction, allowing fewer horses to pull heavier loads at higher speeds A French engineer living in New York, Alphonse Loubat, was the first to lay tracks flush with the surface of the road. Returning to Paris in 1853, he set up a trial run of his "American railroad," the first of its kind in Europe. By the turn of the century electric-powered tramways, pioneered in Germany and perfected by Frank Sprague in the United States, began to replace the horse-drawn omnibus. By increasing the distance city dwellers could travel in a reasonable amount of time, tramways forced the classic European walking city to grow, breaking through its old physical limitations. Paris's outermost swirl of *arrondissements*, from the 12th to the 20th, all date from the 1860s or later, after electric tramways became common.

About a mile and a half from Notre Dame, Rue Saint-Jacques passes the former site of the Wall of the Farmers-General (1784), a customs barrier whose tollgates would become the target of mob fury during the Revolution. Paris, for most of its history, has grown less like a tree trunk, through the accretion of successive rings, and more like a crab, which regularly bursts through its constrictive exoskeleton to grow a larger, roomier shell. (Such walls, because they required large cleared areas on either side, also provided natural conduits for the transportation needs of modernizing European cities; Brussels and Vienna would build "ring streets," their versions of boulevards, where fortifications once stood.) The hated customs wall lasted until 1860, when it was torn down by Baron Haussmann, the man responsible for shaping modern Paris.

Georges-Eugène Haussmann was the Robert Moses of nineteenth-century Paris. As Prefect of the Seine, he had unprecedented powers of expropriation, and drove broad avenues through the convoluted streets of the Latin Quarter and Belleville, allowing Napoléon III's troops to penetrate notoriously seditious *quartiers*. His massive building program filled central Paris with the unified facades of "Haussmannien" apartments, with their ground-floor shops, four or five floors of middle-class apartments, and low-ceilinged garrets for servants. In the name of symmetry and geometry, Haussmann razed entire neighborhoods to allow uninterrupted vistas of the Opéra, the Arc de Triomphe, and other picturesque monuments. He even shifted Paris's historic *cardo*, making the northern stretch of Boulevard Saint-Michel, two hundred yards to the west of Rue Saint-Jacques, the new gateway to the city.

Like Robert Moses, Haussmann caused enormous social upheaval;

over his career, he displaced 350,000 Parisians.* But Parisians by and large acquiesced to the transformation of their city: at the height of redevelopment, one-fifth of the population was employed in the construction trades, and many acknowledged that the congested and disease-ridden city was in need of some modernization. Had Haussmann come to power during the automobile age, Paris might now be a Warsaw, Birmingham, or Moscow, strangling on highways and traffic. But he was building during the age of steam, ensuring that such railway stations as the Gare du Nord and the Gare Montparnasse became the true gateways to the capital. His 100-foot-wide boulevards, while designed to facilitate the circulation of omnibuses, private carriages, and troops, also provided promenades for *flâneurs*, terraces for cafés, and meeting grounds for people of all classes.

Unlike Moses's gutting of New York City, Haussmann's reimagining of Paris did not result in a middle-class flight to the suburbs. Parisian urban development, in stark contrast to the American version, saw workers and industry—as well as the expropriated poor—moving to the periphery, aided by omnibuses and tramways, while the middle class and wealthy clung to the central *arrondissements*. In *Bourgeois Utopias*, historian Robert Fishman writes that the middle-class flight to the 'burbs was "an Anglo-American phenomenon, with some influence in northern and central European cities but very little in those European or Latin American cities which took their lead from Paris."

As a model of urban form, the Haussmannized city of bourgeois apartment buildings and vibrant street life spread east to Vienna, to be copied by Budapest, Bucharest, and other cities of central and eastern Europe; south to Barcelona, and through Latin America to Buenos Aires; and eventually to any of the dozen cities known as the "Paris of the East," among them Casablanca, Beirut, Hanoi, and Shanghai.

Where Rue Saint-Jacques crosses Haussmann's Boulevard de Port-Royal, you will see a small ticket hall of red and buff–colored brick, whose "Entrée" and "Sortie" signs are spelled out in a serpentine Art Nouveau typeface. It is one of the entrances to line 6 of the métro, which opened in 1906; if you peek through the fence down to the open-air platform, you might see the roof of a train flashing past as it enters the station.

---

* Moses was a fan, and wrote approvingly of the Baron in a 1942 *Architectural Digest* article. But whereas New York's master butcher boasted of taking a "meat-ax" to the metropolis, Haussmann fancied himself a baker, opining that it was "easier to cut through a pie's inside than to break into the crust."

The métro was the next great revolution in Parisian transportation. As with New York's subway, decades of debate preceded its construction. Paris's mainline railways, which required huge yards and terminal stations, had been built far from the center to spare historic neighborhoods. The railway companies, supported by the French state, had long wanted to connect their far-flung termini; municipal officials, meanwhile, argued for a network of closely spaced stations within the city limits. Fortunately for the citizens of Paris, it was the city, not the French state, that planned and oversaw the project. (This is why it is known as the *Métropolitain*, and why stations within city limits are so closely spaced: from the start, the métro was meant to serve the people of the metropolis, rather than facilitate an exodus to the suburbs.) Fearing a slippery slope into socialism, however, the state refused to allow municipal operation of the system. While planning and oversight remained in municipal hands, a Belgian industrialist was chosen to build and run the system, and the *Compagnie du métropolitain de Paris* was founded in 1898.

It took just over a decade to build a half-dozen lines. The Universal Exposition of 1900 spurred the construction of the first. A one-armed engineer from Brittany called Fulgence Bienvenüe—the name can be loosely translated as "Lightning Welcome," fitting for a man who brought electricity to the underground—oversaw construction, which required a workforce of 3,500, and temporarily made a shambles of the city. As in New York, most lines were built using the cut-and-cover method, which meant tearing up the paving stones of Rue de Rivoli and other elegant avenues. Caissons were sunk in the Seine, tracks were laid through the buried vaults of a seventeenth-century canal, and to ensure that the cogitations of the members of the Academy were not disturbed, line 1 was rerouted to circumvent the Institut de France. The early métro had its share of setbacks. A fire in a train in the Couronnes station claimed seventy-seven lives when passengers who remained too long on the platform demanding ticket refunds for their interrupted journeys were asphyxiated. When the Seine overflowed its banks—the high-water mark can still be seen in lines marked "1910" painted on the sides of Latin Quarter buildings—employees had to punt between inundated stations on rafts.

But Parisians quickly embraced the new system. In London's Underground, the world's first when it opened in 1863, trains spewed coal fumes into subterranean tunnels, but Paris's métro was electric-powered, and thus smoke-free, from the start. On the eve of the First World War, half a billion passengers used the métro annually. With more stations than Berlin's or New York's, Paris's underground was the world's most modern and elegant, the elliptical arches of its platforms and its organic *édicules* a welcome contrast to the stern geometry of the Haussmannian city.

While the New York subway spawned midtown skyscrapers and spread the population of lower Manhattan to the outer boroughs, Paris's métro was added to a city that, for all intents and purposes, had already been built. Like all well-conceived urban subway systems, it became the skeleton undergirding the soft tissue of the streets above, lending Paris integrity in times of crisis. Even during the Second World War, when private automobiles all but disappeared from the street, the métro kept running; new construction even extended some lines.* In spite of France's reputation for constant strikes, the métro has only rarely failed to keep functioning year-round, twenty hours a day, in its 110 years of existence. (After national strikes disrupted service for three weeks in 1995, laws were passed that require workers to provide a minimum level of service, even during labor actions.) While new transport—especially the automobile and freeways—depopulated American downtowns, the Métropolitain, built to serve the city, kept central Paris intact.

But the métro had one great failing: it did nothing to help suburban commuters. Even today, only a few métro lines extend any distance beyond the old city gates.

To see the next great innovation in Parisian transit, you'll need to take a slight detour from Rue Saint-Jacques. Walking along 200 yards of tree-shaded boulevard to the west of the city's old *cardo* will bring you to the curved stone facade of the Gare de Denfert-Rochereau, the entrance to the RER, or Réseau Express Régional. If you hopped one of the double-decked trains of line B of the RER at this station, you could ride to Charles de Gaulle airport in the north, and farther along transfer to line C, which would take you to the Palace of Versailles, or line A, which runs to Disneyland Paris in the west. All told, five RER lines serve major hub stations in central Paris before thrusting into the most far-flung suburbs. When the French state began building the RER in the early 1960s, it had specific development goals in mind: the *Schéma directeur*, a kind of regional mas-

---

* During the Nazi Occupation, when Jews were forced to wear yellow stars and ride in the last car, the métro became a meeting place for the Résistance, and was feared by German soldiers— especially after an officer was gunned down on the platform of the Barbès station in 1941.

ter plan inspired by Stockholm's suburban mass transit system, called for new RER stations to concentrate the population in such satellite towns as Cergy-Pontoise, Évry, and Marne-la-Vallée. Paris's suburbs would continue to grow, but it would be railways, not highways, that would carry the bulk of the traffic, serving suburban university campuses, airports, and the new high-rise employment centers at La Défense.

The goal of the RER was to limit urban sprawl, and it worked. While suburbanization continued—in the six years after line A opened in 1969, central Paris would lose 400,000 inhabitants—the city did not bleed into its hinterland anything like a London or a Moscow. The RER prevented low-density development by encouraging suburbanites, very few of whom use cars to commute, to live within walking distance of stations. The satellite towns in the outer surburbs are remarkably compact, and the three departments that make up Paris's inner circle of suburbs are actually denser than central San Francisco. Thanks largely to the RER, the metropolitan area of Paris, with over 10.2 million residents, takes up no more space on the earth's surface than Jacksonville, Florida, a freeway-formed city with fewer than 800,000 residents.

Walking along Paris's old *cardo* as it drives deeper into the 14th *arrondissement*, where cars are thicker on the ground, can test a stroller's patience. Paris may be one of the world's great walking cities, but it has a serious drawback: it is plagued by Parisian drivers, probably the most caffeinated and vindictive in the world. The Gallic love affair with the car started early. At the beginning of the twentieth century French roads were considered the world's best, the Michelin tire company published the first guidebook for automobile tourists, and Paris's suburban fringe was the capital of the nascent global automobile industry. Parisian taxis shuttled reinforcements to the Battle of the Marne in the First World War, and in the '20s the shaft of the Eiffel Tower was lit up with giant letters spelling out "Citroën." But gasoline shortages during the Nazi Occupation brought bicycle-taxis and horse-drawn carriages to the streets of Paris, and it wasn't until the '50s that automobiles were anything more than playthings for the upper classes. When the Renault 4 CV, the French equivalent of the Volkswagen, was introduced in 1949, there were only 80,000 cars in Paris. Thirty years later, that number had increased tenfold, making Paris's streets deadly, with cars killing an average of two hundred people in the city a year by the late '70s.

Much of historic Paris was sacrificed in the name of greater convenience for drivers. To improve traffic flow, in the 1930s the sidewalks of the *grands boulevards* were narrowed, their shade trees and street vendors banished. To prevent jaywalking on the busier arteries, pedestrians were channeled into crosswalks by waist-high barriers, and directed to gloomy underground passages to keep them away from the traffic around the Arc de Triomphe. And because Les Halles was blamed for city-center jams of delivery trucks, the iron and glass pavilions of the legendary food market, where Parisians went to eat onion soup in the early hours, were razed in the '60s and relocated to the suburbs.

It could have been worse. The planned expressway over the Canal Saint-Martin was part of a more ambitious scheme dreamed up by Georges Pompidou. Elected president in 1969, and known for being chauffeured around in an outsized Citroën convertible with a V6 motor, Pompidou famously declared: "Paris must adapt itself to the automobile. We must renounce an outmoded aesthetic." In the place of a historic train station, he erected the Tour Montparnasse, at 59 stories France's tallest skyscraper. He allowed the construction of the riverfront highway that still cuts Parisians off from romantic strolls on the Right Bank of the Seine. And he actively encouraged sprawl by subsidizing an own-your-own-home scheme that saw 70,000 cheaply built detached houses going up on the urban fringe. Had Pompidou not died in 1974, a webwork of urban highways would have put eight lanes of high-speed traffic within a hundred yards of the Madeleine church, and transformed Haussmann's boulevards into urban speedways.

Pompidou's technocrats were nonetheless successful in building their most grandiose megaproject: the Périphérique, a 22-mile-long ring road, in some places 150 feet wide, that cinches Paris in a continuous belt of eternally rushing traffic. From its opening in 1973, the Périph' averaged an accident per kilometer a day, did nothing to reduce congestion, and created a barrier, both psychological and physical, between Paris and its suburbs. By then, a backlash had begun: students set fire to that supreme object of consumer aspiration, the automobile, during the street riots of May 1968. Pompidou's successor, after killing several planned urban highways, came out in favor of improving the "attractiveness of the quartiers," and the OPEC embargo and the energy crisis of the '70s put a damper on car sales.

Living in Paris in the early '90s, when the city was still in thrall to the automobile, I remember how rushing traffic meant that I had to stay constantly alert when crossing even the narrowest street. But a revolution began a couple of years after I left. The traffic jams caused by the 1995 strikes that shut down public transport were a revelation: many Parisians invested in bicycles after realizing how quickly they could get around their compact city on two wheels. Rue Mouffetard, a market street on the Left Bank, and the banks of Canal Saint-Martin were closed to traffic on Sundays, and the city started building a network of bike paths that now totals 275 miles. Real systemic change came in 2001, with the election of Mayor Bertrand Delanoë, a socialist who declared open war on the "the hegemony of the automobile." To the shock of drivers, he shut down Pompidou's riverbank highway during the summer, and covered the asphalt with sand, making the Right Bank of the Seine into a beach—complete with, this being France, topless sunbathers. In 2007, Delanoë introduced Vélib', the world's largest bike-sharing program, which allows anyone with a credit card, and now a métro pass, to borrow a sturdy gray bicycle from any one of 1,450 stands around the city. Under Delanoë's mayoralty, driving in Paris has gotten a lot harder, as reserved busways have removed lanes from Rue de Rivoli and other major thoroughfares.

Just before the old *cardo* reaches the Périphérique, it crosses Boulevard des Maréchaux, which constitutes the final ring of boulevards circling Paris. If your timing is good, you may glimpse an apparition. Every few minutes, a streamlined jade-green streetcar, powered by overhead wires and gliding on steel wheels, runs down the tracks set into the grassy meridian. This is Tramway 3, which started operating in 2006; it is one of four lines in Greater Paris that run spacious, fast-loading streetcars. These modern tramways mark the return of the "American railway," last seen on the city's streets in 1937.

The disappearance of America's historic streetcar networks is often cast as the consequence of the arrival of a superior technology, the automobile. But in Paris, it is now the car that is in retreat, and some tram lines are carrying 100,000 passengers a day; by 2014, the city plans to have 60 miles of tracks in operation. Lately, there has even been talk of banning cars from Paris's four central *arrondissements*. In the near future, Rue Saint-Jacques might be restored to its original purpose: as a pathway for pilgrims and pedestrians, rather than a thoroughfare for impatient drivers.

Two and a half miles south of Notre Dame, a modern-day pilgrim on the historic *cardo* comes up against the Périphérique, with its 12 lanes of rushing traffic—certainly the most insuperable barrier in Paris's long history of wall-building. The Périph' had one positive impact; it so shocked

Parisians that not a single new mile of highway has been built within city limits since its opening. However, unless it is roofed over to create an outer ring of boulevards apt for strolling—a plan that has been seriously mooted in recent years—this brutal ring road may prove to be the toughest crab shell of all, and the one Paris has the hardest time shedding.

Public transport didn't structure central Paris the way it did New York or Los Angeles, which grew and evolved simultaneously with their subway and streetcar lines: with infinite care, the métro was shoehorned into an ancient walking city. It was the extensive RER system, which allows suburbanites to live within walking distance of train stations, that played the greatest role in transforming modern Paris, permitting the creation of dense suburbs while limiting urban sprawl. The métro, in contrast, preserved the integrity of the historic city. Why build expressways, after all, when an efficient, reliable, and comfortable alternative could always be found underfoot?

And *that* is how the métro saved Paris.

Le *Supermétro*

My instructions were clear: be on the platform at République station, no later than 11:40 a.m. A giant of a man, wearing an *Exile on Main Street* T-shirt under his blue RATP cardigan, emerged from the *loge de conduite*— the driver's cabin—shook my hand, and with a conspiratorial grin invited me aboard his métro train.

With his shaved head, François, who stands six foot six in sneakers, cuts an impressive figure. We had been introduced by my old Parisian friends, Guillaume and Alexandra, at a bar in Montmartre; as we bonded over glasses of beer, François mentioned he was a driver on line 8 of the métro, and told me to give him a call if I ever wanted to take a ride.

François took his position in the driver's seat, propping his knees against the dash. While looking at a convex mirror mounted on the platform which gave him a view down the side of the train, François pressed a button to activate the *vibreur*, the buzzer that warns the train is about to leave, and turned a key to close the doors. With a *ding!* and a mounting electric hum, we began to accelerate into the tunnel. The speedometer, I noticed, went up to 120 kilometers an hour—just under 75 miles an hour. I asked François if the train ever reached its maximum.

"Never! In the suburbs, I sometimes hit seventy kilometers an hour.

But you have to be careful. One of the worst accidents happened a few years ago, when a train arrived in a curved station at sixty kilometers an hour. The driver was supposed to be doing twenty. The train derailed, but there were no deaths, which was a miracle."

Only 45 seconds after we'd started, we began to decelerate—stations in the center of Paris are often no more than three hundred yards apart—coming to a stop at the head of the Filles du Calvaire platform.

I complimented him on the smoothness of the ride. "I'm not the one who's driving!" he said. "Almost all the lines are operated by automatic pilot. Once I've closed the doors, all I have to do is press this green button, and the train drives itself."

Demonstrating, he took his hand off the throttle; we continued to accelerate. "I just have to remember to press on a foot pedal every thirty seconds to let the train know I'm still alive." Running between the tracks ahead of us was the plastic band housing two cables that relay information to receivers on the underside of the train, allowing optimal acceleration and braking for each section of track. The entire system is monitored from a central command post, where supervisors oversee the real-time position of every train on every line. Adopted in the '70s, the remarkably robust autopilot technology, which operates on the majority of métro lines, has never been implicated in an accident.

For the time being, drivers like François still have some work to do. At the Daumesnil station, he pointed out two signs at the head of the platform. "PSV"—*personnel sur voie*—indicated there were workers on the tracks, which meant François had to revert to "CM," *conduite manuelle*—manual operation. After turning off the autopilot, he throttled slowly into the tunnel, giving two workers inspecting the adjoining track two friendly blasts of the horn, before accelerating to forty. But this was the exception: for most of the route, François functioned more as a supervisor, a comforting presence at the front of the train, than an actual driver.

At the last stop, Créteil Prefecture, five miles southeast of the Périphérique, François got out, stretched, and bought himself a coffee from a vending machine. It was twenty to one, and his day was over. Since punching in at 5:30 that morning, he had completed three return trips of 28 miles each, for a workday of just over six and a half hours. I asked him if driving a métro train had been a boyhood dream. "Not at all!" he said. "This is just a way of earning a living." His annual salary of €41,000 and relatively short workweek, he volunteered, allowed him to pursue his real

passion, photography. And his commute back home was easy: his apartment is only a ten-minute walk from Balard, the station at the western end
of the line.

We rode back to Paris in another train with Michel, a young driver
who sported a Celtic cross in his left earlobe and a shock of blue hair over
his forehead. The drivers' union had announced a 24-hour strike, and
François thought he'd participate, but Michel hadn't made up his mind
yet. (Nationwide strikes over the issue of pension reform would erupt a
couple of months later, limiting service on some transit lines.) What was
really bothering them, though, was what was happening on line 1. At
great expense, and without interrupting service, the first-born of Paris's
métro lines was being converted to all-automatic operation. Automation
is a step beyond autopilot: the new trains wouldn't need drivers at all, and
an entire line can be run by only six employees.

"Obviously, we're disgusted by what's happening," said François. "I think
our careers will soon be over."

The new system, which requires the installation of suicide-preventing
platform doors, promises to reduce accidents and, by allowing shorter
headways between trains, to increase the line's carrying capacity by up to
15 percent. As more urban rail systems around the world are automated,
drivers like François and Michel are likely to go the way of elevator operators. I was sympathetic to their plight, but I have also seen how automation
can improve service. The métro's all automatic line 14, known as Météor, has
been in operation since 1998, and is a pleasure to ride. With no partitions
separating its wagons, you can wander to the front of the trains and watch
the lights in the tunnel beneath the Seine flash past, the view unimpeded
by any driver. In cash-strapped North American cities, where unionized
employees' salaries can be one of the chief obstacles to expanding transit
systems, opting for automated technology makes a lot of sense.

François admitted something had to change. Many Parisian métro lines
are now strained to the limit. While line 8 trains get crowded at rush hours,
they are positively roomy compared to the infamous 13, where François
worked as a driver for two years.

"It runs from the suburbs in the south to Saint-Denis in the north.
Some of the poorest parts of Paris. On the thirteen, you've got major train
stations, and big connecting stations, like Place de Clichy and Champs-
Elysées. It's the busiest line, and it's a pain in the ass to drive." The platforms got so crowded that he lived in constant fear of a child falling onto

the tracks, and he got so tired of passengers yelling at him about delays that he would hide in his cabin when the train was in the station. "If you can drive the thirteen," said François, "you can drive anywhere."

Waving good-bye to François at République, whose platforms were already filling up at two in the afternoon, I reflected on how much the experience of riding the métro had changed. When I lived in Paris twenty years ago, I had a fair chance of getting a seat, even at rush hour. When I visit these days, I'm almost always a standee, one of many. Since 2000, ridership has been increasing from 3 to 5 percent annually—the equivalent of a town of 150,000 added to the system every year. The north-south line 13, one of the few to project beyond the Périphérique and deep into the suburbs, now runs at 116 percent capacity, even with headways of only 100 seconds between trains.

Fortunately, the city that invented the *carosses à cinq sols* is poised to launch the next revolution in transit: a high-speed automatic métro system completely centered on the suburbs. It's about time. The city most tourists visit is not the city where the vast majority of Parisians live; fully 82 percent of the region's population live in the high-density suburbs outside the Périphérique. Unlike many American cities, Paris has no high-rise downtown business district; its employment centers are scattered in dense nodes outside the historic center. Even the RER, explicitly designed to serve the suburbs, can no longer handle the strain. A chronic lack of affordable housing has forced many Parisians to move to apartments in the east, around Disneyland, while they continue to work at La Défense and other office complexes in the west, forcing a daily commute in uncomfortably crowded RER trains across the entire breadth of the city. It is a problem shared by many modern metropolises: getting from one suburb to another almost inevitably means traversing a crowded central city.

The proposed solution is the *supermétro*, whose route was announced in the summer of 2011 after months of public consultations and debate between left-wing regional authorities and the right-wing national government. The building of the €21 billion Grand Paris Express will create a roughly figure-8-shaped double loop of fifty-seven stations; the inner loop will circle the Périphérique at distances of one to three miles. The trains will mostly run underground—some of them 24 hours a day—and will be automatic (meaning that drivers like François will be out of luck). Funding will come from the regional and national governments, loans, and new real estate taxes. The stations of Grand Paris Express, expected to be completed by 2025, will be closely spaced enough to be within walking distance of most households in the innermost ring of suburbs. Yet with trains running at 40 miles an hour, it will put any passenger within an hour's ride of almost any point in the Greater Paris area.

A Paris-style *supermétro* serving the suburbs is the next logical step in public transport, and exactly what such cities as Los Angeles, Philadelphia, Chicago, Toronto, and Boston, as well as dozens in the developing world, need. A circular line linking the radials that already extend from city centers would enable suburb-to-suburb travel, allowing transit to match the flexibility of cars and seriously cut down on traffic in metropolitan areas.

As transit historian Mark Ovenden told me, "When you talk to people in France, Spain, the Netherlands, and Germany, the dedication to funding public transport is not even a question. People understand that if you have urban areas, you have to have some way of getting around. It's just sensible."

Fully one-quarter of the Paris region's €4.7 billion annual budget goes to roads and transit, and a transit-specific payroll tax on any company with more than nine employees has long guaranteed the revenue stream that keeps public transport constantly improving.

In Paris they have done the math: if you want a city that works in the future, you have to build smart transit in the present.

A Sale of Two Cities

I would rather ride the métro than any other subway system in the world, and that's not just because the streets of Paris happen to be above it. As a model of elegance and efficiency, Paris's transit system is the network to beat.

That doesn't mean I think the people who brought us the métro should be running every urban transit system in the world, yet that is exactly what some French transport companies are aiming to do. In a turnaround that would have intrigued Milton Friedman, once-statist Europe is now leading the global drive toward transit privatization, and is even putting the moves on municipally run public transport systems in the United States.

I became aware of this drive-to-privatize by accident, during my travels over the last few years. As I waited outside the train station in Malmö, Sweden's third-largest city, I noticed that local buses were operated by Veolia, a private French company. Boarding a bus in Mesa, Arizona, I was surprised to see it was being run by a French conglomerate originally founded by Napoléon III. On the streets of my own city, Montreal, I've lately spotted intercity buses with the logo of Transdev, another French corporation.

The privatization of public transport is a recent development, but it has roots in the nineteenth century. While New York's early elevated and subway lines, like Los Angeles's streetcar lines, were built with private capital, governments in Britain and most of Continental Europe, though they paid lip service to the principles of laissez-faire capitalism, oversaw the design of transit networks to an extent unimaginable in the United States. In the era of the tramways, Paris and other European cities granted 50-year concessions to private street railways, after which tracks and tunnels would revert to the municipal authorities without payment, and the city would be given the option of buying the rolling stock. Across the Channel, six private companies built and ran the various lines of the early London Underground—a situation that often forced commuters to walk aboveground between stations and buy new tickets when changing lines—until it was integrated into a single system in the 1930s, and nationalized by Labour in 1948. Though Paris's métro was built and operated by a Belgian industrialist, and two lines were actually built and run by an independent company, planning remained in municipal hands. Private operation failed to provoke widespread public resentment, as it did in New York—probably because the trains never got too crowded. Nonetheless, Paris's métro and bus lines were also nationalized in 1948, and since 2005, strategic and tactical oversight has been in the hands of the *Société des transports de l'île de France* (StiF), a regional planning body, while the RATP retains responsibility for operations.

Since the Second World War, in fact, transit in most of the world's great cities has been run by publicly owned agencies. The argument for public ownership of transit is two-pronged. First, that transit systems and railroads are an example of a natural monopoly; like electric utilities or sewer systems, they can optimize expenditures and increase efficiency if they are under a single management. Second, since a decent transport system has external benefits like increasing property values and reducing congestion and pollution, it is best managed not to maximize owners' profits, but in the public interest. The early history of the subways of New York, Paris, and London shows that private companies have no trouble efficiently building, and running, profitable lines. They encounter problems when the individually run lines merge into a network and a private monopoly emerges. Historically, this has led to owners cutting service on unprofitable lines, followed by overcrowding, the emergence of popular disgust with greedy owners profiting from the misery of commuters, and the inevitable call for public ownership.

Here's where things get interesting: an ideologically driven move toward privatization is now sweeping the European transportation sector. It started with a little-known European Union directive, which broke up national rail monopolies by requiring independent ownership and management of rolling stock—the actual trains—from rail infrastructure—the tunnels and tracks—thus separating "wheels from steel." In France this has meant the SNCF, the newly privatized national rail company, is being charged user fees to run the wheels of its bullet trains over the tracks of the French Rail Network, a state-controlled authority. (To cover costs, the French Rail Network has jacked up track use fees, which means ticket prices, low in comparison to other European countries, are now increasing.) European railway networks, the thinking goes, should be as open to free-market competition as the airline industry: in the future, "RyanTrain" or "EasyRail" high-speed trains could be competing for service on the same tracks from, say, Brussels to Berlin, or Lisbon to Marseilles. Italy's privatized Trenitalia is already bidding to provide service between French cities.

Amazingly, the drive-to-privatize might one day include urban transit systems, among them Paris's métro. The RATP, though it is still a public authority, has privatized many operations, which allows it to run Florence's tramways, Johannesburg's airport train, and some city buses in East London. The corollary, of course, is that new métro, bus, or tram lines in Paris could be run by Danish, Portuguese, or German companies. The RATP is not even a shoo-in to win the contract to build the planned suburban *supermétro*. To the chagrin of StiF, the regional government's transit authority, the RATP also plans to create distinct companies to oversee infrastructure and operate trains. Critics see this separation of wheels from steel as another step by Nicolas Sarkozy's right-wing government toward the total privatization of transit.*

---

* Some commentators believe this privatization is in fact "corporatization." Making a show of following EU regulations, transit systems and national rail companies have split themselves into separate corporations that do business with each other but merely pretend to compete with foreign companies, while contracts are awarded as usual. If Paris's métro seems to run pretty much as

The recent attempt to privatize London's Underground ended in failure. Refusing to break with their Conservative predecessors' promise not to increase spending, Tony Blair's Labour government looked for a way to involve the private sector in transit—mostly to get the costs of a planned refurbishment of the Underground off the government's books. The result was a public-private partnership that sold off the Tube to three infrastructure companies, each of which was given a 30-year lease to maintain track, signaling, and trains on different lines. A new company called London Underground, controlled by the city's Transport for London, was to be responsible for running the trains. From the start, the partnership was a disaster. Pitting the people maintaining the tracks against the people running the trains led to bizarre conflicts: the infrastructure companies, trying to fulfill their obligation to repair tracks and escalators on the cheap, pressured London Underground to stop running trains on weekends. The partnership began in 2003, but after only five years the infrastructure companies walked away, citing skyrocketing costs. The usual argument for privatization is that it will spur innovation and growth, but under the private companies' watch, the network was not expanded by a single mile. In the end, only lawyers and arbiters profited: drawing up the contracts alone cost half a billion pounds. While riding the Underground was never cheap, lately it has become criminally expensive: the lowest cash fare for the shortest possible ride is now £4 (two and a half times what a métro ticket costs). Today, a renationalized Underground has returned to square one: maintenance is now managed in-house by a single public authority, Transport for London.

"In Britain, all these public-private partnerships have collapsed and gone back to the public sector," Christian Wolmar, the nation's leading commentator on transportation issues, told me. "Separating infrastructure and operations creates this totally unnecessary interface, which just leads to endless, arcane disputes, when what you really need is a seamless operation between the two. From everything I've seen, we would have saved billions of pounds if we hadn't privatized our rail network."

Privatization is clearly in the short-term interest of European corporations, which are already world leaders in the transport sector. Apart from the RATP, two giant French conglomerates are now aggressively expanding

---

it always has, it is because the RATP, through canny negotiations with Brussels, has delayed the onset of complete privatization until 2030.

into the global public transport market. Keolis now has 40,000 employees, and runs commuter trains in Virginia as well as Melbourne's tramway system. A 2009 merger between Veolia Transportation and its rival Trans-dev created the world's largest private urban transport company, a $48 billion multinational with 119,000 employees in twenty-eight countries that carries 3.3 billion riders a year (equal to the combined ridership of Paris's métro and New York's subway). Among the French conglomerate's recent acquisitions are New Orleans's buses and streetcars, Las Vegas's bus rapid transit system, Boston's Massachussets Bay Commuter Railroad, and San Diego's Sprinter light-rail system. Free-market pundits could claim this as a triumph of the private sector—if such corporations were truly private. But Keolis is a subsidiary of SNCF, France's passenger rail company. Veolia Transdev is owned by a company that was founded by Napoléon III as the Compagnie des Eaux in 1853. And Transdev, Veolia's new partner, is a sub-sidiary of a massive pension fund started under Louis XVIII. Such compa-nies are backed by state guarantees unavailable to their competitors in the private sector.

According to the Australian transit scholar Paul Mees, the French pri-vate transit industry has "become an oligopoly dominated by three large companies, where collusion has been more common than competition." I asked Mees about his native Melbourne, whose tram lines were privatized in 1999. "Two French companies bid for contracts to operate the tram and train lines," he told me. "They won by lowballing. They were indif-ferent to whether projections of profitability were true or not, because all they had to do was threaten to leave and they knew they'd be bailed out by the government. After learning the ropes in their home country, they're now experts at manipulating public transport contracting. It's basically a carpetbagging industry." Not only has transit service in Melbourne wors-ened since privatization, said Mees, but every year the government has had to increase its subsidies to the private companies, which now approach a billion Australian dollars a year.

As Christian Wolmar sees it, "The key flaw in the privatization con-cept, as it is practiced today, is that it is ersatz capitalism. When they built the first rail lines back in the nineteenth century, it was rough-and-raw capitalism: you invested money, and you could lose it if you misjudged the market. Now you have this pretend capitalism where private companies know the government will never allow a transit service to be shut down."

The most corrosive aspect of this pseudo-privatization is hidden behind talk of private-sector efficiency. Employees of truly state-run transport enterprises have won decent salaries and benefits through decades of labor action. Acting as private companies, pseudo-private transport companies can outbid their rivals precisely because they offer lower salaries and fewer benefits.

I've taken Keolis- and Veolia-operated buses and trains, and the service can be good, the ride comfortable. But it does seem strange that, in the name of cutting costs, politicians in Arizona, Virginia, and Louisiana are willing to let the dimes and quarters their citizens drop in local fare boxes end up in the coffers of a French multinational, rather than go to pay decent wages and benefits locally. And when recession hits, and profits vanish, entire transit systems risk being abandoned, leaving taxpayers footing the bill. The notorious inefficiency of publicly owned American transit agencies may have more to do with history than ideology. In the United States, where public takeovers tended to happen in the '60s and later, cities inherited bankrupt private systems, and never had the opportunity to develop efficient operating cultures. (The record of transit agencies in Toronto and other Canadian cities, which were municipalized much earlier in the twentieth century, tends to be a lot better.) The danger is that, in the name of fostering privatization, the United States may allow France—or its state-supported, pseudo-private transport companies—to bid for one of the last bastions of truly public-spirited enterprise, the big-city transit authority. In 2009, New Orleans became the first major American city to hand complete control of a public transit authority to a private company. Reports on service since Veolia Transdev took over are contradictory, but ridership still remains far below pre-Hurricane Katrina days, and it might strike some as strange that a French company has received tens of millions of dollars in public stimulus money.

Frankly, I'm a little worried about the future of those clattery old trolleys I've ridden up St. Charles Avenue. If profits decline and the government's willingness to subsidize a private company disappears, they might one day go the way of the streetcar named Desire.

I'll admit it might be interesting to see how the company that runs the Paris métro would go about remodeling, say, Chicago's El; a little Art Nouveau ironwork could make an attractive addition to the Loop. But I'd rather be able to rely on consistent service. One of the pleasures of traveling as a straphanger, after all, is riding on a network with its own local character—preferably one whose employees can count on a decent wage.

Is Paris Burning?

When I visit Paris these days, I always spend a few days with my friends Alexandra and Guillaume, and this trip was no exception. Guillaume, an elementary schoolteacher, is from Normandy, and Alexandra, who works as a librarian, was born and raised in Paris. They own a one-bedroom apartment in the 18th *arrondissement*, which they share with their cat Piedsec and their infant son Étienne.

Their apartment, a walk-up on the fifth floor of a ninety-year-old building, is small, but somehow they make it work. The computer is on a desk in the bedroom, which has a window overlooking the building's courtyard. The washing machine is next to the bathtub, and the kitchen, dining room, and living room—well, they're all the same room. I remembered how, in Los Angeles, Joel Kotkin had disparaged such Old World residences as "Hobbit houses." What people fail to realize is that European city dwellers are willing to trade square footage for urban amenities; who needs a baronial foyer and a home theater, after all, when you've got the Louvre and the cinemas of the Left Bank practically in your backyard? Outside Alexandra and Guillaume's apartment is an outdoor market, and Montmartre, with its vineyards and bench-filled squares, is a ten-minute walk away. There are café terraces to linger on, bookstores to browse, leafy parks where they can take Étienne for a stroll, and hundreds of bistros offering affordable *prix fixe* meals.

What's more, the entrance to the Château Rouge métro station is 200 yards from their front door. For Guillaume and Alexandra, the métro is the key to the city, and indeed, all of Europe. Once they are on line 4, it is a short ride to any one of Paris's major train stations, and from there, high-speed lines radiate out to London and Amsterdam, Marseilles and Berlin. Like most Parisians I know, Guillaume and Alexandra have never owned a car. Gas and insurance are expensive, and parking on their narrow street is a headache. "A car?" Guillaume once said to me, incredulously. "What would be the point?"

Alexandra, who when I first met her got around on a little Dutch bike, introduced me to the pleasures of cycling in Paris. These days, when I revisit Paris, I get a kick out of using the city's cheap and ubiquitous rental bicycles, and marvel at how bike paths now crisscross every part of the city, even the once car-dominated Rue de Rivoli.

Riding along the Right Bank thoroughfare on this visit, my progress on the bike path was briefly blocked by a doorman opening the door of a Bentley outside the Hôtel Meurice. As I stifled a scowl, I was reminded that, during the Occupation, this was the hotel the Nazis commandeered to use as their headquarters.

As the Allies advanced on Paris on August 7, 1944, an erasure more definitive even than Le Corbusier's Plan Voisin was being coordinated from this spot. The Nazis had wired everything from the Eiffel Tower to the bridges on the Seine with explosives. As he awaited his orders from Berlin, the military governor, Dietrich von Choltitz, admitted to Paris's mayor that the city was slated for destruction. As the story goes, the mayor realized he only had one chance to convince Von Choltitz to reconsider. When the asthmatic general was seized by a coughing fit, Paris's mayor led him to a balcony for some fresh air.

In an appeal to Von Choltitz's sentimentality, the mayor gestured toward the golden dome of Les Invalides, and the gossamer of the Eiffel Tower. Then a vision appeared: a lovely girl riding a bicycle down the Rue de Rivoli. How, the mayor wondered aloud, could the general contemplate destroying a city this beautiful?

Von Choltitz was genuinely moved. Lying to his superiors, he wired Berlin that the destruction was already under way; a few days later, he surrendered the intact city to Charles de Gaulle's army.

It's a miracle worth commemorating. Though Paris was threatened by bulldozers and cars in the twentieth century, its closest brush with annihilation came at the hands of the Nazis. It was saved by a woman on a bicycle.

Zone 2 / Zone 1   Zone 1

ndevang Fasanvej rederiksberg orum Nørreport Kongens Nytorv Christianshavn Amagerbro Lergravsparken Øresund Amager Str Femør K
ØLBJERG

Cycle tracks will abound in Utopia.
—H. G. Wells, *A Modern Utopia*, 1905

Islands Brygge

Zone 2 | Zone 1   Zone 1

DR Byen   Zone 3
UNIVERSITETET

Sundby

Bella Center

5. The Copenhagen Syndrome

Copenhagen, Denmark

Zone 3 | Zone 4

T raveling in Europe was giving me an inferiority complex. It had nothing to do with architectural glory, art galleries, or artisanal cheeses. It was simply the experience of riding on the continent's high-speed train network. I found myself wanting to be a European, if only so I could move like a European: comfortably, cheaply, and quickly.

There is now a train in Spain that is faster than the plane. The platypus-nosed AVE covers the almost 400 miles between Barcelona and Madrid in just two and half hours. The same trip done by jet, counting airport transfers and security line, takes at least three. (I have taken the AVE. The ride was so smooth that even as we topped out near 215 miles per hour the Rioja in the stemless glass on the tray table in front of me barely rippled.) In Europe, high-speed trains have cornered the market for short-haul travel between cities that are three or fewer air-hours apart. In the last few years, Spain has laid 1,200 miles of high-speed tracks, a figure expected to increase fivefold by 2020, when 90 percent of the population will live within 30 miles of a high-speed rail station. In Germany, bullet trains now *average* 150 miles an hour, and have almost completely superseded the market for flights between such major cities as Berlin and Hamburg, Frankfurt and Stuttgart, and Bremen and Cologne. In contrast, the fastest train in North America barely averages 88 miles an hour. When it comes to transportation, a serious gap has developed between the Old World and the New. With our crumbling freeways and chronically late, diesel-powered locomotives, we might as well be riding in stagecoaches.

I was reminded of how seamless and pleasant overland travel could be as I embarked on a 1,000-mile journey from Paris to Copenhagen. Checking out of my Left Bank hotel late one morning, I trundled my wheeled suitcase around the corner to a métro station, and rode to Gare de l'Est, where I bought a ticket for a *train à grande vitesse*, the TGV, France's bullet train. I had my pick of departures: there were nineteen leaving that day for Strasbourg, and the next would be pulling out in ten minutes. After lining up for a croissant in the bar car, I dozed off in my reclining second-class seat. Two hours and 20 minutes after leaving, we pulled into Strasbourg's train station, only a minute behind schedule, which meant we had averaged 105 miles per hour. (The next generation French bullet train, already in production, has a top speed of 223 miles per hour.) After stuffing my baggage into a coin locker, I set out to explore Grand Île, the city's medieval core, an ovoid island of high-pitched roofs, timbered facades, and church spires encircled by two arms of a tributary of the Rhine.

Strasbourg, the seat of the European Parliament, is the hub of a region straddling the German and French borders whose population is almost 900,000. On that Saturday afternoon, it felt as if they had all decided to come downtown at once. In Place Kléber, which was closed to automobiles, workers were setting up bleachers in preparation for the evening's main event, a performance by a swing band to mark the anniversary of the city's liberation by Allied troops. Sweatered and scarved against the

late fall chill, the Strasbourgeois queued up for roasted chestnuts and sha-
warmas, or just sat around fountains, engaging in that most elemental of
human pleasures—watching other humans. Some had clearly arrived by
car—on a few streets, motorists wormed their way among the pedestrians—
but most poured out of the impressive, slant-nosed trams that seemed to
slip through every major street.

Twenty years ago, the center of Strasbourg was polluted and thronged
with cars; on a typical day, fifty thousand automobiles would pass through
Place Kléber, making the city's main square a place in which few people
wanted to linger. Fearing the onset of a vicious circle of downtown decline
and suburban flight, the socialist city council voted to revive the tram lines
that had served the city until 1960. (Merchants and conservative councilors favored a subway, which would have cost four times as much per mile
to build.) After pedestrianizing certain streets, they began to build a network of bike lanes, and, as a concession to business owners, underground
parking lots on the edge of downtown. The strategy worked. Thirty percent
fewer cars now enter the core than in 1990, six tram lines handle 300,000
riders a day on 35 miles of tracks, and the downtown is thriving.

On Avenue de la Paix, I boarded a tram on line E, which runs past the
seat of the European Parliament, a coliseum-shaped building of glass and
steel. Drawing power from overhead wires, it trundled down the middle of
streets, and later followed its own right of way down a grassy median, like a
deliberate, heavy-footed centipede. The ride was smooth, and because the
roomy, tall-windowed Alstom- and Bombardier-made cars have low floors
that open almost flush with the curb, parents had no trouble wheeling strollers draped with shopping bags on board. Its progress was surprisingly fast, a
reminder that the streetcar can be a rapid and efficient means of urban transportation, as it was in American cities up until the 1920s—provided, that is,
the tracks aren't constantly blocked by cars. Most of all, the tram made a
statement; advancing along narrow streets, the imposing vehicles proclaimed
their dominance of the downtown. Without explicitly banning the automobile, Strasbourg has made reaching the center by car inconvenient and
expensive. An all-day tram pass, offering unlimited rides, costs less than
two hours of parking in a downtown lot. Suburbanites now leave their cars
at park-and-rides, where parking is free with a transit ticket, and ride the
trams downtown. Strasbourg's tram revolution has drawn tourists, too, and
is credited with reviving one of the most appealing city centers in France.

Not many cities, it is true, can count Strasbourg's three millennia of uninterrupted human settlement, or have such compact medieval centers. (In the United States, Sacramento, Charlotte, Denver, and a dozen other medium-sized cities have launched modern light-rail lines, and many more have walkable cores that could profit from a Strasbourg-style street-car revival. None, however, have paired track mileage with car-limiting policies the way Strasbourg has.) But I had heard about a more ambitious— and arguably more universally applicable—municipal transformation occurring a couple of hundred miles to the south, on the German side of the Rhine River, where the people of Freiburg claim to have built the world's first car-free suburb.

A short hop on a local, two-car shuttle train took me to Offenburg, where I changed platforms and rode for a half hour through the Black For-est on an Inter-City Express, alighting at Freiburg's main train station. The city center was flattened when British Lancaster bombers dropped 2,000 tons of explosives one night in 1944—only the Gothic-spired cathedral was spared—but it was soon rebuilt, in the painstaking German way, following the old medieval street plan. After leaving my suitcase at a hotel, I caught the No. 3 tram on Kaiser-Joseph-Strasse to the suburb that is helping to redefine urban mobility.

Even for Germany, the neighborhood of Vauban is hyperbolically, almost comically, green. Eco-pilgrims come to marvel at the Heliotrop, a cylindrical house that swivels like a sunflower to catch the sun's rays. The first thing I saw after passing through the thirteenth-century tollgate that once marked the Freiburg city limits was the *Sonnenschiff*, or solar boat, a block-long commercial complex with a pharmacy and organic grocery at street level and a roof tiled with photovoltaic cells. On a pine-covered hill-top nearby, the blades of a dozen wind turbines whirled lazily, their speed limited lest they injure the bats of the Black Forest.

I had not come to worship at Vauban's alternative energy altar, how-ever. What intrigued me was its residents' claims that they were reinvent-ing suburbia. Wandering between buildings, I followed leaf-covered paths that led past handmade playgrounds. Four-story buildings, some arranged like row houses, others like small apartment blocks, dominated the tract, facing each other across grassy courtyards. School was out, and parents were pedaling home, towing their children in polyester-covered bicycle trailers. I did see one car creeping behind two cyclists; as long as residents progress at a walking pace, they are allowed to park outside their own homes to load and unload their cars.

Until the reunification of Germany in the early '90s, Vauban was a French military base, and many of its larger buildings are refurbished barracks. In a restaurant called Süden, which was formerly a mess hall, Andreas Delleske, one of the community's founders, explained the facts of life in Vauban.

"Strictly speaking," said Delleske, "we are not a car-free district. People with cars are still welcome, but they have to buy a parking space when they move in." Nine solar-powered parking lots are dotted throughout Vauban, most of them less than a 300-yard walk from apartments. At €17,500, however, a parking space is expensive; most new residents decline the option, and a solid majority have chosen to sell their cars. "We have reduced car use by seventy percent. Over two-thirds of all trips are now made by bicycle," he said.

What were the advantages, I asked Delleske, to living car-free?

"The main one is cost. I save easily four hundred euros a month by not owning a car. The kids can play in the middle of the road without fear of being run over. And one very practical benefit is that, since we can walk in the road, we don't need sidewalks, which cost money to maintain." Delleske pointed out that residents further saved because they had developed the site on their own. "We formed *Baugruppen*, or construction groups, and hired architects to build our apartments. It was not a developer who built Vauban, but families. We saved twenty percent on the purchase price of our homes."

At first, Vauban looked more like a village of teachers' residences on a college campus than any subdivision I'd ever seen. (Delleske pointed out that 10 percent of Freiburg's workforce is employed by its university and hospital.) But Vauban is definitely suburban; it is located two miles from Freiburg's center, and is filled with more parks and playgrounds than most family-oriented subdivisions in North America. As I spent another day getting to know the place, I began to appreciate its low-key charms. Without traffic noises, I could hear birdsong, somebody practicing scales on a piano, and parents calling from ivy-covered balconies. Near the neighborhood's communal brick bread oven, a young woman in a tight track suit teetered by on a unicycle, and, in the courtyards, children played in piles of yellow and red autumn leaves. Population density is forty residents per acre, about the same as older row-house neighborhoods in Brooklyn or Boston, but with all the green space Vauban resembles such bosky garden suburbs as Philadelphia's Chestnut Hill and Chicago's Riverside.

Vauban, I realized, is what a suburb looks like when you remove all the land-gobbling driveways, garages, lanes, and cul-de-sacs. It is also the answer to all those who claim owning a car is essential when you start raising a family. With a third of its population under eighteen, Vauban may be the closest thing to what suburbia was meant to be before it was overrun by cars: a paradise of unsupervised free play for children.

Without Freiburg's citywide network of tramways, Delleske acknowledged, living car-free in Vauban would be a challenge. Freiburg has the highest transit ridership of any city in Germany, and the stalwart little trams, most of which are thirty years old, seem to go everywhere; two-thirds of the city's homes are within a three-minute walk of a stop. The trams also allow residents and visitors to easily access intercity trains, opening all of Europe to those who don't own cars. The No. 3 whizzed me back to my hotel, the No. 5 dropped me in front of the train station, and within 15 minutes, I was on an Inter-City Express bullet train, which took only six hours to cover the 500 miles to Berlin. After an overnight visit with friends, I was on another express train, this one headed north to Copenhagen.

Train travel's superiority over cars and planes, particularly in mid-distance intercity trips, has only increased in the era of high-speed technology. Since Europe's trains cater to business travelers, you can now Skype your family, answer emails, or just wander to the bar car for a decent meal and a bottle of beer. For a visitor who wishes to savor the scenery, bullet trains can sometimes seem a little *too* fast: our sheer velocity made even the middle-distance into a blur, and the bare-branched oaks of late fall, tangled with cats' cradles of mistletoe, seemed to strobe past like some never-ending magic lantern of dancing skeletons.

As we continued to rush electric-powered over welded rails, passing the endless wind turbines of northern Germany, invidious comparisons sprang to mind. Why, I wondered, do the Europeans do urban and intercity transport so well? And why are North America's passenger trains—with the exception of the Northeast's Acela, California's Capitol Corridor, and the Pacific Northwest's Cascades—so uncomfortable, so unreliable, and, to put it bluntly, such an egregious embarrassment?

It didn't help that the book on my lap was *Waiting on a Train*, a by turns dispiriting, by turns hopeful account of the state of passenger rail in the United States. In the year author James McCommons spent traveling the country by Amtrak, he encountered disintegrating stations, constant breakdowns, and horror stories like the New Orleans-to-Los Angeles Sunset Limited, which typically runs *twenty* hours late. Outside of a few heavily traveled corridors, most intercity Amtrak trains offer only a single departure a day. Every long-distance rail journey I've made in North America, from VIA Rail's Montreal-to-Halifax Ocean to Amtrak's Seattle-to-Los Angeles Coast Starlight (known on the West Coast as the "Star-late"), has been marked by indifferent service and repeated and usually unexplained delays.

The reason for this abysmal service, according to McCommons, is simple. In contrast to Europe, where the vast majority of cargo is moved by truck, North America's rail infrastructure is owned by seven major freight companies, and almost all of them consider the Amtrak and Via passenger trains that run on their rails an unmitigated nuisance. The next time you spend an hour or two sitting in a cornfield, sidelined by a Pennsylvania coal carrier, an 80-car tanker carrying crude oil from Alberta's tar sands, or what railroaders call a "Wal-Mart Chinese Doodad Train," blame it on companies like Union Pacific, Canadian National, and Burlington Northern, who prioritize on-time goods delivery over the travel needs of human beings.

At Puttgarden, where Germany runs out of land, our Inter-City Express slowed to a crawl as we advanced over a specially adapted wharf and, without stopping, directly into the belly of a Scandline Ferry. I hadn't been expecting it, but the next leg of the trip was to be by train-ferry, those specially adapted boats, still fairly common in Northern Europe, that carry cars as well as trains. As we drew up alongside a Mercedes semi-trailer, a multilingual announcement asked us to enjoy ourselves in the restaurants and duty-free shops of the upper decks during the 45-minute crossing. After traversing a strait in the Baltic Sea, we continued to the east coast of the island of Zealand, pulling into Copenhagen at 4:43 in the afternoon. Not counting stopovers, my meandering, 1,000-mile journey from Paris to Copenhagen had taken 17 hours and cost just 193 euros ($260).

According to the Web site of Deutsche Bahn, Germany's state rail operator, making the same journey by car would have taken an hour and a quarter longer, and would have cost twice as much in gas and tolls (not counting car rental fees and insurance). Traveling by plane, of course, would have been faster, but even using budget airlines, it would have been 25 percent more expensive.

The most sobering statistics came in graph form. Had I made the journey by kerosene-fueled jets, my carbon dioxide emissions would have amounted to 560 pounds, and by diesel-powered car, 640 pounds—a third of a ton of carbon released into the atmosphere. By choosing to travel by electric-powered train, I had released only 160 pounds of carbon dioxide. It was a reminder that rail is by far the most sustainable means of long-distance travel. Even the swiftest bullet trains produce less than a quarter of the emissions of jets.

And I hadn't been forced to endure security lines, body scans, or turbulence. I didn't get lost, or fined for speeding or running a red light. When I wheeled my suitcase into the main hall of Copenhagen's magnificent, wood-beamed central station, I was rested, well-fed, caught up on my reading—and three minutes ahead of schedule.

Copenhagen Has Been Taken

I was prepared to admire Copenhagen, grudgingly, as you might a doughty Lutheran aunt who prides herself on her strong opinions and sensible shoes. I didn't expect to become infatuated with the place, jealous of those who got to live there year-round, and, to my wife's annoyance, an advocate for an eventual emigration to Scandinavian climes.

I've been to more striking cities. Copenhagen is like a greatest hits of more glamorous destinations: it has the canals of Amsterdam, the squares of Florence, and the Baroque architecture of Vienna; there is even a single, New York–style modernist skyscraper (the SAS building, all of twenty stories). I've been to more exciting cities. Copenhagen's biggest attraction is the Tivoli Gardens, a nineteenth-century amusement park complete with Ferris wheel and carousel, though the Lego Store and the Bodum Hus, where you can splurge on interlocking plastic bricks and functional coffeepots, are close runner-ups. And I've definitely been to balmier cities. Copenhagen is windblown and rainy, and because it is at the same latitude as Ketchikan, Alaska, the winter sunset—when the sun deigns to appear at all—tends to come at midafternoon. Yet the scale of the place is perfect: Copenhagen is big enough to keep you interested, but small enough that you feel comfortable. In truth, though, the depth of my affection probably comes from the *way* I discovered Copenhagen.

During my first couple of days in the city, I walked and rode the two-line Metro. The brand-new system has state-of-the-art platform doors in its deep underground stations, and gleaming automated Italian-made trains, the kind that allow kids to sit in the front and watch the lights in the tunnel rush by. This being Northern Europe, there are no turnstiles, and passengers board on the honor system. (When I blundered on ticket-free on my first day, a platform attendant smiled indulgently and rode the escalators back to street level to give me a lesson on the proper use of the ticket machines.) From the central train station, eleven commuter train lines, run by Danish State Railways, extend deep into the suburbs. Cheerful orange buses, with low floors to allow easy entry for strollers and wheelchairs, run along most major streets. In fact, Copenhagen is the only city I've been where people complain there is *too* much public transport. When the Cityringen, a circle line that will add fifteen new stations, is completed in 2018, only the residents of the city's most isolated districts will be more than a 600-yard walk from a Metro station.

"My problem with the Cityringen," one longtime Copenhagener told me, "is that this is a small, uncongested city that already has a very good transit system. You can easily get to most places in twenty minutes or less, so I don't really see the point in investing a huge amount of money and disrupting the city with ten years of construction when things work just fine as they are."

The Cityringen may well be overkill. The city's medieval core, tightly wound around the parliament building and stock exchange on the island of Slotsholmen, is so compact it can be crossed on foot in under an hour. More to the point, Copenhagen has reinvented its streets so they are now served by the most decentralized, affordable, and efficient mode of mass transit ever invented: the bicycle.

They are everywhere, the bikes of Copenhagen. Gray-haired senior executives ride black Flying Dutchmen to downtown offices in three-piece suits, slacks clipped to their calves and briefcases strapped to their backs. Women in late middle age do their shopping on pastel-hued Verlorbises whose baskets are stuffed with bread and produce. All of life seems to happen on bikes: Copenhageners have mastered the art of sending text messages, drinking cans of Carlsberg, smoking Prince cigarettes, and flirting on two wheels. On weekday mornings, the distributors of the free newspaper *Metro* stand curbside, holding out rolled-up copies for cyclists to grab, and recycling bins are oriented toward the bike lanes, their mouths positioned at the perfect height for a passing cyclist to lob a can. Even the homeless have bikes—*nice* bikes. Outside a Burger King, I saw a ruddy-faced gentleman asking for spare change, the handlebars of his classic

Batavus hung with shopping bags filled with cans and bottles. When I finally happened upon the statue of the Little Mermaid in the harbor, I was a little surprised to see she was perched on a boulder, rather than straddling a Raleigh.

Bicycles here actually outnumber humans. At the last tally, central Copenhagen counted 560,000 bikes, but only 519,000 people. In the greater Copenhagen area, 37 percent of residents get to work or school by bicycle— a proportion that jumps to 55 percent in the central core—and these numbers are rising every year. To put this in context: more people commute by bicycle in greater Copenhagen, population 1.8 million, than cycle to work in the entire United States, pop. 310 million. After a couple of days of watching streams of fit, stylish Danes pedaling their hearts out, the Metro lost its appeal. I needed to find a bike of my own and join the parade.

Happily, my hotel made a dozen loaner bikes available to guests. Lasse Lindholm, the head of communications for the municipal bicycle program, had volunteered to give me a tour of Copenhagen's bicycle infrastructure, and on a weekday morning, I mounted my sturdy black three-gear bicycle and followed him out to the bike lanes.

"In Copenhagen, being a cyclist is not an explicit identity marker," Lindholm explained to me, as we merged into the flow of morning commuters. "If you asked the first hundred Copenhageners you met to define themselves, I can guarantee none of them would say 'I'm a cyclist.' Riding a bike here is as natural as brushing your teeth or tying your shoelaces. We don't even think about it."

People ride in their work clothes, men in polished shoes, women often in heels. The typical Copenhagen bicycle has high handlebars, which allow for a comfortable upright posture, a basket on the headset, a mud guard over the chain, and a rat-trap above the rear fender. They are cheap enough to be practically disposable; the exceptions are cargo bikes, which have become something of a status symbol. These sturdy tricycles, with two small, swiveling front wheels and deep round cargo bays that call to mind pelicans' bills, look like sleeker, more maneuverable versions of the bikes that ice-cream vendors pedal. They have become the SUVs of Copenhagen; Lindholm said a quarter of all Copenhagen families with two or more kids now own a cargo bike, and a new Nihola, one of the most coveted brands, can cost $4,000. Even Denmark's crown prince Frederik is regularly photographed ferrying his youngest son around in a Nihola bike.

"You can easily carry three children in a cargo bike, and a week's worth of groceries," said Lindholm, as we pulled to the curb in the back-streets of Vesterbro, a working-class district undergoing rapid gentrification. Outside a six-story apartment building, a pink fiberglass shelter in the shape of an automobile took up a parking spot that would normally have been occupied by a car. A pilot project of the municipal bike program, the shelter, which looked something like a Studebaker spun out of cotton candy, was divided into flaps that could be lowered and locked to provide secure overnight parking for four cargo bikes. "We love that cargo bikes have exploded in popularity, but they are difficult to park at regular bike racks. This way, we take away street parking from cars, but we are also illustrating that four big bikes can fit in the same space as one small car."

After crossing a swing bridge, which the municipal government had built to provide a shortcut across the harbor for cyclists and pedestrians, Lindholm showed me where to lock my bike outside the Rådhuset, an impressive crenellated town hall guarded by sculpted dragons. In the basement, he showed me a cavernous room filled with hundreds of neatly racked bicycles; municipal politicians had been parking their bikes here, Lindholm said, since 1905. The real spectacle, though, came a few minutes later, when we paused on a bridge on Nørrebrogade, one of the main thoroughfares into the downtown. It was a quarter to nine, and a never-ending succession of cyclists streamed past, often four or five abreast, bound for downtown offices. Some talked on cell phones, some listened to MP3 players; only a handful wore helmets. When the hordes of bicycle commuters were forced to stop by a red light, a young woman with a campaign button on her lapel strolled among them, handing out pamphlets for the upcoming municipal elections.

"I'm a candidate for the Social Liberals," she told me, returning to the curb as the light turned green. "Our transportation policy is actually quite controversial. We would like to add more lanes for bikes on bridges like these. We would like cars out of the city altogether."

On the other side of the bridge, a monolith-like counter with a bright LED display kept a running count of the passing cyclists. So far that year, 1.8 million bicycles had crossed; in the summer, said Lindholm, the tally typically reached 35,000 a day, making Nørrebrogade the busiest bike route in Europe. Though it was a drizzly morning in mid-November, with the temperature only a few degrees above freezing, cyclists waiting for the light to change had backed up halfway along the bridge: I realized I was witnessing rush-hour bicycle congestion. Unlike automobile traffic jams, though, nobody here seemed particularly frustrated.

"People still ride when it snows," said Lindholm. "We send the plows out to clear the bike lanes before they plow the roads for cars."

Though Lindholm and I were often riding on busy streets, I never felt threatened by rushing cars. The broad bike lanes are positioned a few inches higher than the roadway, yet lower than the sidewalks, and are physically separated from automobile lanes by a low curb, offering a real sense of security. In North American cities that have bike paths, a single, bi-directional lane tends to be confined to one side of the street, which means that cyclists going in opposite directions rush past one another, often with inches to spare. In Copenhagen, unidirectional bike lanes run down either side of major streets, allowing cyclists to relax (which may explain why so many were steering with one hand and holding cell phones in the other). On the few roads that offered on-street parking, the bike lane was located inside the line of parked cars, offering further shelter from traffic. Where the bike lanes crossed busy roads, a bold blue stripe showed the way across the intersection.

Lindholm said that, though it was mid-November, the city hadn't seen a single cycling fatality that year. (In contrast, about twenty cyclists die every year on the streets of New York.) Drivers, I noticed, were exaggeratedly cautious, coming to a full stop, craning their necks and waiting until the bike lane was completely clear before turning right. In Denmark, as in Holland and Belgium, a policy of strict liability applies to motorists: in accidents, the presumption of guilt is on the driver, who is considered to be the operator of a potentially lethal piece of heavy machinery. Opening a door on a cyclist is a serious offense, and—except in extreme cases, where a bike rider blindsides a stopped car—it is the driver's insurance company that has to cover all the costs. (Drivers are also taught to reach for their door handles with their right hands, which forces them to swivel and look back for approaching bikes before opening the door.) If anything, I felt less intimidated by the motorists than by my fellow bike riders. In Copenhagen, coming to a halt on a busy bike lane can be tricky: to prevent a pile-up, you are well advised to signal a stop by holding up your right hand, crooked elbowed, before easing your way over to the sidewalk.

Lindholm left me at a waterfront community center, after introducing me to the director of Copenhagen's cycle program. Over coffee, Andreas Röhl explained how the city's technical and environmental administration was trying to make Copenhagen a paradise for cyclists.

"I work with the bicycle as mass transit," explained Röhl. "It's all about what makes a nicer city to be in. Bicycles are fast, they don't make noise, and they are cheap for the city. There is no cost of running the system— you just have to give people the infrastructure, and they use it. For a city like Copenhagen, with the kind of climate and layout we have, the bike is by far the most cost-effective mode of transport for moving large numbers of people."

Röhl figures bikes are beating cars in Copenhagen thanks to a classic system of incentives and disincentives. A "green wave" times traffic signals on thoroughfares so a cyclist maintaining an average speed of 12 miles an hour won't be stopped by a red light. At over a hundred intersections, bicycles are given a 15-foot, six-second headstart over cars, an initiative that Röhl says has cut down significantly on right-turn collisions. In some areas, bike lanes are even marked by flashing green running lights embedded in the pavement, and cyclists are allowed to go the wrong way down one-way streets without risking a ticket. Copenhagen's municipal authorities have set a high price for parking, but the national government is responsible for the most effective disincentives. Gas in Denmark is expensive—during my visit, the equivalent of $7.50 a gallon—and there is a 180 percent registration tax on new cars. For many people, car ownership just doesn't make financial sense.

With 220 miles of bike lanes, Copenhagen's network is close to being built out. "The thing is," said Röhl, "it's easy to add miles. The hard part is putting bike lanes where people want to go." Röhl pointed out that bike paths in other cities are often threaded through parks or alongside rivers. In Copenhagen, bike paths follow the most direct possible routes to downtown, while drivers are forced to detour along one-way streets.

The growing popularity of biking actually had Röhl a little worried. "Now we're experiencing rush-hour congestion, which isn't good for traveling speed or feelings of safety. Our goal is to have fifty percent of people in the greater Copenhagen area commuting by bicycle in the next five years. That will mean fifty-five thousand more people riding bicycles to work or school." The next step, he said, was to widen existing bike paths, which would mean taking even more road space away from cars.

Röhl acknowledged that cycling may not be a year-round solution for every city. "Remember, though, Copenhagen is rainy and cold, and gets snow, and it is also quite spread out. Yet we are finding that people are routinely cycling twelve miles one-way to get to work. In places like Phoenix or Houston, which were built for cars, you might have an uphill battle getting many people on bicycles. But you need to go for the low-hanging fruit, places like Manhattan or Chicago, which are quite flat and densely populated. With the right kind of infrastructure, bike riding could easily become a major form of mass transit in the United States."

It is clearly a boon for public health. I have to admit I was a little skeptical when Röhl cited studies that showed commuters who got to work by bike rather than car had a 30 percent lower mortality rate than motorists. But as I pedaled around the harbor, encountering bike-riding Danes of all ages, red-cheeked and strong-limbed, I began to suspect there might be some truth to the stats. Routinely cycling a dozen miles a day as you take your kids to daycare, do your shopping, or ride to work would give you all the exercise you needed. As Lindholm pointed out, why spend an hour and a half in the gym when the act of commuting alone could make you a healthier person?

It might even make you a happier one. I know that, after just a day of pedaling the streets of the world's best bicycle city, I was grinning like a seven-year-old who'd awakened to find a brand-new Schwinn next to the Christmas tree.

A Quiet War on Cars

For a city dweller, bike riding makes good sense as public transport; for a traveler, it is a revelation. Copenhagen's Metro is efficient, but like all subways it fragments your experience, whisking you under the streets between neighborhoods without allowing you to see how a city is stitched together. And as great as walking can be, it tends to limit you to exploring a handful of districts in a day. By riding on a safe and well-connected network of bike lanes, I felt as though I was quickly grasping the layout of Copenhagen in a way I had never been able to do in New York, London, or Paris.

I knew I was approaching Freetown Christiania, Copenhagen's legendary urban commune, when spray-paint began to crop up on the normally impeccable brick facades of apartment blocks, soon followed by long stretches of elaborate murals. Like Vauban in Freiburg, car-free Christiania was also built on a former military base (which makes sense: closely spaced barracks tend to preclude roads), but this community's origins go back to the early '70s, when anarchists first squatted on the hundred-acre site. Filled with warehouses, slumping wooden shacks, fantastic houses with huge shutters that look as if they were built by elves, and some fairly strung-out looking wastrels, Christiania occupies prime urban real estate and has long been hated by right-wing politicians. After strolling down Pusher Street, where bricks of Nepalese and Moroccan hashish were neatly laid out on cloth-covered tables, I poked my head into Christiania Bikes. In 1984, a blacksmith named Lars Engstrøm built a front-loading cargo bike for his wife, Annie, to ferry their kids around Christiania. His design was adopted by the Danish post office and would later inspire the Nihola cargo bike. I saw examples of the commune's ingenious mode of transportation, often emblazoned with the distinctive three-dotted Christiania flag, outside day care centers and organic bakeries.

Leaving Christiania, I pedaled to the western side of the downtown and along the Søerne, a series of interlinked rectangular basins dotted with swans and lily pads, until I reached the "Potato Rows," a half-dozen parallel streets of buff-colored brick row houses. In the 1860s, shipyard workers, priced out of tenements by speculation, founded their own building society and hired an architect to build five hundred identical row houses in an area that had once been potato fields. It was a story that reminded me of Vauban's *Baugruppen*, in which the people of Freiburg banded together to build their own subdivision without the help of a developer. (Scholars have traced the birth of the Scandinavian welfare state back to such union-organized co-housing initiatives.) The results were similarly idyllic. Though a dozen cars were parked at either end of the narrow streets, a several-hundred-yard stretch of the center of each block was entirely car-free. What normally would have been space taken up by street parking was filled with swings, planters filled with flowering shrubs, and picnic tables.

Outside one of the houses on Eckersbergsgade, I met Niels, who was bringing his four-year-old son Julius back from kindergarten in a cargo bike. He invited me inside his house for a quick tour.

"Our house was built in 1883," said Niels, as we walked through airy, sunlit rooms to a grapevine-covered balcony on the top floor. It was a spic-and-span three-story dwelling, with the functional but tasteful moldings and cabinetry you'd expect in a house designed by shipbuilders. "Three families would have been living here, with the outhouses in the garden." The houses in the Potato Rows were now highly sought after, million-dollar properties occupied by professionals (Niels's wife is an architect).

He said the absence of cars allowed his two sons to kick around a soccer ball unsupervised, and neighbors to meet in the middle of the street for drinks in the summer.

Not all of Copenhagen is open to bike riders. Arriving in the medieval center, I had to dismount and walk my bike along the Strøget, Europe's longest uninterrupted pedestrian street. From the vast square in front of the Rådhuset to Kongens Nytorv, the nearly mile-long Strøget is the spine of the city's medieval center. It meanders through the downtown, widening and contracting like a river, pouring pedestrians into adjoining squares via cobblestoned alleys. In some European cities, such pedestrian zones are no-man's-lands; when only a few streets are closed to traffic, they can become a haven for beggars and packs of vagrants with feral dogs. While Copenhagen has its share of street people, they were vastly outnumbered by well-dressed strollers, shoppers, and students. Though the weather was cool and autumnal, the scene was as lively as a summer day in an Italian piazza. In the squares, Copenhageners sat on terraces, drinking beer and smoking, cozy beneath heavy blankets provided by café owners. Next to a fountain where a trio of storks were sculpted in perpetual lift-off, I bought a *ristretto* from a barista who had transformed his Nihola bike into a mobile coffee bar, a gleaming espresso machine sitting atop the modified cargo bay.

"Not so long ago," recalled Jan Gehl, "sitting around in cafés was considered un-Scandinavian behavior. People said Copenhagen was too cold and too far north for sidewalk cafés, it could never happen here. Now there are seven thousand outdoor café and restaurant seats downtown, and you can find people enjoying them twelve months of the year." After locking my bike, I had met Gehl in a sunlit conference room in a nineteenth-century apartment building that had been converted into offices for his architectural firm. As a consultant to city hall, Gehl was instrumental in the pedestrianizing of the Strøget that had revitalized downtown Copenhagen.

Back in the '60s, Gehl explained, Copenhagen was just another car-clogged European city.

"Two forces emerged to destroy the city," said Gehl, who speaks fluent English with a marked Scandinavian singsong. "Modernistic city planning ideas and the invasion of the automobile. At the same time there was the silly architecture of ideologists, with their vertical garden cities, and there was a distinct policy of getting rid of bikes, because the car invasion was causing lots of accidents." Bucking the trend, and against the protests of merchants, the city made the Strøget car-free in 1962, though delivery vehicles were, and are, permitted in the morning. More streets and squares were added a few years later, and the OPEC embargo of the '70s, which hit energy-poor Denmark particularly hard, accelerated the process. Protests killed a plan to cover the beautiful artificial lakes west of downtown with a four-lane highway, and tens of thousands of cyclists converged on the square in front of city hall in a grassroots demonstration against the growing dominance of the car. (The refrain for a popular Danish children's song of the day went: "I love my bicycle / It doesn't pollute like those oil-burning bastards.") Today, a 25-acre swath of the downtown is closed to motor vehicles.

"I got a research grant to study how people use public space, which hadn't really been done before," said Gehl. "Of course, there was old Jane Jacobs looking out of her window in Greenwich Village, but we started counting pedestrians on the Strøget on a regular basis. We found that people's use of the city was very rhythmic, and entirely predictable." With photographs and charts, his 1971 book *Life Between Buildings* enumerated the urban design features that went into fostering lively street life; every decade Gehl's firm publishes the results of follow-up surveys. "The mayor's office loves them. Sometimes, a shop owner still tries to claim his business was ruined because the city removed four parking spaces. But now the mayor can point to real figures and say: 'There are six thousand more people passing your shop a day than there were five years ago. Are you sure you're a good businessman?'"

The fact is, ever since cars were kicked out of central Copenhagen, the downtown has been thriving. "For a while now, Copenhagen has had a policy of taking away three percent of the inner city parking every year, on the theory that if people can't park, they won't drive. If you do it slowly enough, nobody notices. I always say that the quality of a city shouldn't be determined by counting how many pedestrians you have, but by the number of people who have *stopped* being pedestrians, and have decided to sit down and stay awhile. We found that for every fourteen square meters you take away from cars"—about 150 square feet—"you can count on one extra café terrace seat. That means for every parking spot removed, you get two more people sitting and enjoying life."

These days Gehl, who has advised municipal leaders in seventy cities on creating attractive public spaces, spends much of his time abroad.

With New York City's transportation commissioner Janette Sadik-Khan, he worked on pedestrianizing Broadway and Times Square, and is especially enthusiastic about how Melbourne has embraced his ideas. "They pedestrianized the downtown, and took shabby, garbage-filled lanes, and filled them with terraces of cafés and bars. Now there are ten times more people living in the center. Melbourne has become the second nicest city in the world—after Copenhagen."

Gehl believes that cities that continue to plan for the car are in deep trouble. "Individual four-wheel drive has no future," he said. "You can never solve the problems of a Mumbai, a Beijing, or a Lagos with the dream of automobiles for everybody. Cities like Phoenix, Atlanta, and Houston still haven't figured this out. But New York, San Francisco, and Seattle are finally starting to address the situation.

"But you can't do it halfway—you can't set aside only two blocks, as so many North American cities have done, going from nowhere to nowhere, and expect it to work. You need a complete walking system, which is what we have with the Strøget in Copenhagen."

Gehl recalled the way he and his wife celebrated their forty-fifth wedding anniversary in Copenhagen: "We decided to have dinner downtown, so we rode on our bikes for several miles, side by side, on safe bicycle lanes. And we walked around the inner city to see which restaurant we would prefer, before finding a place in the harbor, where we had a nice bottle of wine and a wonderful meal. Then we bicycled home. We are in our seventies, and without even knowing it, we rode sixteen miles, in comfort and style. When we were first married, an evening like that would not have been possible."

Gehl clearly relished the part he had played in this civic transformation. I could see how, as a lifetime achievement, making your hometown demonstrably safer, healthier, and more attractive—and in the process chipping away at the legacy of the likes of Robert Moses, Frank Lloyd Wright, and Le Corbusier—had a lot to recommend it.

A Virtuous Cycle

When it comes to encouraging people to give up their cars, transportation planners often face a seemingly intractable challenge: the last-mile problem. Commuter and intercity rail is good at moving people along major corridors, but it fails to get them the final few blocks to their homes or offices. Thanks to Copenhagen's good bicycle infrastructure, the last-mile problem is a virtual non-issue. People just hop on a bike.

Danes, in fact, seem to have an instinctive knack for hybrid and inter-modal transportation. By law, all taxis in Denmark are required to have a rack for carrying two bicycles. A single, transferable transit pass allows Copenhageners to ride buses, the Metro, and mini-ferries across the harbor. Commuters who ride the Metro or S-train downtown often own two bikes, a utilitarian model they lock outside Central Station and use to get to work, and a fancier one for riding to their home in the suburbs.

Good city planning helps. In 1948, politicians came up with the Finger Plan, in which new development and transportation routes would be channeled along five corridors, extending from the palm of the downtown like fingers splayed for a game of mumblety-peg. Greater Copenhagen has grown following this plan, with each finger bone serving as a transit corridor of S-train lines, thoroughfares, and bike lanes, separated by parks and other green spaces.

Copenhagen's greatest contribution to solving the last-mile problem is probably Bycyklen, or City Bikes, the world's first large-scale bike-share program, founded in 1995. The free loaner bikes work on the model of a cart in a supermarket parking lot: the bike is freed with a 20-krone coin, a deposit you get back when you return your ride to one of over a hundred stands in the central city. Its most notorious predecessor was the White Bicycle plan, launched in the mid-'60s when an anarchist group scattered several hundred free bicycles around Amsterdam. Cynics cited the fate of the White Bicycles—many ended up in canals after drunken joyrides—as proof that human nature would always trump such utopian schemes. Copenhagen solved the problem by incentivizing the return of the City Bikes with a small deposit. Beginning in 2005, the French city of Lyon launched Vélo'v, in which bikes locked in computer-controlled stands could be liberated after paying a credit-card deposit. Once you'd bought a daily, weekly, or yearly, membership, the first thirty minutes were free; subsequent half hours cost only one euro.

I missed using Copenhagen's City Bikes by a couple of weeks, as the city takes the stands off the streets over the winter, but I have used bike-share programs in many cities. The most ambitious scheme is Paris's Vélib'. To combat a persistent problem—Vélib' bikes tended to accumulate near the Seine, a downhill ride from outer districts—Paris now gives users credits for free rentals if they return a Vélib' to a stand at a higher elevation. GPS systems allow for better tracking of missing and stolen bikes, and there are plans to introduce "pedelec" or e-bikes—bicycles whose pedals are assisted by electric motors—in some cities. Washington, D.C., Minneapolis, Boston, and Chicago have their own, much smaller, versions of Vélib', and at last count there were 120 bike-share programs worldwide, ranging from the sixty Green Bikes on Chicago's St. Xavier University campus to the 5,000 bikes in the Chinese city of Guang'zhou.

So many Copenhageners already own their own bicycles that City Bikes are mostly used by tourists and business travelers, but systems like Paris's Vélib' have transformed a significant number of Parisians into enthusiastic cyclists. For cycle advocates, bike-share systems function like Trojan horses in car-besieged cities. At minimum expense, they introduce people to an alternative to driving.

In many cities, including my hometown of Montreal, stands are located next to subway or métro stations, allowing for true intermodal transportation. Lately, I get a lot of satisfaction in maneuvering my borrowed bike into an unoccupied dock with a resounding *thwack*, before heading straight for the métro turnstiles.

Taming the Bull

I'd arranged to meet Mikael Colville-Andersen outside my hotel in the district of Vesterbro. Looking dapper in a tailored charcoal car coat, he rolled up to the Savoy on his trademark white Bullitt. He explained it was a modern version of the Long John, the long-framed two-wheel cargo bike Danish deliverymen once used to carry bricks and 200-pound sacks of cement. Normally, Colville-Andersen perches his son Felix and his daughter Lulu-Sophia in the low-slung box in front of the saddle, but tonight his wife, Susanne, was taking care of the kids, so I took it for a spin around the block. For such a long bike, it was surprisingly easy to maneuver, and incredibly fast.

We locked our rides outside a small, smoky café. Over pints of high-octane Christmas beer, Denmark's most tireless propagandist for bicycle culture made a spirited case for the exportability of Copenhageners' preferred mode of mass transit.

"The Danish are very modest, right?" said Colville-Andersen. "They know they've got a good thing going with their bicycle superhighways, green waves, and infrastructure, but they don't spend much time marketing them abroad." That's where Colville-Andersen, who was born to Danish parents in western Canada, comes in. His award-winning blog Copenhagen Cycle Chic features photos of Danes cycling in all kinds of weather: blond beauties wearing cotton dresses and high heels, or wrapped in heavy knit scarves; picturesquely wrinkled men nattily attired in fedoras, tweed jackets and wingtips; and teenagers in tight jeans and Converse sneakers, all of them balanced on heavy, high-handlebar bikes.

"Cycling should not be about bombing down the street in and out of traffic, that whole New York bike messenger mentality: 'Yo, fuck you in the car!' You need to get people riding nice and easy, upright on their bikes, where their center of gravity is in the same place as when they're walking. When you think style over speed, cycling is going to be safe."*

In the United States, Colville-Andersen said, cycling is perceived either as a leisure activity or the transportation choice of marginalized subcultures. "We have to re-democratize the bicycle. Forget the hipsters on fixies with their messenger bags, forget the spandex-clad men riding around in packs, forget the vehicular cyclists.† In Paris, they had no existing subculture of messengers or urban cycle gear, so, when Vélib' came to town, there was no stigma attached to cycling. The people you see riding Vélib', in their suits and skirts, are the same people you see riding the métro." Though environmental consciousness runs high in Denmark, Colville-Andersen insisted that Copenhageners didn't ride to be green. "When they survey Copenhageners, only three percent say they're doing it to save the planet, and only one in five say they do it because its good exercise. The vast majority ride because it's quick and easy."

Copenhagen, Colville-Andersen believes, has an important lesson to teach other cities: put bike lanes where people actually want to go, rather than where they happen to be convenient. "When Copenhagen started building bike lanes, it routed them through quiet neighborhoods, which

---

* Colville-Andersen is known for the controversial position he has taken against the use of bicycle helmets—in fact the one helmet you can see on his Web site has been upended and filled with ice and bottles of beer. He believes that promoting helmets puts the emphasis on the dangers of cycling, and cites cases where the introduction of helmet laws produced a precipitous drop in cycling rates. In Copenhagen, of course, bicycle paths are physically separated from the road, and the sheer mass of cyclists makes for safety in numbers; fewer than one in ten cyclists wear helmets. In my hometown, Montreal, where cyclists are vastly outnumbered by drivers, I often wear a helmet in the summer, and always in the winter.

† "Fixies" are lightweight, fixed gear bikes, often without brakes, popular among messengers in American cities. Vehicular cyclists disdain bike lanes and subscribe to the suicidal credo that bicycles should act like cars, claiming entire lanes on busy streets.

added like fifteen minutes to every journey. It was a massive flop. We're *Homo sapiens*, we instinctively want to get from point A to point B as quickly as possible. So we began building safe bike lanes on the city's busiest streets, direct routes to the downtown, and we never looked back." After years of trial and error, Colville-Anderson believes, the Danes have established the best practice for building bicycle infrastructure. "Building Copenhagen-style separated bike lanes—it's pretty much cut-and-paste. You could easily export them to other cities."

Nonetheless, in North America, even well-designed bike lanes are controversial. Residents of Brooklyn's Park Slope, for example, have filed a lawsuit to remove the Scandinavian-style bike lane on Prospect Park West, arguing that it snarls traffic and is a potential danger to pedestrians. I brought up an argument I'd heard many people make: that European cities with their compact cores were intrinsically more suited for bicycle riding than American cities. Colville-Andersen wasn't buying it:

"I'll admit that's true for Amsterdam. When you're standing next to one of those canals, you cannot visualize a North American city in its place. It has a strange, unique layout. But Copenhagen is completely different. It's true we have a medieval core, but it's tiny. A hundred and fifty years ago, we tore down the city walls, and with the industrial revolution Copenhagen began to explode outward. Now we have extensive urban sprawl. We have wide boulevards. When people come here from the United States, I say, can you visualize your city when you're standing here in Copenhagen? And most of them say, 'Yeah, this works for us.'" Amazingly enough, Copenhagen's average metropolitan density of 11.5 residents per acre is virtually the same as Los Angeles's, which is 11 per acre.

Colville-Andersen conceded that the fact the city is flat helps. "But Aarhus, Denmark's second city, is as hilly as Seattle or Portland, and they have twenty-five percent of the population riding bikes. Look," he pursued, "we can't talk about bikes without talking about the sacred bull in society's china shop: the automobile. We go around bubble-wrapping cyclists, making people wear helmets, when what we should be doing is taming the bull. It can be done easily, through traffic calming, congestion charges, giving priority to cyclists at intersections." He insisted he wasn't fanatically anti-automobile. "At a lecture in Washington, somebody said to me, 'Here in the United States, we go for bike rides on the weekend, what do you do in Denmark?' I told her: we go for *car* rides. A lot of my friends own cars. The difference is, in Copenhagen, we get our first car when we're like thirty-five, after we've had a couple of kids. We use them to go to our sum-mer houses, or take the kids to Grandma's house for babysitting duty. But we don't use them seven days a week, for commuting or running every little errand. We're weekend drivers."

Butting out a cigarette, Colville-Andersen took a final pull on his beer. "The bicycle is the most fantastic tool we possess as a society for traffic calming, for reducing carbon emissions, for making our cities more liv-able. If you make bikes the quickest way to get around your city, which is all we did in Copenhagen, everybody and their dog will get on board."

It turned out that Colville-Andersen and I had a lot in common. We were both in our forties, had both grown up in western Canada, and had spent much of our twenties and thirties traveling the world. He invited me over for dinner at his house a few nights after our first interview, where Susanne served us a macaroni casserole and seven-year-old Felix drew me a picture of Darth Vader. They lived in a fifth-floor apartment in a hand-some nineteenth-century building in Frederiksberg. It had no elevator. When I said that schlepping the kids up and down the stairs must be exhausting, Colville-Andersen looked surprised.

"No, not at all. Living in Copenhagen, you stay in good shape. The couple below us never complain about the stairs, and they're in their seventies."

After dinner, we took a stroll to a local high school gymnasium, where Copenhageners were lining up to cast votes in the municipal and regional elections. The ballots, which were the size of beach towels, included candi-dates running for the Nihilist People's Party under the slogan: "It's all meaningless anyway, so waste your vote on us." As we walked back to his flat, a compact car made a jerky exit from a driveway, braking just inches short of clipping the stroller he was pushing his two-year-old daughter in. Whistling reproachfully, Colville-Andersen held up a finger and a thumb, indicating how near she'd come to taking out his Lulu-Sophia.

Looking suitably contrite, the driver, a middle-aged woman, raised a hand to her mouth. It was a close call: society's sacred bull had almost claimed another victim.

The Happiness Factor

I was starting to worry myself. Normally, I find northern European envi-ronmental rectitude a little aggravating; nothing is more tedious, after all, than a Scandinavian harangue about living clean and green. But the

Danes were different—I had to *ask* why their cities seemed to work so well; mostly they just pedaled around, looking healthy and happy. I seemed to be succumbing to the Danish equivalent of Stockholm syndrome, where, after intense exposure to an alien ideology, you develop excessive sympathy for your captors. When it came to the urban issues that stumped every other city on the planet—transportation, energy policy, reducing congestion— Copenhageners seemed to have it all figured out. *Of course*, I said to myself, a city needs to invest in high-quality bike paths and the best subway and commuter train network it can afford—it made getting around so much easier. *Of course*, a city that wants to encourage livability should favor pedestrian spaces and discourage car use—it only stands to reason. And though I had no reason to stay, I found I didn't want to leave. Copenhagen seemed like an ideal place to settle down and raise a family. Everything just made so much sense.

Take the way Copenhageners heat their homes. While 16 percent of the nation's power comes from wind and solar energy, nine in ten Copenhageners rely on district heating, in which heat generated by electricity production is channeled through super-insulated pipes to homes throughout Greater Copenhagen. While most Danish electricity plants still burn coal, district heating is so efficient its carbon footprint is lower even than electricity from hydro dams. (The steaming manholes of Manhattan, by the way, are a legacy of the New York Steam Company's district heating system, which dates from 1882 and still provides heat to about 2,000 customers.) Though their economy has grown by 70 percent in the last thirty years, Danes use the same amount of energy today as they did in 1980.

Contrasting German, Dutch, and Danish cycling levels with the low levels of bike use in American and British cities, Rutgers University planning professor John Pucher has observed, "The differences are enlightening because all of them are democratic, capitalist, affluent societies with nearly universal car ownership. The success of cycling does not depend on poverty, dictatorial regimes or the lack of motorized transport options to force people onto bikes." Bicycles were once seen as symbols of underdevelopment—the pedaling hordes of Chinese cities under Chairman Mao, dreaming of the day they would be free to buy a Honda or a Ford. Yet Denmark, where unemployment currently sits at half the American rate, is regularly ranked in the top ten of the world's most competitive societies. Most households do have access to a car—Copenhageners just choose not to use them in their city.

If we want to "Copenhagenize" our cities—to borrow the buzzword favored by Jan Gehl and Mikael Colville-Andersen—or build car-free communities like Vauban, a good way to start the process would be to introduce bike-share schemes and gradually limit downtown parking, while slowly pedestrianizing certain streets. The lesson of Freiburg, Strasbourg, and Copenhagen, however, is that no single initiative is enough to bring real change: it takes intelligent transport policy, linking streetcars, buses, and metros with bike lanes and intercity rail, to create a truly integrated transport network. The biggest impediment to changing cities in the United States is not the physical realities of New World urban structure, but in our habits of thought. The communitarian traditions that made such co-housing projects as Freiburg's Vauban and Copenhagen's Potato Rows, bike-share schemes like City Bikes, and urban communes like Christiania natural developments in Northern Europe tend to be rare on the ground in North America—a continent founded, after all, by individualists who were often fleeing the demands of community in crowded, class-stratified, premodern cities. But times have changed, on both sides of the Atlantic, and there's a lot we can learn from the way Europeans are making their cities more liveable.

You might figure that a gloomy, rainy northern capital like Copenhagen would push its citizens to depression. Taxes here are astronomically high: 59 percent in the upper echelons, half of which goes to the city. Fortunately, the Danes know how to enjoy themselves—if they weren't so busy smoking like chimneys, drinking like fish, and stuffing themselves with buttery baked goods, they would probably be the healthiest people on earth. As it is, they seem to be the happiest. When sociologists undertake international surveys of life satisfaction, the Danes consistently come out on top. What's more, Danish happiness levels have been steadily rising over the last twenty years, while in the United States they remain flat. Yet you don't hear many Danes boasting about their well-being. It's as though, after discovering the formula for a felicitous and fulfilling urban life, Copenhageners decided to just get out and enjoy it.

On one of my last nights in Copenhagen, I put a bottle of wine in my backpack and pedaled up Nørrebrogade to visit a couple I'd met at a close friend's wedding. Maibritt was born in Denmark, but her husband, Jon, had emigrated from Canada ten years before. As their baby played on the floor, I asked for their take on the whole question of Danish happiness.

Like any modest Dane, Maibritt reacted with a laugh and a shrug, but Jon had a theory.

"I tell you, since we moved here, I've been biking about twenty miles a day to and from work," he said. "Maibritt's been using bikes for transport her whole life. When it's cold and dark, somehow you get a real high out of the challenge. In Copenhagen, people take pride in managing to bike in all weather. I know this may sound simplistic, but I actually think Danes are happy because they ride their bikes so much. It definitely contributes to people's sense of well-being. Being outside, getting that little bit of exercise every day—somehow it makes a huge difference."

It wouldn't surprise me at all if riding a bike was one of the secrets behind Danish happiness. Even though the temperature never rose above the mid-40s during my stay, I felt as relaxed after a week of cycling in Copenhagen as if I'd been on a vacation to a tropical beach resort. For most of my life as a cyclist, I've felt like an afterthought on the civic landscape, a barely tolerated nuisance forced to adopt the guerilla tactics of a courier to survive the daily obstacle course of car doors and swerving taxis. In Copenhagen, I began to feel as though we cyclists were small, fleet-footed mammals among the city's few remaining saurian automobiles, a species doomed to go the way of the *Diplodocus*.

Unfortunately, there is a downside to the Copenhagen syndrome: it can ruin you for other cities. A ride on the high-speed trains of Europe, and a visit to the world's first post-automobile city made me realize how mired in twentieth-century thinking we are in North America. Auto dependency is a vicious circle: if you live in sprawl and drive all your life, by the end of your life the only thing you're fit for is driving. (The corollary is equally true: the more time you spend walking and cycling in a day—or walking up a few flights of stairs—the healthier you're likely to be. The Danish obesity rate is three times lower than the American rate.) Escaping from congestion and pollution will almost certainly involve building multibillion-dollar transit and intercity rail networks. But initiating the virtuous cycle of municipal transformation might be as simple as what the happy Danes have been doing for a while now.

Hopping on a bike, and starting to pedal.

Why the modernization of the Soviet Union
started with the hanging of chandeliers beneath the earth I didn't know. But I did know
that when I was underground, I felt free.

—Alexander Kaletski, *Metro*, 1985

6. Fools and Roads

Moscow, Russia

I knew I was in for a wait when my taxi driver leaned back and offered me a cigarette. I declined, so he shrugged and lit one himself, dangling his sun-mottled left hand out the window while tracking the progress of a leggy woman in a tight dress on the opposite sidewalk. I didn't complain about the smoke. There was a good cross breeze going, and the Marlboro was an improvement on the exhaust from the Soviet-era truck idling next to us. I watched as skeins of white seed puffs wafted down the street and accumulated around the tires of immobile Ladas and Renaults like snow-drifts.

We were stuck in traffic in one of the middle lanes of Moscow's Garden Ring Road, the interlinked boulevards that circle the Kremlin at a distance of about a mile and a half. I was running late for a meeting at a café near Red Square, so I had the desk clerk at my hotel phone call me a taxi. The alternative was a *chastnik*—one of the private, unmarked cabs that can be hailed almost instantaneously by stepping to the curb and extending a pointed hand downward—but I didn't trust my haggling skills. The driver of the taxi, a yellow Ford Focus II, furrowed his brow at my accent, but when I pointed out my destination on a map, he said, *"Da, da,"* and gestured for me to get in the back. After three blocks of good progress, all pretense of mobility ended, and for ten minutes we remained at a dead stop. The woman in the tight red dress was long gone. Putting her long legs to good use, she had disappeared into a pedestrian underpass.

Being stuck in Moscow traffic is the modern version of waiting in a Soviet breadline—a limbo apt for the rueful contemplation of the failure of systems. In the final decades of Communism, box-shaped Ladas and Moskvitches were pumped out in such Russian Detroits as Tolyatti, but the waiting list for a car of one's own could stretch to ten years. The fall of Communism brought an end to the hated *propiska*, the permit that restricted residency in Moscow, and in its absence Ukrainians, rural Russians, and Central Asians poured into the capital, all of them in the market for that long-denied emblem of personal sovereignty, the privately owned automobile. Imported Japanese and German cars flooded the market, and then Ford, Toyota, and Renault set up their own factories on Russian soil to avoid import tariffs. In 1990, there were 400,000 cars registered in Moscow. Today, there are four million, a figure the Russian Transportation Ministry expects to double by 2015.

There just isn't room for all of them. In North America's most sprawling car-based metropolises, transportation infrastructure—the freeways, arterials, and side streets designed to make mobility possible—accounts for up to 30 percent of land area. Transport infrastructure in Moscow makes up only 9 *percent* of its surface area. Yet new cars continue to pour in, at the rate of 300,000 a year. Muscovites are apparently under the collective delusion they can squeeze an Atlanta or a Houston into a city the size of a Paris or a Berlin.

The result, predictably, is traffic hell. In central Moscow, average car speeds have now fallen to 13 miles per hour, the same as Manhattan's pokiest crosstown buses. As there is no paid street parking, drivers park their cars in crosswalks and up against the doors of apartment buildings, forcing pedestrians into the street. Municipal politicians have seriously considered a German scheme to lay roadways over the roofs of residential apartment buildings, or erect double-decked highways above the tracks of Russian Railways. Muscovites now suffer the world's longest traffic delays: at least once every three years, they report being stuck in traffic for two and a half hours at a time, and congestion costs Moscow's economy $1.3 billion a year. Three days before New Year's 2011, a combination of snow and holiday shoppers caused a backup of cars that, had they been stretched bumper to bumper, would have reached over the Alps and all the way to Barcelona. Many Muscovites simply walked away from their cars, returning to shovel them out a couple of days later.

I had come to Moscow, in part, to see what the traffic in a developing economy with rapidly rising car ownership looked like. In such megacities as Lagos and Bangkok, average traffic speeds have slowed to a walking pace; in São Paulo, where daily backups routinely reach 160 miles, the rich have taken to traveling by helicopter; and in Mumbai, motorists now have to budget three hours' travel time to make it to crosstown appointments. (At the 2010 South Asian Games, India's champions actually failed to appear at the closing ceremonies because they were stuck in traffic.) The view from a car window in the center lane of an expressway in Moscow, I quickly realized, is about the same as it is in Shanghai, Hyderabad, or Johannesburg: multiple lanes of cars, trucks, and vans, going nowhere, filled with pained passengers and even more aggravated-looking drivers. From megacity to megacity, only the smell of the exhaust and the makes of the vehicles seem to change.

But in Moscow, it turns out, there is one surefire way to cut through even the densest traffic. Behind us, a siren whooped, and red-and-blue lights flashed in our rearview mirror. Three black Mercedes surged past us, playing a sustained game of chicken with oncoming traffic. Muttering something under his breath, my driver flicked his cigarette in the direction of the sinister cortege as it bullied a channel for itself between lanes with its obnoxious sound-and-light show.

"*Migalki?*" I echoed, imagining he'd uttered the family name of some oligarch.

"*Migalki! Migalki!*" he repeated, pointing to the cab's roof as he imitated the whooping sound.

Migalki are the rooftop lights that flash with epileptic fit–inducing insistency on the roofs of the BMWs and Mercedes of the Russian elite. Officially, fewer than one thousand VIPs in all of Russia, among them Vladimir Putin and the Patriarch of the Orthodox Church, have the right to use the flashing lights, and then only when they are on official business. But one Web site has posted amateur photos of 1,200 distinct *migalki*-bearing cars in the Moscow area alone. Muscovites say that black-market permits for the flashing lights can be bought for as little as $10,000—a not unreasonable premium to pay for guaranteed mobility. In one widely reported case, when a young woman refused to pull over for an unmarked Mercedes being escorted by police cars, the driver followed her home and threatened to have her license revoked—anonymous tipsters later pointed to the twenty-one-year-old son of Russia's prosecutor general. In another incident, the vice president of the country's largest oil company slammed his siren-bearing Mercedes into a Citroën, killing the driver and her daughter-in-law, both of them doctors. Widespread disgust with such elite misbehavior has led a group called the Blue Buckets Society to stage spontaneous protests, printing up bumper stickers that read, "Servant of the people, take off your flashing lights!"—its members have also rampaged, with buckets over their heads to hide their identities, over the roofs of luxury sedans double-parked outside the Kremlin.

At this point, I was already half an hour late for my appointment. Stranded in the middle of twelve lanes of traffic, I began to long for the sidewalk as a raft-bound sailor must for a seashore belted by dangerous reefs. Then I saw it: less than two hundred yards away, a stylized red "M" on a pole, with an arrow pointing to a staircase that disappeared beneath the sidewalk.

Leaning forward, I pointed to the sign: "*Metro! Metro!*"

The driver understood immediately, and in a matter of minutes he'd worked his way over to the curb. I tipped him a hundred rubles and ran toward the Metro.

Russia, wrote Nikolai Gogol, has only two misfortunes: fools and roads. I'd completed my first Russian lesson: in Moscow, only fools use the road. Real life, and actual movement, is elsewhere—namely, underground.

Gulag Baroque

I'd come to Moscow not only to see the hell emerging on its streets but also to see the paradise beneath them—and because no straphanger's round-the-world journey would be complete without a trip to the legendary Moscow underground. New York's subway has grit, London's Tube has history, and Paris's Métropolitain has glamour. But Moscow's Metro, I'd been told, had something I'd never seen in an urban transit system: full-on, unabashed splendor.

I knew I would need a guide to this sprawling museum. Anastasia, in her late twenties, fluent in English and French, had volunteered to play the docent, and we'd arranged to meet at the terrace of a café surrounded by musical conservatories, a ten-minute walk from the Kremlin gates.

I apologized for arriving late. "You took taxi?" she said. "From now on, take Metro. Is fastest. With Metro, you can be anywhere in Moscow in thirty minutes. When you take car, you can never be sure."

The tour began at Komsomolskaya station. After pausing to applaud a sloppily dressed string quintet's precisely rendered version of Mozart's *Eine Kleine Nachtmusik*, we followed the crowds to a line in front of a ticket booth in a high-ceilinged vestibule. As my turn approached, Anastasia whispered a magic incantation into my ear; I repeated it, and the woman behind the glass handed me a cardboard ticket.

"*Diesyet bileti*," ten tickets, is the "Open, Sesame" that unlocks the gates to Moscow.

Every Metro station, explained Anastasia as she strode ahead of me, shares a few common features. First, you will encounter banks of turnstiles, inevitably overseen by grim-faced women in late middle age. When things are quiet, these uniformed babushkas sit in plexiglass booths doing the Cyrillic version of word-search puzzles. When rush hours approach, they run about like fierce little dogs, blowing their whistles at fare skippers and rule breakers. (We watched as one such attendant yelled, in vain, at a long-haired woman in flower-print bell-bottoms and a matching linen jacket who strode willfully through the gates, preceded by a giant black poodle.) Second, you will see escalators, many of whose risers are still topped with wooden slats, which move fast and go deep. (*Really* fast and *really* deep. To give you an idea: though the escalators at Park Pobody, the world's deepest subway station, are one and a half times faster than those in the London Underground, they still take three full minutes to reach the platforms, which are located 32 stories beneath street level.) As we scrolled diagonally past businessmen in ties, school kids in uniforms, and workers in paint-splattered overalls, the thrumming under our feet felt like an extended drumroll, preparing us for the third and main act: the *Zal* or central hall that precedes the platforms of most stations, like the victory hall in a baron's mansion.

"Every *Zal* has different decoration," said Anastasia, as we entered a secular temple of late-Stalinist kitsch. Two rows of marble-faced columns topped with Corinthian capitals supported a canary yellow barrel-vaulted ceiling, from which dangled immense circular electroliers, leading to a bust of a supercilious Lenin beneath the gilded coat of arms of the Soviet Union. It was subterranean Gulag Baroque—Liberace's basement ballroom if it had been decorated by master propagandists. The theme of Komsomolskaya, Anastasia explained, was the Russian fight for freedom through the ages, from Alexander Nevsky's Battle on the Ice to the Soviet troops' raising of a red flag over the Reichstag, all rendered in elaborately framed ceiling mosaics. When the station opened in 1952, the last of the eight mosaics showed a half-dozen Soviet luminaries casting the banners of the defeated Nazis in front of Lenin's tomb. As each politician suffered reverses, his likeness was excised, tile by tile: first Stalin's chief of secret police disappeared, then Deputy Premier Molotov, and finally Lazar Kaganovich, the man responsible for building the Metro's first lines. Nikita Khrushchev's de-Stalinization campaign brought the ultimate retouch: all human figures were replaced by a scowling Mother Russia, who can be seen raising a hammer and sickle in her left hand while crushing a swastika and eagle beneath her bare feet.

"Come, come," beckoned Anastasia, as a train arrived on one of the side platforms. "We have many stations to see." We slipped into a Circle Line train, half empty in midafternoon. There is nothing remarkable about the Metro's aging rolling stock—the heavy-duty trains are painted gun-metal gray and run on wide-gauge tracks on a third-rail system, piloted by grim-faced, underpaid drivers—except for the unforgiving doors, which slam shut with guillotine-like ferocity. What amazes is their frequency. At the mouth of every tunnel, a wall-mounted display counts the seconds since the last train left the station; I rarely saw the counter get past two minutes, and during the rush hours, headways were as brief as 90 seconds— the kind of efficiency normally achieved only by automatic, driverless systems. Most trains are eight cars long, and the Moscow Metro maintains an average throughput of 6.5 million passengers a day—nine million on busy days—giving it the highest ridership in Europe. Globally it is surpassed only by the two separately owned companies that run Tokyo's Metro.

Anastasia said that rush hour crowding could be awful. "When there are many people, I dislike taking Metro," she said. Her worst experience happened not on a train, but in the station, as she attempted to leave. "It was Friday evening, on the way to railroad station. Everybody was in a hurry to get a train, but only one escalator was working. I got stuck in the crowd, and spent one hour just trying to exit. I missed my train, of course!"

Our next stop was Novoslobodskaya. "In my opinion," said Anastasia, "this is the most beautiful station." I could see its appeal. The *Zal* was decorated by Latvian artists, who had assembled stained-glass tributes to the life of the mind—a pianist in a tuxedo and tails seated at a piano, an intellectual at a desk bent over a newspaper, a palette-wielding painter at his easel—and the brass frames, pinkish marble, and warm lighting contributed to a sensation of being in an airy, skylit atrium.

The impression of lightness, I found, was strongest in Mayakovskaya station, named after Vladimir Mayakovsky, the globe-trotting Futurist poet who, disillusioned by the realities of Stalinism, committed suicide by shooting himself in the chest after being denied a visa to travel abroad. The station's theme was "A Day in the Land of the Soviets," and the ceiling of the central hall featured three-dozen cupolas, each dimpled at its center with an oval mosaic medallion. Anastasia showed me how you had to position yourself below a medallion to view it properly, just as you would to see the all-seeing eyes of the Pantocrator on the dome of an Orthodox cathedral. Each showed an inspiring image of the Russian sky: a zeppelin soaring above a red star–topped skyscraper, a bomber overflying electric power lines, ski jumpers in crimson suits airborne over pine trees. Impressively, the palate changed as you moved down the platform, progressing from the blues and grays of pre-dawn gloom to yellows and whites corresponding to midday in the center, and back to crepuscular tones at the far end.

The Moscow Metro, in the words of its master builder, Lazar Kaganovich, was meant to be a rebuke to the "gloomy, monotonous, and dismal" subways of the capitalist world. He deliberately built its ceilings twice as high as those in Berlin's U-Bahn or New York's subway, and decorated it in a manner that "provides comfort, better spirits, and artistic delight" to its passengers, making them feel "as if in a palace." As we continued to explore, marveling at arches clad in stainless steel, and marble shipped from the Caucuses and Urals or stripped from the original Cathedral of

Christ the Savior, I had to concede that the planners of the Communist subway had succeeded where others had failed. For all its lapses into bad taste, the Moscow Metro is the one subway system explicitly designed to ennoble and uplift the long-suffering straphangers of the world.

And Muscovites remain fond of their Metro; people linger on the platforms, and arrange to meet friends in the cavernous *Zals*. Our last stop was Revolution Square, where seventy-six life-size statues of heroes of the Soviet Union—engineers with rolled blueprints, a schoolgirl with a book in one hand and a rifle in the other—crouch or squat on square plinths beneath arches of red and brown marble. Noticing that the nose of a sculpted German shepherd with erect ears, nestled beneath the arm of a border guard, had been burnished shiny, we asked a young woman in tight jeans why she was giving his snout a good rub. "For good luck, of course!" she told Anastasia.

Our tour ended in the octagonal vestibule of the Kurskaya station, on the Circle Line. Above the heads of striding commuters, pallid caryatids extended their arms toward black Cyrillic characters that circled the room above the capitals of columns.

I asked Anastasia what they meant. "That's the words of anthem of Soviet Union." Swiveling her head, she read aloud: "'Stalin raised us on loyalty to people. He inspired us to labor and be heroes.' Those are old words. I think they are changed now."

She hummed a few bars of her nation's de-Communized anthem, which now speaks of "a holy nation" and "a free Fatherland."

"Yes," she said, with a wry smile. "The music stays the same, but the words have changed."

Back at street level, among the 24-hour Dunkin' Donuts, Mercedes billboards, and girls in miniskirts handing out free cans of Coke, we exchanged cheek kisses and said our good-byes. Two all-day tickets to this museum of forgotten ideology—this Louvre of the Revolution—had cost us 44 rubles, or less than 78 cents each.

The Building of the Socialist Subway

The Moscow Metro is transit with a thesis. It was meant to prove that Communist central planning could do a better job of serving the daily transportation needs of people than the crowded, inefficient subways built by capitalists.

By the 1920s, Moscow's very existence was in question. The early city had grown as a series of concentric forts emanating from the Kremlin, that ultimate stronghold located, in one form or another, on the Moskva River since the fourteenth century. Abandoned as the capital in favor of master-planned, Europeanized St. Petersburg in the eighteenth century, Moscow became an undergoverned patchwork of onion-domed churches and monasteries, "gentry nests" of Parisian-style apartment blocks with shops on the ground floor, and highly inflammable wooden buildings that regularly caught fire and razed entire neighborhoods. After 1850, railway building spurred the development at the outskirts of dacha zones, clusters of summer cottages that soon enough became grimy industrial villages. In the chaos following the 1917 Revolution, Moscow became a Bolshevik ghost town, losing half its population of two million as citizens fled the collapsing city for the countryside.

When Muscovites gradually returned to the new Soviet capital, they found a transportation system in chaos. Private horse-drawn cabs and the few motorized taxis had been confiscated by the state, and the tramway system, which had been municipalized at the turn of the century, failed to keep pace with the hundreds of factories and mills being built in the Soviet drive to industrialize. On the overcrowded streetcars, deaths and severed limbs were daily occurences, and even after the Moscow City Railroad Trust was put under "proletarian control," workers still faced four-hour commutes. Meanwhile, an influential group known as the disurbanists, who called for the abandonment of crowded cities in favor of the healthful countryside—a plan that recalls Frank Lloyd Wright's Broadacre City— questioned the very need for mass transit, claiming that the London Underground and New York subway were exploitative of the working class and made commuters into "human porridge." Building a subway during a housing shortage, these utopian socialist planners argued, was tantamount to "buying a silk top hat for a man without trousers": if you had to prop up dying cities, rubber-wheeled buses would be cheaper and more efficient. (H. G. Wells agreed, and advised the Soviets to invest in a thousand London buses.)

Far from dying, by the early 1930s Moscow had become a victim of its success. As peasant refugees arrived in search of work, Moscow, like London in the 1850s and New York in the 1880s, hit a wall, as pervasive traffic jams stifled progress toward the workers' utopia. By 1931, the newly ascendent Stalinist leadership had decided the disurbanists' plans were semi-fanatical nonsense, and declared cities—and with them subways—the key to the Communist future. The handsome and charismatic Lazar Kaganovich, Stalin's second-in-command, was put in charge of building the "world's best metro."

Unfortunately, nobody seemed to know how to build a subway; only a very few Russians had even used one. Kaganovich was a bootmaker by trade, and the nation's only subway expert was in prison for economic sabotage. (In his memoirs, Nikita Khrushchev, who began his career as Kaganovich's deputy, confessed: "We thought of the subway as something almost supernatural. I think it's probably easier to contemplate space flights today than it was for us to contemplate the construction of the Moscow Metro.") The building of the first station began in November 1931, with a dozen men hacking at the frozen ground with shovels and pickaxes.

Yet the overseers of Soviet Moscow had two enormous advantages over their capitalist peers: limitless powers of expropriation, and access to a huge labor pool. After months of sluggish progress, the Metro was declared a "shock" project, and its engineers were given priority access to supplies and personnel. To build the first line, dozens of churches and tsarist monuments were razed, as was Hunters' Row, a convivial all-night market street. Early on, construction of shallow stations broke water mains, opened craters in the street, and caused buildings to collapse; to avoid further chaos in the streets, Stalin decreed that the Metro be dug deep, in the apparently stable layer of Jurassic clay that started 45 feet beneath the surface. The jailed subway expert was freed, and in 1933 thousands of *Komsomoltsy*—members of the Communist Youth League, many of them women who faced daily taunts and harassment from male coworkers—began to work in the tunnels. Progress further accelerated when tens of thousands of *subbotnik* workers pitched in—in return for voluntary work for the glory of Mother Russia, these "Saturday people" were given a subway ticket, good for one free ride when the subway was completed. At its height, a workforce of 74,000, with an average age of twenty-three, was employed building the first line of the Metro. In the absence of pneumatic drills, the tunneling was done almost entirely with picks, shovels, and muscle power.

Unlike other Stalinist shock projects, like the Moscow-Volga Canal, which was dug by Gulag prisoners, the Moscow Metro was not built with forced labor. But workers were obliged to live on daily rations of a few hundred grams of meat, bread, and cooking oil and walk miles from under-heated, hastily built barracks. Many spent all day in tunnels filled waist-deep with water, where oxygen levels were often so low matches wouldn't light. Even the idealistic Young Communists were appalled by such conditions, and almost half the recruits failed to report for work.

Yet the first line was completed in 1935, with the Soviet leadership crowing that Soviet ingenuity had permitted the world's greatest construction project to be achieved in record time. Actually, the seven-mile line took twice as long to build as the Paris métro's line 1, which was virtually the same length but required a workforce just one-twentieth the size. And Soviet engineers proved more adept at industrial skullduggery than genuine innovation. Given a sample subway car by Siemens in anticipation of huge sales, they completely dismantled it, built a copy, and returned the original to the German firm with their sincere thanks. Stringing along salesmen from escalator maker Otis with promises of big orders, they managed to milk them for enough technical details to build their own versions. (The Metro's famous escalators are virtually identical to those in the London Underground.) The technology of the tunneling shield came from England, and the process for freezing earth before pouring concrete was borrowed from Germany. The new socialist transit system was not even all that rapid—the trains reached 16 miles per hour, barely a third of the speed that New York City's express trains had attained thirty years before.

And, at least at first, the people who built the Metro could not afford to ride it: a single token cost 50 kopecks, which, in relation to the income of the average worker, was ten times higher than New York's nickel fare. (The price would drop to five kopecks after the Second World War, and today it is one of the world's cheapest big-city subways.) The stations were far apart; the average distance between stops is still a mile, which means many Muscovites face a long and, in winter, cold walk to get to transit. All told, building the first line consumed one-fifth of the municipal budget during a time of nationwide famine and a citywide housing shortage.

Yet there was something undeniably special about the Moscow Metro. "It is the first subway in which beauty has been attempted," conceded a *New York Times* reporter upon its opening. It was famously immaculate: a Muscovite, it was said, would sooner spit on somebody else's coat than on the marble floors of the Metro. Though not conceived for the purposes of defense, its deep stations did double duty as bomb shelters—almost three hundred children were born underground during the Second World War—and the Kirov Station became Stalin's military command post.*

The Koltsevaya, or Circle, line was completed in the early '50s to link the lines radiating from the center. (An almost certainly apocryphal story holds that the line was built after Stalin slammed down a coffee cup on a planner's map in disgust; the resulting stain was interpreted as a command, and the Circle Line was born.) Under Nikita Khrushchev's rule, Stalinist excess was replaced by modernism and clean lines, but lately there has been a return to the tradition of more elaborate station design. Opened in 2010, the Dostoyevskaya station on line 10 features a wall-sized portrait of the author of *Crime and Punishment*, and is surely the only transit stop in the world whose official decor includes a mural of a would-be nihilist ax-murdering an elderly pawnbroker.

Most of all, Moscow's Metro proved that an urban subway network did not have to be a gloomy, claustrophobia-inducing warren. "It was a place where a government had elected to honor the heart and soul on par with politics and profit," writes the Russian-born author Boris Fishman, "where the Soviet citizen, otherwise forced to live a double life of faked enthusiasm, could for a moment feel a harmony between his private and public self; where even the Soviet dream remained alive."

Today, of course, it has become the mausoleum of that dream. Yet in spite of the immense social cost, the Moscow Metro was a farsighted investment. Beneath the billboards and Bentley dealerships of the new Moscow, the old Stalinist gear works keep turning. And the Metro may be the one space where you can still find a semblance of the value system the Soviet system claimed to embody.

One morning I was standing on one of the Circle Line trains above a teenage girl who was sitting on a bench seat, tapping her feet to the electronic pop on her MP3 player. At the Belorusskaya stop, a tiny and very ancient woman made a beeline for the bench seat and, planting herself

* Since the 1950s, there have been persistent rumors about something called "Metro Dva," or Metro-2. The four lines of this secret metro are said to center on the Kremlin, with stations up to 700 feet deep, encompassing twenty bunkers and fifteen factories. Stalin was rumored to have a private entrance, and his henchmen apparently used it to travel around the city quickly, keeping Party members in a state of constant panic. According to legend, each twentieth-century premier added or extended lines, so that even Boris Yeltsin could take a train directly to his dacha. Though some Muscovites I met had heard rumors about Metro-2, none knew where it was, nor knew anybody who had seen it. Nor could any confirm another intriguing urban legend: that some of Moscow's large population of feral dogs had learned to ride the Metro to commute to better scavenging grounds.

directly in front of the girl, gave an upward tick of her chin that eloquently conveyed both command and reproach. The girl leapt up as if she'd been hit by a cattle prod. With great satisfaction, the old woman settled into her rightful place. I saw similar scenes repeated daily. Underground, there are no *migalki*, no flashing lights giving priority to the wealthy; an older social hierarchy prevails, one where the elderly, the weary, and the disabled still get the consideration they deserve.

Fortunately, government officials are fully aware of how crucial the Metro is to the capital's continued functioning. The system now counts 182 stations on twelve lines, more miles of track are being added every year, and fares account for 70 percent of revenue, which means the Metro requires only modest subsidies from the state.

Though Moscow Metro's builders failed to prove that the idealism of Communist workers would inevitably result in the world's best subway, they showed that dignity and even grandeur could be engineered into mass transit—and that is an achievement that transcends ideology.

Terror Underground

It's something you notice right away. Not only do Muscovites like their Metro; they are actually proud of it. Even bombs won't stop them from using it.

On March 29, 2010, at the height of the morning rush hour, a bomb went off as commuters were leaving a crowded train at Lubyanka station, killing twenty-six; forty minutes later, a blast at the Park Kultury station killed fourteen more and injured dozens. Caught on security cameras, the culprits, whom the media dubbed "Black Widows," turned out to be female Islamist separatists from the Caucusus who had detonated explosive belts as they stepped onto the platforms.

The slaughter and ensuing panic—each bomb was packed with bolts and screws and the equivalent of three pounds of dynamite, and provoked stampedes in which dozens were trampled—would have been enough to completely paralyze any other metropolis. But even after the second bomb went off, the Metro's managers refused to shut down the system; to do so, they confessed, would have meant chaos in the streets of Moscow. As it was, rush hour traffic on the streets was so impenetrable that ambulances couldn't reach the bomb sites; the wounded had to be helicoptered to hospitals.

Visiting Moscow two months after the blasts, I feared I would find the system deserted, or used only by gray-faced wraiths with their heads down. But in the vast central halls, which are cool when the city above swelters in summer heat, and warm and bright when the streets are slushy and dark, people waited for friends, texted on cell phones, and generally treated the Metro like the most welcoming of public spaces. A plastic-wrapped red rose, left on the floor in the *Zal* of the Lubyanka station, was the only reminder of the bombings. Intrigued by this apparent indifference to danger, I asked some Muscovites if the bombings had changed their attitude to riding the Metro.

Just outside Lubyanka station, where the first bomb had gone off, a woman in her early sixties, dressed in faded jeans, sandals, and a blazer made of roughly sewn leather patches, was removing a stack of pamphlets from her purse. Behind her loomed the intimidating mustard-yellow facade of the former KGB headquarters, now the head office of the Federal Security Service.

Her name was Valentina Pavlova; she said she had been riding the Metro since she was a child. She now lived on Moscow's northern outskirts near Sergiyev Posad, one of Russia's greatest monasteries. Every weekday, she rode a commuter train to Komsomolskaya Square; there she transferred to the Metro. The trip took about an hour and a half.

"I have an aunt who lives in the center of Moscow, she's eighty-four," Pavlova explained. "There's nobody to watch her, so I take care of her. That's the way we'll all be one day—you can't always be young."

To supplement her pension, Pavlova handed out flyers to passersby. When the bomb went off at Lubyanka, she was already out on the street working. "Within ten minutes, everybody knew something bad had happened," she said. "People came out of the Metro, they were all in shock." I asked her if she rode the Metro home that day. "Of course! Only the center part of the city was involved. The rest was good." I asked her if she'd been afraid. "No! I'm more afraid to be in a car in Moscow. It is more dangerous. My husband had a car, but he has been dead for twenty years. The Metro is the best way of traveling. There is never a problem. Sometimes a train is too crowded, but you just wait a minute—always another train comes."

Excusing herself, Pavlova said she had work to do. I left her on the sidewalk, a tiny, gray-haired woman, trying to get rushing businessmen to accept pamphlets for a weight-loss program.

Outside the Park Kultury station, where the second bomb had gone off, Maria Agalarova was catching a bit of sun. The eighteen-year-old, whose eyes were hidden behind huge round sunglasses, was trying to calm her nerves before an exam at the Moscow State Linguistic University, where she attended classes. She said her commute, on the Gray Line from her parents' apartment near the Prazshkaya Metro Station, was not too hard: six days a week, she left home at eight in the morning, and was at school by nine.

"I was sick, thanks God, the day of the bombing," she said. "I'm lucky, I guess. Two people from our university died that day. People gave charity to their families, and for nine days there were flowers in the Metro station." She knew some students who avoided the Metro for a few days after the bombing. "But not everybody has money to take a taxi every day." I asked her if she hoped to buy a car. "I don't think so. Even if someone gave me one, I think I wouldn't use it. There's too much traffic, and the Metro is faster." I told her that had a similar incident happened in North America many people would have sworn off transit. "Russian people are kind of brave, I guess. But really, there is no other choice. Life has to go on."

Such professions of sangfroid were common. Igor Vladimirovich, a construction site manager, was on the Metro the morning of the attacks. "I missed the second bomb by fifteen minutes. I had just left the station, here at Park Kultury," he said. In his late fifties, with a thick but whitening mustache and wearing a neatly pressed blue shirt, he stood aloof and erect, calmly scanning the crowds outside the station for a colleague's face. "I saw the Special Intelligence forces, all dressed in black, rushing to the station. But then I left, because I had a meeting." Did he get back on the Metro the same day? "*Da*," he said. "It was no problem. I was a colonel in Afghanistan, a tank commander, in the eighties. I saw much worse in the war." Vladimirovich owned a Ford Mondeo, but he said he didn't use it in Moscow. "In the day, it's impossible to get around by car. You will miss every appointment. I park it and use the Metro." I asked if there was any stigma attached to riding public transport, as there is in some American cities. "*Nyet*," he said. "You see middle managers and even big businessmen riding the Metro." Warming to the subject, he continued: "I have seen other metros, like Kiev's and Berlin's. They are simple, like American subways, without any beauty. Stalin wanted to build a great metro, and he did."

The stoicism of Muscovites may strike some as cold-blooded, but from

Basque explosives in Madrid department stores to IRA pub bombings, Europe has a long history of urban terrorism. Bombs in Madrid's main railway station in 2004 killed almost two hundred, and explosions in London's buses and Underground the following year killed over fifty.

There are those who condemn subways and buses because they create dense crowds and provide tempting targets for terrorists. But you can say the same thing about cruise ships, the Stanley Cup play-offs, shopping malls, or Daytona Beach at spring break. It is the same bunker logic that led Frank Lloyd Wright to promote Broadacre City as a way of protecting Usonians against aerial bombing, or freeway proponents to advocate low-density subdivisions and bomb shelters as a safeguard against nuclear attack. To give up on cities because they happen to bring people together is to give up on civilization itself.

I had seen cell phone videos of Lubyanka's bloodied marble and smoke-filled halls, and I confess to feeling the occasional twinge of dread as I waited on the platform. Terrorists, of course, are betting their desperate efforts will provoke just such fear—enough to shut down an entire metropolis, if only for a few days. That this has utterly failed to happen is a tribute to the vitality of urban life. In Europe, abandoning the city has never been a serious option. Madrileños, Londoners, and Muscovites have shown that the best way to cope with terrorism is to simply get out of bed the next day and get back on the subway, bus, or train.

Their reasoning is sound. A study published by the Victoria Transport Policy Institute after the London bombings of 2005 showed that, even factoring in all the terrorist incidents of the last decade, riding transit is still ten times safer, per passenger mile, than traveling by car anywhere in the world. In Russia, which accounts for two-thirds of Europe's road fatalities, one hundred people die in automobile accidents every day. This means that, in one country alone, cars kill more people *every four days* than have died in all the attacks targeting public transport in Europe since 1990. The real terror, I figured, wasn't underground. As I walked back toward the Park Kultury station, I saw it was all around me on the streets of Moscow, where speeding oligarchs, road rage–filled skinheads, and the vodka-drunk of the new Russia could be seen cutting each other off, trying to bribe traffic cops, and driving their armor-plated BMWs up onto curbs.

Fortunately, I still had a few rides left on my Metro card.

The Ideology of Transit

One of the Cold War's most famous encounters occurred at Sokolniki Park, not far from where the Metro's first station opened. In 1959, then vice president Richard Nixon met premier Nikita Khrushchev in the kitchen of a model home, a replica of an actual ranch-style suburban from Millburn, New Jersey, that had been shipped overseas to give the Soviet people a glimpse of the American way of life. Nixon boasted that the General Electric oven and range, the washing machine topped with Dash detergent, and the government-backed, 25-year mortgage were all within reach of the average American steelworker. Scoffing at the electric lemon juicer, Khrushchev satirically asked if Americans also had machines that would spoon-feed them their dinner and chew it for them, too. Eyewitnesses say the kitchen debate, as it became known, had no clear victor, but Nixon, photographed confidently jabbing Khrushchev in the chest as he stressed America's lead in material goods, ended up winning the propaganda battle.

The next day, the Soviets struck back. First deputy premier Frol Kozlov, who had traveled extensively in the United States, told the assembled press that the New York subway was "lousy." He observed that in America "the subways are dirty and the air is bad—very bad." When a reporter asked how it could be improved, he replied: "You would just have to reconstruct it, I think." Indeed, riding the New York subway, with its forty-year-old trains and dirty stations, had by then become a depressing experience. Moscow, meanwhile, continued to open subterranean "Palaces for the People," and in the years that followed Leningrad, Prague, Bucharest, and other Eastern bloc cities would build modern and efficient metros. Such Cold War propaganda skirmishes still echo. In North America, cars and freeways continue to be associated with consumer choice and free markets, while subways and other forms of transit get linked to socialism, big government, and planned economies.

Authoritarian regimes do have an edge when it comes to building transportation networks: in the name of progress, they can marshall vast social and material resources, requisition workers like serfs, and wield eminent domain to clear away buildings or lives that happen to stand in the way of "progress." Contemporary examples abound: Singapore's Mass Rapid Transit system, whose futuristic Alstom trains snake between palm trees, housing developments, and corporate headquarters on elevated tracks, is a model of efficiency; to build it, Lee Kuan Yew and his People's Action Party razed shophouses and relocated countless families to brutalist housing developments. Shanghai's metro, which took only fifteen years to become the longest subway network in the world, was also built by bulldozing historic neighborhoods. While many Western transportation experts profess an admiration for Chinese efficiency, few condone Chinese methods. Wages for workers are low, hours are long, benefits few. Expropriated in the name of the "public good"—a concept that is broadly defined in China—residents who cling to their shops and homes have been beaten by thugs or driven to suicide. And Shanghai is just one example. By 2015, China will have spent $150 billion on rapid transit rail lines in twenty-five cities—a program of subway building unprecedented both in its scope and its impact on human lives.

As quickly as China digs subways, of course, it is also building new dams and roads. Which is a reminder that authoritarian states are at an advantage when it comes to building *any* vast public works project— including expressways. Fascist governments were among the earliest champions of car culture: Benito Mussolini opened the world's first true freeway, the *autostrada*, in 1924, and Adolf Hitler, who kept a portrait of Henry Ford in a place of honor at National Socialist headquarters, conceived his network of *autobahns* as a means of quickly mobilizing Nazi armies, with mass ownership of Volkswagens as the way of the future. Any agency that concentrates power, from Robert Moses's Triborough Bridge Authority to the Moscow Soviet, has an edge when it comes to coordinating big public works—precisely because it can brush aside the rights of citizens in the name of progress and the greater good. But mass transit no more leads to the tyranny of the masses than freeways and a free market in cars guarantees unfettered freedom of movement. Fascists have built plenty of freeways, and capitalist enterprise was responsible for most of the early horsecar, trolley, elevated and subway lines in the industrial cities of the West.

The twentieth century provided ample evidence that dictatorships can build impressive transportation systems. In the twenty-first, the challenge is to build good transit in democracies, with real buy-in from the public.

In the end, Muscovites don't favor their Stalinist Metro because it is filled with hammers and sickles and other symbols of a discredited ideology. They ride it because it is fast, cheap, and gets them where they want to go with comfort and dignity. In this, Moscow's straphangers show that transportation can no longer be about left and right; it has to be about what works—and, on an increasingly urbanized planet, what is sustainable.

The Passenger

There were times, I discovered, when driving on the broad boulevards of Moscow could be a pleasure.

I was being chauffered to Domodedovo International Airport, 26 miles southeast of Moscow, in extreme comfort. Catching one's plane in Russia, I had been warned, can be a challenge; more than one politician has missed his flight after getting stuck in traffic. But my driver seemed to be blessed, and we hit a never-ending succession of green lights. Occasionally, we would pass a rectangular city bus, as aerodynamic as a shoebox, but generally the roads were empty, and our progress steady.

There was no denying it: coccooned in the backseat of a Mercedes minivan, I appreciated the comfort and speed of private transportation. If you are willing to pay the price, you get convenience and a sense of security.

In the past, nobility meant mobility. Aristocrats in pre-revolutionary France used to send lackeys running ahead of their carriages with burning torches to warn peasants off the roads. In the days of the tsars, the passing of the carriage or sleigh of a Russian nobleman was announced by the manic jingling of bells. The Soviet *nomenklatura*, those *über*-proles in the dictatorship of the proletariat, appropriated aristocratic rights-of-way to barge through the streets in motorcades of Volga limousines.

"Russia has almost never belonged to the Russian people," author Boris Fishman has noted. "Historically, its bounty has been hoarded by a select few."

Today, oil oligarchs and upper-level bureaucrats use an electronic version of the aristocratic bells and torches in the form of sirens and flashing *migalki* to clear the hoi polloi out of their way. This has always been the appeal of the automobile, which is merely the nabob's carriage, democratized by industrialization: it removes its occupant from distasteful contact with the city—not to mention his, or her, fellow citizens.

It should come as no surprise that in authoritarian regimes the lucky few award themselves priority of movement. But in democracies, privileged mobility for the rich—whether it's in the form of Lexus lanes on California freeways, or the helipads on the roofs of Brazilian penthouses—is corrosive of all professed ideals of egalitarianism. (And this is why such subway-riding politicians as New York's Michael Bloomberg or Ken Livingstone, former mayor of London, make more than an empty gesture when they take public transport to work.) Separated from the places they govern by panes of glass, the thoughts of the chauffeur-driven naturally turn to ways to improve their own mobility—which usually involves building more parking lots and increasing road capacity. Moscow's latest Genplan, which programs the city's development to 2025, calls for the building of at least five-dozen buildings of over twenty stories and two million new parking spaces in central Moscow. To keep the city's cars moving, foot traffic is increasingly being directed into underpasses; rather than use a crosswalk, pedestrians are forced to traverse multilane boulevards by descending into gloomy, street-spanning passages. (The underpasses are often filled with tiny shops retailing bread, liquor, locks, and, this being post-Soviet Russia, the vendors of cell phones and porn DVDs.) For the convenience of drivers, the latest Genplan calls for the building of a hundred more such underpasses, turning the city's pedestrians into troglodytes.

Congestion caused by rapid motorization may be a global phenomenon, but while every metropolis with an emerging middle class is rushing down the same dead-end street, Moscow is the first European metropolis to hit the wall. Fortunately, Moscow has an ace up its sleeve, one that will keep the city moving, even if its leaders bring the streets to gridlock. As long as its Metro is maintained and expanded, Moscow stands a chance at continued mobility. Encouragingly, the latest mayor, elected in 2010, has announced plans to extend existing lines outside city limits and build a second circle line.

In the end, my driver got me to Domodedovo in time. In fact, I was an hour early for my flight. I'd taken a cab because the Metro was closed, and it was four o'clock in the morning. Which is just about the only time you are not a fool for being on the road in Moscow.

> Underneath nostalgia about glamorous 1930s passenger trains, lonesome steam whistles echoing at midnight, and Lionel toy trains rumbles something vastly more important: the landscape that people created around the railroad may have been better than the sprawl the automobile engenders.
>
> —John Stilgoe, *Train Time*, 2009

7. City of Trains

Tokyo, Japan

Tokyo Metro Ma
Tokyo Metro Hi
Tokyo Metro To
Tokyo Metro Ch

Tokyo, for me, will always be the city of trains, a place where you can see a subway car emerging from the the third floor of a department store, a driverless elevated train wending its way past a replica of the Statue of Liberty, or four futuristic bullet trains on parallel tracks racing past parks where people have gathered to drink beer and watch cherry blossoms fall.

In previous visits, I'd noticed how Japanese cities were structured by tracks and tunnels, rather than freeways and overpasses. And the train

network, though confoundingly complex, always seemed to work beautifully: I'd never been in a place where so many people used subways and
trains with so little friction. A question nagged me, though: Is a megacity
built by and for trains any better than one built by and for the automobile?

In search of an answer, I decided to thrust myself directly into the
inner circle of what the Japanese call *tsukin jigoku*, or "commuting hell." It
was the morning rush hour in Shinjuku Station, and the crowds swirled
around me. Fortunately, I had found a Virgil to lead the way: Kiyoshi
Sakamoto, a researcher for East Japan Railways (JR East), and a man with
strong opinions about proper commuting behavior.

"This is the busiest train station in the world," Sakamoto told me as yet
another eleven-car train disgorged its payload of commuters onto the south-
bound Yamanote line platform of Shinjuku. Sakamoto is a compact, precise man in his early forties, who speaks rapid-fire English with a slight
midwestern accent picked up from his two years of studying at the University of Cincinnati. "Private companies like Odakyu and Keio come
here, as well as four lines of the Tokyo Metropolitan Subway. Japan Railway's trains alone bring one million passengers to Shinjuku each day."

I had joined Sakamoto outside Shinjuku's south entrance. Following
him into the maelstrom of the morning rush hour, I was immediately
impressed by his ability to navigate the currents of humanity. Intuitively
sensing ebbs and eddies in the tides of commuters, Sakamoto forded the
torrents of black-suited salarymen pouring from the sluice gates of the
turnstiles, arced his back to dodge a convoy of schoolgirls in sailor outfits
going up a flight of stairs as he was going down, and finally, spotting a few
square feet of unoccupied platform, led us to safe moorage beside a trackside pillar. Thus sheltered from the crowds, we had a privileged spot from
which to view one of the legendary mob scenes of modern times. According to the hands on the clock over our heads, it was 7:58 a.m.: just a couple
of minutes shy of the height of the weekday rush hour in the congested
heart of Tokyo, the earth's most populous city.

To our left, a yellow-striped Chuo-Sobu Local, twice the length of a
standard London Underground train, arrived on track 13. A few seconds
later, a pea-green Yamanote train, some of whose cars were fitted out with
folding seats to boost peak-period capacity, came to a halt on track 14. Both
trains were packed with standing straphangers; Sakamoto estimated they
were operating at over 200 percent capacity. In other words, as many as
3,000 passengers—the equivalent of seven fully-loaded Boeing 747s—were

about to spill onto a narrow platform that was already filled with as many people as a decent-sized midwestern town. I raised my camera, anticipating chaos.

Since the 1960s, when the first *oshiya*, or pushmen, began working at Shinjuku, the image of the impossibly congested Japanese commuter train has been fixed in the global imagination. During rush hours, white-gloved "passenger arrangement staff" strained to cram bodies into commuter trains that, to Western eyes, already seemed filled beyond capacity. Though the occasional station attendant still rushes to tuck a purse or a backpack into closing doors, the days of the pushmen have passed. Which is strange, because Tokyo's trains carry more people than they ever have. Three and a half million commuters pass through Shinjuku's two hundred exits a day—and Shinjuku is just one of 882 rail stations in the Tokyo metropolitan area. New York's Penn Station, the busiest in the United States, has a throughput of 600,000 passengers a day. Shinjuku can process the same number in just three hours.

Sakamoto directed my attention to the scene at the head of the Yamanote train.

"You see the way people are standing? As far as we know, nobody ever told Tokyo people to stand like that." Green lines set near the platform's edge indicated the position of doors on the arriving train; in front of each line, people waiting to board were lined up in four orderly columns. As the Yamanote train doors opened, the columns split down the middle, allowing departing passengers to reach the center of the platform and join the tail end of the Chuo-Sobu Local crowds, already shuffling toward the stairs. Only when the train was almost empty did people start to enter the cars.* The process seemed almost organic, as if the pressure from all the bodies leaving the train was abetting the osmotic rush of the platform crowds into the emptying train.

The blue-capped conductor, who had emerged from the cab to oversee the boarding process, pressed a button on a pillar near the head of the train, which set off a recording of an urgent little song indicating that the doors were about to close. (Each station on the Yamanote line has its own

---

* Such orderly behavior is not universal in Asia, nor even in Japan. The citizens of Osaka, famous for their impatience, make a pretense of queuing on the platform, but tend to break ranks and crowd the doors when a train arrives. They also, according to a survey by the International Association of Traffic and Safety Sciences, start boarding the train 3.2 seconds before the last person gets off. More disciplined Tokyoites average 1.3 seconds.

signature tune; in Ebisu Station, it is the nostalgic "Yebisu Beer-Drinking Song," reminiscent of the zither solo in *The Third Man*. I always looked forward to Takadanobaba Station, where they played the rousing theme of the *Astroboy* cartoons.) Over a microphone, the conductor made a short speech in the affectedly nasal, subservient tones employed for public announcements in Japan.

"He is saying the train's scheduled time, 8:12, and announcing that it is leaving a little bit late, at 8:13." If the train had been more than five minutes late, JR East employees would have appeared to distribute date-stamped proof-of-delay cards, to be handed to the boss with a penitential bow.

An athletic-looking salaryman in his twenties, deciding there was still room in the car closest to us, stepped onto the train backward, facing the platform. Taking a determined stance, he spread his feet on the ledge and raised his arms, palms against the upper rim of the door. He bowed his body backward, compressing the people behind him with his hips; as the doors whooshed shut, narrowly missing the tip of his nose, the tiniest smile of triumph was visible on his face. The train slid out of the station, carrying with it the conductor, his head poking out of the tail end of the last car, right forearm resting on an open windowsill. After the train's departure, an attendant walked to the edge of the platform, and, peering down, swept a white-gloved index finger the length of the tracks, indicating they were clear of all obstructions.

The passengers that remained on the platform didn't have long to wait: two minutes and twenty seconds later—less time than it would take to walk the length of the platform—another train had arrived, and the process was repeated.

Similar scenes were happening at every stop on the Yamanote, the 22-mile circle line that connects Ueno, Shinagawa, Tokyo, Shibuya, and the other major stations of central Tokyo. At the height of the morning rush hour, fifty trains, operating with headways of as little as two minutes, circulate on the Yamanote at once, half running clockwise, half counter-clockwise, each train carrying upward of 1,500 people. Yet the Yamanote is just one of 35 lines operated by JR East in the Tokyo region. And JR East is just one of 12 rail companies in Tokyo: among them are Tokyu (2.9 million daily riders), Seibu (1.7 million), and Tobu (2.4 million). Then there are the 13 lines and 8.5 million daily riders of the Tokyo Metro, the mostly underground system that originally operated within the Yamanote loop, but whose tentacles now draw commuters from Chiba, Tama, and the other far-flung *bedtowns*, or bedroom communities, of Tokyo. Poky streetcars, rubber-wheeled monorails, and fleets of feeder buses gather commuters into the orbit of the Yamanote—a single line whose daily ridership is equal to that of the entire New York subway system. All told, people in the Tokyo area take 43 million daily rides on public transport a day—almost 16 billion a year—the equivalent of two and a half times the volume handled by all the transit systems in the United States. It is this fantastic clockwork, with the Yamanote moving at its center like a gigantic cogwheel, that reliably delivers workers to the center of the city, keeping the economy of the world's most productive mega-region thrumming. Tokyo is the world's best example of a transit metropolis—or rather, a transit megalopolis, for it is home to a quarter of Japan's population—a city built, and now kept running, by its trains.

As we followed the crowd toward the concourse, I told Sakamoto how impressed I was by the crowd's discipline. There had been no pushing, almost no collisions; everything flowed smoothly.

"That's because people in Tokyo are professional at commuting. They know how to behave in a station."

In fact, if the fantastic machinery devoted to transporting people to and from work operates this well, it is not because Tokyoites are endowed with some gene that makes them natural born rail riders. It is because transit companies here have devoted sustained energy to streamlining the commuting process, steadily reconfiguring stations, introducing more comfortable and capacious rail cars, constantly seeking to entice commuters away from toll highways and the private automobile. Sakamoto, whose research for JR East focuses on the analysis of rail passenger traffic flow, had come up with a sophisticated system for recording the behavior of commuters once they stepped into a station. Near Shinjuku's south exit, he explained how it worked.

"The challenge was to follow an individual passenger's trajectory on the concourse." In the JR East section of Shinjuku, the main concourse terminates in a white-walled, fluorescent-lit rectangular hall, where rushing commuters mingle as they head for the stairs or escalators that lead to the fourteen tracks above. During peak periods, it is not an area where any sane person would voluntarily linger: in the big stations of the Yamanote, hundreds of faces strobe by every second; the sheer weight of caffeinated humanity, eerily silent in its focus on commuting efficiency, seems to generate its own energy. (Not just seems, but does. Across town, in a JR East pilot project, the vibrations created by all the commuters walking over mats set into the concourse floor were being converted into enough electricity to power all the lights at Tokyo Station.)

Sakamoto found that overhead video cameras, their lenses trained on the crowns of people's heads, could not capture the complexity.

"Their fidelity is too high. They tell you everything that happened on the concourse, but the data is too heavy. You'd have to install hundreds of cameras on the ceiling to record everybody's trajectory."

Sakamoto decided to experiment with new technology. At strategic points on the periphery of Shinjuku's main concourse, he set up German-made laser scanners, small blue boxes housing rotating mirrors that sent beams of light fanning outward in a 180-degree arc. When passing ankles broke the fan of light, the laser beam was reflected back to a sensor. Each data point, correlated to a precise point on the concourse, was then relayed to a computer attached to the scanner.

Though the millions of commuters who pass through the main Shinjuku concourse every day make for a lot of data points, eight scanners, Sakamoto found, were enough to cover the whole concourse. The software clustered the points into flow lines, which served as visual traces of an individual passenger's progress across the concourse; a yellow flow line representing a passenger moving from left to right, a blue line a passenger moving from right to left. Red dots stood for commuters who—lost, confused, or distracted by the ringing of a cell phone—had come to a full stop. When blue and yellow lines met, a white dot appeared, a visual record of the moment when a rushing commuter dodged to avoid a collision.* When all the data was combined, Sakamoto found he could generate an overhead view of Shinjuku, a vermicelli-like tangle of fine blue and yellow lines, poxed at key points with red and white spots. The result was not a simulation; it was a kind of snapshot of the real behavior, in 50-second increments, of the actual route passengers had taken to cross the concourse throughout an entire day.

Sakamoto led me to the entrance of the JR East concourse. We watched

---

* Tip for travelers: Do like the Japanese, and use the gesture called *tegatana o kiru*, or sword hand, to signify the direction of your dodge. It involves briskly slicing your hand, fingers together, downward toward your waist in the direction you wish to take, as if executing an abbreviated karate chop. It can look rude and abrupt, but is considered an efficient way of indicating your planned path.

the commuters passing a bank of waist-high barriers, some pressing their wallets or phones to a sensor with a practiced flourish, confident that the correct fare was being automatically deducted from their commuting passes or smartphones. Suddenly, two hidden wings on the barriers snapped shut with a ding-dong chime, and a middle-aged woman grimaced as she was forced to stop in her tracks. Reddening slightly, she retreated through the pool of commuters behind her, and headed toward a counter to buy a ticket.

"She didn't have enough money on her card, I guess," said Sakamoto. "She would have appeared as a red dot on our image."

Sakamoto pointed to a bank of LED monitors displaying train information that spanned the width of the concourse, a couple of dozen yards beyond the barriers. It was here that many commuters came to a full stop as they paused to check which track their train was departing from. Sakamoto's scanners showed that two diffuse clusters of red dots tended to form at Shinjuku's south entrance, representing a virtual dam of stalled commuters, in turn creating a morass of white dots as people slowed and swerved to pass. At peak times, it was enough to turn the currents passing through the barriers into a bare trickle.

Solving the problem proved simple. JR East redesigned its signs, so the information for the most popular train lines was displayed on the right, forcing those who needed to consult the monitors to gather on one side. The wall of standing commuters was changed into one easily sidestepped hot spot, and foot traffic began to flow smoothly through the barriers again.

"My technique is new," said Sakamoto. "It's still in the development stage. But in ten years, it may be used to change the layout of stations, even big ones like Shinjuku." As JR East progressively refurbishes its stations, making them more accessible to the elderly and handicapped—a crucial move to maintain ridership in an aging society—the laser scanners will be used to identify hot spots and reposition elevators, news kiosks, moving sidewalks, and noodle stands.

Sakamoto's system for analyzing passenger flow is just one innovation among many. At the time of my visit, JR technicians were developing self-healing concrete that would automatically repair itself when water entered through cracks; a system that would spray jets of warm water onto bullet train tracks to melt ice and snow; and seismic isolation techniques that would allow the construction of comfortable hotels beneath elevated train tracks. Some Tokyo Metro trains now monitor the load being carried by their wheels, and spray a special lubricant on the track on sharp curves to reduce friction and squealing (a measure with potential applications on many New York subway lines). The genius of Japanese railways lies in such incremental improvements, ceaselessly integrated into an ever more elaborate system.

Sakamoto glanced at his wristwatch, and took a last look at the concourse.

"I'm sorry it's all going so smoothly," he said. He knew I'd been expecting a Dantesque tableau of crowding and congestion. "The best way to move passengers successfully is to operate a stable transportation system. If the trains are on schedule, we have no problems—no problems at all. Even when over three million people are using the station a day."

I watched the Virgil of Shinjuku as he rushed to catch the 8:36 to Omiya, becoming one black suit among hundreds. In my mind, he had already transformed into one of his own blue flow lines, gracefully curving around red and white dots.

Traintown

Tokyo's railways are the standard by which all others must be judged. Simply put, there is no better place on the planet to be a straphanger.

On the Shonan-Shinjuku line, JR's twin-level, first-class Green Cars have plush reclining seats, and attendants wheel carts down the aisles during the evening commute, serving ice-cold beer. Most lines are exquisitely climate-controlled; conditioned air blows cool in Tokyo's muggy summer, and heated bench seats gently warm your loins in the winter (which is why you are liable to find the head of a dozing neighbor lolling on your shoulder between stations). Trains run frequently, quietly, and quickly: barely out of central Tokyo, limited-express commuter trains accelerate to 80 miles an hour, faster than the maximum speed of all but a few intercity Amtrak trains. The fare machines speak to you—in Japanese or English—and display cartoon images of workers bowing as they issue your ticket.

Tickets are increasingly rare, though. Many Tokyoites carry metallic cards in their wallets called Pasmo or Suica. The cards carry chips that draw enough power to operate when they pass within four inches of a radio field generated by readers at railway and subway barriers. There are 40 million such cards in circulation in the Greater Tokyo area, carrying balances of up to $250, and they can now be used in convenience stores, buses, vending machines, and even taxis. The card readers on some private train lines automatically send a text message to parents' phones, informing them when their children have passed through the turnstiles.

Make no mistake: the Japanese love their trains. On strategic curves in the tracks of major lines, I spotted hordes of trainspotters—here known as *densha otaku*, train geeks, though they prefer the term *tetsudo fan*, or rail fans—jostling with their telephoto lenses to get the money shot of a streaking *shinkansen* or a streamlined limited express. Trains have worked their way into the sex life of Japan in the form of *chikan densha*, or "pervert-train clubs." At "Shibuya Pink Girl's Club," aspiring *frotteurs* enter a replica of a subway car, complete with recorded announcements, where they pay to grope women dressed as schoolgirls or office receptionists. A series of *manga* based on the real-life hobby of a travel writer who spent fifteen years visiting Japan's nearly 10,000 train stations became a huge bestseller; the *anime* based on the *manga* sparked a national passion for visiting *hikyo-eki*, secluded stations, often in remote mountain regions.

"It's simply the best train system in the world," André Sorensen, the author of *The Making of Urban Japan*, the definitive English-language text on Japanese city planning, told me. "It's *way* out there, in terms of the density of the lines, cleanliness, reliability, and the convenience of getting around." Now a professor of urban geography at the University of Toronto, Sorensen lived in Japan for nine years and still marvels at the country's public transport. "They do something in Tokyo that nobody else in the world has ever done. The private commuter rail lines actually link seamlessly with the subway system. You can hop on a private Tokyu train in Yokohama, to the west, and it will duck underground through the tunnels of the public subway system in the center of Tokyo, and then come out onto private tracks on the east side of the city. All you have to do is wait for the right train and it will drop you right off at home. Fantastic!"

If commuters here are now the world's most pampered, it's because Japan is densely populated enough to make running trains profitable, which in turn allows rail companies to plow profits back into constantly improving service—whether that involves using laser scanners to reconfigure stations or new tunnel-boring technology to dig whole new subway lines. Of course, if Tokyo is as dense as it is today, it's because its twentieth-century growth was almost entirely driven by electric traction rather than the internal combustion engine.

Which reminded me of the question that had brought me back to Tokyo. Was it really any better to live in a city built by trains than in one built by cars?

The Express and the *Chin-chin*

One of my oldest friends lives in Japan. Scott and his wife, Jennifer, have now been in Tokyo for eight years, long enough for them to have learned the language and adopted a Japanese daughter. By visiting them, and seeing Japan through their eyes, I've discovered a culture that otherwise would have remained closed to me.

When I arrive in Tokyo, jet-lagged and stiff-kneed after fourteen hours in the air, it can take a while for my head to adjust to the dimensions and densities of the Japan metropolis. The Express from Narita International Airport was my first, stroboscopic glimpse of Japanese urbanism, and taking the train to Tokyo still unsettles and entrances me. Narita airport, built in the '70s amid the sometimes violent protests of farmers whose fields were expropriated to make way for runways, is 40 miles east of the downtown. In the first ten minutes or so of the hour-long ride, rectangular rice fields, rimmed by narrow roads, flash by against a backdrop of low forested hills, some topped by tiered pagodas. Soon enough, clusters of two- and three-story suburban homes surrounded by compact cars and minivans appear, condensing into multistory apartment buildings and shopping centers near station platforms. By the time the Express stops in Chiba, a satellite city of almost a million, all traces of countryside have been supplanted by multilevel bicycle parking lots, mesh-wrapped golf driving ranges, concrete-banked rivers, webworks of telephone and electrical lines, and the coruscating neon of pachinko parlors. But the Narita Express only ventures into the *Blade Runner* realm of outrageously asymmetrical skyscrapers and giant video screens in the last minutes of the journey, around the major stations of Tokyo, Shinagawa, and Shinjuku. For most of the trip, you travel through a seemingly endless landscape of closely spaced low-rise private homes, peppered with occasional outcroppings of four- to six-story apartment units, office towers, and department stores. Yet given its population Tokyo is hardly a land gobbler. The Tokyo Metropolitan Region, with 36 million residents, covers only slightly more land than Sydney, Australia, a city of 4.5 million.

The journalist Robert MacNeil, traveling on the outskirts of Tokyo in the '90s, saw only "a formless, brutal, utilitarian jumble, unplanned, with tunnels easier on the eyes." But the charms of Japanese cities are rarely visible from the window of an express train. They lie within the intimate warrens of a city's *chos*, or districts. Scott and Jennifer have helped me appreciate Tokyoites' unparalleled flair for urban living by directing me to neighborhoods most visitors don't see. To really understand the deep patterns of civic structure that have persisted through quakes, firebombs, and economic bubbles, you need to take a ride on a train slower than the Narita Express.

At the beginning of the eighteenth century, Tokyo, then called Edo, was the largest city in the world. One million people lived on the great bay on the Pacific coast of Honshu Island, building their canals of stone and houses of wood on soft alluvial soil. In 1868, after the overthrow of the shogunate, Emperor Meiji moved the imperial residence from Kyoto. The powerful territorial lords known as *daimyo* settled, along with retainers and samurai, in the *yamanote* districts on the highlands; commoners lived in the low-lying *shitamachi* areas in land reclaimed from the delta of the Sumida River. At the center, then as now, was the vast, moated Imperial Palace. As Roland Barthes observed in *The Empire of Signs*, it has always been inaccessible to ordinary citizens, making the core of Tokyo, an area larger than the grounds of the White House, "empty"—particularly in contrast to Western cities, whose centers are, by design, *full*: of opera houses, cathedrals, triumphal arches, and other semantically freighted edifices. Tokyo's transit map is a testament to the force field that emanates from the city's sacred center. The necklace of the Yamanote circle line, which was completed by 1925, is pearled with railway termini that stop well short of the palace grounds. Even today, no subway line is permitted to undermine the home of the emperor.

In Old Edo, people walked, or took ferries across the wharf and warehouse-lined canals that crisscrossed the *shitamachi* districts. The world's first rickshaws began to appear in the mid-nineteenth century, and were well suited to Tokyo's narrow streets, but they almost immediately faced competition from a new technology: the railroad. Among the cargo carried on Commodore Matthew Perry's second visit to Japan in 1854—the arrival of the American Black Ships the year before provided the shock that would bring a xenophobic feudal society into modernity—was a quarter-scale steam locomotive. The newcomers set up a circle of track, and took an official of the shogunate for a spin, setting his robes flapping in the wind as the train accelerated to 18 miles an hour. The Japanese were eager adopters of the new technology, and by 1902, private enterprise had built trolley lines from the Western-style brick town of Ginza to the stables and brothels of Shinjuku and beyond to the rice fields of Tama in the west. Four years later, the government—the samurai class of old had become suit-wearing, salaried administrators—nationalized Japan's 3,000 miles of private railways.

According to planning historian André Sorensen, "The private entrepreneurs were the ones who really knew how to build railways, and they plowed the money back into building even more private commuter railways around Osaka, Nagoya, and other big, lucrative markets." This pattern of private construction and nationalization would be repeated throughout the twentieth century, with Japan Government Railways, the ancestor of today's Japan Railways, building a strategic network of rail lines to carry arms and troops in the militarization that preceded the Second World War.

Tokyo was railroaded into modernity by steam trains and electric trolleys, but it took more than steel tracks and pantograph wires to wipe the architecture of Old Edo off the map. The fires that followed the great earthquake of 1923 razed almost half of Tokyo. Tokyoites rebuilt, again in wood, and the Second World War ended with waves of B-29s dropping incendiary bombs that killed 100,000 and burned 16 square miles of the city to the ground, mostly in the commoner districts of the east.

If much of what has been built since then looks shoddy or downright ugly—the norm tends to boxlike homes of water-stained concrete festooned with stick-on plastic bricks and exterior air-conditioning units—it is partly because Tokyoites have not had much experience with permanence. Literary flaneur Donald Richie, who has observed Tokyo since the end of the Second World War, has written that this city, more than others, "lives with an apprehension of its own destruction." Sprawling over nineteen major faults, Tokyo remains a predominantly low-rise city because building upward is expensive and risky. Atomic bombs and firebombs, tsunamis and doomsday cults, earthquakes and conflagrations, Godzilla and Mothra— urban apocalypses are all too vividly imagined here. (After my latest visit, the great earthquake and tsunami of 2011, which devastated the north coast and rattled my friends in their Tokyo home, showed once again that Japan's *deus ex machina* lurks uncomfortably close to the surface.)

The city that has grown since the war can seem beguilingly chaotic. Since arriving in Tokyo, Scott and Jennifer have lived in three different areas; I have stayed in all of them. In the first, Kita-Kogane, which was an hour and three separate train rides from Central Tokyo, they lived on the ground floor of a flimsily built two-story apartment building, serviced by kerosene heaters and a septic tank. I remember thinking that the district— where the rice paddies and vegetable fields that shared country lanes with scrap metal recyclers, billboards and industrial incinerators would suddenly run up against towering, ultra-modern shopping centers—looked like something that had just *happened*, without the oversight of any rational planner. Their second home was a low-ceilinged apartment in a multistory building in a highly urban neighborhood on the Chuo line; they shared their street with pachinko parlors and the cramped quarters of Chinese workers. On their third move, they got lucky. The neighborhood where they now rent an old two-story house with a garden, near the Mejiro station on the Yamanote line, is Japanese urbanism at its intimate, mixed-use best.

In Mejiro, sinuous streets wind past closely spaced multimillion-dollar mansions of poured concrete, older wooden homes, small fishmongers, and hole-in-the-wall beauty parlors and shops selling used household goods. Elderly women sweep the paths of ingeniously arranged pocket parks; homeowners green the roadsides with bonsai pines and potted plants; the branches of trees are hung with wooden signs indicating their Japanese and Latin names. A sense of custodianship, of a neighborhood enlivened by tiny aesthetic flourishes, prevails. In Mejiro, there is no need for European-style traffic-calming measures: the few cars that appear pick their way gingerly through streets as narrow as alleys. The neighborhood is a paradise for cyclists and cats.

Mejiro is just one of many such districts. This is the great secret of Japanese cities: away from the main arteries, the streets tend to be remarkably peaceful, and much more intimate and walkable than those in cities built around freeways and cars.

"Much of Tokyo is a grand warren, a twisted tangle of alleys and lanes," Donald Richie has observed. "The Japanese, like the English, prefer the cozy, and consequently the streets of new Tokyo are as crooked and twisting as those of old London. There is a corresponding sense of group: our cozy warrens are just for us, not for those of you outside." Today's expressways cover ancient canals, and major avenues follow the ridge and valley roads of ancient Edo. "In Europe, cities grew by repeatedly breaking through and expanding beyond the hard shell of the city walls," Jinnai

Hidenobu wrote in his classic study, *Tokyo: A Spatial Anthropology*. "In Edo, by contrast, the location of the temples and shrines and their use of the land around them meant that the city's life solidified inside a series of soft shells." In European cities, stone walls were built to protect the people; in densely settled Japanese cities, the *people* served as the walls.

This kind of fine-grained urban fabric, and Tokyo's overarching lack of architectural unity, leads some Westerners to conclude that zoning as they understand it does not exist in Japan. In fact, land use rules and urban growth boundary laws based on German models were on the books as early as 1919, even before zoning became widespread in the United States and Canada. Modern North American zoning laws work in broad strokes, aggressively separating residential, commercial, and agricultural uses, virtually guaranteeing long commutes to the mall and the office. In all but the most exclusive areas, Japanese zoning allows bakeries, tofu factories, driving schools, public baths, and other small businesses to operate in residential neighborhoods. Light industry zones can creep amoeba-like into blocks of apartment houses, and agricultural zones have been grandfathered into factory districts. According to planning historian Sorensen, these high-density, mixed-use central areas help ensure that Tokyo has the most sustainable pattern of regional development among any of the world's megacities. Not all of this is by design: the national government often prioritized industrial growth over the quality of life of urbanites. In many neighborhoods, it is a long tradition of self-reliance that makes for districts as charming and human-scaled as Jane Jacobs's Greenwich Village.

"The repeating pattern in Japan," Sorensen told me, "is these patches of planned city set in a sea of unplanned sprawl." Over half of all metropolitan growth in Japan has occurred in the form of haphazard, plot-by-plot development along rural roads—the kind of landscape I saw in Kita-Kogane—with sewers, schools, and parks built as afterthoughts, often at a horrendously elevated cost to taxpayers. Though Tokyo has many expressways, they are not structuring elements; they were added, often clumsily, to a city whose basic form was already set by earlier modes of transportation. Only the rail network, Sorensen believes, benefits from really effective, long-term regional planning. "Tokyo's railway system allows a city that would otherwise be an utter nightmare to work really, really well. It's just assumed that the core of every new development will be a rail station you can walk to. If you get transit right, then the stuff that we are obsessed with in North America—the detailed regulation of suburban development—becomes much less important. Tokyo shows that good public transport systems end up mitigating the most serious problems of cities."

A corrective to the vision of Tokyo as unrelenting sprawl offered by the Narita Express is a ride on a *chin-chin densha*, or "ding-dong train." At their peak a century ago, Tokyo's trams carried two million people a day on 220 miles of track. The Toden Arakawa line, built by a private company to ferry cherry-blossom viewers to Asukayama Park, is one of the few survivors. Now run by the Tokyo Metropolitan Government, it still trundles from Waseda University, the training ground for Japan's political elites, to Minowabashi, a working-class neighborhood that was a red-light district in the days of old Edo.

Early one drizzly afternoon, I boarded a forty-year-old, single-car tram from a sheltered platform in the middle of the street at the Waseda end of the line. A motorman in a white surgical mask pointed to the fare box; I dropped a couple of hundred-yen coins into the slot, and took a seat next to the door. The *chin-chin*'s bell ding-donged, the motorman ratcheted the brass throttle to the right, and, as the tram accelerated, an electric hum mounted against the clickety-clack of steel wheels over rail joints. The Arakawa cars can carry fifty passengers, seated on benches of green baize, or gripping rings of plastic dangling from old-fashioned straps, though at this time of day every passenger found a seat. A pair of elderly women in flowered kimonos shuffled aboard, furling their umbrellas with stately grace. Across from me, a dexterous young woman held a compact in her left hand and crimped her eyelashes with her right hand, all the while clenching a Louis Vuitton bag between her nyloned calves. When we arrived at the Shakomae stop, the motorman stood up, stretched, gathered his pocket watch from the control panel, and left the tram, bowing to his replacement on the platform.

The tram's route offered a back-door glimpse into Japanese neighborhood life. Ramen houses, public baths, and bicycle repair shops were wedged among the detached wooden homes that backed onto the tracks. At a narrow level crossing ahead of us, a pair of teenager boys rushed their bikes across the rails, ducking beneath the striped bars of the crossing gates as they dropped. On a third-floor balcony, a boy clapped his hands in delight as the carp-shaped streamer his father was tying to the railing swelled with wind. The passengers on the train were mostly people of retirement age, taking in the passing scene with serene smiles.

By the time I arrived at the last stop, Minowabashi, the rain was coming down hard. I sought shelter in a *shotengai*, a shop-lined street covered by a glass roof, whose apartments on its upper floors made it seem like a working-class version of a Parisian arcade. Snacking on deep-fried zucchini and yams bought from a tempura shop, I explored this oasis of old Tokyo at the end of the line. Seated on stools, construction workers in dusty, balloon-legged *tobi* pants laughed and yelled over beer and grilled eel. A gruff shopkeeper totaled up his sales with an abacus, barking quips and jibes at a colleague across the street. Aproned housewives, the baskets of their bikes brimming with groceries, wove between pedestrians.

Scenes like this can be found beneath the viaducts at Ueno Station, near the level crossings of Shimo-Kitazawa, in the smoky backstreet *yakitori* stands and ramshackle ten-seat bars of "Drunkard's Lane" and "Piss Alley" outside Shinjuku. The blueprint for the cozy warren seems to be encoded in Japan's national DNA. The bullet trains flash by such neighborhoods; expressways actively destroy them. In spite of earthquakes and firebombs and decades of reckless development, Tokyo's *shitamachi* spirit lives on, apparently most at home when it is tucked alongside the tracks and stations of the pokiest *chin-chin* trains.

Road Tribes vs. Rail Fans

Railway culture is so entrenched in Japanese cities that it is easy to forget that Japan is also one of the world's great automobile-producing nations.

There is a toy-like quality to the cars you see on the streets of Tokyo: they look utterly unscuffed, as though they had just been removed from their packaging. There are bubble-shaped Toppos, Pleos, and Alto Lapins that look like overinflated Austin Minis, and taxis, complete with dainty lace antimacassars on their seat backs, with names like the "Cedric Brougham" and the "Crown Comfort." Nissan recently introduced the Pivo 2, whose wheels swivel 90 degrees, allowing sideways entry into parking spots; the three-seater also has a dash-mounted robot head whose "eyes" can read a driver's expressions and play his favorite music if it catches him frowning. The rate of commercial vehicle ownership in Japan is the highest in the world, and the traffic in central Tokyo sometimes seems to consist entirely of small trucks, scooters, delivery vehicles, taxis, buses, and limousines. There is a good reason for this: owning a car in Tokyo is prohibitively expensive.

The coming of *maika*—"my car," the privately owned automobile— happened later in Japan than most places. Tokyo's first parking lot only opened in 1959; the country's first expressway, between Tokyo and Osaka, four years later. But Japan, whose postwar constitution limited military expenditures, made up for lost time, pouring the money it might have spent on armed forces into extravagant infrastructure projects. The billiard-table smooth Metropolitan Expressway, which swoops between downtown skyscrapers and plunges into tunnels deep beneath the streets, is just part of an impressive nationwide network of toll roads. Highway building here is pork-barrel politics at its worst: politicians award contracts to cronies, and Japan's "road tribes," kept nourished by high gasoline taxes, are notorious for building bridges-to-nowhere in remote prefectures and expressways that connect industrial parks to ports and airports that industry does not want to use. To pay for budget overruns, Japan's three highway companies (collectively $340 billion in debt) run the world's most expensive expressways, with tolls two and a half times those in France. In terms of square mileage of asphalt to usable land, Japan now has at least four times more road than any other developed nation.

Yet Japan is the first industrialized economy to experience widespread demotorization. Vehicle sales, since peaking at 8 million annually in 1990, have gone into steep decline; in 2010, the Japanese bought only 4.6 million cars, a thirty-three-year low. And the people who do own cars tend not to use them very much: it is not uncommon to find ten-year-old cars with less than 60,000 miles on the odometer. These days, only a quarter of Japanese men say they want to own a car, down from half in 2000. The trend is particularly pronounced among the young.

"The main reason I don't want to own a car is that in Japan, the parking cost is high," explained Yuki Takei. In his early thirties, Takei works for a company that imports furniture from China; he learned Mandarin living in Shanghai and Beijing, where he met his Vietnamese wife. A fit young man with a crusher of a handshake, he had ridden his bicycle from his apartment to meet me at a café near Funabashi Station, on the Sobu line. "If you are in Tokyo, you have to pay more than fifty thousand yen a month for parking"—almost $650—"It's too much!" Curb parking has been illegal in Tokyo since the early '60s, and everyone who buys a new car has to prove he has access to his own parking space. Though Takei commutes by train, he is occasionally forced to deliver furniture samples with a truck at work. "The traffic is terrible. Very crowded. And the roads are narrow, so it can be dangerous. Though drivers are very disciplined here—they understand the rules. In China, it's the opposite—there are wide roads, but the traffic lights don't work, and the drivers are crazy."

Takei said he and his wife were not interested in buying a car. "If we have a child, we might want a car to go on vacation. But now, with the Internet, you can rent a car, or do car-sharing. The trains are always timely, and you seldom have delays." Takei showed me his bike, a five-gear "Offroad Collection" with half-size wheels, which can be folded up to take on a train.

I took it for a little spin, a gangly *gaijin* on an undersize bike weaving in and out of weekend shoppers. The station was surrounded by two-level bike racks offering 100 yen ($1.30) parking on weekdays. Weekend parking was free, and many people had simply left their bikes on kickstands, unlocked, outside the station. In Japan, as in Copenhagen, park-and-ride almost always means leaving your bicycle, rather than your car, at the train station. What Takei and many other Japanese people of his generation are saying about automobile ownership should have the world's carmakers deeply concerned. After the asset price bubble of the '80s, Japan has seen two decades of deflation and economic stagnation, a climate not conducive to the conspicuous consumption of big-ticket items like cars. A growing environmental awareness is also having an impact on auto sales. A Japanese automobile emits about ten ounces of carbon dioxide for every mile it carries a passenger. A JR train, in contrast, emits only two-thirds of an ounce of carbon per passenger mile. Though the nuclear disaster that followed the 2011 tsunami highlighted the extent to which Japan depends on atomic power—30 percent of the electricity that powers Japan's trains comes from plants like Fukushima, the rest from gas and hydroelectricity—transit's energy needs are surprisingly small. (During peak hours, Tokyo's pachinko parlors alone consume more than twice as much electricity as the city's main subway system.) The sheer volume of passengers transported, and the efficiency of the trains, help the equation. Over the course of a year, the average Canadian is responsible for emitting 22.1 tons of carbon; thanks largely to widespread transit use, the share of the average Tokyoite is only 4.8 tons.

Among the young, there are signs that cars are becoming deeply uncool. The celebrity entrepreneur Shiho Fujita, an idol of the *gyarus*—Japan's high-consuming post-adolescent "gals," fond of fake tans and blond hair extensions—recently proclaimed: "If I was with my friends and my boyfriend pulled up in a car to pick me up, I'd feel kind of embarrassed." A survey of college students in 2009 found that cars ranked 17th in the list of the 25 most popular products and services, behind makeup, televisions, and foreign language lessons. Many of the young Japanese people I interviewed cited concerns about carbon emissions and pollution as one of the main reasons for not buying cars.

I asked Noboru Harata, a professor at the University of Tokyo's urban engineering department who specializes in modeling travel behavior, whether he thought the automobile had a future in Japan.

"In the past, when people made a lot of money in Tokyo, they wanted to buy a single house and own a car in the suburbs. It was the original dream. Nowadays, younger people don't think so—especially those who were born in the suburbs! A car and a suburban home was the *end* of the dream of their parents. Young people today think it's better to live inside the city, where they don't need a car."

The government, which has never stopped building highways, continues to send mixed messages about car ownership. I had planned my visit so I would miss Golden Week, the period in spring when several national holidays coincide and trains and highways fill up as people leave the cities to visit distant temples and parks. To encourage domestic tourism during Golden Week, the government decided to reduce the tolls between expressway gates to the equivalent of twelve dollars—a bargain for Japan.

The incentive, I would later read in the *Daily Yomiuri*, worked only too well. While ridership on JR trains dropped by 7 percent, the entire country was crippled by 58 major traffic jams. Drivers in the outbound lanes of Tomei Expressway from Tokyo to Nagoya spent precious hours of their holiday stuck in 40 miles of backups, a new record. At least they had a view of Mount Fuji while they waited, just north of the expressway. Or they would have if that weekend it hadn't been obscured behind a thick scrim of smog.

Tokyu, Tokyu, Tokyu

Before the First World War, America's street railway companies extended their tracks to "electric parks," the fairgrounds they owned miles from the center of great cities; the space in between was filled in by streetcar suburbs. In early twentieth-century Japan, the attractions at the end of the lines tended to be outdoor baths, giant statues of seated Buddhas, and parks where you could sip sake while watching the cherry blossoms fall. While freeways in the United States supplanted streetcars, in Japan they never stopped laying tracks. Modern Tokyo is the streetcar suburb, writ large.

The pattern for all development to come was set in Osaka. In 1910, the Hankyu rail company built a department store at its Umeda terminus and a hot spring resort at the other end; along the tracks, they built housing estates, office towers, and hotels, turning a barely profitable line into a huge moneymaker. Japan's up-and-coming railway barons took note: the people-moving business could be profitable, but by building communities where people would live, an energetic entrepreneur could also build an empire.

The suburban dream, Japanese style, was always more modest than the American version. The detached single-family home, whose symbolic entrance gate and perimeter wall surrounds a small garden, is more miniature homage to the fortified samurai estates of the Edo period than an Asian version of a lawn-moated Levittowner or picket-fenced California bungalow. The rail conglomerates, which earned higher fares the farther they carried people, made the dream of such suburban fortresses attainable by extending their lines deep into Tokyo's rural hinterlands. In the mass suburbanization that followed the Second World War, entire communities became the domains of such rail conglomerates as Keio, Odakyu, and Seibu. The greatest of them all, though, was the Tokyu Corporation.

The company's early directors aggressively bought up private railways west of Tokyo. At big terminal stations like Shibuya, where commuters changed from national railways or subways to Tokyu trains, the company built huge department stores. Tokyu formed cooperatives that consolidated farm property and returned developed plots to the original landowners, who were willing to give up as much as 45 percent of their acreage in return for parcels fully serviced with sewers, streets, electricity, and access to railway lines. This sideways approach to urban growth, known as land re-adjustment, was the way the suburb crept into the countryside, contributing to Tokyo's distinctive pattern of rail-based growth. The Tokyu Group became one of Japan's largest corporate empires, and land readjustment— which eventually accounted for 30 percent of all land in urban areas—came to be known as the "Tokyu Method."

Shibuya, a district that is home to one of the Yamanote line's biggest stations and the headquarters of the Tokyu Group, is Tokyo at its most intense. Scuttling across the pedestrian scramble in front of the station plaza, overlooked by a chattering, 30-foot-tall *anime* penguin on the screen above, I was keenly aware that I was in Tokyu territory. Behind me was a high-rise shopping complex shaped like a silver silo, topped with the glowing red figures *109*—clever shorthand for "Tokyu": the Japanese character for 10 is *to*; 9 is read *kyu*. Towering above Shibuya station was an exclusive Tokyu hotel; up the street was an outlet of Tokyu Hands, a multilevel department store and do-it-yourselfer's paradise. Running between the skyscrapers were the elevated tracks, the foundations of Tokyu's fortunes, that kept Shibuya humming with a constant supply of commuters from the western suburbs. Today, Tokyu is Japan's largest rail-based conglomerate, with annual revenues of $12 billion.

It seemed entirely possible, I pointed out to Shiroishi Fumiaki, a senior planner for Tokyu's transportation and development department, to live in a Tokyu apartment building, ride a Tokyu train downtown, and work all day in a Tokyu-owned high-rise.

"Tokyu, Tokyu, Tokyu!" he agreed, chuckling. We were sitting in a café in the Tokyu department store. Laying out the company's route map, Shiroishi traced the seven Tokyu lines that shuttled passengers from the suburbs to the major Yamanote line hubs of Shibuya and Meguro. "Tokyu has one hundred stations, and only one hundred kilometers of lines. Three million passengers use our lines a day, so we have to run a lot of trains, sometimes with headways of under two minutes." In other words, this single private railway carried as many passengers a day as the entire London Underground—on less than a quarter of the length of track. "The problem on our two main lines, the Den'-en Toshi and Toyoko lines, is congestion. At rush hour, we are usually at two hundred percent capacity. To solve the problem, we are building new sets of tracks along existing lines."

As we rode an express Tokyo Metro train running on Tokyu's tracks to Tama Plaza, the commercial center of Tama Den'-en Toshi, a development ten miles southwest of Shibuya, Shiroishi explained that the area Tokyu served was younger and wealthier than the rest of the city. "The population in Tama is expected to continue increasing for the next twenty-five years. And people along our lines make good money; incomes are fifty percent higher than the national average." Tama was analogous to a high-density version of the richer suburbs of Los Angeles, minus the traffic jams; at shopping meccas like Futako-Tamagawa, you could browse for $300 melons, minke whale steaks, or jewel-encrusted Cartier watches.

At Tama Plaza, we rode escalators to the fourth floor of a shopping mall overlooking the construction site of the station, a high-ceilinged atrium of glass and steel with a dramatically curving roofline. It looked more like one of the international terminals at Shanghai or Singapore airport than a suburban railway station.

Shiroishi explained that new construction techniques were allowing Tokyu to develop the space over the tracks. Within a year, the station would be at the center of a brand-new complex of department stores, food courts, supermarkets, and office buildings.

"Forty years ago, this was simple mountain fields; only farmers lived here. Tama City didn't exist. Now the population is over half a million."

Starting in the '70s, government planners tried to make Tokyo less dependent on its center. "Technopolises" like Tama City, Chiba New Town, and Tsukuba Science City would be places where people could live and work, obviating long commutes to the central city. But Japanese technocrats, like their peers in France, never got the balance between housing and jobs right. The magnetic pull that originally shaped Tokyo continued to emanate from such Yamanote-line subcenters as Shinjuku and Shibuya, which are now coming close to coalescing into one giant central business district. In Japan, unlike North America, the burgeoning of the suburbs wasn't accompanied by the withering of "downtown": the exurbs attracted residents, but the jobs remained within the Yamanote line. Even Yokohama, 16 miles from Shibuya and a separate city whose population rivals Los Angeles's, is now largely a *bedtown* of Tokyo.

"One thing about a rail-based system in terms of urban form is that it reinforces the center," urban planning historian André Sorensen told me. "Tokyo is hugely monocentric for its size, and that's only possible because of the rail system. Tokyo's network reinforces centrality because, like all rail systems, it's radial: all the lines feed into the central Yamanote line." Major government agencies have always clustered around the Imperial Palace, and corporations still build their headquarters as close to these centers of influence as possible.

Central Tokyo lost population to the suburbs through the '70s and '80s even as its dominance as an employment center increased. As in many sprawling American cities, the ring of fastest growth spread outward, like a shock wave from a bomb blast, to a radius of 20 to 40 miles from the center. Suburbanizaton hit the wall when the bottom fell out of the economy, with the band of greatest growth almost immediately falling to within a 12-mile radius of the center—about where Tokyu's Tama Plaza is located.

Since then, Metropolitan Tokyo has been playing catch-up, building infill to plug the gaps left over in the period of unchecked growth. It reminded me of the pattern I'd seen in Los Angeles, where Metro was turning vacant lots in Pasadena and Hollywood into new apartment complexes.

The Tokyu Corporation, whose rail lines helped Tokyo grow, is taking full advantage of this demographic shift back to the center and inner suburbs. The third stage of Tama Plaza, Shiroishi explained, was set to open next year: "Our target is young to middle-aged people. Young people don't drive anymore, so we're building high-density apartment complexes, of several hundred residences each, within a ten-minute walk of the station." All paths lead to the train station—which then leads, via railway, to Tokyo. The new generation of train stations include day care centers, so parents can drop off their children before they ride the train to work.

I had contacted Shiroishi in the hopes of getting a tour of the latest in transit-oriented development in Tokyo. As I rode back to Shibuya, looking out over the apartment complexes, department stores, and bicycle parking lots, I realized how naive my request had been. In a city built around trains, the real challenge is to find any development that is *not* transit-oriented.

Before visiting Tama, I'd asked Noboru Harata at the University of Tokyo whether he thought it was possible to apply Tokyo's methods of centering development around transit in North American cities.

"*Everywhere*, I think it is possible," he told me. "The kind of lifestyle you want to have in the future depends on your values, your way, your decisions; whether you are willing to pay more money to support public transport. Car-dependent cities are very comfortable for the car people. But there are people who cannot use cars, and they have to have choices, too. A city should provide that choice."

I'm not sure, however, that the Tokyo model is exportable. Among cities, it stands alone: it is the only major metropolis where private corporations can profitably run rail transit without government subsidies. Conglomerates like Tokyu do so by packing a lot of people on their trains, which run at extremely high frequencies, through the high-density residential neighborhoods they built for their passengers. It is as though Los Angeles had chosen trains over freeways, and Henry Huntington's Pacific Electric had not only continued operating its network of interurban Red Cars into the twenty-first century but also laid out most of the subdivisions in Southern California.

That's not how we are used to doing things in North America, where—

for the time being—most highways and transit systems are publicly owned. In Tokyo, the men who ran the trains were also the ones who built the city, a concentration of power that wouldn't have been possible in Western democracies. The fact that transit happens to be profitable in Tokyo isn't an argument for its privatization. It is just more proof, if any were needed, that Tokyo is a world unto itself.

Land Jets

I couldn't leave Japan without riding a *shinkansen*, or bullet train. At the station in Kyoto, where I'd gone for a day of temple visiting, my inner *densha otaku*, or train geek, emerged as I snapped pictures of a 300-series *shinkansen* pulling into the platform. It was one handsome train: sleek, white, with a snub nose that sloped toward its high-glassed brow, it looked like a Jumbo Jet wearing wraparound sunglasses.

I took a window seat in the thirteenth of the sixteen cars on the Hikari Super Express. We left at 9:56 a.m., exactly as scheduled, and by the time we'd reached the end of the platform, we were already doing at least 50 miles per hour. Before the train had even passed through the first tunnel, my eardrums were popping. As we left the outskirts of Kyoto, smoothly accelerating to our top speed of 143 miles per hour, I felt my head being pressed back against the linen antimacassar. Yet the Hikari was neither the newest nor swiftest of the *shinkansen*. JR East's latest bullet train, the Fastech, has been clocked at 227 miles per hour, and JR is working on a magnetic-levitation train capable of making the Tokyo-to-Osaka run in an hour—top speed 360 miles per hour. These are no longer trains: they are more like jets on land.

Except that traveling by *shinkansen* is a lot more fun than flying. Young women, lavender aprons over pink shirts, their hair in buns, wheel carts of whisky, *o-bento* lunch boxes, and cold coffee drinks down the aisles, bowing to passengers as they enter and leave each car. Stops are preceded by five xylophone tones and a crisp, British-accented woman's voice announcing the station name. The ceilings are high, the seats recline. You can wander the train freely, and I did, swaying only slightly through the three virtually all-male smoking cars, inspecting the Japanese-style squat toilets and envying, but only fractionally, the executives in the spacious Green Cars, where the rows have four rather than six seats.

Strictly speaking, *shinkansen* are intercity transport. But like Europe's high-speed trains, they have shrunk distances, allowing people to live in one city and work in another. At the University of Tokyo, one of Noboru Harata's colleagues showed me his monthly Utsunomiya-to-Tokyo *shinkansen* pass (expensive at $1,000 month, but still cheaper than commuting by car and partially subsidized by the school); he pointed out that he did almost all his class preparation and work during his 125-mile commute. As in Europe, good rail connections between cities reinforce transit within cities, making a car-free life possible.

Mount Fuji, out in all its flat-topped glory that day, filed by to my left; the Pacific shimmered to my right. We passed landmarks like Nagoya's Solar Ark, a gunmetal-toned boomerang of a building covered with 5,000 photovoltaic cells. The tracks followed the Tokaido Highway, the old post road that went from Kyoto to Edo, a 300-mile journey that used to take several days. Our trip took exactly two hours and 44 minutes; we arrived back at Tokyo station within ten seconds of our scheduled time.

I didn't want it to end.

Blood on the Tracks

There were times, I'll admit, when I saw the sinister side of Japan's famously efficient public transport.

After I'd gotten into the habit of riding in the lead car, which offers a view to the tracks ahead, I began to suspect the drivers were a little insane. Alone in their cabs, usually veiled by surgical masks, they would gesticulate vigorously and seemed to be involved in a spirited conversation with themselves. When the doors closed, they'd shout: *"Doa, shimete-aru!"* Throttling up, they'd cry: *"Yoshi, ikou!"* (OK, let's go!) Whenever they passed a green signal, they'd lift an index finger and shout: *"Jyonai shinku!"* and arriving in the station, I could hear them saying *"Jyuro tesihi ichi, yoshi!"* (Ten-car stop position, OK!) It was like watching sufferers of OCD in the grip of their compulsion.

There was method, I would learn, to this apparent madness. The system is called *shisa kanko*, or pointing-and-calling. It originated in the early days of steam rail, when an engineer who was losing his sight started calling out the status of approaching signals to the fireman beside him; in response, the fireman would shout back a confirmation. Encoded in Japanese railway manuals as early as 1913, and now adopted by bus drivers and factory workers, pointing-and-calling has been shown to reduce on-the-job errors by as much as 85 percent.

All well and good, but the discipline brought to bear on rail employees can be extreme. In 2005, a JR West train speeding between Osaka and Kobe jumped the rails, slamming into a trackside condo high-rise; the driver and over one hundred passengers were killed. The train had been running a minute and a half behind schedule; in an effort to make up lost time the driver accelerated to almost 80 miles an hour before a tight curve. The investigation that followed exposed a corporate culture of humiliating punishments, where drivers who had caused delays were forced to endlessly rewrite reports and undergo months of "reeducation"; one driver hanged himself after managers yelled at him continuously for three days. The phenomenal punctuality of Japanese trains apparently comes at a price.

Standing behind the driver's cabin on a Chuo Rapid, watching the speedometer edge up to 120 kilometers (75 miles) an hour as the tracks stretched out before us, I found myself dreading a *jinshin jiko*, or "human-body accident," which is JR's euphemism for a suicide. Among expatriates the Chuo is known as the "Chuocide" line, because its long, straight tracks allow trains to reach high speeds, making its stations suicide hot spots. Suicides remain one of the most tenacious sources of delays; statistics are hard to come by, but it is thought Tokyo averages three hundred "human-body accidents" a year, almost all resulting in death. To discourage suicides, rail companies seize inheritances or insurance money from victims' families as compensation for the disruption—in one case, $64,000, though apparently the practice is far from routine. JR East has also installed mirrors on the far side of the tracks in some enclosed stations, on the theory that jumpers are given pause when confronted with their reflections. The most effective remedy is also the most expensive: new subway lines have platform doors that only open once the train has arrived in the station. By 2017, JR East plans to retrofit all the stations on the Yamanote line with such suicide-preventing platform doors.*

---

* There is a grim logic to suicide-by-train. Tokyo can sometimes feel like a relentlessly grinding machine of metropolitan proportions. The overstressed and overwhelmed might imagine that their last act, throwing flesh and blood into this Moloch's gears, would bring the system to a complete stop. It does, but only briefly. JR East prides itself on getting bodies off the tracks and trains running again in as little as forty minutes.

204 ■ Taras Grescoe

Tokyo's trains were also the target of the biggest mass homicide attempt in transit history. On March 20, 1995, during the morning rush hour, five members of the religious cult Aum Shinrikyo boarded Tokyo Metro trains on three different lines and, as they approached stations scattered throughout the city, punctured plastic bags filled with sarin, a poison twenty-six times as deadly as cyanide. As the liquid vaporized, commuters went into convulsions and foamed at the mouth; twelve people died, and thousands were injured. The doomsday cultists—perhaps history's only Buddhist terrorists—believed they were giving their victims a fast track to nirvana by killing them. In *Underground*, an oral history of the attacks, novelist Haruki Murakami chronicled startling scenes: one commuter continues reading his newspaper as the syrupy smell of sarin fills the car and people around him hack and vomit, refusing to leave his seat until the train arrives at his stop. Murakami also speculates about why the attacks were so deeply traumatizing: by targeting the Tokyo Metro, Aum struck at the dense heart of Japanese identity. If their goal was to hasten doomsday by causing panic and social breakdown, however, they failed. Some station attendants were so devoted to duty they had to be dragged from the turnstiles even as they succumbed to the effects of the gas.

In the dozens of interviews Murakami did for *Underground*, an interesting detail emerges: crowding on Tokyo's trains used to be a *lot* worse than it is today. Murakami's subjects describe routine overcrowding so horrific that eyeglasses were often broken, ribs crushed, and hips thrown out of joint; during a regular rush hour at Kita-Senju Station, one man recalls being forced to release his grip on his briefcase, which is then swept away by the crowd, for fear that his arm will break. It is an accurate picture of commuting in Tokyo in the early '90s, when congestion was at its worst.

The Japan Railway's definition of crowding is telling. At 100 percent capacity, there is a person in every seat, and a hand on every strap. At 150 percent, shoulders are brushing, but a standing commuter is still able to read a newspaper; at 180 percent, he or she can "more or less" read a newspaper—provided it is folded. At 200 percent, we are in the realm of the Crush Load, when there is "substantial pressure" from body contact. Above 250 percent, people are so packed they can no longer move their hands, and if the train jolts a passenger will lurch helplessly "into an inclined position and be unable to move."* In the last twenty years, the railways have started running more cars, with shorter headways, and thanks to the efforts of people like Kiyoshi Sakamoto, stations have been redesigned to reduce clotting and bottlenecks. Yet cattle-car conditions still exist on some lines, like the Tozai, which averages 199 percent capacity in the morning rush hour. My friend Scott tells me the sense of compression is noticeably worse in winter, when people wear heavy coats.

This kind of body-to-body crowding has led to the recurring problem of the groper, or *chikan*. It is not new—there were women-only cars on the Chuo Line as early as 1947—nor is it confined to Japan: there are buses for *mujeres*, indicated by a pink circle, in Mexico City, and women-only cars on Mumbai's trains, where "eve-teasing" is a problem. But with over 2,000 reported cases a year in Japan, this form of abuse remains common enough. Scott says when he rides in a car that has reached Crush Load, he keeps both hands raised at all times; many foreigners have been accused, rightly or wrongly, of groping.

One Friday night at 7 p.m., I found myself waiting for a Yamanote line train at Shibuya station. The platform, which is sharply curved, was already full; the lines reached down the stairs. The discipline of the morning rush-hour commuters I had seen at Shinjuku had broken down: red-faced salarymen, who had clearly stopped for drinks after work, cursed and jostled; one growled as he slid in a "platform pizza," a pool of vomit. I queued next to a quartet of schoolgirls who were giggling as they shared a single Krispy Kreme donut. As trains arrived at two-minute intervals, absorbing swaths of the crowd in increments, we were slowly pushed closer to the tracks. Finally I was swept inside by the weight of the crowd, performing a last-second hop over the rather significant gap between the platform and the train.

For four stops, I experienced the full compression of the upper limits of the Crush Load. My hands were pinned at my side, which meant that when the train lurched, I lurched with it. Fortunately, everybody else went diagonal at precisely the same time, righting themselves only as the train

* Engineers have had to invent a new category for the commuter trains of Mumbai, whose Western Railway Line is the world's single most crowded public transport corridor. When fourteen or more people are standing per square meter—above 275 percent capacity—the train has attained "Super Dense Crush Load." In Mumbai, of course, this means people are actually sitting on the roof and hanging out the open doors.

accelerated. Resisting the pressure at first, I felt a sense of panic as obscure muscles protested, but then I recalled the advice for successful roller-coaster riding: don't fight, just go limp. As I became one with the crowd, I began to enjoy the experience. The car was eerily quiet; I could hear the tinny buzz from the earbuds of a junior executive next to me. A manboy in the exaggeratedly nerdy attire of an electronics geek held his smart-phone close to his horn-rim glasses, reading an ebook—a format ideally suited for crowded trains. As we lurched again, I felt sorry for the tiny schoolgirl beside me, crushed up against a sweaty foreigner. Just as I was beginning to worry about being accused of being a *chikan* myself, a woman in the seat in front of me gathered up her shopping bags, twisted around the pole, and got out at Takadanobaba. Gratefully sliding into her place, I idly admired the way a business-suited woman rocked back and forth, apparently asleep on her feet as she drooped from a strap. Soon my own head was drooping.

Japanese trains tend to do that to me. Provided you can find a seat, you can relax and enjoy the ride, knowing you are in good hands. Serious accidents or crimes on trains make for huge headlines, precisely because they are so rare. In Japan, statistically speaking, you are more likely to perish after your pajamas have caught fire than to die in a train crash. Since the first *shinkansen* began running in 1964, there have been precisely zero fatalities from collisions or derailments on bullet trains.*

Westerners tend to experience the quietness of Tokyo's crowded trains as a symptom of numbing conformity, but I have come to see it as a heightened form of civility. Recorded announcements regularly ask people to switch their cell phones to "manner mode," and they actually do it. (What's more, it is catching: when my cell phone trilled one day as I sat on a bench seat on the Sobu line, I found myself blushing and bowing apologetically as I fumbled to turn off the ringer.)

"To use public transport," Noboru Harata of the University of Tokyo told me, "is to know how to cooperate with other people, how to behave in public space."

After a few days in Tokyo, the sight of children as young as six riding trains to school unaccompanied by adults seemed completely normal to me.

* In China, a shocking collision between two bullet trains in the summer of 2011, which killed forty people, has led Beijing to cut back maximum speeds and temporarily halt new rail construction.

That tens of millions of people come face to face, and shoulder to shoulder, in the same rail cars every day, rather than slipping past each other in metal cocoons on freeways, ends up reinforcing this sense of civility. For the Japanese, riding public transport is a daily reminder that they are all in this thing—their community, their city, their society—together. Even a poison gas attack by a death cult failed to provoke widespread panic and social breakdown; as in Moscow, terrorism only briefly disrupted train service.

And trains like these, crowded as they sometimes were, allowed for the evolution of an urbanism that was superior in almost every way to the version built around cars. If Tokyo was any guide, planning for rail transit allowed immense populations to live in settings that favored sustainability and walkable neighborhoods while limiting sprawl and pollution.

As the heated seat of the Yamanote line JR train gently warmed my backside, I began to doze, lulled into sleep by the clickety-clack of steel wheels over rail joints. It was only at Ikebukuro, awakened by the urgent tones of the station song, that I leapt to my feet.

I was proud of myself. I'd gone through the first rite of passage of the true Tokyo straphanger. I'd slept through my stop.

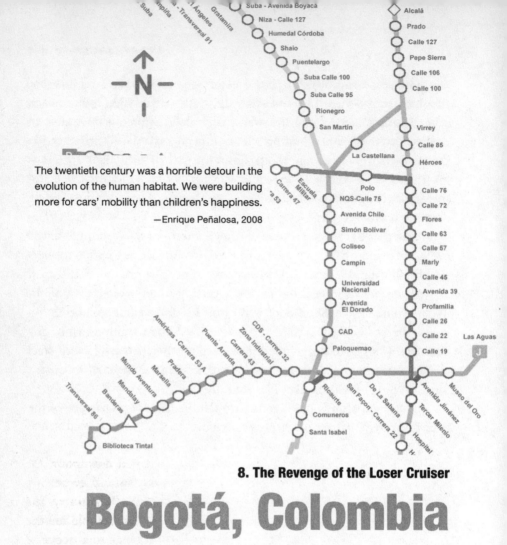

The twentieth century was a horrible detour in the evolution of the human habitat. We were building more for cars' mobility than children's happiness.

—Enrique Peñalosa, 2008

8. The Revenge of the Loser Cruiser

Bogotá, Colombia

When it comes to modernist architecture and modern cities, form follows function. At least that's what I *thought* I knew, and every place I'd been so far seemed to confirm the idea that cities are structured by their transportation networks.

New York, though it came close to being undone by Robert Moses's parkways and expressways, had clearly grown up dense and vertical around elevateds and subways. Paris's suburbs were saved from sprawl by the state-planned RER system, and Moscow was structured by its broad ceremonial boulevards, Stalinist metro, and contemporary ring roads. Farsighted transport planning, and four decades of advanced urbanism, had not only kept Copenhagen walkable, but lately made it into the world's most bikeable city. Transit didn't always make for a compact city—Los Angeles, I'd discovered, owed its dispersed form to its historic streetcar and interurban network, and Tokyo covered a lot of ground because railroad companies were paid more the farther they carried their passengers— but it almost always made for a dense city. When every commuter has to be within easy striking distance of a station or stop, building monster homes on huge lots doesn't make a lot of sense.

In almost every city I'd seen, subways, buses, and trains promised a way out of congestion, pollution, and sprawl. (The exception was Phoenix, a case study in how a city predicated on freeways can become an irredeemable monster of unbridled growth.) Since I'd started my travels, though, urbanists and transport experts kept telling me about a city that had followed a different path. Without making any significant changes to urban form, the capital of Colombia had engineered a revolution in mobility by gambling on an innovative form of transit. My work wouldn't be complete, they said, until I'd visited Bogotá.

My plane touched down in the midst of a torrential downpour, the onset, it turned out, of La Niña year flooding that would eventually destroy 5,000 homes and affect two million people across the country. The man at the currency exchange counter at El Dorado airport told me the only way to get to my hotel was by taxi, and directed me to a queue of bleary-eyed, jet-rumpled passengers that snaked around three walls of the fluorescent-lit arrivals hall. It took an hour to work my way to the front of the line. Outside, the rain was coming down so hard it actually ricocheted; in the half-dozen steps between terminal and trunk, I was soaked. The driver let out a constant string of *"Carajos"* and *"Coños"* as we drove, often up to our wheel wells in floodwater, through dimly lit streets of tightly serried apartment blocks, where burglar bars fronted every window and razor wire topped every roof. Balefully eyed by teenage soldiers with machine guns on their shoulders and muzzled rottweilers at their feet, I walked up a cobblestoned street to my hotel, and wondered if I had been misinformed about Bogotá. It looked like an improbable template for a municipal renaissance.

Bogotá has long had a sinister reputation. In the '80s, the conflict that pitted Marxist-Leninist guerillas against right-wing militias made the capital of Latin America's oldest democracy the world's most dangerous city. In the run-up to the 1990 elections, no less than three presidential candidates were assassinated. A few blocks from the neoclassical City Hall and Parliament buildings could be found the stalls and shanties of El Cartucho, the Western Hemisphere's most violent urban slum, a place even the notoriously corrupt police feared to enter. While workers spent an average of four hours a day commuting from the poor south to the rich north, the powerful got around in armor-plated cars, driving over sidewalks and parking in crosswalks with impunity. The authorities, such as they were, could count on four traffic fatalities and a dozen homicides a day—and that was on a good day. With its abandoned parks filled with the twitchy casualties of smokable cocaine paste, overrun by narco-terrorists and kidnappers, and so polluted that asphyxiated birds regularly rained from the sky, Bogotá—which by the early '90s was as populous as London—rivaled wartorn Mogadishu, Beirut, and Belgrade for the title of hell on earth.

Yet, just two days after I'd arrived, I was riding a rented bicycle through what looked like an urban paradise. The canopy of rain clouds had receded from the lush green mountainsides that mark the city's eastern limits, revealing red-brick apartment buildings ascending toward the white-spired church perched high atop the peak of Monserrate. All around me, Bogotanos—venturesome children on mountain bikes, Lycra-clad middle-aged men on Italian racing bikes—pedaled down the middle of Carrera Séptima, a thoroughfare normally clotted with taxis and minibuses. Eighty miles of the city's busiest arteries were closed to automobile traffic for the Ciclovía, an event that draws a million participants every Sunday of the year. Traffic cops were posted on side streets to prevent incursions by errant drivers, and every few blocks people were oiling chains or pumping up tires at city-run bike repair stands. After following a broad bicycle path through a riverside park, I bought a snack of fat-kerneled grilled corn and freshly squeezed mango juice from a streetside vendor on a grassy meridian, and marveled at the scene—people on foot and bicycle, wearing the kind of relaxed smiles usually seen on sun-soaked seaside boardwalks. Glancing at the pavement, I noticed someone had scrawled an English-language graffito into wet cement, now hardened into a permanent homage: "I love Bogotá."

I'd expected to find a Third World city putting on a brave face, but on this Sunday, Bogotá felt more like an equatorial Amsterdam. Dotted with appealing squares and well-groomed parks, and green enough that it has United Nations approval to sell carbon credits to more polluted cities, the city has become a model of advanced urbanism in the tropics.

How, in little more than a decade, did Bogotá go from being one of the most chaotic, crime-ridden, and congested cities on the planet to one of the best managed—a place people now say they are proud to be from?

It all started with a pair of visionary mayors, the likes of which no North American city has ever seen. But it never would have happened if it weren't for that most maligned of vehicles, the humble city bus.

The Subway on the Street

I had a confession to make to Carlos Pardo, who had volunteered to introduce me to the system that kick-started the transformation of Bogotá.

"I don't like buses," I told him. "Actually, I hate them."

I laid out my objections. While there is something aristocratic about riding the rails, in most of North America a ride on a standard-issue city bus is a second-class experience. After being forced to wait outside, in all kinds of weather—or, at best, in some malodorous Plexiglas shelter—you pay for the privilege of boarding the slowest, bulkiest vehicle on the road, one whose progress is impeded by every double-parked car and FedEx truck with its flashers on. You grit your teeth as yet another passenger fumbles for change, causing the driver to miss yet another green light. If you are forced to stand, as you usually are, you totter with every lurch. If you do manage to find a seat, you are inevitably the recipient of sidelong glances of pity from the drivers zipping past you. In some North American cities, I told Pardo, the bus is known as the "loser cruiser."

He nodded sagely. Trained as an urbanist at the London School of Economics, Pardo is now an adviser to the Institute for Transportation and Development Policy, a New York–based nonprofit group that provides technical assistance to cities trying to develop sustainable transport programs. Though a lifelong Bogotano, and proud of what his city has become, he was used to hearing gringos' hang-ups about bus travel. He assured me that TransMilenio, Bogotá's revolutionary bus rapid transit system, would change my mind about buses. I, in turn, assured him it would be a hard sell.

We were accompanied by a half-dozen South Africans, on a Latin American fact-finding tour to improve bus service in Johannesburg. Outside their hotel, Pardo gave us a security briefing.

"Leave behind your passports," he said. "Don't worry, the police never ask for them. Put your wallets inside your jackets. And if you are carrying a camera, be careful. The pickpockets in Bogotá are very good."

It was the tail end of the morning rush hour, and as we walked down Calle 90, we encountered waves of commuters in skirts, suits, and ties headed for the office towers of northern Bogotá. At the southern end of the street, we stepped onto an impressive piece of urban infrastructure: aluminum-floored walkways that switchbacked up to a pedestrian overpass above the city's main north-south highway, before sloping back down to a ticket booth in the center of six lanes of traffic. After lining up to buy a fare card, good for ten trips at 1,600 pesos (about 85 cents) a ride, we filed through electronic turnstiles into a long, enclosed station. On either side, passengers waited in front of glass doors labeled with route numbers. Every few seconds, an articulated bus, painted a deep red, pulled up to the station. See-through platform doors slid open, in tandem with three sets of bus doors, and passengers poured onto the platform. Because everybody had paid before entering the station, and the platform was level with the bus floor, boarding took all of ten seconds—people just stepped forward as though entering an elevator, the doors slid shut, and the bus was on its way. The station was long enough for a half-dozen buses, each capable of carrying 160 passengers, to load and unload at once. At one point, I was astonished to see a tidal wave of commuters emerging from a yellow behemoth of a bus. Pardo said it was a Biarticulado, a bus manufactured by Volvo with two pivoting joints, four axles, and five sets of doors. The latest addition to the TransMilenio fleet, it is as long as a Boeing 737, and with a capacity of 270 passengers, is currently the longest bus in the world.

As our F14 bus, an express service, pulled out of the station, I realized that TransMileno operated like a ground-level subway, with rubber tires in place of steel wheels. The TransMileno routes ran down major avenues or highways, occupying the two center lanes for most of their lengths. Stations were about 700 yards apart, and because there were passing lanes near each station, our bus was able to skip stops, much like the express trains on the double-tracked New York subway. Physically separated from six lanes of automobile traffic by low walls, TransMilenio's dedicated bus lanes worked like a railroad right-of-way, eliminating the frustrating stop-and-start progress that occurs when buses mix with cars. As we got closer to the Candelaria, Bogotá's historic center, signal priority technology changed red lights to green at our approach, and our bus sailed past cars stopped in bumper-to-bumper traffic. Pardo explained that about four hundred small feeder buses, painted green, gather customers from outlying districts, depositing them at terminals where the system's thousand red TransMilenio buses begin their runs on seven intersecting trunk lines. The main line, which we were riding, handles 45,000 passengers per hour in each direction during peak periods, a throughput only a few subways in the world can match.

TransMilenio is fast—we crossed half the city at rush hour in just 25 minutes; the same journey by taxi would take at least three-quarters of an hour. Globally, city buses manage a pathetic 7 miles per hour; TransMilenio's buses average 17 miles per hour, making it far and away the fastest means of moving around Bogotá. Unfortunately, TransMilenio is also fantastically crowded. Every seat was taken, and as more passengers piled in at every stop, we approached the kind of Crush Load I'd recently experienced in Tokyo. (I could see why TransMilenio would be a paradise for pickpockets; compressed on all sides, it wasn't long before I couldn't tell who, or what, was touching me.)

When TransMilenio started operating in 2000, approval ratings were high; one of the new millennium's hottest Christmas toys was a scale model of a red articulated bus. Of the 240 miles of lanes originally planned, however, only 52 have been completed, and though route mileage has not budged since 2007, ridership has increased by 300,000 daily passengers. TransMilenio now moves 1.7 million commuters a day, and it does so without government subsidies, making it the only big-city transit system outside of Japan to turn a profit. As crowding surpasses six passengers per square meter, however, Bogotanos are growing disenchanted with the system, and many are looking for alternatives.

At Avenida Jiménez, we changed lines, walking through subway-like corridors between platforms, before boarding a bus that actually had a few empty seats. I asked Jeff Ncgobo, the manager of Johannesburg's Rea Vaya bus rapid transit system, what he thought of TransMilenio. "It's pretty slick," he conceded. "In Joburg, we don't have anywhere near this ridership. We still have less than fifty buses, and we're only carrying forty thousand passengers a day." Johannesburg's 15-mile bus rapid transit line, which carries mostly black workers from Soweto to downtown, faces special challenges. Until recently, commuters relied on the relatively expensive private minibus taxis that clogged the streets.

"The minibus owners over there are a real mafia," confided Carlos Pardo, who had worked as a consultant on the South African transit system. "They don't like bus rapid transit at all, because they see it as stealing their business. On the day the Rea Vaya service began, two of the city's drivers were shot. That's how they deal with competition in South Africa—they tell drivers that if you work for the city's bus system, you will die!"

As we drove up a sinuous transit mall to the terminal at Las Aguas, following the course of a river that cascaded through interconnected concrete troughs, I began to see the appeal of TransMilenio. The buses, built by Mercedes, España, and Volvo, had large windows, high ceilings, and spacious, comfortable seats. The sleekly designed stations, all glass and aluminum, provided welcome shelter from Bogotá's frequent downpours. And a bus has one obvious advantage over a subway: it allows you to see the city you are traveling through. Riding TransMilenio was giving us a glimpse of the messy vitality of Bogotá's streets, from the big-busted transgender prostitutes pacing Avenida Caracas to the vendors of cheese-filled *arepas*, cell phone minutes, and pirated copies of Gabriel García Márquez novels on every sidewalk.

As we paused next to a multilevel bicycle parking lot the city had built for transit users, I admitted to Pardo that TransMilenio was changing my opinion of buses. "TransMilenio has been wonderful, from the start," Pardo said. "And if you compare it to what public transport was like in the nineties, it's *still* wonderful. People know they can walk to a station, catch a bus, and arrive where they need to. It's a full transport system, completely formal and completely legal. So when you see a driver, he's being paid for his vacations, he's being paid for health care, he's being paid for his pension. All the maintenance is being done regularly. Previously you would not have that at all." Waning commitment from the municipal government, he believed, was the cause of the current crowding. "In the beginning, people said, it's so fast I don't care that it's crowded. Now they're saying, it may be fast, but I don't want to be touched or pickpocketed any more." If Trans-Milenio was going to survive, it was clearly going to have to evolve.

But really appreciating what bus rapid transit has done for Bogotá requires some knowledge of what this city was like before TransMilenio—and that involves a ride on a very different kind of bus.

The Penny War

The following evening, I was standing on a street corner, a few blocks east of TransMilenio's main trunk line on Avenida Caracas. It was Tuesday at 6 p.m., and along Carrer 11, hundreds of *busetas*—40-seater minibuses—trolled the curbs of Bogotá's financial district in search of customers. The drivers cruised along with their doors open, shouting out destinations. There were no formal bus stops; the *busetas* would alight anywhere, for anybody who raised a hand. Spotting a woman in a business suit and heels, the driver of an aging Chevrolet, which spewed black smoke from a rusty exhaust pipe, swerved to the curb, narrowly missing the fender of a Japanese-made Daihatsu; he slowed, but didn't stop, and she just barely managed to hop on board. Steering with his left hand and collecting pesos and *centavos* with his right, each overworked driver fought for every fare; to leave a customer behind on the sidewalk was tantamount to refusing money. In spite of their drivers' exertions, most of the buses left the financial district half empty. Headed for working-class neighborhoods on the outskirts of the city, the *busetas* coalesced into long, slow-moving files on the diesel-choked Carrer 11.

This is the daily insanity of the *guerra de centavos,* the "penny war." Until the coming of TransMilenio, the privately owned *busetas* were the city's only form of transit; though less common today, they still turn the streets of some districts, particularly northern Bogotá, into congested, dangerous free-for-alls. The bus drivers cover the cost of diesel and pay a daily fee to the owners, who in turn pay the private bus companies a monthly rent. Each bus company owner is issued a permit, good for life, to operate a given bus route by the notoriously ineffectual Secretariat of Mobility—a federal authority whose reputation has been tarnished by a succession of corruption scandals. There are currently 20,000 bus owners in Bogotá, and 68 separate bus companies. As it is in each owner's interest to put as many revenue-earning buses on the street as possible, the city suffers from an absurd oversupply; and each new *buseta*, because it increases congestion, has the perverse effect of decreasing the gross revenue of the bus owners, while boosting commute times. In Bogotá, the average return-trip commute on a *buseta* now takes three hours.

This, of course, is how public transport worked in New York, Paris, and London in the nineteenth century, with dozens of horsecar and omnibus companies competing for customers—until civic paralysis made the construction of elevateds, metros, and subways inevitable. It is still the way transit functions in many developing-world metropolises. In Manila, for example, colorful jeepneys—a melding of leftover American military Jeeps and jitneys, the unregulated shared taxis that competed with streetcars in the United States at the end of the First World War—dominate public transport. Middle-class Filipinos almost never ride the slow, crowded, and labor-intensive jeepneys, which crowd busy avenues but rarely serve the suburbs. Jeepneys and *busetas* are the libertarian ideal of competition-in-the-market made manifest: public transport is left to the free market, with a minimum of public oversight. As picturesque as they can be, such systems are a disaster for any major city, causing exponential increases in congestion, pollution, and carbon emissions.

Enrique Peñalosa, the man who created TransMilenio, has vivid memories of the chaotic Bogotá of the '90s. "I have never been in a city where people had less self-confidence," he told me from behind a desk in a penthouse office that offered a spectacular view of the Andes. White-haired and white-bearded, with a booming voice, Peñalosa is a tall man with a commanding presence. "Bogotanos used to constantly deprecate their own city. There were no parks, and when they rebuilt the big avenues, they wouldn't even put in sidewalks. The whole downtown was dying, and it was so filled with drug addicts and mafias that it had actually become a barrier, dividing the north from the south. We had one of the highest murder rates on the planet. This was the Bogotá of the past, a city without hope, without vision, getting worse all the time."

The dysfunctional transport system, Peñalosa said, was symbolic of how deeply inegalitarian Colombian society had become. "I had a secretary whose only daughter was killed by a *buseta*. The driver was in a crazy race, and drove right onto the sidewalk, running her over. The drivers worked for fourteen hours at a time, collecting fares, letting people out, constantly getting into fights. I myself saw a driver, who after getting cut off, came out and broke all the windows on the other bus with a metal bar while all the passengers were still inside. Anybody with power or money had a car, and they would simply park on the sidewalks. It was beyond imagination."

Peñalosa first ran for mayor in 1994. The son of a liberal senator who had redistributed land to peasants during the agrarian reform of the '60s, Peñalosa studied economics and history at North Carolina's Duke University, where he became disenchanted with socialism. Capitalism, he decided, could work if cities fostered universal belonging for all citizens—a process he believed could be initiated through a revolution in the concept of public space.

Peñalosa represented a new force on the Colombian political scene, where, until 1990, mayors had been appointed by the president, rather than elected by popular vote. Breaking with tradition, he spurned candidates' debates and handed out flyers in the streets. He was outflanked, however, by an even more unconventional politician. Antanas Mockus, the son of Lithuanian immigrants, burst onto the public scene when, as the dean of the national university, he dropped his pants and mooned an auditorium full of unruly students. The bowl-cut, long-bearded, bicycle-riding Mockus was an outsider who promised a radical break with the past. Funding his campaign with the $10,000 he raised from selling his car, the forty-three-year-old professor of philosophy and physics became mayor in 1995 with 64 percent of the popular vote.

Working with a tiny budget and no support from district councilors, Mockus focused on improving "citizen culture" and undermining cycles of violence through jester-like interventions in daily life. He dismissed the notoriously corrupt traffic police and hired four hundred mimes to shame drivers into stopping at crosswalks. He launched an anti-gun campaign, in which 1,500 illegal weapons were melted down into baby spoons, and orchestrated symbolic public inoculations against violence, where prominent citizens, after taking drops of sugar water on their tongues, vowed to resolve conflicts peacefully. Taxi drivers were encouraged to become "Gentlemen of the Crosswalks," and every new traffic fatality was marked with a black star prominently painted on the pavement. To discourage road rage and honking, he distributed a quarter of a million World Cup–style penalty cards to pedestrians and motorists, a red thumb's down to signify disapproval, a green thumbs up to express thanks for a kind act. Incredibly, these loopy, low-cost initiatives brought real hope to Bogotanos, and real change to the city. Seeing tangible evidence of municipal progress, citizens once again began to pay their property taxes. Violent deaths decreased by a third during Mockus's mayoralty, and the once-bankrupt city's finances began to recover.

Mockus's revolution in citizen culture laid the groundwork for Peñalosa's physical transformation of the city. Elected mayor as an independent candidate in 1998, Peñalosa quickly realized that in a city of Bogotá's size and density, where less than 20 percent of the population owned cars, the private automobile was never going to be an equitable or efficient mode of transportation.

"When I was elected, I was given a study by the Japan International Cooperation Agency. They proposed building seven elevated highways, at a cost of twenty billion dollars, to solve Bogotá's traffic problems. We rejected their plan, and decided to build the Alameda, a twenty-four-kilometer highway for pedestrians and bicycles only." (It wasn't the first time foreign technocrats set their sights on Bogotá: in 1947, Le Corbusier drew up plans that would have replaced the Candelaria district, home to some of South America's most glorious colonial architecture, with widely spaced high-rises and high-speed roads.)

"I believe a city is more civilized not when it has highways," continued Peñalosa, "but when a child on a tricycle is able to move about everywhere with ease and safety. In the developing world, that kind of quality of life is our competitive edge—we may not be able to give high income, but we can give people quality of life."

Championing the prevalence of public good over private interest, Peñalosa and his youthful team, many of them women, focused on building a livable Bogotá. Relocating the residents of El Cartucho, he turned the violent city center slum into a well-policed and popular square, and expropriated Country Club de Bogotá, the nation's most elite recreational institution, transforming its polo grounds into public soccer fields and basketball courts. He built hundreds of miles of bike paths, not only to protect cyclists, but "because they showed that a cyclist on a thirty-dollar bike was equally important as a citizen in a thirty-thousand-dollar car." Using the newly flowing revenue from property taxes, his administration bought large parcels of land on the urban fringe and handed them to private developers on the condition they build affordable housing. He also set up a new library system, brought running water to the city's poorest districts, and created over 200 acres of new parks and public squares.

"We wanted to make people look down on the values of the criminals in our society. We were saying, 'You, with your big cars and fancy jewels, we think you are *stupid*, we think you are *animals!*'" Peñalosa rose from his chair, sweeping an arm over his desk. "What we respect is *music*, and *sports*, and *libraries*. For us, the neighborhood hero was not the mafioso with the big motorcycle and the flashy clothes, but the young man who played sports and read books and rode around on an old bike."

Peñalosa began his campaign of change with a simple and venerable urban traffic control measure: the bollard. A bollard is a short vertical post—a famous example is the *Amsterdammertje,* the triple-crossed red bollard of Amsterdam, originally cast from old cannons—and a low-tech way of protecting sidewalks from the incursions of automobiles. By putting bollards on every major thoroughfare, Peñalosa's team instantly returned the sidewalks to pedestrians.

"A car on a sidewalk is a very powerful symbol of inequality and lack of respect for human dignity," said Peñalosa. Motorists perceived the bollards as a declaration of war, and enraged businessmen launched a petition that almost got the new mayor impeached, but Peñalosa forged on, introducing a sweeping traffic mitigation scheme. Known as *pico y placa*— literally, peak and plate—the measure banned weekday travel during morning and evening rush hours according to the final digit of car owners' license plates. By forcing motorists to leave their cars at home twice a week, and finding other ways—taxis, buses, or bicycles—to get to work, *pico y placa* immediately reduced congestion by 40 percent.

But Peñalosa's most ambitious initiative, and his attempt to provide an alternative to the daily insanity of the Penny War, was TransMilenio. The last time Bogotá had a formal transit system was 1948, when riots following the assassination of a presidential candidate led to the permanent closure of the city's streetcar network. Peñalosa knew he would have to act fast—at that point a mayor's term lasted three years, and Colombian law forbade successive terms—and that for TransMilenio to succeed, the powerful owners of the *buseta* companies would have to be brought on board. Relying on the expertise of Brazilian and European consulting firms, he came up with a scheme by which operating concessions would be granted to over 60 bus companies, organized into four conglomerates. The private operators would be responsible for providing buses and drivers; dispatching and route design would be handled by a new public company, which would pay the conglomerates based on the distance logged by their drivers, rather than the fares collected. In return for pulling 5.5 *busetas* off the road for every red TransMilenio bus they operated, Peñalosa promised the conglomerates a minimal annual return of 14 percent. The city would be responsible for building stations and other infrastructure, paid for with a federally imposed tax of 25 percent on each liter of gas. On December 17, 2000, the first phase of TransMilenio—the name means "across the millennium"—went into operation. Bogotanos were delighted to be offered an alternative to the *busetas*, and Peñalosa left office the following year with an astonishing 85 percent approval rating.

For Peñalosa, TransMilenio was a crucial victory. "If, in a democracy, all citizens are equal before the law, then a bus with one hundred passengers should have the right to one hundred times more road space than a car carrying only one person. When a fast-moving bus passes cars stuck in a total traffic jam, it is an unconscious and extremely powerful symbol that shows that democracy is really at work, and it gives a whole new legitimacy to the state and social organization."

Peñalosa endorsed Mockus's successful reelection campaign, and his successor continued to expand TransMilenio. But the current mayor, Samuel Moreno, of the left-wing Democratic Pole party, had been elected on his promise to build a subway, and the public's growing disenchantment with Peñalosa's brainchild was clearly causing the ex-mayor pain.

"You know, the main problem with TransMilenio is that it is identified with me. Moreno, who hates me, doesn't have the slightest interest in solving TransMilenio's problems. The best thing that could happen to the system is that I will be run over by a truck tomorrow."

Fortunately, Peñalosa had a surefire plan to save TransMilenio, one that didn't involve dying in traffic. Its success was contingent on his being reelected mayor of Bogotá.

His campaign, he told me, would start in a few months.

The Triumph of the City Bus

TransMilenio is an example of a revolutionary development in public transport. Bus rapid transit—or BRT as it is known in the acronym-loving transportation world—is sweeping the cities of the developing world, where large populations mean even low rates of car ownership can create incessant traffic jams.

In 2010 the Chinese city of Guangzhou opened a BRT system, linked to a bike-share program and the city's eight-line subway, which within weeks was moving 27,000 passengers an hour in each direction, a throughput second only to Bogotá's. A single lane of Istanbul's Metrobüs system moves as many people as seven lanes of automobile traffic, and has restored mobility on the perennially jammed Bosphorus Bridge that links Europe to Asia. Tehran now has an award-winning BRT network that carries 1.8 million Iranians a day. Though Caracas, São Paulo, Santiago, and Buenos Aires all have metro systems (the Argentinian capital's *subtérraneo* has been in operation since 1913), seventeen BRT networks have recently been inaugurated in Latin America, and ten more are under construction. Though Europe has so far proven allergic to BRT, there are now 84 full or partial systems in the world, from Ahmedabad's, which carries a mere 35,000 passengers a day, to São Paulo's, which handles six million.

Bus rapid transit appeals to politicians because it is quick to implement, efficient, and inexpensive: a single line can easily move three to four times more commuters than a lane of highway, and, mile for mile, the infrastructure can be cheaper than a subway by a factor of 30. For politicians eager to leave a legacy, a BRT system can be kicked off in a matter of months, rather than the years or even decades it takes to complete a single subway line.

The mother of all BRT systems can be found in Curitiba, a Brazilian city known for its modernist high-rises and abundant green space. In a move that recalled the lightning pedestrianization of downtown Copenhagen, Mayor Jaime Lerner turned several downtown blocks into a car-free zone over a single weekend in 1972. A year later, he rationalized the city's chaotic private bus system and opened the first dedicated express bus lane. The citizens of Curitiba now wait in ribbed glass tubes that serve as boarding platforms for articulated buses that race down broad avenues flanked by parallel one-way roads serving local traffic. The five-line system is stunningly efficient, and in spite of having one of the highest rates of car ownership in the nation, Curitiba consumes 30 percent less gasoline than comparably sized Brazilian cities. But Curitiba's story may be unique. Lerner, trained as an urbanist and appointed to his post by the military dictatorship, was able to impose his will with little public consultation, enjoying the kind of latitude granted to the planners currently reshaping Chinese cities. Land use and transportation development were coordinated by the same agency, and as Curitiba grew, developers were guided by strict zoning rules and encouraged by financial incentives to build mixed-use high-rises along BRT corridors. Like New York with its subway and elevated lines, Curitiba developed in tandem with its transit system. As a template for transit-led urban transformation, the Curitiba model may only be relevant to boomtowns in the early stages of their development.

Bogotá is a very different kind of city. Settled by Spaniards, mestizos, Indians, and slaves in the sixteenth century, it is spectacularly sited on a plateau of drained wetlands, 9,000 feet above sea level. Its glass-walled skyscrapers and red brick high-rises huddle up against the eastern range of the Andes, which rise east of the city like palisades erected against the Amazonian jungle. In terms of urban structure, Bogotá, like many Latin American capitals, owes more to Paris than it does to London, Chicago, or Los Angeles: the well-to-do have remained close to the center, often in multi-story apartment buildings that allow them to share the cost of security, while the poor are concentrated in neighborhoods of one- and two-story buildings on the southern outskirts. (A few gated suburban communities are now cropping up in the far north.) Fully half the city developed spontaneously and illegally. With a population of 7.4 million, in densities approaching those of Madrid and London, Bogotá can easily supply the ridership necessary for subways and heavy rail. It also happens to have hundreds of miles of broad avenues and city-straddling multilane expressways, ideally suited for fast bus service.

"TransMilenio is like Curitiba on steroids. It's the first BRT system in the world to handle so many passengers, a volume you normally see in metros," Dario Hidalgo told me, as his housekeeper brought us a pot of strong coffee. Hidalgo was responsible for implementing TransMilenio during Peñalosa's mayoralty, and as a consultant for the Washington-based Center for Sustainable Transport, he has since toured the world doing comparative studies of BRT systems. "I'm a transport engineer, and I was educated to create space for cars. When you go to school, they give you the highway capacity manual, and you're supposed to calculate the number of cars and create the number of lanes the cars need. It's the standard way of doing transport in the United States, Canada, and Australia. But it's not something that works in our society. When less than a fifth of your people own cars, you can't dedicate most of your funding to roads." Hidalgo agreed with Peñalosa that a BRT system like Curitiba's would be an ideal fit for Bogotá.

"To make a real bus rapid transit system," said Hidalgo, "you need dedicated bus lanes, separated from the rest of traffic. Your buses can't be moving through mixed traffic." The best, he believes, are busways, lanes physically segregated by curbs, rumble strips, guide rails, or other barriers. "Then you need real stations. Not just bus shelters, but stations with level boarding and prepayment, so you pay before going into the station and, when the bus arrives, you just walk in like you do a metro." Prepayment speeds up boarding, and permits headways of as little as ten seconds. "You need information technologies to support the operation of the system. In

Bogotá, every privately owned TransMilenio bus has a GPS that sends its location to a control center, which is run by a government agency." Information technology also allows the use of contactless fare cards, whose sale is overseen by a separate private company. "Finally, you need a strong image. You don't run the same old *busetas*. You run really well-designed buses with their own colors, you brand the infrastructure with a name like TransMilenio. Only when you have all these components can you really call your system BRT."

Under Hidalgo's definition, most systems currently operating in North America don't qualify as bus rapid transit. The Orange Line, which I rode in Los Angeles, is what transit commentators call "Light Rail Lite": built along a politically expedient former railway right-of-way, with widely spaced stations, it functions more like a light-rail line, one that happens to run on rubber tires. The Select Bus Service that follows 207th Street in the Bronx has had some success, but because its marked lanes aren't physically separated from traffic, it means they too often get blocked by delivery vehicles, double-parked cars and even police cruisers. (New York City's Department of Transportation plans to open a river-to-river bus transitway, complete with separate lanes, along Thirty-fourth Street by 2012.) The Transitway system in Ottawa, which has been running since 1983, is an influential early attempt at BRT, but there are few enclosed stations—a real drawback in the frigid Canadian capital—and buses slow to a crawl when they mix with downtown traffic. Hidalgo gives high marks to Cleveland's HealthLine, which runs articulated buses along a corridor of universities and hospitals. It not only meets all the criteria of BRT, but there is evidence it has fostered billions of dollars' worth of new development along Euclid Avenue. The best example of BRT in the developed world, according to Hidalgo, is the Busway network in Brisbane, Australia, which follows the TransMilenio model of segregated busways, enclosed stations, and passing lanes.

The simple fact is that buses, those much-hated "loser cruisers," remain a hard sell in North America. Many transit advocates see BRT as rail transport's poor cousin, or at best a stepping-stone to light rail. But in cities that can't afford rail transit, a fully implemented BRT system can be an efficient and sustainable form of transit. Even in Bogotá, though, there are signs that BRT is running into problems. After our coffee, Hidalgo invited me out for a stroll to take a look at his system in action. It was rush hour, and a crimson stream of fully loaded buses flowed down Avenida Caracas.

There was no denying TransMilenio's efficiency, but I pointed out there didn't seem to be much residential development on the street; we were standing in front of a flood-lit soccer pitch, for example, whose forecourt had been converted into a private parking lot. Hidalgo said: "The city could have used real estate development as a funding mechanism to build transit infrastructure, as they do in Hong Kong and Singapore. When he was mayor, Enrique Peñalosa asked us to do urban development around Trans-Milenio stations. But we had only three years to implement the system, so we had to ask him: 'Do you want a perfect city or something?'" Unlike Curitiba's BRT, which was built in tandem with specially designed roads, TransMilenio was retrofitted into major arteries that had existed for decades. "Maybe we missed an opportunity to do transit-oriented development. But the city has rezoned some areas, and private developers are doing taller, mixed-use buildings close to TransMilenio, so it may be happening organically, not as a project managed by the city."

Viewed from sidewalk level, it was impossible not to notice Trans-Milenio's heavy-handed presence in the city. The system's main trunk lines threw imposing barriers across Bogotá, creating raging cataracts of traffic that pedestrians can only traverse by using circuitous overpasses. In its way, TransMilenio was as disruptive as any urban expressway, and the air on Avenida Caracas seemed as bad as what you would breathe on the shoulder of a Los Angeles freeway. I told Hidalgo I probably wouldn't want to live next to his BRT line.

"TransMilenio uses diesel," said Hidalgo, with a sigh. "It's a sad thing, I know. Diesel in Colombia still has five hundred parts per million of sulfur. There are plans to reduce it to fifty, which is the standard in North America, but that won't happen for at least five years. There are all kinds of issues with particulate matter and respiratory disease." (The United Nations allows TransMilenio to sell carbon credits to other cities not because it uses clean fuel, but because the system has removed so many *busetas*, which are even more polluting, from the streets.) Diesel-electric buses, acknowledged Hidalgo, would be the best alternative; they pollute less and consume 90 percent less gas than regular buses, but cost three times as much to buy. Cleveland uses them on its HealthLine, but its fleet is fifty times smaller than Bogotá's.

TransMilenio's other challenge, of course, is that it has become ridiculously crowded. Every bus we watched leaving the station was filled to capacity. As we walked back up Calle 72, Hidalgo was quiet for a couple of blocks. I asked what was on his mind. "It's just that I would have preferred the system to run much better than it is running." It was a startling admission to hear from the man responsible for implementing one of the most studied and highly praised BRT systems in the world. "I mean, six standees per square meter, that's not good. People still use TransMilenio, because it's the best alternative for them. But it's running at a level of service that is not acceptable to users. *Something* has to be done."

For some Bogotanos, I would discover, that "something" meant improving and expanding TransMilenio. For others, it meant investing in an entirely new form of transit. One thing was pretty clear: in Bogotá, where transit is king, there was no shortage of ideas.

A Victim of Its Success

It was about to rain. You could tell because vendors, clutching handfuls of rolled umbrellas, suddenly appeared in every alley and doorway in the Candelaria.

Then the downpour began, chasing scores of commuters into the shelter of the TransMilenio station near Bogotá's emerald district. As they waited out the flood, I talked to some of them about what, if anything, could be done to solve the city's traffic problems.

Julia Maria Gomez, a print shop employee in her mid-forties, said she had been riding TransMilenio since it was inaugurated in 2000. Compared to a *buseta*, it shaved an hour off her commute every day. "It's faster, but it's getting more crowded, and people don't have as much respect as they used to. There used to be all kinds of education campaigns; for example, to encourage people to help handicapped people. Now it is so crowded everybody just pushes in. And when the buses are late, the station starts to get really packed." She said that even if somebody offered her a car, she would not accept; driving in Bogotá was too stressful. But she didn't think building a metro was the answer. "A metro is only going to serve high-income neighborhoods. It won't reach the really dense parts of the city, the people that really use public transport. And we citizens will have to pay the costs for years to come."

The current mayor, Samuel Moreno, had defeated Enrique Peñalosa in 2007 by promising to build a metro. One of the proposed routes was along Carrera Séptima, Bogotá's version of Los Angeles's Miracle Mile, which extends from the Candelaria toward the wealthier neighborhoods in the north. Building this single line would cost the equivalent of four billion dollars over the next twenty years, 70 percent of which would be paid by the federal government. But Moreno's term was coming to an end, and he had yet to sign a single contract. TransMilenio's infrastructure, meanwhile, was already showing its age. In many places, slabs of asphalt had subsided and cracked, forcing drivers to proceed at a crawl. The only new phase under construction, a line set to reach the airport in 2012 that was currently a muddy trench along Calle 26, was $300 million over budget, and contractors accused Moreno and his brother of accepting kickbacks in exchange for fast-tracking approval of the project. (In 2011, Moreno was suspended from his duties as mayor and formally charged with fraudulent contracting, embezzlement, and extortion.)

Neglect of TransMilenio was just the start. Moreno's lack of a coherent transportation policy had undone most of the advances secured under the Mockus and Peñalosa mayoralties. The *pico y placa* restrictions, widely applauded when they were first introduced, worked well when they were limited to rush hours. But Moreno extended the restrictions to the entire day, which had the perverse effect of convincing many families to invest in a second and even a third car so they could drive all week. (Though a new car in Colombia costs $20,000, drivable used cars can be found at a tenth the price.)

Inside the Avenida Jiménez station, I talked to Diego Lombana, a professional translator in his late thirties. Though Lombana owned a car, he was riding TransMilenio because his license plate ended in nine—which meant the *pico y placa* rules barred him from driving that day. "Look, TransMilenio is a good system," he said, speaking English with a South End accent he'd picked up after living in Boston for several years. "It's only going to take me thirty-five minutes to cross the city today. It would take longer in my ca'. The only thing is, riding it standing up, it's not fun. And the asphalt plates they did keep on crackin'. If they don't improve TransMilenio, it's gonna be obsolete pretty soon." I asked him what he thought should be done. "I think we need a metro system. But it's not like it's going to happen any time soon. It's a solution for the next twenty years."

Did Bogotá's only hope lie in an expensive metro? Naturally, Enrique Peñalosa didn't think so. During our interview, the former mayor had stood up and pointed to an eight-story apartment building visible across a leafy park from his office. "Look!" he said. "That's my home. They are planning to build a metro station next to it. It would be perfect for me, so easy to get around! But a metro is not the solution. Naturally, all the old ladies who meet for tea around here think the *busetas* are terrible, and that a metro would help clear them off the street. But they don't have the slightest intention of using the metro. They will be driven around, as they always are." He accused European railcar manufacturers such as Siemens and Alstom of aggressive behind-the-scenes lobbying for the metro. Peñalosa's solution, not surprisingly, was to improve and expand his brainchild, TransMilenio.

"We can increase capacity in three ways. We have to make the stations bigger, so there aren't these horrible lineups. We have to put more access points in each station, so people can buy tickets at different entrances. And we need to build underpasses at some intersections, so car traffic doesn't interfere with TransMilenio." Most important, all the originally planned phases of TransMilenio had to be built. "A subway will reach only five percent of the population, but TransMilenio will go everywhere. And we need TransMilenio everywhere!"

Most of the analysts I talked to agreed that TransMilenio was caught in a trap. Conceived as a public-private partnership, the system was planned for passenger volumes high enough to make the system profitable with revenue from passengers' fares alone. But there's no incentive for the four conglomerates that operate the system to provide TransMilenio with more buses and drivers; in fact, running as few buses as possible allows them to keep costs down. The result, inevitably, is overcrowding.

"We're paying too high a price for TransMilenio's profitability," said Ricardo Montezuma, a transit commentator and director of Bogotá's non-profit Humane City Organization. "TransMilenio started off really well, but every day, people are looking for cheaper, faster alternatives and leaving the system. They buy cars, they buy motorcycles." I had noticed the abundance of motorcyclists on Bogotá's streets. Obliged to wear helmets and fluorescent vests bearing a license plate number—a legacy of the days streetbike-riding gunmen carried out assassinations—they could be seen roaring ahead of traffic at every intersection.

"Nobody used to ride motorcycles in Bogotá, because it rains so much. But the number of motorcycles has increased tenfold in the last fifteen years. There are two hundred thousand of them now, and a million cars." Montezuma believed the only way to stem the defection of bus riders to private transportation was to charge drivers entering the city a fee, similar to London's congestion charge, that would be used to subsidize better Trans-Milenio service. (He also favored replacing the polluting TransMilenio buses with rubber-tired electric trolleys, powered by Colombia's abundant hydroelectric power—an elegant, if dauntingly expensive, solution.)

TransMilenio was caught in the same trap the New York subway had been in the 1920s, when the contractually guaranteed nickel fare brought overcrowding and declining service, and led compressed straphangers to defect to automobiles. Dario Hidalgo told me that using a congestion charge, parking revenues, or increased gas taxes to subsidize Trans-Milenio's operating costs would give the private operators the financial leeway to run more buses, which might be enough to stem the overcrowd-ing that was tarnishing the system's image. "The truth is that the subway advocates, the bus advocates, the light-rail advocates, spend too much fighting about public transport modes, when the real fight is with the car. I would love subways to be less expensive than they are. But we need to find solutions with the resources we have."

The whole debate reminded me of the rhetoric that pitted the Bus Riders' Union against Antonio Villaraigosa, Los Angeles's "Subway Mayor." The well-to-do in both cities favored a subway, mostly because it would serve rich neighborhoods, and had the potential to remove troublesome buses from the roads—in turn making life a whole lot easier for motorists. I appreciated the symbolic value of BRT: it would be a triumph for social justice if several lanes of every freeway in Los Angeles were exclusively devoted to high-speed buses. But a TransMilenio-scaled BRT network is about as likely to come to Southern California as a late-spring ice storm. While the political stars are in alignment, Angelenos should probably jump on the opportunity to build their new subway—the best transit their tax dollars could buy them—which could serve as a long-term backbone for a much bigger system.

Bus rapid transit makes a lot of sense in cities without the resources to build rail transit, but there is no denying that it can be as disruptive to neighborhood life as a freeway. It was a sign of the times, I figured, that Ottawa, the pioneer of BRT in North America, had recently announced it was replacing its twenty-five-year-old bus transitways with a light-rail system, much of it underground.

The Exit from Tragedy

Globally, carbon emissions from transportation are expected to rise by over 50 percent by 2030, and the bulk of the increase will occur in the burgeoning metropolises of the developing world. By removing 7,000 old, polluting *busetas* from the streets of Bogotá, TransMilenio reduced annual carbon emissions by a quarter of a million tons, and showed that a streamlined transport system could improve mobility in even a poor and chaotic city. Bogotá was also the first metropolis I'd visited where transit alone—without significant changes to urban structure—had decreased congestion and fostered the growth of new public space.

But bus rapid transit owes its success to conditions that may be unique to the developing world. In the Brazilian city of Curitiba, it was implemented by a mayor appointed by a military dictatorship, who could impose urban reform with little public consultation. In Bogotá, the situation was more complex. Constitutional reform in the early '90s gave sweeping powers to municipal governments, and, as Eleonora Passota has observed in her study *Political Branding in Cities*, mayors such as Mockus and Peñalosa broke with the old political machine in favor of "brand politics," using the media to communicate directly with citizens, while sidestepping consultation with district councilors. Bogotá's mayors continue to enjoy an independence, prestige, and latitude unknown in North America. Some commentators say only term limits prevent them from wielding dictatorial power. (As a candidate for the Green Party, Mockus ran a close second in the presidential elections of 2010.) Had either Mockus or Peñalosa had Robert Moses's inclinations toward freeway-building, Bogotá might be a very different place today.

By claiming road space from cars, TransMilenio brought the clash between public good and private interest into the political discourse. In a city whose low motorization rate means that, for the vast majority, *every* day is car-free day, TransMilenio showed you can win popular support for ambitious schemes that limit the use of automobiles, even when they are the preferred method of transportation of the rich and influential. The lessons of Bogotá are relevant to other cities, particularly in the developing world, because, from sidewalk-blocking bollards, to bike paths, to BRT, they map out an incremental process of municipal transformation.

On my last day in Bogotá, I was about to cross the street on my way to the Gabriel García Márquez Center in the Candelaria, when a cop on a motorcycle, its siren blaring, blocked my path. Another swooped to a halt, barring the side street, and two more roared ahead, holding back the traffic a block ahead. A line of pedestrians and vehicles formed—*busetas* filled with workers in overalls, students from the nearby university, a horse-drawn cart piled with bags of cement. After half a minute's wait, the reason for the roadblock became apparent. A troika of black Toyota V6 SUVs thundered past, armored sides gleaming and tinted windows repelling gazes, headed in the direction of the presidential palace, congress, and city hall—the center of power in Colombia. The motorcycle cops, their work clearing a passage for the VIPs done, roared away, finally releasing the tides of apparently far less important Bogotanos.

It reminded me of how the oligarchs of Moscow cut through traffic, *migalki* flashing and sirens blaring. It also made me realize that, if I lived in Bogotá, I would be a proud rider of those crowded red buses.

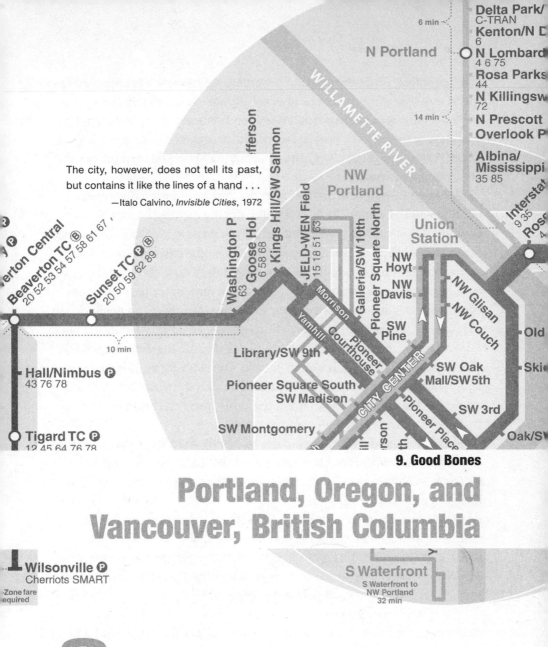

The city, however, does not tell its past,
but contains it like the lines of a hand . . .
—Italo Calvino, *Invisible Cities*, 1972

WILLAMETTE RIVER

Delta Park/
C-TRAN
Kenton/N D
6
N Lombard
4 6 75
Rosa Parks
44
N Killingsw
72
N Prescott
Overlook P
Albina/
Mississippi
35 85

N Portland

6 min
14 min

NW
Portland

Union
Station

Interstat
9 35
Ros

NW
Hoyt
NW
Davis
SW
Pine

NW Glisan
NW Couch

Old

erton Central
Beaverton TC Ⓑ
20 52 53 54 57 58 61 67

Sunset TC Ⓟ Ⓑ
20 50 59 62 89

Washington P
63

Goose Hol
6 58 68

Kings Hill/SW Salmon

JELD-WEN Field
15 18 51 63

Galleria/SW 10th

Pioneer Square North

Jefferson

Morrison

Yamhill

Pioneer
Courthouse

CITY CENTER

SW Oak
Mall/SW 5th

Ski

10 min

Library/SW 9th

Pioneer Square South
SW Madison

SW Montgomery

Pioneer Place

SW 3rd

Oak/S

Hall/Nimbus Ⓟ
43 76 78

Tigard TC Ⓟ
12 45 64 76 78

9. Good Bones

Portland, Oregon, and
Vancouver, British Columbia

Wilsonville Ⓟ
Cherriots SMART

Zone fare
equired

S Waterfront
S Waterfront to
NW Portland
32 min

Some of the cities I'd seen in my travels made me dream of becoming an expatriate.

I envied the people of Tokyo their idyllic residential neighborhoods, those cozy warrens where cats roam free and people run errands on bikes and stroll to nearby train stations. I could imagine raising a family in Freiburg's car-free Vauban neighborhood, and I would love a pied-à-terre in Paris, preferably one within walking distance of a tram line. Even Bogotá had a certain appeal—especially on a Sunday, when the roads are closed to traffic and the entire city seems to pour into the streets to join the parade of pedestrians and cyclists. And ever since I've been to Copenhagen, I've been trying to convince my wife to visit that urban utopia on the Baltic, where people ride cargo bikes instead of driving SUVs and even the elderly are fit enough to pedal.

All these cities share a common trait: they have fostered an enviable quality of life by improving transit and reducing car dependency. I wasn't convinced, however, that you could graft the transport policies of Asian, European, and Latin American metropolises on the cities of North America and expect similar results. European capitals, with their historic metro or tramway networks and medieval cores built for foot traffic, tend to have central-city residential densities that few American cities can come close to matching. In the cities of Japan, which developed largely thanks to their rail networks, the private automobile never became the default mode of transportation, and remains an expensive accessory for running errands and making pleasure trips. And in the dense central cities of South America, where the vast majority of urbanites don't own cars, promising better transit can actually win politicians elections.

The municipal fabric of most cities in North America is vastly different. Since the first Curved Dash Oldsmobile rolled off an assembly line in Lansing, Michigan, in 1901, the mass-produced, gas-powered automobile has put an indelible stamp on the continent. Loop-and-lollipop subdivisions and freeway-interchange edge cities, the most transit-resistant forms of development, have become the template for far too much of the national landscape. From Newport News to New Westminster, the ubiquity of car-centered development can make reverse-engineering our way out of sprawl seem like the most delusional of pipe dreams.

There is at least one city in the United States that points the way to a different kind of future. I know what easterners say about Portland, Oregon. Nice enough, in a crunchy-granola, moss-on-the-shingles, vegan cat-food kind of way. This, after all, is the '50s-style small-town-in-the-city of the Ramona Quimby children's stories, the Keep-Portland-Weird anticorporate haven of author Chuck Palahniuk's fugitives and refugees—the kind of place, famously, where young people go to retire. All right if you want to devote your life to organic beer, secondhand vinyl, or fixed-wheel bikes, but if you've got serious ambitions, or want to make real money, *fuggedaboutit*. Really, though, all the Portlandia flakiness is only skin deep; in many ways, this is a typical midsize American city, one whose economy has lately weathered the transition from shipbuilding, flour milling, and pulp-and-paper processing to pumping out Intel chips, Nike running shoes, and Columbia "activewear." With a population of 600,000, Portland is now just the central city in a metro region of 27 municipalities, whose two million residents are spread over three counties that include their share of strip malls, surface parking lots, and postwar sprawl.

Yet at a crucial point in its development, Portland made key planning and transportation choices that are now starting to pay off. These days, the people of Portland, whose per capita transit ridership rivals that of Chicago, Philadelphia, and many other older, denser cities, are twice as likely to use public transport as the average American; they also travel 20 percent fewer miles a day and spend far less of their household income on transportation. A 52-mile system of four light-rail lines, slated to expand a further ten miles in the next six years, takes commuters through pine forests to distant suburbs, and to within a couple of hundred feet of the baggage check at the international airport. And, thanks to a network of 260 miles of bike paths, Portlanders are now more likely to get to work by bicycle than the inhabitants of any other American city.*

Predictably, when it comes to public transport and transit-oriented development (TOD), the city is getting some things wrong. More assuredly than almost anywhere else in America, though, Portland is charting a course that will allow it to thrive in a future of higher energy prices. And the way Portland is using intelligent transportation policy to escape the worst excesses of automobile dominance shows there is hope for other cities— even young places whose greatest growth spurts occurred after the war.

A Picnic on the Freeway

The center of Portland is alive in a way that few downtowns in the west are. Built on a gridwork of short, 200-foot blocks—a pattern that multiplies the corner lots that showcase heritage buildings, including one of the continent's largest concentrations of cast-iron buildings—it sometimes feels like a Gold Rush mini-Manhattan. Unlike Los Angeles's downtown,

* According to U.S. Census data, in the city of Portland, 6.4 percent of residents were bicycle commuters in 2008—a figure that's more than doubled in a decade, and only a poor showing when you recall the 37 percent of Copenhageners who get to work by bike.

made desolate by too many surface parking lots and blank-faced office buildings, Portland's has real, round-the-clock urbanity. The few vacant lots are filled with gypsy camps of semipermanent food carts offering Turkish lavash, Ethiopian injera, and Latin-Asian fusions like Korean kimchi-quesadillas. The old flagship department stores never fled to out-lying malls, a good percentage of regional employment remains centered in its office towers, and, crucially, people still live here. And I may be biased, but any place that counts a bookstore that sprawls over an entire city block—the astonishing, labyrinthine Powell's—as a prime downtown attraction clearly has a lot going for it.

Yet something is missing from downtown Portland.

I vaguely sensed this absence the first time I visited; this time around, it hit me almost immediately. At Pioneer Courthouse Square, hundreds of revelers were lined up for the Holiday Ale Festival, undeterred by the news that a Somali teenager had been arrested a week before for allegedly plotting to bomb a Christmas tree lighting in the same square. A stray drunken Santa—Portland is known for its gangs of rogue Kris Kringles—paused to wet his beard at a Benson Bubbler, one of the bronze four-armed water fountains, as elegant as anything you'd find on the streets of Paris, donated to the city by a Gilded Age lumber baron. At the outdoor Satur-day Market, I briefly joined a crowd that had gathered to stomp their feet to a raucous ten-piece gypsy-klezmer band. It was only as I crossed Burn-side Avenue toward Union Station, and heard a train whistle ricocheting between the steel bridges spanning the Willamette River, that I realized what Portland was lacking. I'd been strolling downtown for over two hours and had yet to encounter that bane of the North American metrop-olis: the neighborhood-killing, blight-inducing, multilaned freeway.

The few urban expressways the city has are well hidden. Interstate 5, which parallels the Pacific Coast from Canada to Mexico, is routed through the warehouses and used car lots of East Portland, on the other side of the Willamette. The I-405 loop separates the downtown from the wealthy West Hills, but it is buried in a trough, allowing major arterials to span the interstate at grade. And on the downtown side of the river, where any other city would have put an expressway, cyclists pedal on sinuous paths beneath the Japanese cherry trees in Tom McCall Waterfront Park.

When it comes to the suburbanization of the American metropolis, Portland's downtown is the exception that proves the rule. The middle-class abandonment of central cities, the story goes, was the result of flight from civil unrest and widespread consumer preference for spacious suburban living. In fact, in city after city, the onset of urban decline can be dated to a single, epoch-making event: the 1956 signing of the Federal Aid Highway and Revenue Act, which launched the interstate highway system, the largest public works project in world history.

In every way, it is an astonishing achievement. Officially known as the Dwight D. Eisenhower System of Interstate and Defense Highways, it now counts 47,000 miles of limited-access roadways, forming a grid of 62 continent-spanning superhighways with a minimum of two 12-foot-wide travel lanes in either direction, engineered to convey cars and trucks safely at speeds of up to 70 miles per hour. Efficiently linking the nation's 200 military bases, it includes the 8-mile Interstate H-2 on the Hawaiian island of Oahu, and the 3,000-mile Interstate 90 that connects Seattle to Boston, as well as 104 tunnels and 54,633 bridges. By the time the system as originally conceived was completed—with the paving of Colorado's Glenwood Canyon on Interstate 70 in 1992, and twenty years behind schedule—it had cost American taxpayers the equivalent of half a trillion dollars.

Before the twentieth century, roads in the United States were almost exclusively built and maintained by local governments, leading to spectacular variations in quality. It was cyclists, not motorists, who launched the Good Roads movement in the 1880s; the hundred-thousand-member strong League of American Wheelmen was the first group to lobby governments to pave over rutted roads so they could be freed from the "thralldom of mud." Farmers, meanwhile, tended to oppose cross-country highways, which they saw as pleasure paths for idle city dwellers, preferring improved rural roads to markets and railheads. Early in the twentieth century, as historian Owen Gutfreund recounts in *Twentieth-Century Sprawl*, "a dizzying array of interested lobbying groups insinuated their economic interests into the fabric of American political and popular cultures, and into the state and federal legal codes." Though early limited-access toll roads such as the Pennsylvania Turnpike were profitable, they were seen as undemocratic, and a consensus emerged among the highway lobbyists: the new expressways should be public enterprises, charging no tolls—in a word, *freeways*.

The interstate system's origins were military. In 1919, a young Dwight D. Eisenhower was part of a convoy that took over two months to cross the country from Washington, D.C., to San Francisco. Later, as Supreme Commander of the Allied Forces, he witnessed the way the autobahns,

Germany's limited-access superhighways, allowed Hitler's army to zip around the Fatherland, making *blitzkrieg* devastatingly successful. "The old convoy had started me thinking about good, two-lane highways," Eisenhower wrote in his memoirs, "but Germany had made me see the wisdom of broader ribbons across the land."

As the first Republican president since Herbert Hoover, Eisenhower used these broad ribbons to gift-wrap a Cold War present to the American people. At first the interstates, which allowed drivers to drive "coast-to-coast without a stoplight," were greeted with enthusiasm. But it soon became clear that the engineers, many of whom had served under Robert Moses in New York, fully intended to drive their new roads into the hearts of cities, flattening any neighborhood that got in their way. What's more, the draftsmen's T-bars had a suspicious tendency to settle on Jewish, African American, Puerto Rican, and Chinese areas—the high road to suburbia apparently coinciding with the path of least social resistance.

Moses's Cross-Bronx Expressway had already laid East Tremont to waste, but as the technocrats went national, they disemboweled much that was vital in urban America. New Orleans's Claiborne Avenue, home to the longest contiguous chain of ancient oak trees on the continent, and whose front porches attracted jazzmen for impromptu pickup sessions, was permanently darkened by the elevated Interstate 10. In Miami's Overtown, black-owned businesses such as the Cotton Club and Rockland Palace were expropriated to make way for Interstate 95. Detroit's Black Bottom neighborhood, where Aretha Franklin sang in her father's Baptist church, was bulldozed for the sake of the Chrysler Freeway. (Michigan's governor would later testify that he believed freeway construction was a major cause of the 1967 race riots that left over a thousand buildings in ruins and forty-three people dead.) The expressways that made city center life unlivable facilitated the flight to suburban bedroom communities, turning downtowns into little more than "central business districts."

The unstoppable freeway juggernaut soon ran up against the most unlikely of immovable objects. In Greenwich Village, Jane Jacobs had led the community protests that ultimately killed the Lower Manhattan Expressway. In Memphis, an unlikely coalition of "little old ladies in tennis shoes" prevented Interstate 40 from destroying Overton Park, where Elvis Presley had given his first paid performance. Protesters were able to halt virtually all freeway construction in San Francisco, leaving only the stump of the elevated Embarcadero Freeway standing until its demolition after the 1989 earthquake. Were it not for these middle-class obstruction-ists, New Orleans's French Quarter, San Francisco's Golden Gate Park, and the historic center of Boston would now be buried under pavement.

The freeway gang had long held Portland in its sights. In 1943, Robert Moses was invited by a city commissioner to chart out a postwar freeway plan for the Rose City. "Every citizen of Portland," he proclaimed in an 86-page report, "has a right to be proud of the fact that this community is prepared, while there is still time, to face the future with unclouded vision." Moses's vision for Portland, not surprisingly, involved an inner and outer ring of "thruways." In the 1950s, the Oregon Highway Division followed many of Moses's recommendations, building the Sunset Highway and Interstate 5 when federal funds became available. High-capacity tunnels were bored through the West Hills, which had traditionally limited the spread of downtown Portland, initiating the sprawl that would soon over-whelm once-rural Washington Country.

Portland's freeway revolt began with a picnic. "Harbor Drive was this kind of grade-level pre-interstate," urban studies professor Carl Abbott explained to me in his office at Portland State University's downtown cam-pus. "It was built in the forties as a bypass around downtown, and created a barrier to the waterfront. In the mid-sixties, this big white elephant, the *Oregon Journal* building, was finally torn down, and the Highway Division saw it as an opportunity to reengineer Harbor Drive into a freeway." On a midsummer day in 1969, a couple of hundred families staged a peaceful protest. "They spread their blankets and opened their baskets on this bar-ren strip between eight lanes of busy traffic, and carefully tethered their kids to keep them from straying into the cars. They called themselves Riv-erfront for People, and they really changed the agenda by getting rid of the idea of a Harbor Freeway altogether." Today, in the grassy park that now stands on the west bank of the Willamette River, parents let their toddlers wander free.

The next battle was fought over the construction of the Mount Hood Freeway—named after the still active snowcapped volcano that glowers over downtown from the horizon—whose planned route would have cut a 6-mile swath through southeast Portland, taking out almost 2,000 homes. The half-dozen neighborhoods that rose up in true grassroots outrage against the plan had the sympathy of Governor Tom McCall. Born in Massachusetts and raised on a ranch in central Oregon, McCall repre-sented an all but forgotten strain of moderate Republicanism: vehemently pro-environment and anti-growth, McCall railed in the legislature against "sagebrush subdivisions, coastal condomania, and the ravenous rampage of suburbia." In 1974 McCall informed the federal government he would use the money intended for the Mount Hood Freeway to build a regional public transport system.

According to transport scholar Sy Adler, who also teaches at Portland State, "Portland was only the second place in the country, after Boston, to take advantage of this federal opportunity to trade in freeway money for a set of substitute transport investments." Since 1964, the Urban Mass Transportation Act had offered federal funding to cover up to two-thirds of transit equipment purchases—but with the feds offering to pay nine-tenths of freeway costs, cash-strapped jurisdictions had tended to opt for more asphalt. Bucking the trend, the Oregon legislature created the publicly managed TriMet, which took over the assets of Rose City Transit, a bankrupt private bus-and-streetcar company. TriMet started by turning several downtown blocks into a transit mall in 1978; eight years later, it inaugurated a light-rail line along an old railway right-of-way to the city of Gresham, fifteen miles to the east.

After becoming the first city to turn a freeway revolt into a pro-transit revolution, Portland set another precedent by creating Metro, one of the few true regional governments in the United States, and the only one elected by popular vote. One of Metro's first moves was to draw up an urban growth boundary, establishing a twenty-year supply of land that limited Portland's metro area to 370 square miles (the current boundary regulates land use until 2040). It wasn't a new idea; the *Fluchtlinienplan* system had restricted the growth of German cities since the nineteenth century, and town planners in England had been limiting suburbanization with greenbelts—strips of land kept in a natural or undeveloped state— since the 1930s. It remains controversial, however, especially among those who believe government has no business messing with growth.

"The urban growth boundary was established by the state legislature when Portland was still the big kid on the block," pointed out Adler. "It would never happen today, when the suburbs are far more substantial. And because the economy was in the toilet for much of the eighties, it wasn't until ten years ago that the boundary really started to bite." The growth boundary, which has forced developers to fill empty lots and brownfields (former industrial sites) rather than build on farm and forest land, has achieved many of its goals. Though Portland's population has grown by half since 1973, its total area has only increased by 2 percent. Meanwhile, its downtown population has grown at about the same rate as its suburbs, while the suburbs of comparably sized cities have grown three to four times as quickly as their downtowns. Sprawl apologists claim the growth boundary has driven up housing prices, but in relation to median income, houses in Portland remain more affordable than similar homes in Seattle, Salt Lake City, Los Angeles, and other western cities.

Portland's early commitment to transit and regional planning has put the city in a privileged position to weather an era of higher energy prices. Of course, not everybody sees the city's rejection of freeways as some western version of the Declaration of Independence. Some people think what Portland, and all of America, needs is not fewer freeways, but more—a lot more.

The Freeway Counter-Revolutionary

On a Friday morning, I boarded a westbound 56 bus at the corner of Fifth and Alder. Portland's buses, New Flyers running on a blend of diesel and vegetable oil now standard in many fleets, are nothing special, but they attract a ridership you don't see in many American cities. On the 56, a middle-aged woman in a polar fleece jacket on the front bench seat was flipping through a Kindle, and a bearded man in a rain jacket and shorts fished through a blue bin at the front of the bus for a recycled copy of *The Oregonian*. After loading a mountain bike on the rack on the front of the bus, a slender man in a black raincoat pulled a copy of Louis-Ferdinand Céline's *Death on the Installment Plan* out of his backpack. This was the same demographic I saw on the trams of Freiburg or Strasbourg: middle-class, educated, environmentally aware.

As the bus left Portland city limits and entered suburban Washington County, the roadside bike paths ended, and Rite-Aids and Safeways surrounded by land-gobbling parking lots began to appear. I got off at Scholls Ferry Road, and puzzled over how best to approach the Cascades Policy Institute, which is headquartered in a three-story building fronted by a parking lot. From the sidewalk, there was no path for pedestrians, so I had to hop over a landscaped median of cedar chips and bushes. The only conceivable way to approach a libertarian think tank, apparently, is by car.

John Charles invited me into his office. A native of New Jersey, Charles came to Oregon thirty years ago, and has been president of the Institute—a twelve-person research center focused on liberty, property rights, and free markets—since 2005. He is well known in the Pacific Northwest for his op-eds attacking regional planning policies and in support of more freeway building.

"There is *nothing* progressive about Portland," Charles began. "This is the do-nothing city. Since Interstate 205 opened thirty years ago, we haven't built another highway. Every day the number of vehicle miles traveled goes up, and yet the highway capacity is fixed. Every light-rail line that has opened has cannibalized scarce road space and made it tougher to drive. And these people at the City of Portland, Metro, TriMet—they're all interchangeable, it's all incestuous—are still reading off this playbook from the early seventies. 'We killed the Mount Hood Freeway, and now we're going to take this slow, expensive light-rail line, we're going to finance this goofy streetcar, and call ourselves cutting edge.' Here's their big intellectual view: cars are bad."

The light-rail system, in Charles's view, is an expensive toy that serves only a tiny fraction of the population.

"You have this slow train network that doesn't go very many places, and can never hope to imitate the ubiquitous road system, so you're chasing this silly utopian goal that can never be reached. It's not rapid, it's not high capacity, it's not comfortable. The seats are built for midgets. And because of the free rail zone downtown, it attracts a bunch of transients and gangsters, especially in the winter, when it's cold and wet. It's gross."

TriMet, according to Charles, has become a money pit. As Oregon has no sales tax, the agency's main source of revenue is a payroll tax, which all businesses, no matter their size, have to pay. Charles believes most of the money goes to feeding TriMet employees' salaries and fringe benefits.

"Transit doesn't need any more subsidies. We need to *cut* the subsidies. Transit should be self-supporting. What we need is to deregulate to get rid of this behemoth TriMet, and enable private sector transit with niche markets of legalized jitneys again." Like most libertarians, Charles believes that if transit can't pay for itself out of the fare box, it has no business to exist. Privately owned cars should suffice for most people's transport needs; the rest can rely on dollar vans and share taxis.

The flaw in their argument is that the freeways used by private cars aren't self-supporting, and never have been. Apologists for freeways argue that the 18.4 cents of every gallon of gas that goes to the Highway Trust Fund (an amount that hasn't been raised since 1993, and takes only $100 a year out of the pocket of the average driver) represents a user fee—

implying freeway drivers pay for the roads out of their own pockets. This is clearly nonsense: a car commuter in Chicago or Boston who relies on local roads to get to work nonetheless pays for the upkeep of interstates in, say, Montana or North Dakota, with every trip to the pump. And every non-driver who buys a laptop or a can of soup transported by truck is indirectly paying the gas taxes that are built into the sticker prices of all consumer goods. The U.S. Office of Technology Assessment estimates the total public subsidies to automobile and truck users, including road maintenance, traffic regulation, and free parking, are at least $447 billion a year, and could be as high as $899 billion a year. The renowned transportation scholar Vukan Vuchic estimates that motorists pay only 60 percent of the total cost of their highway travel; the remaining 40 percent is subsidized by various levels of government. In other words, freeways are almost exactly as reliant on public subsidies as big-city transit systems.

But Charles has an answer for that one, too: he believes we can save the freeways from congestion by privatizing them. Charging drivers to use roads, he believes, will restore the interstate system to its glory days, when traffic flowed freely. He would like to see new, privately run toll highways in Portland, of the kind that have already been tried in Los Angeles.

"But you could just as easily take the existing highway network," he said, warming to the subject, "and use transponders, electronic tolling and peak-hour pricing, and set the tolling rates to ensure free-flow conditions, and minimum speeds of forty-five miles an hour. Throughput would increase, gas consumption would go down, and motorists would be way happier."

Such a system would certainly ease congestion—for the select few. The express lanes on California's Riverside Freeway, one of the best-known private toll roads, aren't called Lexus lanes for nothing: for ten bucks, an Orange County executive can cruise to his office at 65, while his gardener spends his mornings stuck in traffic.

"You talk about subsidies to motorists," continued Charles. "All I can say is right now we motorists don't even have the *opportunity* to pay. If I'm sitting in traffic I can't just say, 'I'll take out my credit card, I'll swipe it, and I'll get to go around here and go fast.' The view of most of my environmental friends is sort of this Moscow-breadline thing, 'Comrade, we're so egalitarian. We're shoulder to shoulder wasting our time in traffic going nowhere, isn't that wonderful?' No, that's not wonderful, that's stupid."

I'll admit there have been times when I could have been tempted to buy my way past those annoying hordes in an airport security line, at the department of motor vehicles, or on a holiday weekend highway. But I wouldn't want to live in the kind of society where the rich can pay to pre-empt the poor on publicly funded infrastructure. Revolutions have been fought for less.

From the omnibuses of nineteenth-century Manhattan to the jeepneys of contemporary Manila, the free market has shown itself spectacularly ill suited to providing effective transit to cities. As I learned in France, private transit companies make a profit by making unrealistically low bids for service contracts, then billing local governments for cost overruns. In Indiana, Spanish and Australian investors have recently built a multibillion-dollar private highway—which looks like a good deal for the state, until you read the fine print, which shows American taxpayers are on the hook for making multimillon-dollar annual payments to the consortium for the next 75 years. When it comes to transportation networks, operational efficiency is best achieved when a single authority is free to carry out long-term planning, and many of the best have proved to be public agencies like TriMet. Organized public transport isn't the first step toward a One-World Government: it's just common sense.

After Charles had finished making his case, he accompanied me to the Institute's parking lot, where his wife was waiting for him behind the wheel of a silver SUV. He climbed in the passenger side, and they drove away. I walked back to the stop to wait for the 56 bus back downtown.

I wasn't surprised Charles hadn't offered me a lift. Libertarians tend to have a low tolerance for free riders. I didn't mind. It was a sunny day, and I had a good book to read.

The New Suburbanism

After only a couple of days of riding Portland's buses, streetcars, and light rail, I realized that most of John Charles's complaints were exaggerations. He had told me that downtown parking prices were out of hand, but I saw signs advertising all-day parking for only $9, a rate far too low to discourage people from bringing their cars downtown. Charles said the failure to build new freeways has fostered incredible congestion, but according to the Texas Transportation Institute's mobility report, the amount of time Portlanders spend in traffic is lower than average for a city of its size, and has actually been decreasing in recent years. And investments in transit appear to be paying off. Ridership in Portland has doubled over the last twenty years, while increasing only 15 percent nationally.

But some of Charles's criticisms of transit in Portland were justified. The west-side commuter rail line, for example, has failed to attract as many customers as it should, and I found I had to wait far too long for buses, especially outside the downtown. TriMet was the first agency in the United States to introduce the Frequent Network concept, guaranteeing minimum frequencies of ten minutes on key bus routes, but citing declining revenue from payroll taxes it has recently cut service to 17 minutes. Not only is cutting the bus service that feeds the entire system bad policy—and a good way to initiate a transit death spiral—it is also bad public relations, particularly when you are spending hundreds of millions of dollars to extend rail lines to well-off suburbs. People don't want to wait on the street a minute longer than they have to, especially in the rainy Pacific Northwest.

With that said, the MAX light-rail system (the name means Metropolitan Area Express) was a farsighted choice as the backbone of Portland's transit system. The low-floored, two-car MAX trains, which run on rails and are powered by overhead electric wires, are boxy, and have angular, slanted profiles—the height of aerodynamic styling in the '80s. On the Blue Line to Hillsboro one afternoon, a MAX train moved like a ponderous streetcar through the streets of downtown, operated like a subway as it entered a tunnel in the West Hills—at 260 feet, the station beneath the Portland Zoo is the deepest in North America—and then emerged from underground to move like a true light rail vehicle as it accelerated past the cars lined up bumper to bumper on Interstate 26.

Though MAX trains can reach 55 miles per hour for brief stretches, they average 20, including stops. For those who use it—and MAX generates 121,000 boardings a day, almost double what it did a decade ago—Portland's light rail is comfortable and reliable, a good compromise for both the city and the suburbs. But I hadn't come all the way to Oregon just to ride MAX. The Portland metro area is also home to the nation's most celebrated example of suburban transit-oriented development, Orenco Station.

Though previous New Urbanist communities, such as Andrés Duany's and Elizabeth Plater-Zyberk's Seaside and Celebration in Florida, have been praised for their walkability, critics have rightly pointed out that they are entirely automobile-dependent. In spite of the front porches and sidewalks, they remain subdivisions, accessible only by freeway off-ramps. Orenco Station was designed to be the first New Urbanist community to break free of auto-dependency, with a town center within walking distance of mass transit. When the MAX line reached Orenco Station in 1998, then–vice president Al Gore made a speech praising the development's walkability and proximity to transit, and *Sunset* magazine named it the "Best New 'Burb" of 2005.

I wanted to know if Orenco Station lived up to its billing. If good design and planning are enough to encourage suburbanites to start using transit, then it would make sense for planners to devote their efforts to boosting density in reimagined subdivisions. In an age of rising gas prices, Orenco Station could show there's hope for suburbia yet.

After a half-hour ride from downtown Portland, I got off at the Orenco stop. North of the tracks was a park-and-ride with spaces for hundreds of cars, only a dozen of which were occupied. It was a quarter-mile walk, past a vacant lot and a complex of three-story condos called Nexus, and finally across the busy and broad Cornell Road to Orenco Station's town center. It consisted of a supermarket, a post office, a kitchen store, a sushi bar and an Indian restaurant, a premium wine and cigar shop, and the inevitable Starbucks, where I met Debbie Raber, a planner for the nearby municipality of Hillsboro, who collaborated on the Orenco Station project.

"The subdivision's history goes back to 1959," she explained, "when a developer platted out nine hundred quarter-acre lots along Cornell Road. That deal was pretty much a classic land scam. The lots were sold sight unseen to unsuspecting people who were told they could get utilities from the city of Hillsboro, which was over two miles away. When the city said no, the ground just sat empty for thirty years."

Raber's municipality lobbied Metro to bring the MAX Blue Line to downtown Hillsboro, and master developer PacTrust, owned in part by the Oregon and Washington public employees retirement system, teamed up with Costa Pacific homes to develop the 200 acres at a significantly higher density than most suburban neighborhoods.

"Orenco abuts an older development, with single-family dwellings on ten-thousand-square-foot lots. The consternation in that neighborhood, when they learned the developer was planning to build houses on six-thousand-foot lots, could scarcely be overstated. It was like: 'What do you mean? There will be *renters*.'"

If anything, Orenco Station has raised local property values; houses here are worth 30 percent more than those in nearby subdivisions. Raber walked me down Orenco Station Parkway, whose three-story Victorian-style brownstones, fronted with broad sidewalks planted with wrought-iron lampposts, were designed to recall Boston's Back Bay neighborhood. The Parkway continued past live-work row houses to Orenco's Central Park, a grassy oblong surrounded on three sides by two-story houses on small lots. Down an alley, Raber showed me the garage-top "Granny flats"—also known as Fonzie suites, an allusion to the *Happy Days* rebel's apartment on top of a carport—which some Orenco residents rent out as bed-and-breakfasts. Parking is limited to one side of each narrow street, with garages in the back, so houses do not present blank faces to the street; all have deep porches, with front doors close to the lot line. Density in Orenco Station is about seven dwellings an acre in the single-home areas, and twenty per acre in the apartment and town house zones—a number high enough, in theory at least, to provide a decent ridership for light rail.

"When Orenco Station first opened," said Raber, "there were very few kids, because people weren't used to the idea of having no backyards." We were walking past a small park with a playground, empty except for a dog walker. "We're seeing more families as time goes on, but household sizes are definitely smaller here than in other suburbs. We find there are a lot of single women in Orenco Station. They're drawn by the security of the area, the good visibility and lighting and low crime rates."

With its sidewalks and parks, Orenco Station is far more walkable than most suburbs. On summer Sundays, there is a farmers' market in the parking lot of the supermarket. But the developer chose to locate Orenco Station's commercial strip along busy Cornell Road, rather than near the MAX station, and the walk to the light rail involves crossing five lanes of traffic, followed by a soul-deadening slog through the park-and-ride. And the question remains whether it really lives up to its billing as a transit-oriented suburb. On that score, residents give Orenco Station mixed reviews.

Tom Tiernan, whom I found taking notes on a biography of John Adams at a table at Starbucks, said he'd come to Orenco from Massachusetts six years ago, and currently owned a work-live town house on the Parkway. Single, in his mid-fifties, Tiernan appreciated the intentions behind Orenco. "I'll walk down to the post office to get my mail, and do some grocery shopping." But he didn't use light rail to commute. "I work from home. And the reality is, the area is pretty spread out, so you need to drive. I might use the MAX a half-dozen times a year to go to Powell's bookstore, music events, or the zoo. But mostly I drive." He pointed out his Acura, parked in the lot behind us.

At a small restaurant in the forecourt of the supermarket, I talked to Solomon Kinard and Donna McGregor, who were finishing off plates of pasta. They had owned a house together in Orenco Station for the last four years, but McGregor said neither of them commuted by light rail. "We'll use MAX on special occasions," said Kinard, "like a big downtown event, when we don't want to drive, or we want to drink, or we want to catch a plane out of town. You can ride the MAX from here to the airport, instead of leaving your car overnight. It's definitely convenient for that." Kinard worked as a programmer at the nearby Intel campus. "My commute's about ten minutes. I have ridden a bike to work before, I have walked, but I prefer to drive." He recalled that Intel had offered him free MAX passes, but he hadn't taken them up on it. Even though he was studying part-time at Portland State University three days a week, he still used his car to get downtown. "I would probably save time if I took MAX, but I still drive. Parking is free. I mean, it *feels* like it's free. If you're a student, it's built into your tuition fees." The couple had two cars, and even though gas prices were high, they planned on holding on to them. Said McGregor, "We've got kids, and a couple of dogs. You just *need* cars out here."

A study by Lewis and Clark College sociologist Bruce Podobnik confirms that, in spite of their proximity to transit, most Orenco Station residents continue to drive. Though more people here said they biked, walked, or carpooled to work than in nearby suburbs, only 15 percent commuted by MAX or bus, and fully 64 percent continued to get to work by car. Robert Cervero, the director of Berkeley's Transportation Center, sent a team to study Orenco Station and concluded that such suburban TODs simply offered too much parking. Developers, obviously wary of scaring off buyers, provided far more spaces per unit than were necessary, resulting in acres of park-and-rides and surface lots.

The real problem is that MAX doesn't take Orenco Station's residents where they need to go. The area's most important employer is Intel, and the computer chip maker has campuses dotted throughout the area—which has been dubbed the "Silicon Forest"—none of which are within walking distance of light rail. The front door of Intel's sprawling Ronler Acres, located to the north of Orenco Station, is over a mile from the MAX line. The company operates a shuttle bus service from the station, but it is woefully under-used.

Before leaving, I talked to Anne Reed, a nurse from Chicago in her mid-thirties who had moved to Orenco Station just a couple of weeks before; her husband, Ron, was scheduled to follow her in a few days. She confessed she was feeling a little skeptical about moving to the suburbs. "Coming from Chicago, I like the idea of living closer to the city. I'm not sure if I can get used to the pristineness of Orenco Station. When Ron gets here, we might want to move into downtown Portland."

I sympathized. Orenco Station trades on a manufactured quaintness that I find a little sinister—such nostalgic aesthetics, enforced by home-owners' associations, was exploited to good effect in *The Truman Show*, a movie shot on location in Florida's Celebration. Homes in Orenco Station are expensive, and such developments fail to create the mix of classes that make real city neighborhoods so vibrant: a national survey of New Urban-ist developments found that just 15 percent included any housing afford-able to households earning the median income for that region. I figured a more accurate label for these kinds of compact subdivisions, which have adopted the style but not the substance of urbanity, was actually "New Suburbanist." I asked myself whether I would want to live in Orenco Sta-tion. Somehow, I couldn't see Erin and me raising a family in a simulated Big-City Town house in the pine forests of the Pacific Northwest.

But I could easily see us moving to Old Orenco, a very different kind of community located just over the railway tracks from Orenco Station. Founded by the Oregon Nursery Company for its workers in 1906, Old Orenco is a classic company town. Migrant nursery workers from Hungary and Poland built rambling bungalows on a 1,200-acre tract located next to the old Oregon Electric interurban line. Wandering its potholed streets one afternoon, I fell in love with this exemplar of transit-oriented development, before the term existed. In Old Orenco, the Craftsman-style homes are the real thing, not some developer's clever simulacra; dogs sleep in the streets; and overgrown yards with pickups on cinder blocks are shaded by the spreading branches of century-old American elms. You are far enough out in the country to keep chickens and raise vegetables, but still within walking distance of a rail line should you need a dose of urbanity in downtown Port-land. In other words, the best of country and city—not something in between, a place, like Orenco Station, that so obviously yearns to be something it's not.

One thing is obvious: Orenco Station is no Vauban, the Freiburg suburb whose residents can live genuinely car-free lives thanks to a citywide network of tramways and intercity trains. Part of the problem is the mismatch between residences and job centers, but the bigger issue may be the sheer dominance of a landscape built by, and for, cars and freeways.

"Once you get outside the downtown, East Portland, and a couple of pockets like Orenco, Portland is like any other American city," conceded Berkeley planning professor Robert Cervero, one of the nation's leading experts on TOD. "It's low density, strip commercial, single-family detached. But you have to keep in mind that MAX and the streetcar are the beginning links of what will hopefully become a full-blown network. At this point, comparing rail with freeways is just not fair. If you're in a car, you've got the connectivity and coverage to go everywhere in the region. With Portland's current rail system, you might be able to serve ten percent of possible destinations. It's a very partial system that, one day, if it becomes like the Parisian métro and RER, will really be able to mimic the regional coverage of the motorway system. Hopefully our grandkids are going to inherit a mature, full-blown system." For the time being, Cervero suggested that a flexibly routed bus rapid transit network that connected with MAX lines might be the most sensible solution for Orenco Station and other Portland suburbs.

I was beginning to wonder if suburban developments, no matter how dense or close to transit, were really the way to go. In the wake of the subprime real estate crash, why focus on growth at all? Wasn't overbuilding suburban housing exactly what had gotten us into this mess? Portland, it seemed to me, had charted the way a generation ago when it introduced its urban growth boundary, challenging the value of the developers' "growth machine" as the foundation of a metropolitan economy. At a time when millions of homes are sitting empty, maybe we should be asking whether pursuing constant growth at the urban fringe—even when it's neatly wrapped up as Smart Growth—isn't a waste of valuable societal resources.

The planners of Portland, it turns out, were way ahead of me.

The Legacy of Good Bones

Portland, as the urbanists like to say, has good bones: it grew up around a pre–Second World War transit network, along arterials lined with small businesses, and the houses and apartments in its center and innermost suburbs were built within walking distance of old streetcar lines. The easiest way to revive such districts, many urbanists believe, is to restore and improve the frequent transit service that blew life into them in the first place.

Portland's Pearl District, which is located immediately north of the central business district, is a striking example. Fifteen years ago, it was a dicey area of abandoned warehouses and aging factories, sandwiched between Chinatown and Interstate 405. Today, American-made streetcars modeled on Czech trams glide between art galleries and ground-floor shops topped by five- to twenty-story condo towers, and the streets bustle with people heading for supermarkets, gyms, cafés, and scores of restaurants. Since the Portland streetcar began running in 2001, $3.5 billion in new development has been built within a two-block radius of its route. Though not all this growth can be attributed to the streetcar, it is clearly an amenity appreciated by residents of the Pearl District. Operating in a loop and free to ride in the downtown, the streetcar, which is run by the City of Portland rather than TriMet, is used by locals for making short hops; every time I rode it, it was filled with shoppers laden with bags from Safeway and Whole Foods.

As pleasant as the Pearl District is, I can't imagine Erin and I living there. Though the city has worked hard to build in abundant affordable housing, "Alimony Flats," as it is known to Portlanders, can feel like an urban playground for affluent empty-nesters. (The South Waterfront, a streetcar-served high-rise neighborhood that was walloped by the recession, can feel downright desolate.) East Portland would be more our style. It includes the bungalows of the African American district of Albina, the Hawthorne District, with its Victorian and Foursquare homes, and such traditional urban villages as Hollywood and Ladd's Addition. These neighborhoods of older, single-family homes are becoming denser as new apartment buildings go up along commercial arteries served by buses and MAX lines. After devoting much of its resources to suburban projects like Orenco Station, the Portland area's regional planning agency, Metro, has shifted its focus to developing transit-oriented projects in East Portland and other central city districts.

I met Megan Gibb at Metro's headquarters, on the east bank of the Willamette River. Originally from Michigan, Gibb, a soft-spoken woman in her thirties, has been head of Metro's TOD program since 2008. She stressed that unlike Los Angeles, whose transit agency owns large stocks of station-side land, Metro is limited to providing incentives to local municipalities.

"Our funds are available for developments close to frequent bus routes, as well as light rail. And what we're seeing with the recession is a lot of smaller projects being built closer in to Portland, in the neighborhoods that used to have streetcars." A good example was the Merrick, a six-story building with ground-floor shops and 185 apartments near a MAX station in the riverfront Lloyd District. The $24 million project, built with $200,000 in incentives from Metro's TOD program, has already produced results far better than similar suburban developments: a study found that only 44 percent of Merrick residents used cars to commute, versus two-thirds in Orenco Station. Gibb said Metro's major problem was keeping up with market demand. "There's all these millennials who want an urban environment, and we're nowhere near being able to meet their needs."

Portland's ongoing success with TOD is only partly a legacy of its good bones. Just as significant is the fact that, a generation ago, Metro limited sprawl with its growth boundary and never stopped investing in transit: there are plans to build a MAX line across the Columbia River to Washington State and construction has begun on a new line south from downtown to Milwaukee. To really bloom, all that the City of Roses needs is a little more tolerance for density in its core, policies—like higher parking rates—that discourage drivers from bringing cars downtown, and for Tri-Met to pay a little more attention to the way it irrigates intact traditional neighborhoods with buses, streetcars, and light rail.

But if Portlanders really want to kick-start the process, they need only look 300 miles to the north, to a Canadian city that has lately become a transit metropolis on overdrive.

"Vancouverism," for Better and Worse

It's hard not to see Vancouver, British Columbia, and Portland, Oregon, as the long-lost twins of Cascadia, separated when they were still young.

Both were born as Gold Rush boomtowns, and both grew up as Pacific Northwest regional centers with thriving ports and economies based on logging and resource extraction. Both developed streetcar and interurban networks, and count smaller areas of postwar suburban sprawl than similar-size North American cities. Both opted for regional governance in the 1970s, Portland with Metro, Vancouver with the Greater Vancouver Regional District (now Metro Vancouver). Vancouver doesn't have a growth boundary, but it has de facto limits to growth, both geographical—the Pacific Ocean to the west, steep mountains to the north and east, and the United States border to the south—and legal, in the form of a large stock of agricultural land forever protected from development. Both have central city populations of 600,000 in regions of just over two million. It is only now, in their early adulthood, that the twins are showing signs of following distinct life paths. Portland remains a regional center, a city comfortable with incremental growth. Vancouver has lately become an international hub, a model for its own brand of urbanism, and a futuristic city of glass towers bound together by the soaring elevated tracks of streamlined rapid transit.

I grew up in Vancouver. It was here, working as a courier, that I witnessed one too many accidents, and developed a lifelong aversion to traffic and cars. My family arrived in the '70s, settling in a neighborhood of single-family homes near the university. Streamlined Brill trolley buses, drawing power from overhead wires, ran down the nearest major artery, Dunbar Street, where only recently streetcars had run. The local housing ran from Tudor-style manses in Shaughnessy Heights, a neighborhood built on an eccentric garden city street plan, to stucco-coated Vancouver Specials, boxy working-class homes with low-pitched roofs and second-floor balconies. Coming from Toronto, Vancouver felt like the edge of the world, an outpost of the British empire experiencing a few timid blooms of alternative culture. This was the place I became a pre-adolescent urbanist, pacing out our block and building a model showing how, if you removed the cars, city streets could be made into parks.

When I visit these days—my parents and sister still call Vancouver home—I barely recognize the place. The shock begins when I get off the plane, walk among the totem poles of the coolly West Coast–themed airport, and wheel my bags to the elevated SkyTrain station. The Canada Line, completed for the 2010 Winter Olympics, whisks passengers in Korean-made electric trains at 50 miles an hour toward the West End. As the driverless light-rail train crosses the Fraser River, I marvel at how thickets of office and condo towers, each cluster corresponding to a SkyTrain station, have cropped up at intervals of about a mile and a half, where once there was only low-rise suburbia. The single-family homes on small lots, which make Vancouver's west side so reminiscent of East Portland, still exist, but they are now bordered by slickly designed, European-inspired condo blocks with names like City Square and Arbutus Walk. Arriving at the station in Yaletown, once a downtown district of forlorn warehouses, I'm surrounded by "see-throughs," the slender condominium towers of pale green glass that rise against the snow-dusted coast mountains. After Manhattan, Vancouver's downtown is now the second densest in North America. In my absence, the backwater of my youth seems to have morphed into a temperate-zone Singapore, a transformation that has spawned a new buzzword among urbanists: "Vancouverism."

To get an idea of where it was all going, I asked Moreno Rossi, a senior planner with TransLink, Metro Vancouver's transit agency, to take me on a SkyTrain tour of the new Vancouver. We boarded an Expo line train from the TransLink headquarters at Metrotown, next to the largest mall in the province; the boxy train pulled out of the station with a mounting electric hum, and we rode southeast away from the downtown on elevated tracks raised on concrete pylons. The train pulled into New Westminster station, three stories above ground level. Overlooking the log floats being hauled by tugboats on the Fraser River, the half-built station area was dotted with the orange hardhats of construction workers; behind us rose three high-rise apartment towers. Rossi said the completed development will include 650 condo units, a drugstore, a supermarket, a multiplex theater, and a doctor's office; most of the retail would be directly accessible from the station platform.

"More and more," said Rossi, "we're seeing these stations are absolutely being wrapped in development. They become an integral part of the neighborhood, rather than something sitting out there and separate."

The contrast with Portland's Orenco Station was striking. Park-and-rides are against TransLink policy, so the station will be surrounded by a transit loop where feeder buses will drop passengers next to the escalators rising to the platforms. Moreno told me about another station where a leading drugstore chain had chosen not to build a single parking spot; instead, customers enter the store directly from the SkyTrain station, and it has become one of the most successful franchises in the chain. Vancouver was building the kind of TOD I'd seen in Tokyo, where commuters can shop for groceries, buy flowers, and pick up their dry cleaning on the walk between station and home.

After a short ride back toward downtown, Rossi left me on the platform of the Joyce-Collingwood station, which overlooks Collingwood Village, a 27-acre development with a population of 4,500 set in a neighborhood of older, single-family homes. Four-story town houses form a street front paralleling the SkyTrain tracks; behind them are 16 mid- and high-rise residential towers. Taking a stroll, I noticed that the greenbelt beneath the elevated SkyTrain tracks had been turned into a community garden, where local residents were tending patches of tomatoes, pumpkins, and lettuce; shops on the ground floors of the condo towers included a Filipino grocery with lacquered ducks hanging in the windows, a walk-in clinic, and a beauty salon advertising "Japanese Straight Perms." The developer had also built an elementary school, a gym, a park, and a neighborhood police station.

What astonished me most, though, was the stream of passengers pouring from the station, some of whom joined the lines for buses at the bottom of the station's escalators. It was half past five, so commuters were returning from downtown, and I stood on the platform counting heads: each four-car train disgorged thirty to forty passengers, with a new train arriving every two minutes or less. At Portland's Orenco Station, I had counted only half a dozen people getting off each rush-hour MAX train, with waits of at least six minutes between trains. The statistics speak for themselves: in Collingwood Village, 56 percent of residents commute by transit, versus only 15 percent in Orenco Station.

When it comes to reducing car dependency, the Vancouver model, which puts high-density residential and retail right up against high-capacity transit, is emerging as the one to beat. SkyTrain ridership is triple MAX's, making it the busiest light-rail system in North America. Over the last decade, transit ridership has grown by 52 percent, pedestrian trips are up 44 percent, and cycling 180 percent. Ten percent fewer cars now enter Vancouver than a decade ago, and the average time people spend commuting to work has actually decreased by several minutes (even while increasing significantly in Canada's largest city, Toronto). Thanks to its transportation policy, Vancouver now has the lowest per capita carbon emissions of any major North American city.*

I asked Gordon Price, a former city alderman and transit blogger, if the lessons of Vancouverism could be applied anywhere but Vancouver. Price agreed that, like Portland, Vancouver's early history of streetcar-driven

---

* The electricity that powers the SkyTrain and the city's fleet of trolley buses comes from hydro dams, one of the cleanest forms of power known. Most of Portland's electricity comes from coal-fired plants.

development gave it certain advantages. A grid system of major arteries at half-mile intervals puts most homes within a few minutes' walk of transit; Vancouver's historic interurban network, the equivalent of Los Angeles's Red Cars, also encouraged the growth of such substantial suburbs as Richmond and Surrey, which now provide the anchors that keep the Sky-Train cars full throughout the day. But the real key, Price believed, was Vancouver's freeway revolt, a more thorough rejection of urban highways than even Portland's.

"There was this planner called Gerald Sutton Brown, an engineer and city manager who since the fifties had been the grand poo-bah of Vancouver." A Canadian Robert Moses, the imperious Sutton Brown came close to implementing his vision of a regional freeway system, until he made the mistake of routing it through Vancouver's Chinatown. "In the late sixties, Chinese businesspeople and the more political unions held marches and raucous public meetings, and a rather ragged coalition of lawyers, architects, academics, and urban thinkers emerged to create a new municipal party. The first thing they did, when they were elected, was to fire Sutton Brown." Most Canadian highways fall under provincial, rather than federal, management, and British Columbia decided against funding such a clearly unpopular plan. "The amazing thing is that, even today, highways don't go through any part of the City of Vancouver," pointed out Price. "They just stop as soon as they reach the city limits." Vancouver, like Portland, opted to use federal highway money for public transport; rather than building a new bridge, the city launched its SeaBuses, bright orange ferries that still shuttle passengers to the north shore mountains for the price of a bus ticket.

Elevated light rail turns out to have been a prescient choice of technology. When I rode the SkyTrain on the opening of Expo 86, a world fair whose theme was transportation, I remember thinking it was nothing more than a toy, a rinky-dink people mover. But the system has proved both robust and popular, and the new, wider trains on the Canada Line operate more like serious mass transit vehicles. "Thanks to the technology," pointed out Price, "we've got a system that gives us headways of as little as ninety seconds, which is incredible. And because it's automated, the labor cost of putting a new train on the line is also incredibly low." Vancouver has also introduced a form of BRT, using articulated buses that run from SkyTrain stations and only stop at major intersections. Students riding the B-line, which serves the University of British Columbia, receive discounted monthly passes paid for out of their tuition fees. The B-line has attracted such a huge ridership that there are now calls for it to be replaced by a permanent light-rail line.

When it comes to transportation policy, Vancouver is getting a lot of the little things right. Downtown parking is expensive: an hour and a half in an off-street lot can cost the same as an entire day of parking in the center of Portland. The city has built broad bike lanes on major bridges and arteries, taking entire lanes away from cars. Michael Shiffer, Trans-Link's vice president of planning, told me he believed another factor was cultural. His last job was as head of planning for the Chicago Transit Authority, where support for public transport was not automatic. "Too often the debate in the United States is about whether transit is a good idea or not. Here, everybody's on board with transit. The debate is, who gets it first, and how are you going to pay for it?"

Funding, in fact, comes from a variety of sources. In Vancouver, passenger fares cover 50 percent of operating costs, while fuel and property taxes pay for the rest. Construction of the proposed Evergreen SkyTrain line will be paid in equal parts by the federal government, the province, and the region. The Canada Line to the airport, in contrast, was the first major piece of transit infrastructure in North America to be built with a public-private partnership, an initiative many commentators say was plagued by corner-cutting. Three stations had to be eliminated from the planned route, and the station platforms that were built were too short to allow future expansion. Thanks to cost overruns, the provincial government will be compensating the private company that operates the line with payments up to $21 million a year until 2025.

Almost everybody I talked to agreed that Vancouver's greatest strength was the concentration of vision allowed by true regional planning. The Livable Region Strategic Plan, adopted in 1996 as a framework for making regional land use and transportation decisions, is now the game plan for the entire region. According to Christina DeMarco, the director of planning at Metro Vancouver, the equivalent of Portland's Metro, the region's twenty-two municipalities are constantly consulting one another.

"Every month since the mid-nineties," she told me, "all the planning directors in the region have gotten together to discuss common concerns, everything from affordable housing to the rezoning of industrial land." They collaborate closely with TransLink, which was created by the provincial government in 1999 to oversee not only transit but also bridges and major roads. The various stakeholders in the process don't always see eye to eye. Metro Vancouver, for example, favored making the Evergreen Line a surface light-rail line similar to Portland's MAX, but the province opted for a more expensive SkyTrain. "The local municipalities are saying, we didn't agree to this train, and now you're asking us to cough up four hundred million to build it. Sort of like, we asked for the Volkswagen and you went for the Ferrari and you're making us pay for it."

There is a broad consensus, however, that the focus will be on regional city centers linked by transit, rather than freeways. When it comes to density, the SkyTrain is proving to be a force multiplier: a true mass transit system, with enormous throughputs, it enables high residential and commercial densities, just as New York's subway created the skyscrapers of Midtown and the apartments of the Upper East and West sides.

Throwing good transit at a city doesn't mean density will follow: think of Phoenix with its expensive light rail, which spends most of its time rumbling past parking lots. The difference is that Vancouver early on limited space for cars, and its planners have worked hard to locate residential towers, bus loops, and shops near transit stops. It provides more evidence that public transport works best when it is overseen by an agency with truly regional scope—preferably one that can work in tandem with a planning body with some degree of metropolitan-level control over zoning and land use.

Some people say that Vancouver, whose economy is increasingly tied to Asia, is hardly a realistic model for other North American cities. One morning I rode the Canada Line to Richmond, a suburb where more than half of the population is of Asian descent—mostly recent immigrants from mainland China, Taiwan, and Hong Kong—and stopped at Aberdeen Center, a mall that could have been airlifted straight from Shanghai, Taipei, or Singapore. Shark-fin soup was the lunch special at the food court, and a Barnes & Noble–size bookstore offered mah-jong sets and books with titles like *Struggling in the U.S.? Move to China!* The lead story in the local paper profiled a real estate agent who was pre-selling entire floors of condo towers to the nouveau riche of mainland China. For its critics, Vancouver has become a kind of productive resort with no indigenous economy—an attractive home base for highly mobile Pacific Rim executives, but entirely dependent on inputs of foreign capital. I could see why, like Dubai or Singapore, it would be a good city for someone with an established career to spend a few years, but a hard place to build a life.

The fact is, the city of my youth has become ridiculously expensive. These days, even a tear-down on a tiny lot can go for over a million dollars; the house my parents lived in was recently listed for *thirty times* what they paid in the '70s. There have been times, particularly in the depths of the Montreal winter, when I've daydreamed about enticing Erin to relocate to Vancouver, which, after all, boasts sandy beaches and old-growth forests within its city limits. In reality, we probably couldn't afford to buy a home in my old hometown anymore.

Brent Toderian, Vancouver's enthusiastic young director of planning, defended the city against charges that it has become an unaffordable haven for the international elite.

"We have about seven thousand kids living downtown, and we're one of the few North American cities to have opened a downtown elementary school in the last decade," said Toderian. "We require developers to include day cares, parks, and neighborhood facilities." Developments like the Woodwards Building, he pointed out, have garnered international praise for including hundreds of apartments priced for poorer families.

Toderian admitted that Vancouver probably had all the condo towers it needed. Echoing Metro Vancouver's Christina DeMarco, he said he hoped the future would bring a more European-style urbanism. That's good news for the Vancouverites who see those ranks of sea-green condo towers as an invading army pushing them out of their hometown.

"What Vancouver has done better than Singapore or Hong Kong," Toderian pointed out, "is slim, separated towers that protect mountain views and allow sunlight in. But we're coming to the end of this lazy interpretation of Vancouverism, which is all about high-rise towers on podiums. I think the future of Vancouver is mid-rise, from four to twelve stories, around transit lines. You'll be seeing much more of that near the new stations on the Canada Line."

There are lessons to be learned from the transit-led renaissance taking place in Portland and Vancouver. Portland is taking things slow—too slow for some tastes. Building denser, transit-oriented suburbs like Orenco Station as a means of transforming the North American cityscape may be a case of too little, too late, particularly in recessionary times. Vancouver, for its part, is undergoing a rapid transformation commensurate with its transit system of choice, the SkyTrain. As a widely applicable model, however, Vancouver may have priced itself out of the market: not only is its wealth of planning expertise simply not available to most cities, there are few places these days that can afford to buy themselves an expensive SkyTrain. A better path, I suspect, lies somewhere between Portland's New Suburbanism and Vancouver's Hyperurbanism.

In other words, in reimagining and rebuilding the kind of cities many of us already live in.

Imagine boarding a train in the center of a city. No racing to an airport and across a terminal, no delays, no sitting on the tarmac, no lost luggage, no taking off your shoes. Imagine whisking through towns at speeds over one hundred miles an hour, walking only a few steps to public transportation, and ending up just blocks from your destination. Imagine what a great project that would be to rebuild America.

—President Barack Obama, 2009

10. The Next Great City

Philadelphia, Pennsylvania

As Amtrak train 68 made its fourth unscheduled stop in as many hours, this time in a field where horses grazed in front of a white farmhouse, I tried hard to envision a day when trains would compete with cars and planes for efficient intercity transportation. For the several hundred passengers immobilized on a weedy siding in upstate New York, the future promised by the White House, when 80 percent of Americans would be linked by high-speed rail, seemed a long way off. After a few minutes, a rusty pickup truck passed us on a dirt road paralleling the tracks, raising a cloud of dust that obscured our vision altogether.

I had boarded the train only ten minutes before our 9:30 a.m. departure from Montreal's Central Station. I stowed my bag, settled into a window seat, and listened to the chatter around me. A half-dozen professors from Rutgers, most of whom spoke with Indian and South African accents, held forth on the pleasures of train travel.

"The train is so much more scenic than the plane," opined a silver-haired man, as the Adirondack slipped from its platform and threaded its way between graffitied warehouses on the industrial fringes of Montreal's downtown.

"Scenery?" chided his younger colleague. "There is *no* scenery on the plane. Once you get up to thirty thousand feet you are in the clouds, and see nothing but the movie on the seat-back in front of you."

A woman piped up from two rows back: "And I understand that soon the airlines will be making us pay to watch even a movie."

On this Sunday morning, the train seemed like the sweetest of deals. The reclining seats offered plenty of leg room, there was no hassle checking baggage, and the view out the window, of rusting bridges over old canals and dozens of silver steeples, inclined one to quiet contemplation. Moreover, the price was right: a ticket on the Adirondack cost a third of the cheapest airfare to New York I could find.

An hour later, though, we were barely out of the southern suburbs of Montreal. After coming to a stop on a rural road for ten minutes, causing a long line of cars to form on either side of our four-coach train, we crept ahead a few hundred yards to the border sheds at Rouses Point. As Canadian and American officials made the rounds, checking passports and collecting apples and oranges, the South African man behind me declared, to nobody and everybody:

"The problem is, the train is too bloody slow."

There was a murmur of assent. The grumbling continued through the customs formalities, which took an hour. And when we came to a stop in the field just after Westport, the couple behind me actually groaned.

Finally, a conductor picked up a microphone. "We'll be waiting on this siding for about ten more minutes," he drawled, "until train 69, the mothership, passes by."

After our Montreal-bound counterpart rumbled past, we finally began to move again. Such delays, which are usually caused by freight trains, are all too familiar to train riders. In most of the United States, Amtrak doesn't own its own tracks; the Adirondack is charged a fee to use the rails owned by freight companies, which means it frequently gets sidelined by freight trains. Only as we neared New York did we start making up time, whistling past the cantilevered span of the Tappan Zee Bridge at a satisfying clip. We pulled into Penn Station at five to nine, fifteen minutes late.

When it's running on time, the Adirondack takes just over eleven hours to cover the 381 miles from Montreal to New York. Provided you've got a day to spare, it's a great way to go. I read an entire book, and learned the life story of my seatmate, a young playwright from Oakland, tender after a sleepless night at a bachelor party in Montreal. But at an average of 34 miles an hour, the Adirondack is painfully slow.

Had I been traveling in 1960, I could have made the same journey a lot faster, and in far more style. Every day of the week at 10:25 p.m., the Montreal Limited, pulled by a streamlined stainless-steel locomotive, eased out of Windsor Station. By midnight, the border crossing would have been complete and, after a drink in the lounge, passengers, their bedding prepared by porters, could retire to roomettes or luxurious double bedrooms in Pullman Standard coaches. Arriving the next morning, a little over nine hours after they'd left, passengers would disembark at Grand Central, well rested and ready to hit the town.

In the not so distant past, train travel on this continent was the envy of the world. By the 1920s, the United States had 380,000 miles of tracks, more than any other nation. As early as 1934, the Pioneer Zephyr crossed a thousand miles of the rural Midwest at an average speed of 78 miles an hour, regularly topping out at 112 in its nonstop run from Denver to Chicago. In the '50s, the trip from Chicago to Minneapolis on the Olympian Hiawathan took only four and a half hours (today, on Amtrak's Empire Builder, it takes more than eight). Fabulously appointed sleeper cars, and chefs that rivaled New York's best, made trains like the Hollywood-bound Super Chief into international bywords for glamour. And North American trains were world-beaters: in 1967, a jet-nosed gas-turbine locomotive called the TurboTrain broke the record for high-speed travel, reaching 171 miles an hour on a track in New Jersey. (A Canadian National–operated Turbo Train actually made a four-hour test run between Toronto and Montreal, but it was limited to 100 miles per hour because it operated on freight tracks.) But the last American railcar builder went out of business in 2008, and the citizens of the nation that invented the electric trolley, the sleeping car, and the pantograph now ride on Spanish-made Talgos, French-made HHP-8s, and hand-me-down Japanese light-rail cars. The United States' infinitely rami-fied rail network, whose veins and capillaries once reached into every small town in the nation, has shrunk to 100,000 miles, the same level as in 1881. In 2010, Amtrak proudly announced a record ridership of 29 million—not a bad showing, unless you compare it to the '20s, when American trains were carrying 1.3 *billion* passengers a year.

The following afternoon, as I sat with businessmen in loosened ties and women in tailored suits in a fluorescent-lit waiting room in a train station in Midtown Manhattan, I wondered when things had started to go wrong. It may have started in the '60s, when so many of the nation's great railway terminals were torn down, among them Atlanta's Terminal Station (which became a concrete bunker for government offices), Mem-phis's Union Station (now a post office surrounded by barbed wire), and perhaps most tragically of all, the original Penn Station. The 1910 struc-ture, with its soaring glass-and-iron train sheds and ceilings of travertine marble, was razed in 1963 to make way for a murky modernist labyrinth beneath an ugly arena. The original waiting hall had been modeled on the Roman Baths of Caracalla; the low-ceilinged lounge of the new Penn sta-tion, where I now sat, felt more like a boarding gate at a second-string regional airport. At ten minutes before six, we were instructed to proceed to the east gate to get in the line for America's only high-speed train.

The Acela, which makes the run from New York to Washington, D.C. in two hours and 45 minutes, is a fine train. Built by a consortium of Bombardier in Quebec and Alstom in France, each train set has two loco-motives, a café car, and four coaches, and draws power from overhead catenary wires. The first coach I walked through was full, but I found a seat in the "quiet car," next to a gray-haired man reading a spy thriller on his Kindle. In the coach ahead of us, first-class passengers were being served steaks and grilled fish from silver carts. As passengers around me dozed or thumbed BlackBerries, the Acela seemed to live up to its name, blazing past the rush-hour traffic backed up on Interstate 95.

Even though one-way peak period tickets can cost $200, Acela trains run full. Amtrak's Northeast Corridor (the only tracks it actually owns) has captured half the combined air-rail market between Boston and Washington, and 60 percent between New York and the capital. "Acela service," Harvard historian John Stilgoe has noted, "is the first evidence that wealthy people might be willing to abandon both automobiles and airliners for high-speed travel over distances between four hundred and five hundred miles."

By international standards, though, the Acela is an underachiever. As I stood in line for a bowl of clam chowder in the café car, I asked a passing conductor how fast he figured we were going.

"We're doing about one-thirty-five right now," he said. "But there was a five- or six-mile stretch back in Massachusetts where we reached a hundred and fifty."

I asked if there were any screens showing the train's current speed, as many European trains have.

"No," he said. "And you know, there *should* be. I guess we're behind on a lot of things here."

After passing the truss bridge across the Delaware River that reads "Trenton Makes The World Takes," we began to decelerate. Though its locomotives are capable of 200 miles an hour, the Acela barely averages 88 miles an hour between New York and Washington. In Europe, the Acela would qualify as a regional express, not a true high-speed train. Even half a century ago, Penn Central's Metroliner routinely covered the same distance in less time.

There are at least two major technological issues preventing American trains from attaining the kinds of speeds Europeans and Asians now take for granted. In 1947, Congress restricted passenger train speeds to 79 miles an hour, except on tracks equipped with Automatic Train Control. (ATC is similar to the system I saw in the Paris métro, where a "dead man's switch" stops a train if the driver fails to touch the controls periodically.) ATC should be standard technology on any modern railroad—it has long been used on the Northeast Corridor—but the freight companies who own most of the tracks oppose its implementation on the ground that it would cost billions. As things stand, North America is the only part of the world to limit the speed of its passenger trains.

The other issue is the failure to electrify. Outside of the Northeast Corridor, almost all North American locomotives run on fossil fuels. Electrification increases reliability by decreasing congestion: because lighter electric locomotives accelerate and decelerate far more rapidly, and require less maintenance than diesels, a line powered by overhead wires can run far more train sets. While Asia and Europe were building the infrastructure for low-emission electric trains—even the Trans-Siberian is powered by overhead wires strung over 6,000 miles of boreal forest and tundra—General

264 of Taras Grescoe

Motors was busy convincing America's few electric railroads to tear down their wires, the better to sell them diesel-powered locomotives, offered on easy credit. Meanwhile, 20 countries have already built high-speed electric networks, and even Brazil, Morocco, and Vietnam are at work on such systems. (Canada remains the only G7 country with no high-speed rail at all.)

The greatest impediment to the creation of a decent network of fast electric trains in the United States, however, is the idea that a transport system that can't pay its way has no reason to exist.* Contrary to popular belief, the Northeast Corridor isn't a moneymaker for Amtrak. In fact, there are only a couple of places in the world—among them the bullet-train routes between Paris and Lyon and Tokyo and Osaka—where high-speed passenger rail turns a profit. In the twentieth century, the United States, as James McCommons emphasizes in *Waiting on a Train*, was the only nation whose rail network remained entirely private, and when that model stopped working, its railroads went to seed. To get big railroads like Penn Central out of the failing passenger business, the Nixon administration created the publicly owned Amtrak in 1971. To be truly competitive with cars and planes, Amtrak's trains need a consistent and dedicated source of funding, equivalent to the Highway Trust Fund. In a good year, Amtrak receives $1.5 billion in federal subsidies, though it actually manages to cover between two-thirds and three-quarters of its operating costs by selling tickets. Contrast this with the freeways, which in 2010 received $52 billion in federal subsidies—and are, of course, free to their users.

These days, the profit lies in freight, and as gas prices increase, so does the competitiveness of rail shipping. A train can haul a ton of freight 400 miles on a single gallon of diesel, making it more fuel-efficient than a truck on a freeway by a factor of 7—which may explain why such far-sighted investors as Warren Buffett have lately gone out of their way to buy control of major freight companies. Some experts believe the fastest way to foster rapid passenger rail would be for the federal government to buy out the major freight companies and nationalize the tracks. Just as it owns the freeways, the nation would own its rail infrastructure, and charge freight and passenger railroads alike user fees. (The moral case for nationalization is based on the fact that today's freight railroads were built on

---

* Only the largesse of the federal government keeps the heavily subsidized aviation industry afloat. Minor airports, for example, benefit from the little-known Essential Air Service program, which provides an average of $74 per passenger to keep planes taking off—almost triple Amtrak's per passenger subsidy.

extensive grants of public land made by the federal government in the nineteenth century.) The other extreme—privatization—has already failed in Britain, and would probably condemn all but the busiest lines to certain death. A less controversial but far more costly option is the vision set forth by the Obama administration: to embark on a national rail-building effort to create a dedicated passenger network of the quality that already exists in Europe and much of Asia.

Only an hour after the Acela left New York, the conductor announced we were approaching Philadelphia—my stop. I rolled my suitcase down the aisle, and as I waited in the passage between coaches for the doors to open, I asked a man in his thirties if he was on a business trip.

"Actually," he said, smiling as he pulled out his earbuds, "I live in Philly. But I work in New York. I use the Acela to commute, three times a week." The older man behind him, in a shirt and tie, volunteered: "Same here, at least a twice a week. It's a great service. There've only been a couple of delays so far this year, when it snowed." I asked if it was common to live in Philadelphia and work in New York. "Oh, yeah," the first man said. "There's lots of us on the Acela. It's kind of like a little club."

The Acela was clearly having the same effect bullet trains had produced in Japan and France: high-speed rail was allowing people to continue living in their hometowns while working in other cities.

Riding an escalator from track level, I gaped upward in frank awe at the marble columns rising to the coffered ceiling of Philadelphia's 30th Street Station, which was completed in 1933, in the depths of the Depression. Just two months before my arrival, Vice President Joe Biden had stood at a lectern next to the station's shoeshine stand and pledged $53 billion for high-speed rail in the six years to come. In the intervening weeks, the Republican governors of Florida, Wisconsin, and Ohio, had refused their share of the money. California snatched up almost a billion dollars of the rejected funding for a program to link the Bay Area to San Diego with 220-mile-per-hour trains. The plan, which would have cut travel time from San Francisco to Los Angeles to two and a half hours, will likely cost $43 billion by 2030—a huge sum, but a fraction of what it would have taken to expand airport and freeway capacity to meet the state's projected population growth. However, House Republicans voted to zero out funding to high-speed rail in the 2012 budget, stalling California's project and casting serious doubt on the future of the Obama White House's vision of a modern national rail network. Future historians may count this as one of the decisive moments in North America's failure to keep pace with advances in Asian infrastructure. The planned network, far from being an extravagance, is actually a common-sense step to cope with ever-growing congestion, and one that is replicable on a national scale. Seventy percent of the U.S. population lives within 50 miles of the East or West Coasts, and the Midwest is about the same size and has about the same population density as Spain, a nation that has built itself an entire high-speed rail network in less than a decade.

Is the dream of being whisked through towns at high speeds, starting and completing your journey with transit, a realistic one? If you believe that taxpayers shouldn't prioritize unsustainable transport systems, the only conceivable answer is *yes*. Freeways and airports cost taxpayers a fortune, and foster pollution, sprawl, and greenhouse gas emissions. As I saw when I traveled from Paris to Copenhagen, a network that enables intercity travel by train, rather than car or plane, slashes carbon emissions while offering significantly more comfort and convenience. (Per passenger mile, even Amtrak's inefficient diesel locomotives emit 60 percent less carbon than cars.)

And if you believe in the future of cities, the answer is a resounding *yes*. By allowing passengers to arrive right in the heart of the cities they serve, trains bring life and commerce to urban centers. A well-frequented passenger rail connection isn't a prerequisite for a thriving central city, but it is a powerful means of encouraging downtown revival. And Philadelphia—in spite of everything you may have heard to the contrary—is one city whose center has held.

Crossing the polished marble floor of the 30th Street Station, I followed the signs to the subway; a token would pay my fare for the short trip to my Center City hotel. From Montreal to Philadelphia, I'd lived the dream, making the entire trip by transit and train. But traveling less than 500 miles had taken me 13 hours, underscoring how far rail travel lags on this continent.

Almost anywhere else in the industrialized world—in France or China, Spain or Japan—covering the same distance would have taken just over three hours.

First City Principles

Our cities, the urbanists say, are too sprawled, too congested, too polluted. How do we fix them?

At this point in my travels, I'd heard this question answered many ways. Civic leaders like Antonio Villaraigosa and Enrique Peñalosa argued that sophisticated public transport is the key to liberating cities from gridlock and congestion. Echoing Frank Lloyd Wright, such defenders of auto-based suburbia as Joel Kotkin believe more fuel-efficient cars and local retail and employment will eventually make the suburbs as vital as the cities they've usurped. Building greater density on the municipal fringe, according to the New Suburbanists, is the best template for harmonious metropolitan growth. In stark contrast, the Hyperurbanists of Vancouver promote a metropolis where high-density residential towers are the way to a sustainable, low-carbon future, a vision reminiscent of Le Corbusier's Radiant City, but redeemed by its reliance on transit, rather than cars.

Though all these visions have their internal logic, I don't find any of them a compelling model for an urban future. Better transportation alone is clearly too simplistic a solution: monorails, modern streetcars, and elevated light-rail trains that move through a landscape of sprawl and parking lots are just so many expensive toys. Densifying cities by building compact neighborhoods on the metropolitan fringe is a glacially slow process, and there is little evidence it reduces car use in the long run. And though high-rise towers permit fantastic urban amenities, not everybody wants to live at Asian-style densities.

Many of our problems, it was becoming clear to me, could be solved by putting what we've already got to better use. There is already almost half a millennium of city-building history on this continent—the Spanish founded St. Augustine, Florida, in 1565—which leaves us with a lot of urban fabric to work with. The long postwar spree of suburb building, which only ended with the subprime mortgage crash, means there is an oversupply of housing: in the United States, 18.4 million homes, 11 percent of the nation's total housing stock, were sitting empty in 2011. Pioneers have been resettling cities for decades now—some people never left—but the trend is about to accelerate as millennials and empty-nesters flood back to cities. Rather than building from scratch, the time has come to recycle and reuse existing neighborhoods, whether they're in central cities or close-in suburbs.

Which is why I'd come to Philadelphia. It's not a place, admittedly, that tends to show up in the PowerPoints of the globe-trotting gurus of urbanism. Deindustrialization hit this city on the eastern edge of the Rust Belt harder than most; from its midcentury high of 2.1 million, it lost 30 percent of its population in fifty years, and a quarter of Philadelphians still live beneath the poverty line. But unemployment here is now below the national average, and in 2010 Philadelphia recorded its first population increase in decades—less than 1 percent, but still an addition of 18,000 new households, most of them downtown, and enough to reclaim its title as the nation's fifth-largest city from foundering Phoenix. One hundred thousand people now live in Center City, making it the third-largest residential downtown in the country, after New York and Chicago. Philadelphia, where 35 percent of households don't own a car, is also the city with the highest percentage of people who commute to work by foot. And, thanks to Mayor Michael Nutter, an extensive network of bike paths means that on any given day in Philadelphia, more people get to work by bicycle than in any other city in the United States.

Philadelphia, it turns out, is a city ideally suited for a transit-led revival. Its bones aren't just good: they're great. The First City owes its structure to one of the New World's most influential works of urban planning. In 1682, the wealthy English Quaker William Penn platted out a "green country towne," divided into quadrants by two broad avenues, on the flatlands between the Delaware and Schuylkill rivers. His plan was a reproach to such crowded Old World cities as London, which had recently been razed by fire: the generous gridwork of streets included four substantial squares and a major park; each detached home was to sit in the center of its plot, surrounded by ample gardens and orchards.* Penn's grid, which would be replicated in countless towns in the upper South and Midwest, was soon overwhelmed by mass immigration. As factories and workshops appeared, residential lots were subdivided and resold, and alleys were interpolated between the main streets. The row house, stately and tall on the main arteries, narrow and cramped in the alleys, emerged as Philadelphia's answer to the New York tenement. Advancing westward in a tide of red brick, by 1840 the row houses had reached the site of the current City Hall, midway between the two rivers. Fifteen years later, development leapfrogged the Schuylkill River into West Philadelphia. The ubiquitous row house kept Philadelphia compact and walkable; nineteenth-century boosters dubbed it

---

* As a structuring element, the orthogonal grid can be traced back to the Roman Empire and beyond to the sacred cities of Imperial China. Penn's grid would influence the New York City Commissioners' Plan of 1811, but the ultimate imposition of rectilinear geometry came with the Homestead Act of 1862, when the entire nation west of the original colonies was divided into a grid of over a million quarter-sections.

the "City of Homes," where even craftsmen and laborers could aspire to homeownership.

As in so many other cities, horsecars and electric trolleys drove Philadelphia's growth beyond the limits of the old walking city, as tracks extended to Spring Garden, Mount Airy, Overbrook, and wherever else the streetcar magnates owned real estate. The once-rural villages of Wynnewood, Narberth, Haverford, and Bryn Mawr became upper-class enclaves, kept within striking distance of such downtown high-society hot spots as Wanamaker's Department Store by the Pennsylvania Railroad's Main Line. By the time the automobile came to Philadelphia, the city had already experienced a century of rail-driven growth. In the '50s, suburban Bucks County became the site of the second Levittown, a prototypical mass-produced suburb, and the Toll Brothers perfected their craft in Montgomery County, before overrunning the country with their trademark high-end sprawl. Though the freeway era bit as hard in Philadelphia as it did elsewhere, a substantial part of the city's skeleton was safeguarded by the bones of iron and steel laid down in the railway age.

If Philadelphia emerged from the twentieth century with its urban fabric intact, it is largely thanks to the influence of Edmund Bacon. The scion of a prominent Quaker family, Bacon worked as an architect in Shanghai before becoming director of the Philadelphia City Planning Commission in 1949, a position he held for three decades. Working in the heyday of freeway building, modernist concrete, and suburban flight, Bacon made many mistakes. Market East, a brutal downtown shopping mall linked to a commuter rail station, sucked the life out of once-thriving Market Street. And under his watch, Philadelphia went from being a city between two rivers to a city between two highways. Interstate 95 scythed the city from the Delaware waterfront, and, in one of the century's great acts of civic desecration, the elevated Schuylkill Expressway turned the riverfront Fairmount Park into a raceway. (Philadelphians have dubbed the Schuylkill, infamous for its tight curves, the "Surekill.")

But Edmund Bacon's concessions to the automobile age were slight compared to Robert Moses's. When neighborhood opposition arose, Bacon backed off from building the Crosstown Expressway along South Street, which remains one of the city's liveliest restaurant-and-nightlife strips. In the Far Northeast, he came up with a remarkable vision for dense suburban row houses, built on curvilinear street plans to respect local watersheds, and linked to the city by mass transit—an example of Smart Growth *avant la lettre.* Asked at the end of the '50s by a local magazine to write an article about what Philadelphia might look like in the year 2009, he predicted, correctly, that a mass transit system would be controlled by a metropolitan authority linking commuter rail, buses, and subways into one coordinated unit (admittedly, he also thought Philadelphians would be traveling by helicopter and moving walkway). By the '70s, Bacon had turned against cars altogether, telling an interviewer, "There is a revulsion against the automobile and the destruction it does to cities and the countryside. The car is losing its luster as something worth sacrificing for." In his retirement, Bacon wrote prolifically about the "Post Petroleum City," and just a couple of years before his death in 2005 at the age of ninety-five, he went skateboarding across JFK Plaza to protest a proposed civic ban on the sport.

Inga Saffron, the architecture critic for the *Philadelphia Inquirer,* sees Bacon's legacy as mixed. "There are two Bacons," she told me, as we sat on the sidewalk terrace of a French restaurant in Center City. "There's the rancid Bacon, who believed cities needed highways. He built Penn Center, which was in many ways a grotesque development, though it created a modern office district that kept corporations happy and prevented them from moving to the suburbs. The good Bacon thought everybody could come into town on rail, and walk through these underground concourses to get to work. He tied the office district and the municipal services district together with regional rail, the subway, and the trolleys. But Bacon's real genius was that he created a way for middle-class people to stay in the city. He was the first planner after the war to realize that old city fabric was valuable and could be renovated and gentrified."

Though Bacon's tenure as city planner coincided with the city's economic decline, his faith in Philadelphia never wavered. Rather than build massive, sterile public housing projects, he championed the Used House Program, which turned renovated row houses into affordable housing for the poor. An early advocate of historic preservation, Bacon fought to save the Center City district of Society Hill from blight. Today, it is a gorgeous neighborhood of tree-shaded laneways and elegant colonial-era town houses, famous for luring middle-class suburbanites back to the city.

In his portrait of Philadelphia in the year 2009, Bacon predicted: "At the same time that large sections of Old Philadelphia are demonstrating the staying power of the brick row house, and the adaptability of it for renewal for attractive urban living, the newer but less well built suburbs just over the city line are deteriorating, forming a ready market for the lower income groups." Bacon's proleptic vision turns out to be dead-on: as the subprime crisis hit Philadelphia's suburbs, shopping malls emptied of tenants and poverty rates in suburban Montgomery County jumped by 50 percent.

"I live in a row house in Center City," said Saffron. "In Philly, we call them Trinities. You know: the Father, Son, and the Holy Ghost, one room on each floor, originally with an outdoor kitchen and privvy. The typical Trinity is sixteen feet wide, like row houses in Amsterdam. We've renovated ours, added rooms, so now it's about two thousand square feet." Saffron believes the city's solid housing stock is one reason Philadelphia's downtown never died. "It's a testament to Philadelphia's great, inherent value that, unlike so many American cities, it never lost its Center City population. Even at the height of suburban flight, there were pioneering gentrifiers here."

At the table next to us, a trio of men in black-framed glasses were getting loud as they dripped ice water from an elaborate fountain into stemmed glasses of absinthe. After paying our bill, Saffron and I crossed Rittenhouse Square, still one of America's great public spaces, passing a crowd of twenty-somethings leaning on their bikes as they watched a breakdancing contest. Saffron pointed out a row house on Locust Street. "That's where Ed Bacon lived for most of his life," she said. It was a narrow-fronted brick Trinity, no different from any other on the block. "He remodeled it with this great modernist interior." Noticing it was for sale, I peered through the window. The current owner had restored all of the original moldings.

In Philadelphia, the process of recycling and reusing never ends.

Getting There . . .

Philadelphia's transit system is a cabinet of curiosities, rife with anachronisms. It is one of the few big city networks that still uses tokens, but just try buying one: the machines in the stations are usually out of order, the notoriously monosyllabic attendants often demand exact change, and an obscure union rule means tokens can only be sold in packages of two. The trolleys here operate on something called Pennsylvania Trolley Gauge—the tracks are laid four inches wider than standard, apparently a measure to prevent the steam companies from taking over municipal railways. Some trolleys are "trackless," the local term for rubber-tired buses that draw power from overhead wires, and one line still runs President

Conference Cars—which were the height of streamlined streetcar performance seventy years ago. Philadelphia also operates a fleet of modern streetcars, which, for a visitor, are terrifyingly unpredictable. One minute you're looking out the window, happily watching West Philly go by; the next, everything goes dark as the trolley dips beneath street level and enters Center City, where it runs for several miles on tracks that parallel the subway trains (even when you're underground, though, you still have to remember to pull the bell cord, or the driver might completely skip your station). The Norristown High Speed Line is one of the stranger lines I've ever encountered: it consists of a single railcar that manically whips between tiny suburban stations. On the outdoor platform of each station, you have to locate a rather poorly marked button, which turns on a lightbulb, signaling the driver he should stop. And Philadelphia is one of the few cities where people go *down* to take the El: the Market-Frankford line, which operates as a subway downtown, becomes an elevated when it leaves Center City.

Until recently, Philadelphians treated the Southeastern Pennsylvania Transportation Authority, or SEPTA—its local nickname is INEPTA or SCHLEPTA—like the punch line to a bad joke. The agency's slogan, "We're Getting There," just about summed it up: it was cobbled together from an eccentric mix of private streetcar companies and commuter rail lines, service interruptions were frequent, and the bloated workforce had a history of walk-outs that shut down the entire city. But in 2009, striking workers signed a five-year contract, new management promised to rationalize an archaic operating culture, and stations finally started benefiting from long-promised renovations. After two decades of crisis, things are finally looking up for SEPTA.

I asked Joe Casey, the agency's new general manager, about the challenges of running a perennially cash-strapped agency.

"Back in the seventies," he told me, "we took over the assets of Penn Central and Reading Railroads, which were basically bankrupt railroads that didn't invest a lot in their passenger services. Last month I had to deal with four catenary failures—these overhead wires that were installed back in the thirties, they just wore out and broke. We've also got a workforce of over nine thousand, and we have to deal with seventeen separate unions."

But SEPTA's main problem, according to Casey, is money. "Our primary funding mechanism is the state sales tax. It covers about half our operating expenses, and we get a much smaller operating subsidy from the federal government and the city. To give you an idea, SEPTA's ridership is comparable to Washington's Metro and Boston's MBTA, but our capital budget, the money we use to maintain the system and make improvements, is only three hundred million dollars a year. Washington and Boston work with more like a billion." Some of SEPTA's regional rail trains, Casey said, were almost half a century old.

This lack of funding is unfortunate, because SEPTA is exactly what the experts say a transit agency should be. Paul Mees, the Australian transit scholar and author of *Transport for Suburbia*, has analyzed agencies around the globe, from the public extreme, where the transit authority is actually a government department (as in Kyoto and Ottawa), to the free-market extreme, with private operation and complete deregulation (common only in the developing world and England's smaller cities). Mees believes that while responsibility for some operations can safely be subcontracted out to private companies, it is essential to keep strategic and tactical planning— the responsibility for setting long-term goals, designing networks, selecting appropriate technologies, and coordinating timetables—in the hands of a public agency, preferably one with a regional scope. (Such public agencies can be surprisingly lean. Mees cites the example of Zurich, a city whose trolleys and buses provide an astonishing half-billion rides a year, yet whose strategic and tactical planning agency has only thirty-five employees on its payroll.) As a public corporation with regional scope that has maintained its powers over strategic and tactical planning, SEPTA is— in theory at least—ideally placed to run transit in metropolitan Philadelphia for decades to come.

The agency's regional scope gives it distinct advantages. As early as 1922, Philadelphia was buying trains, making it the first major city in the United States to have its own publicly owned rolling stock. Like Vancouver's TransLink, SEPTA has authority over almost its entire operating area, and offers additional services in Delaware and New Jersey. (A separate agency, the Port Authority Transit Corporation, runs a single subway line from Center City across the Delaware River to Camden, New Jersey.) In 1984, a downtown-spanning tunnel was opened to connect Penn Railroad's old suburban station and the tracks of the former Reading Railroad. The Center City Commuter Connection, originally championed by Edmund Bacon, allows SEPTA's regional rail trains to run from one distant suburb to another, offering multiple stops downtown. In theory, a passenger can board a commuter train in Trenton and ride it through Center City all the way to Chestnut Hill West, or go from Glendale in the north to the airport in the south. This kind of inter-suburb service, pioneered by Paris's RER in the '70s, gives Philadelphia a degree of connectivity that is only a fond dream for most transit planners. Yet SEPTA has recently opted to kill through-running between suburbs, which means most trains now terminate in Center City.

"SEPTA is the only agency that owns its regional rail system," Vukan Vuchic told me at his office in the Engineering Building at the University of Pennsylvania. "Even in Germany, the commuter rail is owned by the national railway, not the city. SEPTA is unified in ownership, which is unique. Their problem is that they're not capable of running the system."

When it comes to transit, Vuchic wrote the book: his two-volume *Urban Transit* is the standard textbook on the subject in many engineering faculties. As a consultant, he helped rationalize SEPTA's regional rail system, giving suburban lines easy-to-understand colors and labels. Vuchic is frustrated that the agency has opted to kill the one system in North America that permitted genuine suburb-to-suburb travel.

"We are the first city to go from an organized system to a disorganized system. Why? Because SEPTA wants the freedom to send their trains wherever they want, while disregarding passengers' needs."

SEPTA, I pointed out, claims that very few of their customers rode from one suburb to another.

Vuchic cried, "That's because they never did any marketing, they never explained the system to the public!" And unlike European systems, he added, Philadelphia's regional rail operates at frequencies of as little as an hour. "Now, how do you make more frequency? You reduce the size of the crews. Today they have a driver and five conductors on each train, and they are punching the tickets like it was still 1910. If they cut down the workforce, and put in turnstiles like they already have in half a dozen cities, they could afford to run trains every half hour."

Vuchic's criticisms didn't stop there. Trolleys, he said, need to have signal priority and their own rights-of-way when they operate on the streets, and the city should introduce express buses that only stop at major intersections, like Los Angeles's Rapid Buses or Vancouver's B-line.

"But the basic problem is that SEPTA doesn't have stable financing," Vuchic said. "What we really need is a gasoline tax, like they have in Europe, where fifty percent goes to urban transportation. It would improve Philadelphia immensely."

SEPTA's general manager told me some improvements would be coming soon: the agency, Casey said, was working on a system-wide fare card, and new Hyundai-made Silverliner trains would be operating on regional rail by 2012.

As things stand now, SEPTA does a heroic job of providing basic, meat-and-potato service to the people of Philadelphia. Unlike Los Angeles's Metro, SEPTA doesn't own much land around its stations, which limits its ability to foster transit-oriented development. Fortunately, outside of the postwar suburbs, virtually everybody lives within a short walk of a trolley, bus, or rail stop. In other words, thanks to its long history of rail-centered growth, much of Philadelphia is *already* transit-oriented.

All it really needs is better transit.

Carless in West Philly

A few years ago the *New York Times* ran a Style Section piece that claimed Philadelphia as New York's "Sixth Borough." Citing cheap rents and a thriving arts and music scene, the *Times* argued that Philadelphia was poised to become the next Brooklyn.

I could see what the *Times* was getting at. Philadelphia remains a city of neighborhoods, and it has held on to much of the stoop-sitting, watertower-and-vacant-lot grit that has been gentrified out of New York. In Center City, saxophonists seem to play on every other street corner, competing for the spare change of passersby with the shifty types pedaling "loosies" and stolen SEPTA day passes. Once you get beyond the cheesesteaks and hoagies, the city's food culture is cheerful and down-to-earth: bearded Amish farmers sell apple pies at Saturday morning stands in West Philly's Clark Park, and countermen shuck oysters at Reading Terminal, a former railway station that has become a thriving downtown market. Riding the Market-Frankford elevated westbound one day, I was treated to a bird's-eye slide show of rooftop murals, which scrolled past like Burma Shave ads on a bygone highway. They were meant to be love letters, but they read more like disingenuous pickup lines: "Meet me on Fifty-Second, if only for fifty seconds," went one. Another, next to a painting of a cell phone, read: "Prepay is on / Let's Talk / Till My Minutes are Gone." And my favorite, spelled out in outsized fridge-magnet-like letters on a whitewashed wall: "If you were here / I'd be home now."

One day, I rented a bike and pedaled around Old City, Northern Liberties, and Fishtown, the evocatively named river wards that march north up the Delaware from Center City.* These old working-class neighborhoods have undergone a gentle gentrification in recent years. Philadelphia has long been plagued by "black eyes," the estimated 40,000 vacant properties, most of them boarded-up row houses, that dot the city; but as architecture critic Inga Saffron has written, you can now walk for an hour in any direction from City Hall without encountering any significant blight. In the Northern Liberties, the old Schmidt's Brewery, a 14-acre complex of brick buildings, has been sensitively reworked into a complex of condos, restaurants, and shops. New development tends to involve infill, locally known as "onesies" and "twosies": all through the Northern Liberties the spaces between row houses are being filled in by micro-developments of one or two houses—an example of transit-oriented development at its least intrusive. The river wards are anchored by stops on the Market-Frankford elevated line, which puts them within a 20-minute ride of the University of Pennsylvania and the hospitals that remain the city's biggest private employers.

If I were looking to settle here, I'd start my search in West Philadelphia. An easy shot across the Schuylkill River from Center City, it evolved, between the Civil War and the Depression, from a fashionable upper-class country retreat to a middle-class streetcar suburb. Trolleys still fan out through the neighborhood, and apartment blocks parallel the elevated, which reached West Philadelphia in 1907. The housing stock, stately three- to four-and-a-half-story homes, is nothing short of stunning. Queen Annes share blocks with Romanesque Revivals, but most streets are lined with Germano-Georgian row houses, which combine Teutonic and British building traditions. (It reminded me of Brooklyn's Park Slope, with front porches and stepped gables in place of concrete stoops and fire escapes.) After the war, West Philadelphia's substantial manor houses were subdivided into rental units, and as old Anglo-Protestant and Irish Catholic residents relocated to the suburbs, African Americans began to move in. White flight was never as thorough in Philadelphia as it was in Detroit or Baltimore, however; as early as the '60s, urban pioneers committed to staying in the city. Members of the Movement for a New Society, founded by former Quakers, settled around Baltimore Avenue, organizing neighbor-

---

* Some bicycle advocates believe that Philadelphia, a flat and relatively compact city, is poised to become one of America's great cycling towns. The city has over 200 miles of recreational bike paths, and against the protests of drivers, Mayor Nutter recently laid down broad bicycle paths along Pine and Spruce streets, creating a very practical east-west route through Center City.

hood patrols and appointing block captains to reduce crime.* The University of Pennsylvania, whose campus is the economic and cultural focus of the district, also became an agent of revitalization. The turning point came in 1996, after a biochemist was stabbed to death when he tried to stop a purse-snatching and the university began what would become a billion-dollar investment in West Philadelphia.

"When I first lived in this neighborhood ten years ago," said Michael Froehlich, who had agreed to show me around his neighborhood, "there was nothing on Baltimore Avenue. There certainly wasn't a yoga studio, an acupuncture clinic, or an Indian restaurant." We were sitting in the Vietnam Café on 47th Street, waiting for our coffees to drip over evaporated milk. "See that double house across the street?" Froehlich pointed to a three-story twin with bay windows and a huge front porch. "It probably goes for six hundred thousand dollars, depending on the interior. Ten years ago, you could have got it for sixty grand. All those fancy streetlights, the improved sidewalks, the banners on Baltimore Avenue, they come from the university's investment in the neighborhood."

Born in Pittsburgh, Froehlich grew up in Ohio and came to Philadelphia to study political science in the late '90s; now in his mid-thirties, he works as a legal aid lawyer. As we walked down Baltimore Avenue, he listed the neighbors on his block: "On the corner is rentals, first floor is a hairdresser, third floor is an attorney and a librarian; they have a baby. Next door is the Dixons, an elderly white couple who have lived there thirty years. Next door to them are the Tollivers, an elderly black couple; he's a retired security guy, she's a still-working nurse; they've lived here all their lives. Then there's us. Then Dorothy, who has lived there for thirty years, a retired administrator for Penn; she's the block captain. Then there's a Wayne professor, then a rental for college kids."

As we walked up to the front porch of his 110-year-old, four-story brick row house at 48th and Larchwood, Zora, Froehlich's two-year-old daughter, jumped into his arms. In the living room, which doubled as the bike storeroom, Froehlich explained the living arrangements. "My partner Susanna and I bought the house with Alicia, our housemate, three years ago, for just over three hundred thousand. We share the front entrance, and Alicia has the third and fourth floors. It's over three

---

* Block captains, who are officially recognized by the city, coordinate neighborhood watch and community cleanup programs.

thousand square feet, plus a basement, plus a porch, plus a deck, plus a back-yard." Like all the homes I saw in West Philadelphia, Froehlich's had kept its impressive appointments: its wide-slatted oak floors, elaborate moldings, and leaded bay windows gave it the feel of an Addams' Family mansion, minus the cobwebs. There was a separate kitchen on the third floor, and Alicia showed me how she'd turned the unfinished attic into a bedroom with spectacular views over neighboring rooftops.

Nobody in the house owned a car. "There was a six-month period in my early twenties when I owned a beat-up Toyota," said Froehlich, "but I've gotten by without one ever since." In the kitchen, I met Froehlich's partner, Susanna Gilbertson, who was busy trying to dissuade a giggling Zora from wedging herself beneath a set of shelves. "When our daughter was born," said Froehlich, "we thought we'd give it a year and decide if we needed to buy a car."

"We talked about it a lot at first," said Gilbertson. "The few times we've really needed a car, we've used Philly Car Share, which is like Zipcar. That seems to work fine." Gilbertson said she relied on SEPTA more than Michael. "Mike takes Zora to day care on his bike, but I'm still a bit scared of cycling on Philly's streets." She commutes to her Center City job as a domestic violence educator on the trolley, and rides buses to get to workshops.

Gilbertson said she had no regrets about living car-free. Riding bikes and using transit saved the family a lot of money, which didn't surprise me. According to a Brookings Institution study, transit-proximate households in the United States devote only 9 percent of their income to transportation, compared to 25 percent for the car-dependent. Both Froehlich and Gilbertson also told me that living without a car kept them in shape. Because every trip to a bus stop or subway station starts with a walk, transit users in the United States average 19 minutes of walking a day—close to the 22 minutes a day of moderate exercise recommended by the U.S. Center for Disease Control. (And transit may actually be slimming: a study of Charlotte, North Carolina, light-rail riders found that after only half a year, they weighed six and a half pounds less than drivers.)

Yet Froehlich conceded he has some problems with transit in Philadelphia. Until recently, he wrote a blog called "SEPTA Watch," a day-to-day record of the pleasures and pitfalls of taking transit in Philadelphia. He says employees can be rude, and there's a lack of information about routes and service changes for passengers; the fare system could use an overhaul, and regional rail trains should probably run at least once every half hour. But in general, Froehlich feels the system's coverage of the city is excellent.

"If more middle-class riders used SEPTA, SEPTA would improve even more," he said. "But middle-class people are going to be reluctant to use SEPTA until it improves. Unfortunately, with transit it can be a bit of a chicken-and-egg thing.

"I stopped doing the blog because I felt a bit like a poseur," he admitted. "I was moving from being a primary SEPTA user to being a primary bicycle user." Froehlich still uses transit a couple of times a week, but he now finds he can get around by foot and bicycle just as efficiently.

Many of Froehlich's friends also live without cars. In the street, we chatted with Ariel, who grew up next to a train station in Mount Airy. Ariel is thirty, but he has never learned to drive. "Dude," he told me, "I went to a party, and this buddy of mine said there are five people in this room who didn't learn to drive until they were in their thirties. That's totally typical of Philadelphia. The only times I've regretted not having a license have had to do with moving."

The way people in West Philadelphia live their lives may strike some as an anomaly. But it is well to remember that 35 percent of Americans don't even have access to a car: they are too young or too old, too infirm or too poor, or too eyesight-challenged to drive. For the time being, only 6 million of the country's 105 million households are within a half mile of a high-frequency transit stop (though that number is expected to more than double in the next twenty years), which means that if you want to reduce car-dependency, you need to pick the right neighborhood—preferably one that evolved before the age of mass automobile ownership. West Philadelphia is recognized as a historic streetcar district, but almost every North American city has similar neighborhoods. East Portland, Cleveland's Shaker Heights, Berkeley's Ashby Station, Calgary's Hillhurst, Boston's Roxbury, and Washington, D.C.'s Anacostia (which is now being gentrified by middle-class African American professionals) are all classic streetcar suburbs, with highly walkable streets.* Even Phoenix has the F. Q. Story neighborhood, which was served by the city's small prewar streetcar network, and is one of

* An excellent guide to such neighborhoods is the Web site http://www.walkscore.com, which rates urban districts nationwide from 0, for completely "Car-Dependent," to 100, for a "Walker's Paradise."

the few parts of the city whose houses have held their value since the sub-prime mortgage crisis. Planners who aim to foster transit-oriented living would do well to focus on such districts, which tend to have a higher tolerance for density than later suburbs.

Philadelphia is in an excellent position to profit from the coming urban renaissance. It has great structure, it has great neighborhoods like Society Hill, the River Wards, and West Philadelphia, and it has SEPTA, which, in spite of its shortcomings, is well placed to offer exceptional service and coverage. To thrive in the future, it just needs a few more people like Michael Froehlich and his family.

A Kind of Paradise

I expected to feel a little uneasy as I rode transit, and a rented bicycle, around the apparently mean streets of Philadelphia. It is a city, after all, with a reputation. I never had any trouble, though, and while everybody I met had stories about bicycles being stolen, none of the regular SEPTA users I talked to had ever seen a serious crime committed on transit in Philadelphia. The only thing they complained about was the after-school behavior of teenagers—which is the bane of public transport just about everywhere.

Though subways and buses are favorite settings for TV and movie crime, the reality is most transit systems are heavily patrolled by police, and are now monitored by security cameras; statistics show that, even in the crime-plagued '90s, you were safer on a big-city subway than walking the streets above. (Though one category of transit crime has increased exponentially in the past few years: the opportunistic snatching of MP3 players and cell phones.)

I understand why my parents' generation fled the cities for the suburbs. In the '60s, there was a palpable sense that urban neighborhoods all over were in decline. But times have changed. The major crime rate in the United States is now the lowest it's been in forty years. The decline has been particularly striking in large cities. In 2009, the homicide rate in New York reached its lowest level since the city started keeping accurate records in 1963. (In Canada, where the violent crime rate has always been a degree of magnitude lower than in the United States, the overall crime rate in 2010 was at its lowest level in forty years, and the murder rate was lower than it had been since 1966.) From year to year over the last decade, Philadelphia regularly recorded double-digit declines in violent crimes, and the murder rate has dropped by a quarter since the '90s. The one thing that appears to be on the rise, in fact, is *perception* of crime. According to Gallup, every year in the five years leading up to 2010, over two-thirds of Americans reported that they thought crime in the United States was worse than it had been the year before.

Not that I mean to minimize the importance of perception. Nobody wants to live, let alone raise a family, in a place in which they don't feel secure. But demographics are changing, and the reality is big old cities like Philadelphia are safer than they've been in decades. In 2011, *U.S. News & World Report* crunched FBI crime statistics, and came up with a list of the country's most dangerous cities. In order, the top five were St. Louis, Atlanta, Birmingham, Orlando, and Detroit. In St. Louis and Atlanta, you were five times more likely than the national average to be the victim of a murder or robbery, a burglary, or a motor vehicle theft.

It's an interesting list. One thing the nation's worst crime hot spots seem to have in common is that they are highly sprawled metropolitan regions—Greater St. Louis covers almost 8,500 square miles—whose atrophied public transport systems make their residents almost completely dependent on cars.

Any responsible criminologist would protest that only a fool confounds correlation and causation. Fair enough, though this raises another question: Doesn't believing that your transportation and housing choices shield you from crime when they actually make you more likely to be a victim of it mean you are already living in a fool's paradise?

Rubber and Rail

Planners are at ease talking about residential densities, workplace clusters, and transit ridership rates, but they are strangely silent on the role skin color plays in public transport. Yet in many cities around the world, the geography of class, ethnicity, religion, and race can be the most important factor in people's transportation choices. In Philadelphia, it's something you notice the minute you step on a bus.

One morning, I boarded a northbound 23 bus on North 12th Street headed for Chestnut Hill. As we left Center City, every seat was taken, but the bus started to empty out as we passed the low-rise public housing around Temple University. When we reached the corner of Pike Street, our female driver pulled over, and started reading a tabloid—a bad sign, as any transit user who's in a hurry well knows. She had left the door open. It was a chilly day, and the white-haired man in the single seat in front of me, yelled, "At least close the door, driver!"

But then another bus passed by, releasing a SEPTA driver, who, before he settled onto the driver's seat, mumbled an apology to his coworker for being late. After our ten-minute wait, we continued north on Germantown Avenue, past the boarded-up Baptist churches, the murals of Martin Luther King Jr. and Harriet Tubman, the check-cashing stores and tattoo parlors, and the vacant lots bordered by razor-wire-topped chain link. When a woman breezed past the driver talking on a cell phone, he called her back to take a closer look at her fare card.

A voice from the back boomed: "Yo, driver! Don't be checkin' fares! Slow down! You drivin' *reckless*!"

I looked back: the man shouting was wild-eyed, unshaven, in a black hoodie. It was true, the bus had been moving jerkily, and we had even blown through a red light; our driver was obviously trying to get back on schedule.

A couple of stops later, the man in the hoodie stomped to the front of the bus.

"What's your number!" he yelled. "You was drivin' reckless! You got the safety of the people in your hands. I ought to punch you in the face!"

The middle-aged woman across the aisle from me moaned, "Don't punch him! I'm going to be late for work!"

After a tense staring contest, the man in the hoodie jumped to the curb.

As we resumed our journey, the older man in front of me moved to the front bench seat to commiserate with the driver.

"Goddamn crackheads!" he said, shaking his head.

"I'm fifty years old," muttered the driver. "I'm not about to get punched on my own bus."

By the time we reached the upper reaches of Germantown Avenue, the woman across the aisle was the last holdout.

"Driver!" she said. "First you was drivin' too fast, now you're drivin' too slow. I have to be at work by noon. That's four minutes from now! I got the kind of job where you can't be late."

We had been rolling through North Philadelphia, an area notorious for its high-crime no-man's-lands. But by the time Germantown Avenue reached Chestnut Hill, it had undergone a transformation into Main

Street, USA: there were flowerpots hanging in front of antiques stores, and young couples with toddlers sipped iced coffee on the benches in front of an upscale café. I got off the bus and wandered the side streets, where two-story row houses soon gave way to center-hall Colonial Revivals and half-timbered Tudors on five-acre lots. Chestnut Hill was founded in the 1850s as a railroad suburb by one of the owners of the Pennsylvania Railroad, providing Philadelphia's anglophile elite with a haven from the teeming, immigrant-populated city. It remains an upper-class enclave, separated from Center City by some of Philadelphia's roughest neighborhoods.

After an hour, I walked to the Chestnut Hill East train station, whose wooden-roofed platform looked like the inspiration for every train set I'd played with as a child. A regional rail train was waiting on the track. As I boarded, a conductor with a handlebar mustache discouraged a woman talking on a cell phone from entering the "quiet car."

"Everybody's got a cell phone these days," he drawled, rolling his eyes. "It's the new America. I sure miss the old one."

The train returned to Center City, running smoothly on rails through leafy railway cuts, past the substantial backyards of suburban homes. Another conductor came through the train—punching tickets, as SEPTA critic Vukan Vuchic had said, as if it was still 1910.

The one-way fare to Center City was $5. Everybody on the train, including the conductors, was white or Asian.

The price of a token for the 23 Chestnut Hill bus, which covered the same distance in considerably less comfort, was only $1.55. Everybody on the bus had been black.

For some perspective on the differences in service, I asked Adriene Davis—his friends call him Dave—about his experiences riding transit in Philadelphia. I'd first met Dave in Montreal, where he was strolling up our street, smoking a pipe and looking for a decent hamburger. I'd shown him around the neighborhood, and he asked me to look him up if I ever made it to his part of the world. Dave lives in West Philadelphia, and rides the trolley to Germantown most days for rehearsals with the Sun Ra Arkestra, the legendary free jazz combo he's been playing trombone with since the '90s.

"SEPTA, the way it's set up, it's one of the best," Dave told me. "I grew up in Kansas City, where everybody had a car. Here in Philadelphia, SEPTA has got every place covered, every little corner and crack of the city." Dave's only reproach was the lack of information provided to users. He'd been twenty minutes late for our meeting at a bar in Old City because the trolley had gotten stuck in the tunnel. "You just sit there, you wait. Nobody says anything. I could've gone up there and asked the driver, but I just hate being treated rude. "

But in Philly, Dave figured, SEPTA was the way to go. The trolleys, buses, and elevated were cheap, fast, and safe; he had no need to use the more expensive regional rail. "A lot of the trains are people coming from the suburbs. Most of the blacks on the bus are working people, going back and forth to their jobs every day, rather than drive. These are Philadelphia's workers." Dave admitted he was worried about the gentrification of Philadelphia. He lived in an "efficiency," the local term for a studio apartment, near the University of Pennsylvania. "To a degree, it's nice that people are coming back. But then it drives prices up, so the people who have been in the community for years get priced out." When I asked Dave if he wanted to come to Fishtown, where the annual Shad Festival was happening in Penn Treaty Park, he declined. "I've heard it's a pretty racist neighborhood," he said. Dave is African American, and Fishtown is a traditionally Irish working-class district. "A friend of mine, a UPS driver, got beat up in Fishtown because he was black."

It was a reminder that the geography of race can still be an issue in Philadelphia. But there are signs across the country, that the old racial split on public transport is beginning to change. As young people return to the cities that baby boomers fled, the increasingly mixed ridership on transit, particularly on subways and light rail, mirrors the growing racial mix of society at large. Architecture critic Inga Saffron sees this as a sign of the times. "I'm very happy about all the hipsters colonizing Center City and Northern Liberties," she told me. "They're the post–civil rights generation. They didn't grow up with busing, with all the urban riots. They grew up in the suburbs, and they have none of this racial baggage that so many people in my generation have. They're excited to be in the city. They'll ride the subway; they'll ride the buses, without thinking twice."

If this kind of social change is going to continue, public space is also going to have to continue to expand. Just as shopping malls killed main streets and sidewalks, and gated communities replaced real neighborhoods, the private automobile usurped the social space once shared on subways, buses, and trains. When a society eliminates public space— when your only contact with your fellow citizen happens at 55 miles per hour, separated by layers of glass—it stops knowing itself, and can start believing the most outrageous lies: that crime is rampant, that people have no shared interests, that races and classes have no common ground. This doesn't mean that Philadelphia is about to become a placid Zurich or a conflict-free Copenhagen: historic divisions of class, ethnicity, and race run deep here. But there is lots of evidence that geographic segregation and the privatization of public space are slowing. And for better and for worse, subways, buses, and trains have long been a crucial meeting ground for society: when Rosa Parks refused to give up her seat for a white passenger on a bus in Alabama in 1955, public transport provided the shared space where racism could be challenged. It bodes well for the future that the public in Philadelphia never lost the habit of using public transport.

Not everybody is as sanguine about the future. The first person I talked to in Philadelphia was Witold Rybczynski, the distinguished belle-lettrist of modern architecture. I enjoy Rybczynski's elegant prose, but he has a marked tendency to minimize the role of the automobile in the evolution of the North American metropolis, and I was surprised by his dismissal of Philadelphia as a viable city.

"Philadelphia has been in decline for decades now," he told me. "The problem with this city is that it has a lot of poor people, it has a lot of illiterate people, it has a lot of people living below the poverty line, and it has high unemployment." Rybczynski has strong memories of downtown blight. "I remember visiting Old City with a friend, before I moved here, and there were wild dogs in the street. It was a really scary, empty area."

But then Rybczynski is convinced that the natural habitat of Americans is not the city but the suburb. His books, from *City Life* through *Home* and *The Last Harvest*, have consistently made the case for the detached single-family suburban house as a kind of British and American manifest destiny, and he believes suburbs have spread for one reason: because people like them. "Sprawl is and always has been inherent to urbanization," he has written. "It is driven less by the regulations of legislators, the actions of developers, and the theories of city planners than by the decisions of millions of individuals—Adam Smith's 'Invisible Hand.'" To say that the spread of the single-family home on the urban fringe was solely the result of personal choice is to ignore the fact that for a couple of generations after the war government policies made it the *only* practical choice.

And, in his writing, Rybczynski has been silent about the negative forces that formed the American suburb: the freeway-building that gutted so many viable neighborhoods and the redlining of poorer districts that fostered urban decline. Rybczynski's adopted hometown—he moved to Philadelphia from Quebec to teach at the University of Pennsylvania—is a particularly flagrant instance of white flight. By the end of the '60s, almost a quarter of a million whites had left the center of Philadelphia for suburbs like Levittown in Bucks County. When a black couple tried to buy a home in this ur-subdivision in 1957, they were driven back to their old home by two hundred stone-throwing suburbanites. (As late as 2000, less than 5 percent of Levittowners were African American.)

Rybczynski himself lives in the old railroad suburb of Chestnut Hill. When I asked him about the return to Center City and surrounding neighborhoods, he dismissed it as demographically insignificant, and pointed out that the city's orchestra had just gone bankrupt. Which is sad news, to be sure, but hardly incontrovertible proof of urban decline.

I think Philadelphia is on its way back, maybe not in the way people like Rybczynski mean when they talk of urban vitality, but in a far more durable sense, as a city full of decent, livable neighborhoods. Its revival is being driven by people like Kenny Gamble, the pioneering producer of Philadelphia soul, who, after leaving his comfortable home in a Main Line suburb, bought up abandoned houses on the South Side and turned them into affordable housing in an effort to encourage African American home-ownership. It was pioneered by Edmund Bacon, who in the '60s came up with a plan to get blacks involved in the planning process, and whose faith in Philadelphia was shown by the fact he never left his Center City row house. And it will be helped along by people like Michael Froehlich and his family, who are deeply invested in improving their adopted communities.

I'd wager that this urban revival is no mere blip, but the start of a long-term, nationwide trend. Since the beginning of the millennium, the share of residential construction in central cities has more than doubled in 26 of the country's 50 largest metro areas. While single-family house-building has plummeted during the same period, most new construction is in multifamily developments and apartment buildings. The days of the sprawled nation may have passed: when you add together the populations of transit-served central cities, old inner-ring suburbs, and small towns, you now get a solid majority of Americans.

On its own, transportation, even coupled with the most up-to-date urbanism, is never going to be enough to revive a place whose economy is in the doldrums. If there are no jobs for people to get to, the most advanced bus rapid transit and light rail in the world will be useless. But transit is going to be a crucial ingredient in the coming urban renaissance. In an era of rising energy prices, when people are realizing that livable, walkable city neighborhoods make for attractive places to raise families, cities like Philadelphia, with their legacy of good transit and excellent urban structure, will be well placed to thrive. The First City may never attain the international stature of a New York, Shanghai, or London, but my guess is that, pretty soon, Philadelphia will be one great place to live.

It's already well on the way.

[The motorcar] exploded each city into a dozen suburbs, and then extended many of the forms of urban life along the highway till the open road seemed to become non-stop cities. . . . Streets, and even sidewalks, became too intense a scene for the casual interplay of growing up. As the city filled with mobile strangers, even next-door neighbours became strangers. This is the story of the motorcar, and it has not much longer to run.

—Marshall McLuhan, *Understanding Media*, 1964.

11. The Toronto Tragedy

Toronto, Ontario

I'd always planned to end up in Toronto. After all, it was the city where I started.

I was born at the old Women's College Hospital, near Queen's Park station on the Yonge-University line, in 1966. At the time, my parents were renting a top-floor flat in a house on Lytton Boulevard, a short stroller's push from Yonge Street; an auspicious first address for a newborn, it turned out, as it had belonged to one of the inventors of Pablum (his widow spoon-fed me the vitamin-rich baby mush, which may explain why I never developed rickets). When I was only four years old, my parents joined the exodus to suburbia, and we moved to a cookie-cutter bungalow on a curvy street in Burlington, twenty-five miles west along the shore of Lake Ontario from Union Station. I used to wonder if this early exile from the city was the foundational trauma that led to my lifelong bias against subdivisions, but my Kodachrome-hued memories of Riverside Drive—of netting crayfish in the nearby creek, of walking to Frontenac Elementary School, and of pretending I was Bobby Orr in street hockey games—are for the most part fond, and at worst emotionally neutral. My parents tell me they bought the house as a short-term investment, but if they were hoping the suburbs would be a healthier setting than the city, they seriously misjudged Southern Ontario. Less than a mile from our carport were the multimillion-gallon storage tanks of the Oakville refinery, where British Petroleum was busy making jet fuel, and beyond a tiny stand of oaks known as Sherwood Forest Park lay the Queen Elizabeth Way—six lanes of rushing traffic that, in the days before emissions controls, must have created a formidable cancer corridor of leaded gas exhaust. My parents lasted two years in Burlington, before giving up on the land of loops-and-lollipops and bundling my sister and me onto a westbound train.

At a time when downtowns across North America were hollowing out, there was nothing exceptional about my parents' move to the outer suburbs. But it turns out that what made the Toronto area unique in the waning years of the postwar baby boom was the way it was bucking the continent-wide trend toward city-sapping suburbanization. Toronto was the city that Jane Jacobs and her family, despairing of the future in Vietnam-era America, had chosen over New York, settling in the Annex, just one of many inner-city neighborhoods that have never given up their vitality. The city's freeway revolt, led by University of Toronto professors and supported by Jacobs, put the kibosh on the Spadina Expressway, which was part of a larger plan to straitjacket the entire downtown with urban freeways. (The uprising came too late to spare the city the elevated Gardiner Expressway, a leprous eyesore that continues to sever Toronto from its waterfront.) While other cities were putting up district-killing high-rise concrete slabs, Torontonians were renovating old row houses in the central city. And thanks to a decades-long tradition of regional planning and governance, metropolitan Toronto still sprawls half as much as North American cities with comparable populations.

For much of the twentieth century, Toronto was also known as a model of efficient urban transit. The Toronto Transit Commission (TTC), which until the '70s required no government subsidies at all, was generally considered a triumph for public ownership. Over half of the city's workers still get downtown by commuter rail, streetcar, bus, or subway, and transport scholars continue to study the way the TTC extends the reach of its small but efficient two-line subway by using a brilliantly integrated network of feeder buses. While cities like Philadelphia may have potential for revival, Toronto has never questioned its urban birthright: the "City that Works," as impressed visitors used to call it, has long been seen as a Mecca for urbanists, and a shining example of rational transportation planning.

Which is why, when I visit the city of my birth these days, I spend a lot of time shaking my head in sad wonder. In just over a decade, Toronto has lost its lead as a global model for well-planned regional growth, and the TTC is on its way to becoming a case study in how to quickly squander a hard-won legacy of decent transit. Vancouver, meanwhile, has easily outdistanced Toronto as the continent's leading example of progressive transport planning, and even sprawling Calgary can now lay claim to more far-sighted municipal leadership.

When I planned this voyage, Toronto was going to be part of my itinerary; I figured Canada's biggest city still had something to teach North America's most mobility-challenged metropolises about smart urbanism. As my journey draws to an end, however, it is becoming clear that its real claim to fame is as a cautionary tale for other cities. In Toronto, the apposite question has lately become: How did a city that *used* to work so well end up so broken?

The Ford Nation vs. the Bike-Riding Pinkos

It's something you notice the minute you step out of the marmoreal glory of Union Station, Canada's grandest train station, onto bustling Front Street. Drivers in Toronto have serious anger issues. They honk; they lean out the window and yell; they cut off pedestrians. If the latest statistics are any indication, drivers here have every right to be pissed off. According to the city's Board of Trade, the average daily commute is now eighty minutes, which puts Toronto dead last among nineteen major cities in Europe and North America. In IBM's annual commuter pain index, Toronto now ranks ahead of Los Angeles, Houston, and New York when it comes to the anger and stress caused by congestion. Between 1986 and 2006, rush-hour traffic speeds declined by 24 percent, and jams are now estimated to cost the Toronto–Hamilton region $6 billion a year in lost productivity. The Don Valley Parkway, a free-flowing and bucolic river drive when it opened in 1961, is now so congested it is widely known as the "Don Valley Parking Lot."

All this frustration plays out in nasty ways. In one particularly memorable stretch in January 2010, Toronto drivers struck and killed fourteen pedestrians and one cyclist—over a death a day for two weeks. Part of the problem seems to stem from city form: the narrowness of downtown streets, built two centuries ago on the military-style grid devised by Governor John Simcoe, seems to multiply conflicts between cars, transit vehicles, and bikes. Some of the stories behind the headlines are genuinely shocking. On Argyle Street in the city's west end in 2008, a taxi driver was charged with aggravated assault after allegedly pinning a rider on a $5,000 bicycle to a utility pole, reportedly after a heated argument, and leaving the victim with a severely crushed leg.

In another incident, on Bloor Street west of Yonge, after a minor collision between a black convertible Saab and a bicycle, the enraged cyclist grabbed the steering wheel; the man was dragged for a block, before being knocked against a fire hydrant and into the gutter. (The cyclist, a one-time bike courier with a history of run-ins with drivers, died from his injuries; the driver, Ontario's former attorney general, spent a night in jail before being freed on bail. All charges against him were ultimately dropped.) Even as cities like New York and San Francisco earned praise for increasing their cycle path networks, City Hall in 2011 announced it was removing the heavily used bike lanes on Jarvis Street that had been installed only the year before. Lately, Toronto has become the anti-Copenhagen: a city where, day after day, it is actually becoming *more* dangerous to walk or ride a bike.

To an outsider, it is clear that Toronto is in the grips of a culture war, one that culminated in the election, late in 2010, of Rob Ford as mayor. Central casting couldn't have come up with a more perfect car-bound suburbanite: the brush-cut, rubicund Ford, on the obese side of overweight, hails from the suburb of Etobicoke and is egregiously Caucasian in a city where "visible minorities" are within a couple of percentage points of becoming the majority. As a city councilor during the previous administration of Mayor David Miller—whose support of streetcars and bicycles saw him accused of waging a "War on Cars"—Ford made it abundantly clear which side he was on, declaring in a budget debate: "I can't support bike lanes. Roads are built for buses, cars, and trucks. My heart bleeds when someone gets killed, but it's their own fault at the end of the day."

Waging a campaign that promised to lower taxes and "Stop the Gravy Train," Ford got less than a quarter of the votes in Toronto's thirteen downtown wards, but rode to power by sweeping the suburbs of North York, Scarborough, and Etobicoke. Making a speech at the inauguration, Don Cherry, Canada's foghorn-voiced court jester of hockey, declared Ford the clear winner of the culture war. Planting a kiss on the new mayor's cheek, he triumphantly bellowed that he was wearing a pink suit in tribute to "all the pinkos out there that ride bicycles."

The rise of the Ford Nation, as the mayor likes to refer to his supporters, would be just another iteration of the tiresome schism between Canada's Tim Horton subdivisions and its Starbuck downtowns, were it not for the long-term damage Rob Ford is capable of inflicting on the city. In his campaign, he declared his unalterable opposition to the mainstay of Toronto transit: the streetcar. "Streetcars congest traffic, that is the number one issue I hear," he said. He proposed replacing them with buses, adding, "Streets are for cars, trucks, and buses." Ford was sending a clear message to his voter base: car-driving suburbanites whose only interaction with streetcars is as obstacles in their daily commute.

Yet among transport scholars, Toronto is considered remarkable for being the only major North American city that has both retained and expanded its historic streetcar system. These are not revived vintage trolleys for the tourist trade; after protesters saved the original network in the '70s, the Ontario government developed the Canadian Light Rail Vehicle, whose distinctive styling is based on a Swiss prototype. Unlike the vehicles traveling the underused new light-rail lines in Los Angeles and Phoenix, the CLRVs are high-performing workhorses that serve the kinds of dense urban neighborhoods that guarantee high ridership levels. Rolling along eleven routes in their red-and-white livery, they bring European panache to the streets of Toronto, and collectively form the largest street railway system in the Americas.

I used to be skeptical about the efficiency of Toronto's streetcars, but that was because I only knew the Queen Street car. Its stop-and-start progress along the chronically congested stretches of a major crosstown street can be agonizing (and is also a perfect demonstration of how the coming of automobiles to the American city robbed streetcars of their efficiency). On broader streets, though, Toronto's streetcars perform well, and lately the city has done a remarkably good job of laying tracks on dedicated rights-of-way. With signal priority at cross streets, the Spadina Avenue and Queen's Quay cars move fast and even duck into tunnels, allowing transfers to the subway and inter-city trains. The rebuilding of the St. Clair Avenue streetcar route was controversial—laying the tracks on a separate central median put the project tens of millions of dollars over budget, and snarled traffic for years—but it now runs smooth and fast, and has been credited with reviving business on one of the city's major east-west thoroughfares. All in all, Toronto's streetcars are responsible for the kind of heavy lifting that gets done by subways in other cities: each capacious, zero-emissions vehicle can carry 50 percent more passengers than a bus, and the fleet handles almost 300,000 passengers a day, more than all the trains on Philadelphia's subway.

In 2007, then-mayor David Miller announced Transit City, an ambitious plan that would have used $17.5 billion in provincial and federal funds to build seven new light-rail routes, as well as to increase the frequency of buses on almost two dozen major routes. Community groups were ecstatic: the plan would not only have served suburban areas that lacked rapid transit, but also provided superior service to some of the city's poorest neighborhoods. Environmental assessments began, and new light-rail vehicles were ordered from Bombardier. But the provincial government delayed its delivery of funds, and Ford—after killing a vehicle registration tax that would have helped fund public transport—made it one of his first orders of business to cancel Transit City.

I asked Steve Munro, a transit blogger who was a leader in the fight to save streetcars in the '70s, what Transit City would have represented for Toronto.

"There would have been a *major* increase in the amount of surface rail in the city," Munro told me. "The big trunk line, which would have been along Eglinton Avenue, running from the airport in the west to Kennedy station in the east, would have been partially underground, so it wouldn't have interfered with traffic. But the important point is that for decades we looked at transit in Toronto from the point of view of what was the next project we could afford to build. Transit City was something new, in that we were saying: 'Let's not try to spend every penny we have building, say, a single subway line, but look at where network improvements are really needed—and we actually have a fighting chance of finishing in our lifetime.'" All told,

Transit City would have added seventy-five miles of new surface rail routes to the city along dedicated rights-of-way on seven corridors, created 200,000 jobs, and, with its renewed fleet of Bombardier-made Flexity trams, turned Toronto into the Strasbourg of North America—a city on the cutting edge of urban transit.

Ford announced that the money intended for Transit City would go entirely to building new subway lines. The proposed Eglinton light-rail line would be put underground, and the underused Sheppard line, derided as a "Subway to Nowhere" when it opened in 2002, would be extended to the eastern suburb of Scarborough. If built, both would be spectacular wastes of taxpayer money. Outside the central city, Eglinton Avenue is easily broad enough that a couple of its lanes could be devoted to surface rail without losing much in the way of automobile capacity. Transit analysts, meanwhile, have pointed out that building a capacity-increasing extension to the east-west Sheppard line, which feeds into the already overcrowded Yonge subway, would strain Toronto's north-south main line to the breaking point. (Blogger Munro argues that the subway Toronto really needs at this point is the "downtown relief line," a route first proposed in the '60s, which would link the eastern suburbs directly to downtown.)

Ford claimed the multibillion-dollar Sheppard line extension would be built by private entrepreneurs eager to develop land around stations. While this has worked in other cities—Hong Kong's metro was partially funded through sales of city-owned land—Toronto doesn't actually have much station-proximate property to sell to developers. A few months after Ford's election, the chair of the infrastructure agency responsible for putting together subway funding admitted to the press that there was exactly zero private-sector interest in helping to build the Sheppard subway extension. A better way to fund it, he suggested to a *Toronto Star* reporter, would be to introduce an automobile tax—something his boss had just killed.

Neither the Eglinton subway nor the Sheppard extension will be completed during Ford's first term. Ten months into Ford's term, the TTC announced that, even as it anticipated a record ridership of a half billion rides in 2012, it was being forced by City Hall to make Draconian cuts. The delivery of new buses and streetcars would be delayed, an order for new subway trains would be reduced, five hundred jobs would be outsourced, and late-night bus service would be cut. Ford, in other words, is amply delivering on his campaign of negativity: during his term, nothing new will be built, no jobs will be created, and nothing will improve on the streets of Toronto. The only change likely to happen is that the city will be even more congested than it was before, straphangers will have to endure more misery, and the already ravine-deep divide between drivers and transit users will become a yawning canyon.

How did a guy like Ford happen to a nice place like Toronto? Unfortunately, the rise of the Ford Nation, and the gridlock and transport paralysis that are sure to ensue, became inevitable when Toronto's future was handed over to its suburbs. As such, it's a cautionary tale that should be more widely known—if only to prevent it from ever happening ever again.

The Toronto Miracle

Canadians tend to think of the conurbation on the north shore of Lake Ontario as a huge place, an impression borne out by the signs that scroll by—Markham, population 262,000; Brampton, 434,000; Mississauga, 669,000—as you drive westward on Highway 401. But for a metropolitan area of 5.5 million, Toronto is remarkably compact: with central city densities of twenty-eight residents an acre, and an average of eleven per acre over its total area, it beats out San Francisco, Los Angeles, and even New York for the title of densest metro area in North America.* It is only in the newest, outermost suburbs, which Torontonians call the 905 (to distinguish them from the 416, downtown's historic area code) that the densities drop precipitously, to an average of eight residents an acre.

At the end of the Second World War, Toronto covered barely fifty square miles; beyond Steeles Avenue, only eleven miles north of the lakeshore, lay farmland. The city's spread began in earnest with the construction of urban highways. The Queen Elizabeth Way—Canada's first limited-access expressway, started after Ontario's road builders paid a visit to Nazi Germany to study the autobahns—had been completed in 1939, and construction of the elevated Gardiner began in 1955. To the east of downtown, the Don Valley Parkway launched the city on its spread northwards to Lake Simcoe. Expressways in Canada, with the exception of the federally built and managed Trans-Canada Highway, are a provincial responsibility, which meant

* Central-city Toronto is, of course, less dense than Manhattan, but its older suburbs—places like Burlington, where my family's home was shoehorned into a forty-foot-wide lot—are easily denser than their counterparts on Long Island or in New Jersey.

that when protests against the proposed Spadina freeway began in the '70s, the responsible authorities tended to pay attention, with then-premier Bill Davis memorably proclaiming: "If we are building a transportation system to serve the automobile, the Spadina Expressway would be a good place to start. But if we are building a transportation system to serve people, the Spadina Expressway is a good place to stop."* The freeway revolts came too late to do anything about the Gardiner Expressway and the Don Valley Parkway, but Toronto remains less road-bound than comparably-sized American cities, and sprawls far less.

Another factor limiting the city's growth was Metro, which, in its nearly half century of existence, came to be seen as the most effective system of metropolitan government on the continent. Long before Portland and Minneapolis, Toronto was thinking in regional terms: three plans, the first of them drawn up in 1943, effectively channeled orderly development around a compact center in a way far more determinant than the much better known, but in practice less influential, plans created for Chicago and New York. The 1953 birth of Metro, a federation of thirteen municipalities, created a second tier of government that pooled local tax revenues to build sewers, roads, and other crucial infrastructure for the growing city. In jurisdictionally fragmented American metro areas, the lack of regional oversight virtually guaranteed the kind of leapfrog development, often built on septic fields, that fomented sprawl. Metro, which allowed the city to spread only as it expanded its network of roads and sewers, became a powerful force for limiting unplanned growth.

And the version of suburbia that Metro did build was less car-dependent than its American counterpart. Don Mills, a mid-'50s "corporate suburb" whose 8,000 dwellings made it bigger than any contemporary development in the United States outside of Levittown, proved to be hugely influential. Originally called Model City, it placed shopping plazas, schools, libraries, and community centers in the middle of ring roads, all within walking distance of single-family homes and three-story brick apartment blocks. As in Ebenezer Howard's nineteenth-century utopian Garden Cities, workers

---

* Davis, a Progressive Conservative, also launched some early experiments with magnetic-levitation trains and oversaw the building of Scarborough Rapid Transit, an elevated light-rail system that continues to run as a dilapidated offshoot of the Bloor-Danforth subway, Toronto's east-west line. The provincially developed technology was later sold to Detroit as the People Mover, and to Vancouver in the form of the Mark I SkyTrain.

were expected to walk to local jobs; and, like the Garden Suburbs that actually got built, Don Mills fell far short of becoming an independent community: fewer than 5 percent of residents would ever work locally, most commuting, by car, to the offices of downtown. But with its multi-family dwellings, Don Mills was significantly denser than most suburbs, and traces of its impact can still be seen in the street patterns of suburban Canada wherever you find ring roads converging on shopping plazas and community centers.

Even as the region's suburbs grew more slowly and compactly than comparable American metro areas, the central city retained its population. Toronto's answer to the redlining of poor districts—the denial of federally guaranteed mortgages that doomed so many African-American and immigrant neighborhoods in the United States—was "white-painting." In the '70s, proto-gentrifiers, young professionals the *Toronto Star* dubbed "urban adventurers," slapped coats of acrylic on century-old downtown rowhouses, brilliantly proclaiming their intentions to build lives in the city. At the same time, Canadian efforts at urban renewal tended to be far more modest. After experiments with concrete-slab housing projects—among them the blighted Regent Park and St. James Town—proved unpopular, Toronto built a modern neighborhood of low-rise brick row houses called the St. Lawrence community. A textbook example of what would now be called transit-oriented infill, the relative prosperity and low rates of rental turnover of this central-city neighborhood remain a reproach to crime-ridden Le Corbusier–inspired projects in other cities (at least those that haven't been demolished).

The final factor limiting sprawl in Toronto was transit. Private operators had been profitably running electric streetcars in the city since 1891. Unlike American street-railway companies, though, they weren't in the business of real estate development, which meant it was in their interest to keep their trolleys running through those built-up neighborhoods where they could collect the most fares. In order to provide service to less densely settled areas, the city founded the Toronto Civic Railway in 1911; nine years later, the Toronto Transportation Commission (renamed the Toronto Transit Commission in the '50s) was born of a merger of the private and city-run lines. This early municipalization of public transport proved to be a boon. American railroad barons tended to fill their pockets with straphangers' nickels and dimes until the very day they'd driven their trolley and subway companies into the ground—which meant that when public takeovers occurred, U.S. municipalities usually inherited dysfunctional, bankrupt systems. The TTC, in contrast, ran a tight ship from the start, plowing profits back into better service and using the surplus from increased ridership during the Second World War to fund construction of a new subway.

By the time the Yonge-University line opened in 1954, transit planning was a function of Metro; the east-west Bloor-Danforth line, which opened in 1966, was completely overseen by the regional government. Commuter train service, run by the province, started in the same year. I recall watching the GO trains (the name stands for Government of Ontario) zipping by on tracks not far from our home in Burlington. Since then, GO has become the most successful commuter rail service in Canada—with 57 million riders a year, it is over 60 percent busier than Philadelphia's regional rail service—and has played a key role in reining in sprawl by providing a workable alternative to commuting by car and highway. (Canada remains one of the few nations in the developed world to lack a federal program to fund large-scale urban transit projects.)

The way author and former mayor John Sewell sees things, the TTC's troubles began as soon as it was called upon to extend its services into the middle suburbs. For the first fifty years of its existence, the agency had gotten by without any government subsidies: up until 1973, suburbanites had to pay a second fare when they crossed into the older city. (The TTC still covers almost three-quarters of operating expenses out of the fare box, remarkable for North America.) The TTC, Sewell writes in *The Shape of the Suburbs*, was rejigged "to become less of a good local transit service, and more of a regional commuting service," one that, while it mostly benefited suburbanites, was largely subsidized by Torontonians. Downtown service worsened, operating deficits began to accumulate, ridership dropped, and basic maintenance suffered—a situation dramatized when a horrific crash, caused in part by a signal failure, killed three people on the Spadina line in 1995.

Stretched thin in the city, the TTC has done a heroic job of extending its routes into the middle suburbs. Paul Mees, the Melbourne-based transit scholar and author of *Transit for Suburbia*, believes the commission's suburban service is so good, in fact, that it should serve as a model for cities in Australia and the United States.

"I've spent more time wandering around suburban Toronto than any reasonable person should," Mees told me. "The typical pattern of development is that there's a grid network of arterial roads, at one-and-a-quarter-mile intervals. All along the roads, all you see are the back fences of houses and shopping malls, and the subdivisions are designed so it's almost impossible for bus routes to penetrate. The whole environment is very hostile to pedestrians: in many cases there's just a sad little concrete platform for you to stand on. And yet, the fact that enormous numbers of people are willing to navigate this environment shows that by providing extremely high quality bus services to excellent subway lines, you can actually run a transit system that serves suburbia."

On Mees's advice, I rode a northbound subway to Finch station on the Yonge line during the afternoon rush hour. Streams of commuters poured from the underground: in fact, 90,000 people use the station a day, equivalent to the combined daily ridership of all the MAX trains in Portland. At street level, articulated buses were already lined up to pick up passengers, and I joined the queue for a 199 Finch bus heading eastbound to Scarborough. One of the most brilliant features of transit in Toronto is what experts call "free-body transfers": buses and streetcars here pull into loops around subway stations, zones that require a token or farecard to enter. This means that customers, because they are already in the system, can freely transfer between modes without passing through turnstiles or showing a bus driver proof of payment. This significantly speeds up boarding; I strolled on to the articulated bus through the back, as others entered through the middle and front doors, and soon we were on our way. The landscape we drove through—Finch Avenue wends its way through bungalows and past some notoriously crime-ridden housing projects—was as uninspiring as Mees said it would be, but the bus was packed and, stop by stop, it quickly delivered its load of commuters to the surrounding low-density subdivisions. Every morning, the tide is reversed, and frequently scheduled, reliable feeder buses drop commuters outside the escalators at subway stations like Finch—significantly extending the reach of what, after all, is a modest three-line subway system.

The amazing thing, Mees points out, is that Toronto didn't have to build any suburban transit-oriented development, as in the case of Portland's Orenco Station, to achieve these results. Thanks to sophisticated scheduling that closely matches service to patronage by adjusting frequencies—the average Toronto bus carries 23 percent more passengers annually than a London double-decker—the TTC has built a system that provides a true alternative to cars in the suburbs. Torontonians, Mees told me, don't know what they've got: without ever increasing residential densities around stations, Toronto has managed to provide truly effective transport for suburbia. "The fact that Toronto can get very high patronage rates from environments like that," said Mees, "suggests that even highly sprawled cities in the United States might be able to do much better."

Even in the Greater Toronto Area, though, the TTC is limited to providing this level of service to only a few of the inner and middle suburbs. Oakville, Brampton, Mississauga, and several other municipalities elect their own mayors and have their own transit agencies, which are completely separate entities from the TTC. (Collectively they are overseen by Metrolinx, a provincial government agency, which, though it has planning authority over roads, transit, and GO commuter rail in the Toronto and Hamilton area since 2007, lacks the unified authority or predictable revenue stream of Vancouver's TransLink or Portland's TriMet.) Meanwhile, the 905 suburbs, places like Whitby, St. Catharines, and Oshawa, have vanishingly low levels of transit use. These are also the low-density fringes which grew fastest during Conservative premier Mike Harris's so-called Common Sense Revolution in the '90s. Capitalizing on a belated northern version of the anti-urban tax revolt that launched California's Proposition 13 south of the border, Harris downloaded the costs of transit to the municipalities and set a goal of putting 90 percent of Ontario's population within six miles of a major highway. According to John Sewell, the Harris administration explicitly favored Toronto's outer suburbs by lowering commercial tax rates on the metropolitan fringes. Eight years of Conservative government fostered a landscape of starter castles and three-car garages, in stark contrast with the controlled growth that had preceded it. But the single worst thing Harris did, Sewell believes, was to end half a century of effective regional government.

"Metro was a federation of municipalities," Sewell, who was mayor of Toronto from 1978 to 1980, told me. "It required municipal politicians to have a local and a regional bent at the same time. Which is important, because municipal decisions *always* have a local and a regional aspect to them. Metro was required to resolve that tension, and they had to do it publicly. So we were able to debate initiatives like the Spadina Expressway, which had huge implications for both the city and the region. People used to say Metro was the best form of municipal government in the world. I still believe they were right."

Despite Toronto-wide protests and two weeks of spirited filibustering by the opposition, the Harris government replaced Metro with a new "megacity." Since 1998, this megacity has been represented by forty-four city councilors and made up of six previously separate municipalities, from Scarborough in the east to Etobicoke in the west. (All told, the Greater Toronto Area, which stretches from Oshawa to Burlington, is governed by a staggering 244 municipal office holders, including twenty-five mayors.) The impact has been felt hardest in the old city of Toronto, where city staff have been reduced, recreation programs dropped, and streets and parks left uncleaned. Liberated from the regional planning oversight of Metro, low-density sprawl on the fringes has gone into overdrive. But the vast majority of jobs remain in the center, which means long commutes, inevitably by automobile, for the residents of the 905—Toronto's newest, most far-flung, and least transit-served suburbs.

Some outlying municipalities, hiving to populist free-market rhetoric, have contracted what transit services they do offer to the private sector; York Region, for example, handed some of its most profitable bus routes to Veolia. (The French operator has boosted profits by offering lower pay and fewer benefits than the TTC provides to employees doing similar jobs—a fact highlighted by a strike that started in October 2011 and paralyzed the municipality for three months.) Most of the privately run routes are direct-to-downtown commuter lines, though: local transit service on the fringes remains patchy at best, and finding buses that offer frequent service between suburbs is almost impossible. In much of the 905 area code, traffic is now worse than it is on the narrow streets of downtown. This is the demographic that supplies the Toronto region's angriest drivers: not only do they have no access to transit, they see themselves as being robbed of American-style urban freeways by the protests of downtown elitists. For them, driving is the only realistic option, and streetcars and buses are nothing more than slow-moving dinosaurs that clog the roads, while the bicycles they see weaving around their gridlocked cars are so many infuriating gnats—gnats some of them apparently feel inclined to crush.

The dissolution of Metro, the rise of the car-dependent fringes, and the inability of transit to keep up with the spread of the megacity go a long way to explaining why Toronto ended up with a mayor like Rob Ford. While the residents of the 905 weren't responsible for voting him in—the outer suburbs elect their own mayors—there are clearly enough frustrated residents in the transit-challenged middle suburbs of North York, Etobicoke, and Scarborough that a candidate who promised to kick streetcars off the road, reroute bike paths through parks, and generally make life easier for drivers would strike a resounding chord among suburban voters. While it should come as no surprise that the demographic that most supported Ford was male voters over the age of fifty, a 2011 study by University of Toronto grad student Zack Taylor found that the single most reliable predictor of a voter's support for Ford—regardless of age or sex—was whether he or she owned a car.

The tragedy of Toronto, then, is that a city that was so for many years on the right track has lately experienced such a catastrophic derailment. After having its autonomy and power usurped by Mike Harris's Common Sense Revolution, the urban area that is the economic engine of Ontario, and indeed Canada, finds itself a slave to the ideology of suburbia.

"The culture of sprawl has established the upper hand," Sewell concludes in *The Shape of the Suburbs*, "and is now the unquestioned dominant force in the city of Toronto." The rise of Rob Ford is symbolic of this giant leap backward: it's as if a councilor from Levittown on Long Island had been elected mayor of New York City, or Copenhagen had handed over its transport department to an out-of-work freeway planner from Detroit.

For other metropolises, all this should serve as a lesson: if you're lucky enough to retain central-city control of planning and growth, hold on to it with all your might. Because if you permit the anti-urban fringes to gain the upper hand, pretty soon you may not be able to recognize the city you live in.

Cease Fire

My parents tell me that almost as soon as our family moved to the suburbs, they started missing the big city. There was nowhere to walk in Burlington, they didn't make any friends, and my dad seemed to spend his days stuck in traffic on the QEW. They considered moving back downtown, but they also feared for Toronto's future: traffic seemed to be getting worse, the water and air more polluted. They'd already spent a couple of years in British Columbia and liked what they'd seen: in the '70s, my dad likes to say, Vancouver felt like Toronto did in the '50s—a peaceful, slow-paced kind of place, where kids could still play in the streets unsupervised. One morning we had our gray Volkswagen Beetle loaded onto an auto carrier, and we took the long train ride west, settling in a neighborhood of prewar houses where the local park was a patch of temperate rainforest. My parents still live out west, happily ensconced on an island where deer graze in the backyard and bald eagles perch on the fir trees out front.

I still think my parents gave up on Toronto too soon. From what I can tell, it never stopped being a good place to live, and it continues to have one of the most viable, walkable downtowns in North America. When I visit, I love getting to know the ravines that turn Toronto into an upside-down San Francisco, strolling through the markets—whether it's the St. Lawrence, Kensington, or Dufferin Grove Park Farmers'—and listening in on the debates over the singularity of the Beach, the plurality of the Islands and, in this fantastically multiethnic city, pluralism in general.

But I'm glad I don't live in the kind of place that would elect a Rob Ford. These days, I spend my visits commiserating with friends over the latest enormity emanating from City Hall. The river of gravy Ford campaigned against failed to materialize, of course, but the cuts continue to come: City Hall has targeted dental care for the poor, public libraries, city-owned long-term-care homes for the elderly, and even paratransit service for dialysis patients. Meanwhile, councilor Doug Ford, Rob's brother, was trying to sell the city on a waterfront entertainment district, complete with Ferris wheel, mega-mall, and monorail, apparently to be bankrolled by international investors dying to access public land. Most people I talked to were certain Rob Ford would be a one-term wonder. And, as he entered his second year in office, he was proving to have a spectacular anti-talent for public relations: when an actor from the satirical CBC show *This Hour Has 22 Minutes* tried to interview him in his driveway, instead of playing along, as even Canada's most wooden politicos have had the sense to do, Ford called 9-1-1. (The CBC reported that, when the police didn't arrive immediately, he screamed: "I'm Rob fucking Ford, the mayor of this city!") Ever since the TTC's top executive was fired by Ford's henchmen in February 2012, the transit agency's chair Karen Stintz has been in open revolt against the mayor who appointed her, calling for the dissolution of a board dominated by Ford loyalists who support funding the Sheppard subway extension. Toronto may yet get the economical light rail on Finch and Eglinton Avenues set out in the original plans for Transit City.

Mayors come and go, of course; let's just hope Ford goes before he undoes Toronto's historic legacy of excellent transit, or bankrupts the entire city. The TTC is in the process of extending the Spadina line five miles north to York University, and after five years of heavily marketing its next generation of subway trains as "The Rocket," it is poised to put seventy new Bombardier Movia trains into service. Identical to the ones used on the

Delhi and Shanghai metros, they feature more capacious cars, electronic maps that indicate the train's position, and anti-microbial strips on poles that should make even the most paranoid germophobes happier about commuting. Unfortunately, Ford's service cuts will mean the new vehicles will be more crowded than their predecessors ever were.

Some people, clearly, are getting discouraged. When I talked to John Sewell, who is in his seventies, he told me he'd gotten to his office at Queen and Spadina that day by bicycle.

"I used to ride the Queen Street car all the time," the former mayor said. "But they've cut service by a third, so now you've got to wait ten minutes for a streetcar instead of five. Well, that's not good enough for me. I ride my bike all the time now. It's the only rational way to get around downtown."

Unfortunately, the Greater Toronto Area's problems may have more to do with deep structure than any temporary failure of leadership. A city that sometimes fancies itself an Amsterdam or a Barcelona is now surrounded by American-scale sprawl, and a provincially led coup shifted the balance of power to those fringes over a decade ago. Beyond the GTA's middle layer of relatively compact and transit-served suburbs stretches a seemingly endless zone of car-dependent subdivisions—as anybody who has made the long trek to cottage country can attest. These are what architecture critic Reyner Banham, writing about Los Angeles's San Fernando Valley, called the "Plains of Id"—the vast tracts of *Brady Bunch* subdivisions that surround most North American cities, and too often get to call the shots in metropolitan politics. I know the Southern Ontario version of the Plains of Id well; our family escaped from them. People there think bicycles are for kids, streetcars are for losers, and City Hall is for picking up garbage, and they will vote for any vision-impaired candidate who promises to build more roads and keep their taxes low.

Before peace will come to the streets of our cities, these Plains of Id will have to be made part of the polity. The surest way to draw them into the web is with transit, by extending the tendrils of the central city with feeder buses, better commuter trains, and more sensibly routed subways. Until then, the bogus culture war that pits the drivers of the 905 against the walkers and riders of the 416 will only get worse, and blood will continue to stain the streets of Toronto.

On the night before I was going to take the VIA train back home, my friend Justin returned from work with a story to tell. I was staying with him and his wife, Katia, at their flat in Liberty Village, a former industrial area next to the Gardiner Expressway, now being filled with condos. Cycling back from his job at a record store, Justin said, he'd been repeatedly forced into the curb on narrow Dundas Street by the middle-aged driver of a convertible.

"The guy was on his cell phone the whole time," said Justin. "Going on to whoever he's talking to, 'I fuckin' hate bike riders!' Finally I just let him pass. Then he starts doing the same thing to a woman on a bike up ahead. Riding her ass, yelling 'Why don't you buy a car!'

"Thing is, I know that kind of guy," said Justin, who is from Ajax, a suburb in Toronto's 905 that is exactly as industrial as it sounds. "He grew up in Mississauga or Scarborough or Etobicoke, and never left. He used to beat up the goth kids or anyone who was different in high school. Now he sees the same kids are living downtown, having careers, flying around the world, while he's stuck in a suburb with his shitty job, car payments, and a huge mortgage. Naturally, he's going to be pissed off."

I asked Justin if he was tempted to say anything to him.

"I was going to yell, 'Why don't you get a *bike*, asshole!' But it just would have made it worse for the next bike rider he ran into." More to the point, you have to be careful these days: Toronto drivers, after all, have a proven record of flattening cyclists. A heavily tattooed rider like Justin, I imagine, would make a particularly tempting target; he'd already had his collarbone broken a few years back in a late-night hit-and-run.

"Anyway, I didn't have to say anything," Justin continued. "A few blocks later, I caught up with him again. He was stopped dead in traffic. So I cut in front of him, slowed down and gave him a big smile and a wave, and then pedaled across the street nice and slow and disappeared into Trinity-Bellwoods Park."

That's the way to do it. When it comes to fighting traffic, you're always better off choosing philosophical detachment over anger; in any battle between flesh and blood and a couple of thousand pounds of glass and metal, it's the driver, not the cyclist or the pedestrian, who's bound to come out on top. Besides, the minute you think of the streets as a battle-field, you've started to surrender your pleasure in your own city, and it may be time to consider a move.

But I wouldn't advise my friends to relocate to the 905 just yet. As bad as things are right now, there never has really been a war on the streets of Toronto, only people trying to share the city as best they can. And things can get better fast: all it takes is a change of attitude—and, in Toronto's case, of mayor.

Montreal, Quebec

A few months after I came up with the idea of traveling the world on subways, buses, and trains, my then-girlfriend Erin and I bought a home together. It was a big step for us. Up until then, we'd been renters, living in different apartments in the same Montreal neighborhood. At first, we worried that the sudden pressure of making mortgage payments and paying utilities and property taxes would endanger our relationship. Instead, facing the challenges of a shared life solidified our commitment, and a year after we moved in together we got married. (The baby we're expecting, we've recently learned, is a boy.)

I believe the place you choose to live in says a lot about who you are. Fortunately, Erin and I saw eye to eye on the big things. Neither of us was interested in the suburbs, though I could imagine living in a small town, and both of us liked the idea of one day having a cottage on a lake. As Erin had found work as a teacher, she didn't want to live too far from her college, so we confined our search to the city. Helped by a friend who was also a fantastic real estate agent, we trudged up stairs, compared fireplaces and decks, and thought hard about the proximity of parks, markets, schools, and transit. Though we looked all over the city, we kept on circling in on the same neighborhood, even the same few streets. We settled on a place two blocks away from the café terrace where, one unusually balmy afternoon late in October, we'd first caught each other's eye.

Our home is on the eastern edge of Outremont, a middle-class neighborhood a couple of miles north of downtown Montreal. Our street is a mixture of Hasidic Jews, aging Greeks and Italians, French-speaking families, and more recently arrived artists and academics from all over Canada, the United States, and Europe. The Hasids, of whom there are 6,000 in the surrounding blocks, tend to choose such dense neighborhoods because they need to be close to their synagogues on the Sabbath, when they are forbidden to drive. Though some neighbors resent their double-parked minivans and slow-moving schoolbuses, the Hasids provide what Jane Jacobs called "eyes on the street": break-ins are unheard of in our area, and unattended children, some no more than toddlers, play safely in local parks and streets. Given its walkable streets, I wasn't surprised to learn that Outremont, like West Philadelphia, was once a streetcar suburb. Up until the 1950s, a trolley ran up the main thoroughfare, and when the summer gets hot enough for the friction of rubber tires to wear down the asphalt, the old tracks start showing through the pavement, like bones breaking through the civic skin. When the neighborhood kids are out with their pogo sticks, hoops, and scooters, it can feel like 1920—which is about when most of the local housing stock dates from.

Montreal, where Erin was born and where most of her family lives, and where I settled fifteen years ago, has a few things in common with Philadelphia. Both are old cities for North America—Montreal was founded by Catholics in 1642, Philadelphia by Quakers 40 years later—which, after heydays of wealth and influence, went through long periods of economic stagnation. Starting in the '60s, the very real possibility that Quebec would separate from Canada and form its own nation led English speakers, who had historically made up the upper echelons of wealth and privilege, to flee Montreal; some went to the mostly anglophone suburbs of the West Island; others headed for the neighboring province of Ontario. When I arrived in Montreal in the mid-'90s, a couple of months after a provincial referendum on separation was narrowly defeated, it looked like the city had been afflicted by some wasting disease: entire downtown blocks were boarded up, and you could pick up an entire row house for under $100,000. Good jobs were thin on the ground, but if you were a musician, an artist, or a writer, Montreal was a place to revel in romantic squalor, yeasty street life, faded grandeur, and cheap rents. Kind of like Brooklyn in the '90s—or Philadelphia today.

But a funny thing happened to Montreal in the new millennium. Political stability returned, the English speakers who stayed behind learned French, the economy improved, and the abandoned city slowly began to repopulate. Much of the revival could be attributed to Montreal's excellent housing stock. In Philadelphia, the three-story brick row house is the standard residential unit; in Montreal, it is the three-story brick triplex—what Bostonians call a triple-decker—where each floor is a separately owned or rented unit. Originally built for large families, to high prewar construction standards, Montreal's triplexes offer spacious, energy-efficient urban housing.

Erin and I live on the sunlit third floor of a triplex that was built during the Depression. We get all our shopping done on foot, making stops at the baker, the greengrocer, and the fishmonger. Because they know many of their customers don't have cars, the owners of *dépanneurs*, the local corner stores, still deliver groceries using old-fashioned three-wheeled bicycles. Schlepping loads up the thirty-five steps between the sidewalk and our door keeps us in shape, and we're looking forward to raising a child in this neighborhood: day cares abound, and every morning supervisors can be seen leading tethered toddlers to local parks in "walking schoolbuses." The appeal of this old-fashioned urbanism appears to be growing: in less than seven years, condo prices in our neighborhood have doubled, then tripled.

When I first arrived in Montreal, the transportation system was a shambles. The métro the city had built itself for Expo '67 still offered basic service, but it hadn't been expanded in years. A '60s-era infatuation with

brutality and concrete had left the city cross-hatched with hideous elevated expressways, many of which were reaching their sell-by date: in 2006,
an overpass collapsed, killing five people in their cars. (The Turcot Interchange, a massive spaghetti bowl of crumbling concrete, is currently held
together by chicken wire and prayers.) I used the métro and buses when
I needed to, but mostly got around on two wheels, swerving between
potholes on an old racing bike in summer and switching to a bike with
studded tires to negotiate winter slush and ice.

To my surprise, Montreal has lately transformed itself into a city with
some of the most progressive transport and land-use policies on the continent. Parking lots and brownfields that sat vacant for decades are being
filled with new condo developments, often versions of the classic brick
row house reimagined with rooftop terraces and modern fixtures; many
have been built adjoining métro stations and frequent bus lines. On Parc
Avenue, a block from our home, the city has introduced rush-hour transit-
only lanes and replaced old diesel buses with 60-foot-long articulated
buses that run so frequently you can almost always find a seat. A canny
print and television advertising campaign stressing transit's environmental
benefits makes riding the métro seem cool, and an easy-to-use smartcard
has sped up the loading of buses. There is still no train-to-the-plane, but an
express bus now offers frequent service to the airport from downtown, at a
fifth of the price of cab fare. In response to these improvements, ridership
has taken off: on average Montrealers take 224 rides a year, beating out even
New Yorkers for the title of heaviest per capita transit users in North America. The city has extended its métro lines and added new stations without
cutting bus service, preventing the resentment I saw in New York, Los
Angeles, and Portland where riders saw transit agencies building new infrastructure while reducing basic operations. In 2010 Montreal's transit system
was voted the best in North America. City planners get excited about "Vancouverism," but maybe they should be studying the Montreal model as a
more universal template for sustainable urbanism.

Montreal is far from being a car-free city; even before I moved here, I'd
heard about its drivers, who were said to rival even Parisians when it came
to rudeness and impatience. They're still rude and impatient, but a backlash
against the automobile is under way. Luc Ferrandez, the mayor of the Plateau, a large, mostly French-speaking city center borough, has been enacting traffic-calming policies, and his party's leader is the author of *The Black
Book of the Automobile*, a diatribe about the social and environmental

impact of cars. Though Montreal's bike-path network is still rudimentary and poorly designed, more miles are added every year, and a wildly popular bike-share program called Bixi now offers 5,000 heavy-duty bicycles at stands throughout the city. When I'm running late for an appointment, I can grab a Bixi a couple of hundred yards from our front door and pedal it the few blocks to the nearest métro station.

People tell Erin and me that once we become parents, we'll buckle and buy a car of our own. We're not so sure. The rare times we really need a car—to make a run to a furniture store or to visit a friend's cottage—we have a membership with Communauto, the local version of Zipcar. And going to Copenhagen has given me an idea. We've recently spotted a couple in our neighborhood who use a cargo bike, imported from Denmark, to shuttle their young children to and from school. For a fraction of the cost of an SUV, we could pedal our kids to day care, school, or the park. Erin and I have gone from wondering if we could get through our lives without owning a car to wondering why we ever thought we needed one.

Seeing Montreal's gradual rebirth firsthand makes me believe in the future of Philadelphia, and the many other American cities that have walkable neighborhoods at their cores. The revival of New York, which many gave up for dead in the '70s, was the prototypical urban renaissance, and cities like San Francisco, Chicago, Boston, Minneapolis, and Portland never lost their center-city vitality. As the era of cheap fossil fuels that kicked the North American metropolis into a manic state of overdrive comes to an end, the ideology of growth for growth's sake has also reached its limits. When it comes to houses and cities, bigger is not better. Bigger is more McMansions; bigger is subdivisions so sprawled people never get to know their neighbors; bigger is ever longer, ever more soul-sucking commutes. Bigger is *stupider*.

When I started this journey, the future of smarter transportation in North America looked pretty bright. The way the Obama administration was talking, it sounded as if there was hope for, if not a high-speed rail equivalent of the interstate highway system, at least a transport network more equitably balanced between automobiles and trains. But governors with more stubbornness than sense have turned down what little money there was for new rail and public transport projects, and the stimulus money mostly went to roads and cars, before drying up completely. After gaining a majority in Congress, anti-tax Republicans pushed for a one-third reduction in transportation spending in the 2012 budget, which means that federal funds will mostly have to go to keep existing freeways from crumbling. (In Canada, where the role of the federal government in urban matters is much smaller, the Conservative government has shown almost no interest in spending money on transit or passenger rail.) An historic opportunity to balance the continent's half-century-old freeway network with sustainable rail transport has probably been squandered. North America will be paying the price, in terms of lost competitivity, for decades to come.

The change that's going to come will almost certainly have to happen at the city, regional, or state level. Public demand for better urbanism and transportation is growing, and the cities that invest in sustainable transit are going to reap the benefits. Saving our cities from the automobile is going to involve welcoming transit-oriented development, infill in old central city neighborhoods, and multifamily buildings and apartments in what were once low-density areas. It will mean brandishing the stick of congestion and more expensive parking to discourage drivers—a simple way to start would be to heed the "Shoupistas," the followers of University of California professor Donald Shoup, and turn parking minimums into maximums in new developments—while dangling the carrot of safe, comfortable, and frequent transit to draw new riders. For cities, it will involve building high-quality bicycle lanes, pedestrian-oriented urban spaces, and the best public transport money can buy—without cutting back on the frequency or quality of bus service essential to keep rapid transit working. Subways have time and again proven to be the most reliable and efficient mode of transit a city can build for itself, but for places that can't afford it, bus rapid transit and light rail are excellent alternatives. Advances in automation mean that new systems don't need the huge payrolls that were once synonymous with transit—but buses will always need drivers, and there's no excuse for cutting the salaries and benefits of employees who have the public's safety in their hands.

The suburbs, particularly the way they are configured in North American cities, are going to prove a challenge, but that doesn't mean they are a lost cause. The reach of the trunk lines of subway and light-rail systems can be extended by frequently scheduled feeder buses that gather commuters from stops on major arteries (a technique used with great success in Bogotá, Toronto, and Zurich). Existing commuter rail networks such as Philadelphia's SEPTA could be turned into effective suburban transit systems to rival Paris's RER simply by scheduling more trains inbound and

312 ■ Taras Grescoe

outbound—with half-hourly, say, rather than hourly departures. For cities without historic rail networks, bus rapid transit systems, complete with dedicated lanes, signal priority, and express service could link not only the suburbs to downtown but also office parks, malls, and edge cities on the metropolitan fringes to one another.

All this means we'll have to be creative about funding sources. Raising gas taxes might mean career suicide for politicians these days, but transit can be subsidized with parking and congestion charges, highway and bridge tolls, a payroll tax for larger companies, a carbon tax—or all of the above. (Already a few transit agencies, among them Los Angeles's Metro, are taking the lead in developing commercial and residential properties close to transit, rather than selling off property to private developers.) For transit to remain sustainable, we're going to have to ignore the zealots who call for its complete privatization, which has proven such a disaster in Britain and Australia. There is a reason that the transit network of almost every major city in the developed world was municipalized at some point in its history: while private companies can do a creditable job of operating the busiest lines, time and again they have failed to manage complex transportation networks in the public interest. The lessons of history show that public agencies with regional scope and unified planning oversight do the best job of running public transport.

The salvation of cities could start with a rethinking of ill-conceived urban freeways. Milwaukee, San Francisco, Baltimore, and New Haven have already revived neighborhoods by tearing out stretches of inner-city expressways, and Seattle's Alaskan Way Viaduct, New Orleans's Interstate 10, Cleveland's West Shoreway, and parts of Philadelphia's Interstate 95 could be turned into tree-lined, stoplighted boulevards, or torn out altogether. (Kick-starting urban renewal by removing the expressways that initiated blight in the first place would also be sweet justice.)

I've been traveling the world as a straphanger for years now, and I'm not going to pretend it was always an uplifting experience. Riding public transport, you see a bit of everything. In Shanghai, I watched a tiny boy beggar enter a metro car, throw himself on his knees in front of a well-dressed woman on a bench seat, and repeatedly kowtow, bashing his forehead on the floor until she handed him a coin. On a bus on Wilshire Boulevard in Los Angeles, I endured the rant of the woman ahead of me who, clutching a cell phone in her bandaged hand, harangued a series of aid workers about the "avowed Satanists" in her building who had put a curse on her and were leaving dead pigeons on her doormat. In Phoenix, a wild-eyed woman with crooked lipstick and a Minnie Pearl bonnet followed me off the streetcar and stalked me through several parking lots; I finally shook her off in the aisles of a Walgreens. But my only brush with crime was having a cheap cell phone lifted on a bus in Bogotá, something done so artfully I didn't realize it had happened until I got back to my hotel; I never saw any violence, and no serious accidents. Come to think of it, virtually all the death I've seen in my travels—whether it was corpses splayed on Indian highways or bloodstained pavements next to wrecked trucks on the interstate—has been alongside roads.

And for every disturbing image, I saw many more acts of kindness. On the MAX in Portland, a Latino teenager, noticing a blind man with a cane was about to bump into the doorjamb, jumped up and gently steered him by the elbow in the right direction. Outside Kyoto's train station, as I puzzled over the city's bus maps, a wizened old man in a herringbone cap got off his bicycle, and after asking in halting English where I was going, walked me to the correct stop, only moving on after I'd boarded the right bus and was safely on my way. On Berlin's U-bahn, I watched two mothers, one wearing a headscarf, the other with a cross around her neck, board the train at the same time. The first pulled a girl by her hand, the other pushed a boy in a stroller, and they sat side by side on the same bench seat. The gaze of the Muslim woman's curly-haired daughter, who looked to be about four, locked on the smaller boy, and she waved. Eyes widening, he smiled shyly and lifted his hand; the little girl looked at her mother and giggled. They continued peeking at one another for a couple of stops, then as the blonde woman backed her pram toward the door, the boy solemnly waved to his receding friend. The mothers' eyes met and flashed, and they both laughed. Not a word had been uttered: it was a perfect little silent movie, a moment of connection in the city.

I still think of Salvador Dalí's and Margaret Thatcher's dismissal of straphangers as losers and failures. But they were products of the automotive century, an era whose fixation on horsepower is already starting to seem pathological. Though I grew up with romantic tales of gasoline-fueled escape, I'm fine with a slower, more rooted life. What the rebels of the road neglected to mention was that the freeways they followed to get to all that was true and real were the same ones that paved over so much of what was authentic and vital in our cities. Lately, freedom's competing symbol, the train and its lonesome whistle, sings to me sweeter. On the train, you see the country. On the train, you get to know people. On the train, kids wave at you, and you wave back. Tracks stitch places together; freeways tear them apart.

Besides, I've got no big travel plans. I've been out in the world for some time now, thinking hard about the kind of place I want to live, and I've heard a lot of people sharing ideas about ways of making their communities better. Erin and I have made our choice; we've found our community. It's time I recalled the wisdom of my eight-year-old self, the kid in the white turtleneck who used Monopoly hotels to build a model of a city block—one that looked a little less like a parking lot and more like a park.

Sometimes, the best way to get to a better place is to make the place you are in just a little bit better.

Sources

Listed below, by chapter, are the major books, articles, and papers I consulted during my research. A few Web sites provided invaluable background and day-to-day updates on transportation, among them Yonah Freemark's The Transport Politic (www.thetransportpolitic. com), Jarrett Walker's Human Transit (www.humantransit.org), and Reconnecting America's (reconnectingamerica.org) excellent roundup of transit news, The Other Side of the Tracks, curated by the indefatigable Jeff Wood. All Web sites current as of September 2011.

Prologue and Introduction

Anderlini, James. "China's Monster Traffic Jam: A Sign of Things to Come." *Financial Times*, August 23, 2010.

Cadwalladr, Carole. "Top Gear, Please, and Step on It." *The Observer*, July 6, 2008.

"China's Dashing New Trains." *The Economist*, February 4, 2010.

"The Commuter's Challenge: The Impact of Traffic Congestion in the U.S." IBM Corporation, September 2009.

Conover, Ted. "Capitalist Roaders." *The New York Times Magazine*, July 2, 2006.

Ewing, Reid. "Relationship Between Urban Sprawl and Physical Activity, Obesity, and Morbidity." *American Journal of Health Promotion* 18/1 (September–October 2003).

"Fatally Hurt by Automobile." *The New York Times*, September 14, 1899.

Frumkin, Howard. *Urban Spawl and Public Health: Designing, Planning, and Building for Healthy Communities.* Washington, D.C.: Island Press, 2004.

Goodstein, David. *Out of Gas: The End of the Age of Oil.* New York: W. W. Norton, 2004.

"High Gas Prices Fuel Increased Public-Transit Ridership." *Chicago Tribune*, May 20, 2011.

Hessler, Peter. "Wheels of Fortune: The People's Republic Learns to Drive." *The New Yorker*, November 26, 2007.

Ladd, Brian. *Autophobia: Love and Hate in the Automobile Age.* Chicago: University of Chicago Press, 2008.

"A Large Black Cloud." *The Economist*, March 15, 2008.

Lowrey, Annie. "Your Commute Is Killing You." Slate.com, May 26, 2011.

Lutz, Catherine. *Carjacked: The Culture of the Automobile and Its Effect on Our Lives.* New York: Palgrave Macmillan, 2010.

Paumgarten, Nick. "There and Back Again: The Soul of the Commuter." *The New Yorker*, April 16, 2007.

"The Peak Oil-Debate." *The Economist*, December 10, 2009.

Puentes, Robert. "Driving's Back Up . . . Or Is It?" Brookings Institution, *Up Front Blog*, http://www.brookings.edu, March 3, 2011.

Putnam, Robert. *Bowling Alone: The Collapse and Revival of American Community.* New York: Simon & Schuster, 2001.

Roberts, Paul. *The End of Oil: On the Edge of a Perilous New World.* Boston: Houghton Mifflin, 2005.

"Shanghai Air Pollution Reaches Record Levels." *The Independent* (London), May 5, 2011.

Shih, Toh Han. "Beijing Speeds Up Metro Plan Across 25 Cities." *South China Morning Post*, May 14, 2010.

Smil, Vaclav. *Energy at the Crossroads.* Cambridge, Mass.: MIT Press, 2005.

——. *Oil: A Beginner's Guide.* Oxford: One World, 2008.

Sperling, Daniel, and Deborah Gordon. *Two Billion Cars: Driving Toward Sustainability.* New York: Oxford University Press, 2009.

Steiner, Christopher. "A Skinnier, Safer America." *Forbes*, June 16, 2009.

Stuzter, Alois, and Bruno S. Frey. "Stress that Doesn't Pay: The Commuting Paradox." *Scandinavian Journal of Economics* 110/2 (2008).

Surowiecki, James. "Oil Check." *The New Yorker*, June 22, 2009.

"Tata Motors Starts Exports of World's Cheapest Car from April." *The Wall Street Journal*, May 9, 2011.

Tomer, Adie, et al. "Missed Opportunities: Transit and Jobs in Metropolitan America." Brookings Institution, http:// www.brookings.edu, May 2011.

Vanderbilt, Tom. *Traffic: Why We Drive the Way We Do.* New York: Knopf, 2008.

Wang, M., et al. "Projection of Chinese Motor Vehicle Growth, Oil Demand, and CO2 Emissions through 2050." Energy Systems Division, Argonne National Laboratory, http://greet.es.anl.gov/files/rwdz78ca, 2006.

1: The Subway that Time Forgot

For day-to-day updates on the ongoing Second Avenue Subway story, and all matters subway, I relied on Benjamin Kabak's excellent Web site, secondavenuesagas.com. Additional background was provided by meetings and interviews with Jeff Zupan of the Regional Plan Association, William Wheeler, head of planning for the MTA, and Peter Derrick of the Bronx County Historical Society.

Berman, Marshall. *All That Is Solid Melts into Air: The Experience of Modernity.* New York: Simon & Schuster, 1982.

Bobrick, Benson. *Labyrinths of Iron: Subways in History, Myth, Art, Technology, & War.* New York: William Morrow, 1981.

Brooks, Michael W. *Subway City: Riding the Trains; Reading New York.* New Brunswick, N.J.: Rutgers University Press, 1997.

Cangro, Jacquelin. *The Subway Chronicles: Scenes from Life in New York.* New York: Penguin Books, 2006.

Caro, Robert A. *The Power Broker: Robert Moses and the Fall of New York*. New York: Random House, 1974.

Delaney, Paul E. *Sandhogs: A History of the Tunnel Workers of New York*. New York: Union Labor Works, 1983.

Derrick, Peter. "Catalyst for Development: Rapid Transit in New York." *New York Affairs* 9/4 (Fall 1986).

Dwyer, Jim. *Subway Lives: 24 Hours in the Life of the New York Subway*. New York: Crown, 1991.

Fischler, Stan. *Uptown, Downtown: A Trip Through Time on New York's Subways*. New York: Hawthorn, 1976.

Flint, Anthony. *Wrestling with Moses: How Jane Jacobs Took on New York's Master Builder and Transformed the American City*. New York: Random House, 2009.

Goldberger, Paul. "Eminent Dominion: Rethinking the Legacy of Robert Moses." *The New Yorker*, February 5, 2007.

Grynbaum, Michael M. "Mayor Takes Subway—by Way of SUV." *The New York Times*, August 1, 2007.

Hood, Clifton. *722 Miles: The Building of the Subways and How They Transformed New York*. New York: Simon & Schuster, 1993.

"In a Blizzard's Grasp." *The New York Times*, March 13, 1888.

Jacobs, Jane. *The Death and Life of Great American Cities*. New York: Vintage, 1961.

Kennedy, Randy. *Subwayland: Adventures in the World Beneath New York*. New York: St. Martin's Griffith, 2004.

Neuman, William. "Cars Clogging New York? Most Are from the City." *The New York Times*, January 12, 2007.

"New York's First Underground Railway." *The New York Times*, August 28, 1904.

Ouroussoff, Nicolai. "Outgrowing Jane Jacobs." *The New York Times*, April 30, 2006.

Sargent, Greg. "The Line that Time Forgot." *New York*, March 5, 2004.

Sullivan, Robert. "Subway on the Street." *New York*, July 12, 2010.

Theroux, Paul. "Subway Odyssey." *The New York Times Magazine*, January 31, 1982.

Trillin, Calvin. *Tepper Isn't Going Out*. New York: Random House, 2001.

Twain, Mark. Letter sent to *Alta California*. March 28, 1867.

Widdicombe, Lizzie. "Dashboard Divas." *The New Yorker*, January 18, 2010.

2: Only Connect

I'm grateful to William Fulton, urbanist turned municipal politician, for taking the time to give me his measured take on the challenges facing Los Angeles.

Adler, Sy. "The Transformation of the Pacific Electric Railway: Bradford Snell, Roger Rabbit, and the Politics of Transportation in Los Angeles." *Urban Affairs Quarterly* 27/1 (1991).

Axelrod, Jeremiah B. C. *Inventing Autopia: Dreams and Visions of the Modern Metropolis in Jazz Age Los Angeles*. Berkeley: University of California Press, 2009.

Banham, Reyner. *Los Angeles: The Architecture of Four Ecologies*. Berkeley: University of California Press, 1971.

Berkowitz, Eric. "The Subway Mayor." *LA Weekly*, August 18, 2005.

Bottles, Scott L. *Los Angeles and the Automobile*. Berkeley: University of California Press, 1987.

Bradbury, Ray. "The Pedestrian," in *The Golden Apples of the Sun*. New York: Doubleday, 1953.

Bruck, Connie. "Fault Lines: Can Mayor Antonio Villaraigosa Keep Control of L.A.'s Battling Factions?" *The New Yorker*, May 21, 2007.

Crump, Spencer. *Ride the Big Red Cars: How Trolleys Helped Build Southern California*. Los Angeles: Trans-Anglo Books, 1962.

Davis, Mike. *City of Quartz: Excavating the Future in Los Angeles*. London: Verso, 1990.

———. *Ecology of Fear: Los Angeles and the Imagination of Disaster*. New York: Vintage, 1998.

Didion, Joan. *The White Album*. New.York: Simon & Schuster, 1979.

Fulton, William. *The Reluctant Metropolis: The Politics of Urban Growth in Los Angeles*. Baltimore: Johns Hopkins University Press, 2001.

Hall, Peter. *Cities of Tomorrow*. New York: Basil Blackwell, 1988.

Henke, Cliff. "Going Hollywood." *Mass Transit* (April/May 2008).

Hise, Greg. *Magnetic Los Angeles: Planning the Twentieth-Century Metropolis.* Baltimore: Johns Hopkins University Press, 1999.

Jacobs, Chip. *Smogtown: The Lung-Burning History of Pollution in Los Angeles.* New York: Overlook, 2008.

Jones, David W. *Mass Motorization + Mass Transit: An American History and Policy Analysis.* Bloomington: Indiana University Press, 2008.

Kwitny, Jonathan. "The Great Transportation Conspiracy: A Juggernaut Named Desire." *Harper's*, September 1981.

Longstreth, Richard. *City Center to Regional Mall: Architecture, the Automobile, and Retailing in Los Angeles, 1920–1950.* Cambridge, Mass.: MIT Press, 1997.

Manville, Michael, and Donald Shoup. "People, Parking, and Cities." *Access*, No. 30, 2007.

Marshall, Alex. *How Cities Work: Suburbs, Sprawl, and the Roads Not Taken.* Austin: University of Texas Press, 2005.

Mayo, Morrow. *Los Angeles.* New York: Knopf, 1933.

McDonald, Patrick Range. "Black Lungs Lofts." *LA Weekly*, March 10, 2010.

Morris, Steven Leigh. "City Hall's 'Density Hawks' Are Changing L.A.'s DNA." *LA Weekly*, February 28, 2008.

Norton, Peter D. *Fighting Traffic: The Dawn of the Motor Age in the American City.* Cambridge, Mass.: MIT Press, 2008.

Pristin, Terry. "In Westside Los Angeles, a Rail Line Stirs a Revival." *The New York Times*, July 6, 2010.

Richmond, Jonathan E. D. "The Mythical Conception of Rail Transit in Los Angeles." *Journal of Architectural and Planning Research* (November 1996).

Scott, Allen J., and Edward W. Soja, eds. *The City: Los Angeles and Urban Theory at the End of the Twentieth Century.* Berkeley: University of California Press, 1998.

Shoup, Donald. *The High Cost of Free Parking.* Chicago: American Planning Association, 2005.

Zahniser, David. "What's Smart About Smart Growth?" *LA Weekly*, May 31, 2007.

3: The Highway to Hell

The description of Broadacre City is taken from Frank Lloyd Wright's *The Living City* (cited below), sketches and plans in the archives of Taliesin West, and the replica of the original model at the University of Arizona. Data on journey-to-work from the 1980, 1990, and 2000 censuses was downloaded from http://www.census.gov/population/www/socdemo/journey.html.

Augur, Tracy. "The Dispersal of Cities as a Defense Measure." *Bulletin of the Atomic Scientists*, May 1948.

Bogart, William T. *Don't Call It Sprawl: Metropolitan Structures in the Twenty-first Century.* New York: Cambridge University Press, 2006.

Bruegmann, Robert. *Sprawl: A Compact History.* Chicago: University of Chicago Press, 2006.

Brooks, David. "On the Playing Fields of Suburbia." *The Atlantic*, January 2002.

Coontz, Stephanie. *The Way We Never Were: American Families and the Nostalgia Trap.* New York: Basic Books, 2000.

Fishman, Robert. *Bourgeois Utopias: The Rise and Fall of Suburbia.* New York: Basic Books, 1987.

Fulton, William. *The Reluctant Metropolis: The Politics of Urban Growth in Los Angeles.* Baltimore: Johns Hopkins University Press, 2001.

Garreau, Joel. *Edge Cities: Life on the New Frontier.* New York: Anchor Books, 1991.

Hamilton, Mary Jane. "Frank Lloyd Wright & His Automobiles." *Frank Lloyd Wright Quarterly*, 21/1 (Winter 2010).

Howard, Ebenezer. *Garden Cities of To-Morrow.* Cambridge, Mass.: MIT Press, 1965.

Jackson, Kenneth T. *Crabgrass Frontier: The Suburbanization of the United States.* New York: Oxford University Press, 1985.

Kalita, S. Mitra. "No McMansions for Millennials." *The Wall Street Journal*, January 13, 2011.

Kotkin, Joel. *The New Geography.* New York: Random House, 2000.

———. *The Next Hundred Million: America in 2050.* New York: Penguin Books, 2010.

Logan, Michael F. *Desert Cities: The Environmental History of Phoenix and Tucson.* Pittsburgh, Pa.: University of Pittsburgh Press, 2006.

Luckingham, Bradford. *Phoenix: The History of a Southwestern Metropolis.* Phoenix: University of Arizona Press, 1995.

Lucy, William H. *Foreclosing the Dream: How America's Housing Crisis Is Reshaping Our Cities and Suburbs.* Chicago: American Planning Association, 2010.

Mees, Paul. *Transport for Suburbia: Beyond the Automobile Age.* Oxford: Earthscan, 2009.

Pew Research Center. "For Nearly Half of America, Grass Is Greener Somewhere Else." http://pewresearch.org/pubs, January 29, 2009.

Silverstein, Ken. "Tea Party in the Sonora." *Harper's,* July 2010.

Wright, Frank Lloyd. *An Autobiography.* New York: Longmans, Green, 1932.

———. *The Disappearing City.* New York: W. F. Payson, 1932.

———. *The Living City.* New York: Horizon Press, 1958.

4: The Salvation of Paris

Augé, Marc. *Un ethnologue dans le métro.* Paris: Hachette, 2001.

Bell, Kelly. "Dietrich von Choltitz: Saved Paris from Destruction During World War II." *World War II Magazine,* June 12, 2006.

Chevalier, Louis. *L'Assassinat de Paris.* France: Calmann-Lévy, 1977.

Dallas, Gregor. *Metrostop Paris: History from the City's Heart.* London: John Murray, 2009.

Fahey, Bernard. *Metro: A Driver's-Eye View: Lines 5 & 6 of the Paris Métro* (DVD). London: Video 125, 2009.

Flonneau, Mathieu. *Paris et l'automobile, Un siècle de passions.* Paris: Hachette, 2005.

Freemark, Yonah. "Paris Region Moves Ahead with 125 Miles of New Metro Lines." http://www.thetransportpolitic.com, May 27, 2011.

Gaillard, Marc. *Histoire des transports parisiens: De Blaise Pascal à nos jours.* Paris: Horvath, 1987.

Guerrand, Roger-Henri. *L'aventure du métropolitain.* Paris: La Découverte, 1999.

Hopquin, Benoît. "Les naufragés de la ligne 13." *Le Monde,* April 9, 2008.

Jones, Colin. *Paris: The Biography of a City.* New York: Penguin, 2006.

Jones, Joseph. *The Politics of Transport in Twentieth-Century France.* Montreal: McGill-Queen's, 1985.

Lamming, Clive. *Métro Insolite.* Paris: Parigramme, 2002.

Mees, Paul. *Transport for Suburbia: Beyond the Automobile Age.* Oxford: Earthscan, 2009.

Milmo, Dan. "Boris Johnson Told He Must Plug £460m Tube Funding Gap." *The Guardian,* March 10, 2010.

Ovenden, Mark. *Paris Underground: The Maps, Stations, and Design of the Métro.* London: Penguin Books, 2009.

Pascual, Julia. "RER á conduite sous pression." *La Libération,* December 4, 2010.

Studeny, Christophe. *L'Invention de la vitesse, France, VVIIIe–XXe siècle.* Paris: Gallimard, 1995.

Weber, Nicholas Fox. *Le Corbusier: A Life.* New York: Knopf, 2008.

Webster, Richard A. "Passengers in New Orleans Struggle to Adjust to RTA Changes." *New Orleans City Business,* January 11, 2011.

Wolmar, Christian. *The Subterranean Railway.* London: Atlantic, 2004.

5: The Copenhagen Syndrome

Major Web sites consulted: http://www.copenhagenize.com; http://www.copenhagencyclechic.com; and http://www.db.de, for figures on cost and carbon emissions of rail, air, and car travel.

Adler, Ben. "The French Revolution: How Strasbourg Gave Up the Car (and Why Midsized American Cities Can Too)." *The Next City,* Winter 2009.

Buehler, Ralph, and John Pucher. "Sustainable Transport that Works: Lessons from Germany." *World Transport Policy & Practice* 15/1 (April, 2009).

Burnett, Victoria. "Spain's High-Speed Rail Offers Guideposts for U.S." *New York Times,* May 30, 2009.

Connolly, Kate. "High-Speed Rail in Germany: Intercity Planes Are Grounded by Faster Trains." *The Guardian,* August 5, 2009.

Demaio, Paul. "Bike-Sharing: History, Impacts, Models of Provision, and Future." *Journal of Public Transportation* 12/4 (2009).

Gehl, Jan. *Cities for People*. Washington, D.C.: Island Press, 2010.

———. *Life Between Buildings: Using Public Space*. Copenhagen: Arkitektens Forlag, 2006.

Jespersen, Knud J. V. *A History of Denmark*. New York: Palgrave Macmillan, 2004.

Madsen, Hans Helge, et al. *The Award-Winning City*. Copenhagen: Arkitektens Forlag, 2003.

Mapes, Jeff. *Pedaling Revolution: How Cyclists Are Changing American Cities*. Corvallis: Oregon State University Press, 2009.

Mason, Gary. "Energy-Efficient Denmark Makes You Green with Envy." *The Globe and Mail*, October 8, 2009.

McCommons, James. *Waiting on a Train: The Embattled Future of Passenger Rail Service*. White River Junction, Vt.: Chelsea Green, 2009.

Melia, Steve. "On the Road to Sustainability: Transport and Car-Free Living in Freiburg." Report for WHO Healthy Cities Collaborating Center, 2006.

Modoux, François. "Passions solaires." *Le Temps*, September 26, 2009.

Paulsen, Monte. "Off the Rails: How Canada Fell from Leader to Laggard in High-Speed Rail." *The Walrus*, June 2009.

Pucher, John. "Making Cycling Irresistible: Lessons from the Netherlands, Denmark, and Germany." *Transport Reviews*, 28/4, 2008.

Purvis, Andrew. "Is This the Greenest City in the World? (Freiburg, Germany)" *Observer Magazine*, March 23, 2008.

Turner, Chris. "A Step in the Right Direction." *The Globe and Mail*, October 18, 2008.

6: Fools and Roads

Colton, Timothy J. *Moscow: Governing the Socialist Metropolis*. Cambridge, Mass.: Harvard University Press, 1995.

Fishman, Boris. "Metro Blues, or How I Came to America," in *The Subway Chronicles*, ed. Jacquelin Cangro. New York: Penguin Books, 2006.

Hoffmann, David L. *Peasant Metropolis: Social Identities in Moscow, 1924–41*. Ithaca, N.Y.: Cornell University Press, 1994.

Hood, Clifton. *722 Miles: The Building of the Subways and How They Transformed New York*. New York: Simon & Schuster, 1993.

Jenks, Andrew. "A Metro on the Mount: The Underground as a Church of Soviet Civilization." *Technology and Culture* 41/4 (2000).

Kaletski, Alexander. *Metro: A Novel of the Moscow Underground*. London: Methuen, 1985.

Kostof, Spiro. *The City Shaped: Urban Patterns and Meanings through History*. New York: Bluefinch Press, 1991.

Litman, Todd. "Terrorism, Transit and Public Safety: Evaluating the Risks." *Journal of Public Transit* 8/4 (2005).

Siegelbaum, Lewis H. *Cars for Comrades: The Life of the Soviet Automobile*. Ithaca, N.Y.: Cornell University Press, 2008.

Wolf, William K. "Russia's Revolutionary Underground: The Construction of the Moscow Subway, 1931–35." PhD diss., Ohio State University, 1994.

7: City of Trains

Cervero, Robert. *The Transit Metropolis*. Washington, D.C.: Island Press, 1998.

Cybriwsky, Roman. *Tokyo: The Shogun's City at the Twenty-First Century*. New York: John Wiley & Sons, 1998.

Demizu, Tsutomu. "The Motorization of Japan," in *A Social History of Science and Technology in Contemporary Japan*, ed. Shigeru Nakayama, vol. 3. Melbourne: Trans Pacific Press, 2006.

Fisch, Michael. "Blood on the Tracks: Beyond a Politics of Representation." Unpublished paper, courtesy of the author, University of Chicago, Department of Anthropology.

Fuji, James A. "Networks of Modernity—Rail Transport and Modern Japanese Literature." *Japanese Railway and Transport Review,* September 1997.

Gordenker, Alice. "JR Gestures." *Japan Times,* October 21, 2008.

Hidenobu, Jinnai. *Tokyo: A Spatial Anthropology.* Berkeley: University of California Press, 1995.

Hosokawa, Bill. *Old Man Thunder: Father of the Bullet Train.* Tokyo: Sogo Way, 1997.

Inoue, Hirokazu. "JR East Efforts to Prevent Global Warming." *Japan Railway & Transport Review,* February 2009.

Iwai, Hikoji. "Subway Development in Japanese Cities," in *Japanese Urban Environment,* ed. G. S. Golany. New York: Elsevier Science, 1998.

Johnston, Eric. "Answers Elude Hyogo Train Crash Victims." *Japan Times,* April 25, 2006.

Jones, Colin P. A. "Japan's Many Roads to Ruin." *Japan Times,* April 21, 2009.

Kageyama, Yuri. "Cars No Longer Cool in Japan." *The Globe and Mail,* December 30, 2008.

Kerr, Alex. *Dogs and Demons: The Fall of Modern Japan.* London: Penguin Books, 2001.

Lewis, Leo. "Japan's Costly Roads to Nowhere Built on Government Deception." *The Times* (London), December 24, 2007.

McCurry, Justin. "The Fast Buck Stops Here." *Guardian Unlimited,* May 12, 2005.

Murakami, Haruki. *Underground: The Tokyo Gas Attack and the Japanese Psyche.* New York: Vintage, 2000.

Murphy, John. "Japan's Young Won't Rally Round the Car." *The Wall Street Journal,* February 29, 2008.

Okamoto, Kohei. "Suburbanization of Tokyo and the Daily Lives of Suburban People," in *The Japanese City,* ed. Pradyumna Prasad Karan. Lexington: University Press of Kentucky, 1998.

Otake, Tomoko. "The Safety Nets for Would-Be Suicides." *Japan Times,* June 18, 2009.

Richie, Donald. *Tokyo: A View of the City.* London: Reaktion Books, 1999.

Seidensticker, Edward. *Tokyo Rising: The City Since the Great Earthquake.* Cambridge, Mass.: Harvard University Press, 1991.

Silva, Arturo, ed. *The Donald Richie Reader: 50 Years of Writing on Japan.* Berkeley, Calif.: Stone Bridge Press, 2005.

Sorensen, André. *The Making of Urban Japan: Cities and Planning from Edo to the Twenty-First Century.* London: Routledge, 2002.

———. "Subcentres and Satellite Cities: Tokyo's 20th-Century Experience of Planned Polycentrism." *International Planning Studies* 6/1 (2001).

Tanaka, Miya. "Train Crash Reveals Fatal Flaw of Obsession with Punctuality." *Japan Times,* May 26, 2005.

Tiry, Corinne. "Tokyo Yamanote Line—Cityscape Mutations." *Japan Railway & Transport Review,* September 1997.

8: The Revenge of the Loser Cruiser

Ardila, Arturo. "How Public Transportation's Past Is Haunting Its Future in Bogotá, Colombia." *Transportation Research Record* 2038 (2007).

"Can Enrique Peñalosa Restore a Tarnished Municipal Model?" *The Economist,* March 10, 2011.

Despacio, Ando. "Bogotá: Edging Back from the Brink." *Sustainable Transport* (Winter 2008).

Dugger, Celia W. "A Bus System Reopens Rifts in South Africa." *New York Times,* February 22, 2010.

Emblin, Richard. "The Shame of Bogotá." *The City Paper,* November 2010.

Ferro, José Salazar. "Bogotá's Recovery Process," in *Megacities: Urban Form, Governance, and Sustainability,* ed. A. Sorensen. Dordrecht: Springer, 2010.

Gray, Kevin. "Before Night Falls." *The New York Times Travel Magazine,* May 23, 2010.

Hidalgo, Dario. "Modernizing Public Transportation: Lessons Learned from Major Bus Improvements in Latin America and Asia." http:www.embarq.org/en/modernizing-public-transportation, 2010.

Hoffmann, Alan. "Beyond 'Light Rail Lite.'" *Mass Transit* (June 2008).

Lubow, Arthur. "The Road to Curitiba." *The New York Times Magazine,* May 20, 2007.

Medina, Carlos, ed., et al. "Quality of Life in Urban Neighborhoods of Bogotá and Medellín, Colombia," in *Quality of Life in Latin American Cities.* Washington, D.C.: World Bank, 2010.

Moavenzadeh, F., and M. J. Markow. *Moving Millions: Transport Strategies for Sustainable Development in Megacities.* Dordrecht: Springer, 2007.

Montezuma, Ricardo. *Movilidad y Ciudad del Siglo XXI: Retos e Innovaciones.* Bogotá: Editorial Universidad del Rosario, 2010.

———. "La transformation récente de Bogotá et la mobilité urbaine," in *Urban Mobility for All*, ed. Xavier Godard. Lisse: Swets & Zeitlinger, 2002.

Pasotti, Eleonora. *Political Branding in Cities: The Decline of Machine Politics in Bogotá, Naples, and Chicago.* New York: Cambridge University Press, 2009.

Rosenthal, Elisabeth. "Buses May Aid Climate Battle in Poor Cities." *The New York Times,* July 10, 2009.

9: Good Bones

A number of studies have attempted to quantify the total annual subsidies from all levels of government to automobiles and roads in the United States. They range from a low of $378 billion, to a high of $935 billion. A summary of estimates in eight papers can be found at http://www.sierraclub.org/sprawl/articles/subsidies.asp). I have cited figures from Congress's 1994 Office of Technology Assessment Report below.

Abbott, Carl. *Greater Portland: Urban Life and Landscape in the Pacific Northwest.* Philadelphia: University of Pennsylvania Press, 2001.

Adler, Sy, and Jennifer Dill. "The Evolution of Transportation Planning in the Portland Metropolitan Area," in *The Portland Edge,* ed. Connie Ozawa. Washington, D.C.: Island Press, 2004.

Berelowitz, Lance. *Dream City: Vancouver and the Global Imagination.* Vancouver: Douglas & McIntyre, 2005.

Cervero, Robert, et al. "Are Suburban TODs Over-Parked?" *Journal of Public Transportation* 13/2 (2010).

———. *The Transit Metropolis.* Washington, D.C.: Island Press, 1998.

Charles, John A. "The Mythical World of Transit-Oriented Development." Cascade Policy Institute, http://cascadepolicy.org/pdf/env/l_124.pdf, 2003.

Guttfreund, Owen D. *20th-Century Sprawl: Highways and the Reshaping of the American Landscape.* New York: Oxford University Press, 2004.

Ladd, Brian. *Autophobia: Love and Hate in the Automobile Age.* Chicago: University of Chicago Press, 2008.

Lewyn, Michael. "Debunking Cato: Why Portland Works Better than the Analysis of Its Chief Neo-Libertarian Critic." Congress for the New Urbanism, http://www.cnu.org/node/1533.

McNichol, Dan. *The Roads that Built America: The Incredible Story of the U.S. Interstate System.* New York: Sterling, 2006.

Mirk, Sarah. "The Dead Freeways Society: The Strange History of Portland's Unbuilt Roads." *Portland Mercury,* September 24, 2009.

Montgomery, Charles. "Futureville." *Canadian Geographic,* May/June 2006.

Moses, Robert. "Portland Improvement." http://www.portlandonline.com/bps/index.cfm?a=148065&c=44077, 1943.

Palahniuk, Chuck. *Fugitives & Refugees: A Walk in Portland, Oregon.* New York: Crown Journeys, 2003.

Ozawa, Connie, ed. *The Portland Edge.* Washington, D.C.: Island Press, 2004.

Pobodnik, Bruce. "Assessing the Social and Environmental Achievements of New Urbanism: Evidence from Portland, Oregon." Paper presented at the Annual Meeting of the American Sociological Association, San Francisco, 2009.

Schrank, David, et al. "2010 Urban Mobility Report." Texas Transportation Institute, http://tti.tamu.edu/documents/mobility_report_2010.pdf.

Seltzer, Ethan. "It's Not an Experiment: Regional Planning at Metro, 1990 to Present," in *The Portland Edge,* ed. Connie Ozawa. Washington, D.C.: Island Press, 2004.

U.S. Congress, Office of Technology Assessment. *Saving Energy in U.S. Transportation.* OTA-ETI-589, 1994.

Vuchic, Vukan R. "Open Letter from Dr. Vukan R. Vuchic to Secretary Mineta." March 22, 2006, http://discuss.amtraktrains.com/index.php?/topic/5481-open-letter-from-dr-vukan-r-vuchic-to-secretary.

10: The Next Great City

Bailey, Jeff. "Subsidies Keep Airlines Flying to Small Towns." *The New York Times*, October 6, 2006.

Bass, Sam Warner. *The Private City: Philadelphia in Three Periods of Its Growth*. Philadelphia: University of Pennsylvania Press, 1987.

Cheape, Charles W. *Moving the Masses: Urban Public Transit in New York, Boston, and Philadelphia, 1880–1912*. Cambridge, Mass.: Harvard University Press, 1980.

Conn, Steven. *Metropolitan Philadelphia: Living with the Presence of the Past*. Philadelphia: University of Pennsylvania Press, 2006.

Copeland, Larry. "Philadelphia Gains, Pittsburgh Shrinks in Population." *USA Today*, March 10, 2011.

Cudahy, Brian J. *Cash, Tokens, and Transfers: A History of Urban Mass Transit in North America*. New York: Fordham University Press, 1999.

Dewan, Shaila. "The Real Murder Mystery? It's the Low Crime Rate." *The New York Times*, August 1, 2009.

Fishman, Robert. *Bourgeois Utopias: The Rise and Fall of Suburbia*. New York: Basic Books, 1987.

Gertner, John. "Getting Up to Speed." *The New York Times Magazine*, June 14, 2009.

Goodman, Paul. "Banning Cars from Manhattan," in *Utopian Essays and Practical Proposals*. New York: Random House, 1962.

Graham, Troy. "Violent Crime Fell 3 Percent in Philadelphia in 2010." *Philadelphia Inquirer*, December 30, 2010.

Jones, Jeffrey M. "Americans Still Perceive Crime on the Rise." gallup.com, http://www.gallup.com, November 18, 2010.

Knowles, Scott Gabriel, ed. *Imagining Philadelphia: Edmund Bacon and the Future of the City*. Philadelphia: University of Pennsylvania Press, 2009.

Kurtzleben, Danielle. "The 11 Most Dangerous Cities." *U.S. News & World Report*, February 16, 2011.

Lind, Diana. "The Bright Side of Blight." *New York Times*, January 24, 2011.

Littman, Todd. *Evaluating Public Transportation Health Benefits*. Victoria Transport Policy Institute for the American Public Transportation Association, http://www.apta.com, 2010.

MacDonald, John M., et al. "The Effect of Light Rail Transit on Body Mass Index and Physical Activity." *American Journal of Preventive Medicine* 39/2 (August 2010).

McCommons, James. *Waiting on a Train: The Embattled Future of Passenger Rail Service*. White River Junction, Vt.: Chelsea Green, 2009.

Mees, Paul. *Transport for Suburbia: Beyond the Automobile Age*. London: Earthscan, 2010.

Monkkonen, Eric H. *America Becomes Urban: The Development of U.S. Cities and Towns, 1780–1980*. Berkeley: University of California Press, 1988.

Oppel, Richard A. "Steady Decline in Major Crime Baffles Experts." *The New York Times*, May 23, 2011.

Paulsen, Monte. "Off the Rails: How Canada Killed High-Speed Train Travel, and Why We Should Revive It." *The Walrus*, June 2009.

Rybczynski, Witold. *City Life: Urban Expectations in a New World*. New York: Scribner, 1995.

———. "Is Urban Sprawl Really an American Menace?" Slate.com, November 7, 2005.

———. *Last Harvest: From Cornfield to New Town*. New York: Scribner, 2007.

———. *Makeshift Metropolis: Ideas about Cities*. New York: Scribner, 2010.

Saffron, Inga. "The Sensuous City." *Philadelphia Inquirer*, January 8, 2010.

Stilgoe, John R. *Train Time: Railroads and the Imminent Reshaping of the United States Landscape*. Charlottesville: University of Virginia Press, 2007.

Sturm, Roland. "Urban Design, Lifestyle, and the Development of Chronic Conditions, the Built Environment and Childhood Obesity." National Institute of Environmental Health Sciences, http://www.niehs.nih.gov, 2005.

U.S. Environmental Protection Agency. "Residential Construction Trends in America's Metropolitan Regions." http://www.epa.gov/dced/construction_trends.htm, January 2010.

11. The Toronto Tragedy

Agrell, Siri. "Our Commute Is Stalling Us." *The Globe and Mail*, March 26, 2011.

Arthur, Eric. *Toronto: No Mean City*. Toronto: University of Toronto Press, 1986.

Coyne, Andrew. "Stuck in Traffic." *Maclean's*, January 17, 2011.

Dale, Daniel. "TTC Proposes Fare Hike, Job Cuts and Longer Wait Times." *Toronto Star*, September 13, 2011.

Frisken, Frances, et. al. "Governance and Social Sustainability: The Toronto Experience," in *The Social Sustainability of Cities*, ed. Mario Polèse. Toronto: University of Toronto Press, 2000.

Fulford, Robert. *Accidental City: The Transformation of Toronto*. Toronto: Macfarlane Walter & Ross, 1995.

Gee, Marcus. "Backtracking on Transit, Ford Seeks a Handout." *The Globe and Mail*, August 17, 2011.

Jenkins, Jonathan. "Ford's Victory Highlights Urban-Suburban Split." *Toronto Sun*, October 28, 2010.

Lorinc, John. "How Toronto Lost Its Groove." *The Walrus*, November 2011.

Mees, Paul. *Transport for Suburbia: Beyond the Automobile Age*. Oxford: Earthscan, 2009.

Micallef, Shawn. *Stroll: Psychogeographic Tours of Toronto*. Toronto: Coach House Books, 2010.

Miller, Eric J. "We're Talking Mobility, Not Gravy." *Toronto Star*, September 1, 2011.

Sewell, John. *The Shape of the Suburbs: Understanding Toronto's Sprawl*. Toronto: University of Toronto Press, 2009.

———. *The Shape of the City: Toronto Struggles with Modern Planning*. Toronto: University of Toronto Press, 1993.

Wickens, Stephen. "TTC Makes 'Dumbest Decision Ever,' Former Head Warns." *The Globe and Mail*, July 5, 2011.

Further Reading

Amar, Georges. *Mobilités urbaines: Eloge de la diversité et devoir d'invention.* Paris: Edition de l'Aube, 2004.

Downey, Morgan. *Oil 101.* New York: Wooden Table Press, 2010.

Evans, Walker. *Many Are Called.* New Haven, Conn.: Yale University Press, 2004.

Florida, Richard. *The Great Reset: How New Ways of Living and Working Drive Post-Crash Prosperity.* New York: Random House, 2010.

Fogelson, Robert M. *Downtown: Its Rise and Fall, 1880–1950.* New Haven, Conn.: Yale University Press, 2001.

Gilbert, Richard, and Anthony Perl. *Transport Revolutions: Moving People and Freight Without Oil.* Gabriola Island, B.C.: New Society, 2010.

Goddard, Stephen B. *Getting There: The Epic Struggle Between Road and Rail in the American Century.* New York: Basic Books, 1994.

Kargon, Robert H., and Arthur P. Molella. *Techno-Cities of the Twentieth Century.* Cambridge, Mass.: MIT Press, 2008.

Kay, Jane Holtz. *Asphalt Nation: How the Automobile Took Over America and How We Can Take It Back.* Berkeley: University of California Press, 1998.

Kunstler, James Howard. *The Geography of Nowhere.* New York: Touchstone, 1993.

Marshall, Alex. *Beneath the Metropolis: The Secret Lives of Cities.* New York: Carroll & Graf, 2006.

Mumford, Lewis. *The City in History: Its Origins, Its Transformations, and Its Prospects.* New York: Harvest/HBJ, 1961.

Ovenden, Mark. *Transit Maps of the World*. London: Penguin Books, 2007.

Owen, David. *Green Metropolis: Why Living Smaller, Living Closer, and Driving Less Are the Keys to Sustainability*. New York: Riverhead Books, 2009.

Rome, Adam. *The Bulldozer in the Countryside: Suburban Sprawl and the Rise of American Environmentalism*. New York: Cambridge University Press, 2001.

Soderstrom, Mary. *The Walkable City: From Haussmann's Boulevards to Jane Jacobs' Streets and Beyond*. Montreal: Véhicule, 2008.

Acknowledgments

Every book is a voyage, but this one felt like a three-year train trip—on good days by bullet train, but more often by sparking, backsliding, Toonerville trolley. Fortunately, there were people at every station stop to show me the right track; without them, I never would have made it home. (Not all of my travel was by train, of course; all flight mileage incurred in researching this book was matched by carbon offsets bought from the UK-based ClimateCare.)

First of all, thanks to my agent, Michelle Tessler, a woman who can work wonders in the most challenging environments, and Webster Younce, formerly of Henry Holt, who responded so enthusiastically to my *carnet de voyage*. My editor at Holt, Gillian Blake, provided advice, encouragement, and spot-on trimming, and the interest of Jim Gifford at HarperCollins in all things urban made it a pleasure to work with him.

In Shanghai, Toby Skinner did great work at short notice with some very up-to-date reporting on the 2011 Auto Show.

In New York, Jeff Zupan of the Regional Plan Association provided me with valuable background on the metropolis's transit history, and Gene Russianoff, of the excellently named Straphangers Campaign, was as droll and generous about a lifetime of riding the subway as Mark Gorton of Streetsblog was passionate about transforming the streets of Manhattan. Sarah Hoida and Andrew Pink of Brooklyn contributed shelter, great company, and bizarre transit trivia, and David Pirmann, curator of the encyclopedic nycsubway.org, directed me to some of the more obscure corners of the system.

In Los Angeles, Gloria Ohland introduced me to the city's transit campaigners and some fantastic Korean food, and Alexander Kalamaros of Metro was a patient guide to the highlights of the light-rail system. Yuri Aritibise and Tony Arranaga took the time to make the case that Phoenix shouldn't be written off so quickly.

Mille mercis to Alexandra Limiati and Guillaume Blanchaud—as well as the little Étienne—for sharing their life in Paris, and to Bruce and Cécile for a nostalgic picnic on the Canal Saint-Martin. I couldn't have hoped for better guides to the underground than Mark Ovenden and Julien Pepinster, and Gilles Thomas, France's number one *cataphile*, astonished me with his expertise on the Swiss cheese that underlies Paris's paving stones.

On the ride to Copenhagen, thanks to Hans-Georg Herr for setting up a tour of Freiburg on short notice, John Pucher for his tips on Europe's best cycling cities, and to Gwénaëlle Callec and Michael Schaefer for putting up and feeding a feverish traveler in Berlin. In Copenhagen, Maibritt and Jon Lewis introduced me to both the intricacies of Danish transit and the wonders of quorn, and Øjvind Schwedler gave me great background on cycling in Copenhagen.

I'm grateful to Eric Scott and Yakov Rabkin for introducing me to Anastasia Popkov, who proved to be a fearless docent to the Moscow Metro, and a patient interpreter on the streets.

Without the hospitality and guidance of Scott Chernoff and Jennifer Menard I wouldn't have gotten beyond *kon ichiwa* in the labyrinth that is

Tokyo; Scott, thanks for your moral support, your constant updates, and attentive vetting. Of the many people Scott introduced to me, I'd like to thank Beniko Hayazaki, Tomoko Hayazaki, Michie and Hiroshi Shimmoto, Marika and Risa, and Lisa Shikama. Christian Dimmer provided some great perspective on public space, and I'm grateful to Gabriel Banks for his insight into Japanese cities. Thanks also to Keiko Kawamura for her help interpreting, and Chester Liebs for taking the time to talk to me about Japanese cycling habits.

In Bogotá, Carlos Moreno helped when Colombian slang got the best of my rusty Spanish, and Carlos Pardo was a wry and thoughtful source of background on TransMilenio and *pico y placa*.

In Philadelphia, thanks to Lori and Lou of carfreephilly.com (and citykitties.org) for a wonderful bike tour of West Philly.

In Vancouver, thanks to my sister Lara, and her husband Justin Aydein, for airport pick-ups, great Indian take-out, and the occasional late-night Xbox challenge. My parents, Paul and Audrey Grescoe, as always, were a constant source of support. Dad, thanks for the timely updates, links, hyphens, and well-placed words of encouragement. Mom, I'm grateful for your exhaustive (and humorously annotated) research, your close reading of chapters, and your willingness to indulge a headstrong son's intellectual obsessions. Without you two, I wouldn't have had the confidence, or endurance, to write any of my books.

In Montreal, thanks to Zvi Leve, who knows where to find a good cup of coffee, and who shared his contacts in the global transit world. Daniel Rotman and Ryan Osgood proved to be highly overqualified transcribers of rambling interviews; thanks, guys, for your professionalism, speed, and witty asides.

And when this book started to feel like an endless ride on the Trans-Siberian, there was Erin Churchill. I'm grateful to my wife for both her real logistical help—including the thankless task of transcribing—and for accepting my absences, both physical and mental, when I was in the thick of the research and writing of *Straphanger*. Her optimism and love sustained me all the way. Darling, I can't wait for the next leg of our journey together.

Index

income, spent on transportation, 37 and *n*
Independent Subway System (IND), 37–38
India, 3–4, 9
  cars, 3–4, 160
  fuel consumption, 12
Interborough Rapid Transit Company
  (IRT), 28–37, 42
International Energy Agency, 11
Interstate 5, 234, 237
interstate highway system, 235–37
Istanbul, 220
Italy, 126

Jacobs, Jane, 43–44, 48, 191, 236, 289
  *The Death and Life of Great American
  Cities,* 43
Jackson, Kenneth, 89, 91, 92, 95–96
  Crabgrass Frontier, 89, 96, 98, 104
Japan, 10, 90, 213, 232, 262
  economy, 194, 195, 199
  Edo period, 188–92, 197
  population, 182, 187, 188, 199
  Tokyo railways, 178–207
  2011 earthquake and tsunami, 189, 195
Japan Government Railways, 189
Japan Railways (JR), 179–85, 189, 201
jaywalking, 56
jeepneys, 216, 242
Jefferson, Thomas, 88, 98
Jews, 92, 116*n,* 307
jitneys, 58, 216
Johannesburg, 160, 213
Johnson, Lyndon B., 95

Kaganovich, Lazar, 164, 167
Keolis, 128, 129
Khrushchev, Nikita, 163, 167, 169, 174
Kotkin, Joel, 82–85, 91, 103, 130, 266
  The Next Hundred Million, 82, 83
Kyoto, 188, 201, 273, 313

LaGuardia, Fiorello, 37–38, 58
land readjustment, 197
Las Vegas, 128
Latin America, 9, 104, 114, 208, 220–21,
  232. *See also specific countries and
  cities*
Le Corbusier, 105, 106–7, 149, 218
  Radiant City, 106–7, 131, 267

Levittown, 42, 91, 92, 269, 286
light-rail lines, 4, 7, 9, 135, 223, 267, 286,
  311
  elevated, 254–58, 267, 296*n*
  Los Angeles, 51–59, 63–68, 69, 72, 73, 74
  Phoenix, 99–100, 101
  Portland, 233, 238, 240, 243–50
  Toronto, 293–95, 296*n*
  Vancouver, 251–58
  See also specific cities and trains
Llewellyn Park, 89–90
London, 8, 23, 31, 45, 112, 117, 177, 210,
  215, 222, 227, 268
  suburbs, 89, 90
  2005 terrorist attacks, 173
  Underground, 33, 110, 115, 125, 127,
  162, 166, 168, 173, 179, 198
Long Island, New York, 40–43, 45
  suburbanization, 42, 91, 92
Los Angeles, 3, 22, 36, 50–78, 82, 86, 92,
  96, 98, 124, 138, 209, 233, 241, 254,
  261, 265, 274, 312
  buses, 51, 53, 54, 57–58, 61–64, 67, 223
  cars, 50–51, 56–57, 59–62, 67, 68, 71, 74,
  77
  condominiums, 72–75
  downtown, 68–72
  freeways, 50–51, 59–61, 68, 70, 76–78
  light-rail lines, 51–59, 63–68, 72, 73, 74,
  292
  Metro, 51–53, 61–64, 73–76
  Miracle Mile, 69–70
  parking, 54, 57, 71–72, 74, 76
  population, 55, 62–63, 68*n,* 70, 74
  Red Cars, 54–59, 62, 200
  self-image, 76–78
  skyscrapers, 67–68
  sprawl, 54, 67, 68, 71, 74
  streetcars, 54–59, 62, 69, 125
  suburbs, 51, 84–85, 91, 198, 304
  subways, 51–53, 63–67 and *n,* 68, 69, 78
  Subway to the Sea, 65–67 and *n*
  traffic, 59–61, 66, 68, 74
  transit-oriented development, 72–76
  Wilshire Boulevard, 65–66, 69, 70
Los Angeles Times, 57, 74
Lyon, 150, 264

Madrid, 22, 132, 222
  2004 terrorist attack, 173
malls, 9, 13, 70, 87, 102, 284